THE CAUSES OF RAPE

The Causes of Rape

UNDERSTANDING INDIVIDUAL
DIFFERENCES IN MALE PROPENSITY
FOR SEXUAL AGGRESSION

Martin L. Lalumière
Grant T. Harris
Vernon L. Quinsey
Marnie E. Rice

AMERICAN PSYCHOLOGICAL ASSOCIATION
WASHINGTON, DC

Published by
American Psychological Association
750 First Street, NE
Washington, DC 20002
www.apa.org

To order
APA Order Department
P.O. Box 92984
Washington, DC 20090-2984
Tel: (800) 374-2721; Direct: (202) 336-5510
Fax: (202) 336-5502; TDD/TTY: (202) 336-6123
Online: www.apa.org/books/
E-mail: order@apa.org

In the U.K., Europe, Africa, and the Middle East, copies may be ordered from
American Psychological Association
3 Henrietta Street
Covent Garden, London
WC2E 8LU England

Typeset in Goudy by Stephen McDougal, Mechanicsville, MD

Printer: Sheridan Books, Ann Arbor, MI
Cover Designer: Berg Design, Albany, NY
Technical/Production Editor: Gail B. Munroe

The opinions and statements published are the responsibility of the authors, and such opinions and statements do not necessarily represent the policies of the American Psychological Association.

Library of Congress Cataloging-in-Publication Data

The causes of rape : understanding individual differences in male propensity for sexual aggression / by Martin L. Lalumiere . . . [et al].—1st ed.
    p. cm. — (The law and public policy : psychology and the social sciences)
    Includes bibliographical references and index.
    ISBN 1-59147-186-9
    1. Rape. 2. Rape—Psychological aspects. 3. Criminal behavior—Genetic aspects.
I. Lalumiere, Martin L. II. Series: Law and public policy.

    HV6558.C38 2005
    362.883'01'9—dc22   2004015071

British Library Cataloguing-in-Publication Data
A CIP record is available from the British Library.

Printed in the United States of America
First Edition

CONTENTS

ACKNOWLEDGMENTS

The writing of this book and much of our recent research on rape was supported by grants from the Ontario Mental Health Foundation and the Social Sciences and Humanities Research Council of Canada, and by a research contract between the Kingston Psychiatric Hospital and Vernon L. Quinsey. The Centre for Addiction and Mental Health, the Mental Health Centre Penetanguishene, and Queen's University, our home institutions, provided us with much needed support.

Many individuals have contributed up close or from afar to our work on this topic and to the development of this book. Zoe Hilton and Michael Seto are involved in much of our research and are constant sources of intellectual stimulation. Terry Chaplin, Catherine Cormier, and Carol Lang skillfully and assiduously gathered the phallometric and follow-up data in our research, much of which is reported in this book. Martin Daly, Neil Malamuth, Linda Mealey, Randy Thornhill, and Margo Wilson greatly influenced our thinking through their writings and friendly discussions at various research meetings. Joe Camilleri, Karine Côté, Zoe Hilton, Linda Mealey, and Tony Volk read parts of the manuscript and provided helpful feedback and suggestions. Our development editor, Ed Meidenbaur, an anonymous reviewer, and Michael Seto provided detailed feedback on the entire manuscript that greatly improved the final product. Finally, Jessica Bristowe helped us collect the aggregate crime and risk-taking statistics presented in chapters 2 and 4, and Megan Rogers helped us collating and organizing the references. The scientific enterprise is one that requires many good teammates, and we are grateful for all of ours.

THE CAUSES OF RAPE

1

INTRODUCTION

Rape is devastating. Women who have been raped may experience anxiety disorders, depression, somatic disorders, sexual dysfunction, obsessive–compulsive disorders, addictions, loss of self-esteem, financial problems, and many of the symptoms of posttraumatic stress disorder, and they do so to a greater extent than the victims of other violent crimes (Boudreaux, Kilpatrick, Resnick, Best, & Saunders, 1998; Cluss, Broughton, Frank, Stewart, & West, 1983; Emm & McKenry, 1988; Frank & Anderson, 1987; Goodman, Koss, & Russo, 1993; Kilpatrick et al., 1989; Orlando & Koss, 1983; Rhodes, Ebert, & Meyers, 1993; Spitzberg & Rhea, 1999; E. A. Walker, Katon, Roy-Byrne, Jemelka, & Russo, 1993; E. A. Walker et al., 1995). Rape victims are sometimes even blamed for their own victimization (C. Jones & Aronson, 1973). There is no doubt that a reduction in the frequency of rape would prevent much human suffering.

Everyone agrees that reducing the incidence of rape is a worthy goal, but the consensus about rape generally stops there. Few topics have generated more heated debate in the social science literature. Controversies abound in analyses of legal and policy issues, psychological and psychiatric studies of the characteristics of rapists, evaluations of the outcome of treatment for rapists, investigations of sexual motivations underlying rape, explorations of the causal role of pornography and childhood sexual abuse, and so on. This book is about a small part of this contentious literature, that concerned with scientific studies investigating individual differences in male propensity to rape.

Studies of individual differences have produced some consistent and replicable findings. Psychologists know a great deal about the personal characteristics that distinguish or fail to distinguish rapists from other offenders and from other men. They also know that some convicted rapists are more likely than others to commit sexual offenses once again, and they can identify these men reliably. This knowledge has important practical implications. For example, the danger convicted offenders pose to the community can be assessed quite accurately, and judicious decisions can be made regarding their need for treatment, the timing of their release, the conditions of their supervision in the community, and so on (Quinsey, Lalumière, Rice, & Harris, 1995). This information, if used properly, may lead to the prevention of many rapes.

Studies of individual differences also have important implications for developing and testing explanations about why men rape. An explanation that said, for example, that young men who have difficulty meeting and dating women are more likely than others to commit rape could not be true if it were found that sexually coercive men are actually quite successful at dating. Theories about the causes of rape must be consistent with what is known about individual differences.

Our goal in writing this book is to bring to the forefront and integrate some of the recent important scientific findings about men who rape. Theorizing about rape has had an unfortunate history of being unconstrained by empirical knowledge, sometimes with harmful practical consequences. To continue the same example, if one believed that some men are sexually coercive because they have poor interpersonal skills and have difficulties obtaining dates, it might make sense to teach such men dating skills in the hope that they could develop satisfying relationships. But if rapists are actually already quite skilled at getting dates, and if dating frequency were in fact a risk factor for rape, such training for rapists might actually cause harm by increasing the likelihood of rape.

It is likely that prevention and treatment strategies will be successful to the extent that they are grounded in sound explanations. Perhaps because of the lack of empirically supported theories, current treatment programs for sexual offenders have not produced encouraging results (see reviews in R. K. Hanson et al., 2002; Quinsey, Harris, Rice, & Lalumière, 1993; M. E. Rice & Harris, 2003b), and some programs even seem to increase the likelihood that sex offenders will reoffend once released (e.g., Quinsey, Khanna, & Malcolm, 1998). Of course, the link between understanding a phenomenon and controlling or preventing it is not always straightforward. Some phenomena are well understood but little can be done to alter them (e.g., weather patterns), whereas others, such as headaches, are poorly understood (at least until recently) but easily remediable. As we will discuss later in this book, it is quite likely that many rapes could be prevented by reducing the use of alcohol among dating partners, even without knowing much about why some men rape in the first place. Nevertheless, we believe that a good understanding of a phenomenon greatly increases the chance of successful intervention and prevention strategies.

What influences men's propensity to rape? In this book we review major empirical developments in the study of individual differences in male propensity to rape in five areas of research that have proved to be the most productive and conclusive: (a) antisociality and (b) mating effort (chap. 4), (c) atypical sexual interest or paraphilia (chap. 5), (d) psychopathology (chap. 6), and (e) contextual factors (chap. 7). Because of the strong link between antisociality and mating effort, these two topics are covered in the same chapter. Throughout the book we examine the possible sources of individual differences reliably associated with rape, making use of recent conceptual and empirical developments in the study of the origins and the development of antisocial behavior, mating strategies, and anomalous sexual interests.

The field of sex offender research and clinical practice has made little use of recent empirical and theoretical advances in the study of antisocial behavior. Because sex offenders are often considered to be a separate type of criminal, assessment and treatment practices have been little influenced by successful practices in criminology. In this book we argue that rapists share many characteristics with other violent offenders and that most rapists are often violent in nonsexual ways. It follows, then, that understanding the development of antisocial tendencies more generally can have important consequences for understanding rape. On the basis of our recent theoretical work on the origins of delinquency (Quinsey, Skilling, Lalumière, & Craig, 2004), we explain that there are three general developmental pathways to antisocial conduct, including sexually coercive behavior, each with different proximal and ultimate causes.

But before turning our full attention to individual differences, we cover two important areas of research on rape and sexual coercion to provide a more general background for our review and synthesis. Rape is not a uniquely Western contemporary phenomenon and is not even unique to the human species. Indeed, rape has been documented in many cultures over different historical periods, and similar behaviors, often labeled *forced copulation*, have been observed in many other species. In chapter 2 we examine the historical and ethnographic literature on rape. This sometimes puzzling literature provides a glimpse of the individual factors and social conditions that facilitated rape across cultures and time. We also briefly examine recent remarkable changes in the incidence of sexual assaults in North America.

In chapter 3 we examine in detail individual differences associated with forced copulation in other species. Some readers may have heard, at least anecdotally, of sexually aggressive behavior in scorpion flies, mallards, and orangutans, three often-cited species. There is a great deal of good scientific work on forced copulation in many different species, but very little of it is known outside of biology. We identify various mating strategies that underlie and promote the use of forced copulation, strategies that vary from species to species. In some bird species, males that are successful at forming a pair bond force copulation opportunistically on female neighbors. In other species, males that are at a disadvantage in competition for mates resort to forceful mating tactics. These are two of the five main strategies we have identified that describe the use of forced copulation in the species studied so far.

All five strategies have close parallels in the arguments that have been used to explain human rape, and a dispassionate consideration of the theoretical and empirical grounds for inferring the existence of these strategies in nonhuman animals may facilitate evaluation of their relevance, if any, to humans. Our goal, however, is not to develop an animal model of human rape or, worse, to naturalize, trivialize, or excuse human rape. Rather, our goal is to provide a general overview of what is known about forced copulation in the animal world, to introduce concepts that are important when it comes to understanding the sources of individual differences among humans and other species, and to place the study of rape in a wider scientific context.

In chapter 8 we review the literature on the clinical assessment and treatment of rapists. In chapter 9, we provide a synthesis of the book and discuss the implications of some of the findings and hypotheses presented in this book for new practical developments in the assessment and treatment of rapists.

We hope that this book moves the study of rape forward by revealing consilience among several disparate lines of scientific inquiry and by providing new ways of looking at coercive sex among humans. Ultimately, we hope that our analysis leads to improvements in the prevention of rape and the treatment of rapists so as to reduce the prevalence of sexual coercion.

I

GENERAL BACKGROUND

2

RAPE ACROSS CULTURES AND TIME

It has long been known that rape is not a uniquely modern Western phenomenon, but how widespread is it? In this chapter we review the historical and ethnographic literature on rape, paying particular attention to the factors that might explain the cross-cultural variation in the frequency of rape, the contexts in which rape occurred, the characteristics of offenders and victims, the consequences of rape for both offenders and victims, and the role of warfare. This literature provides a helpful empirical and conceptual background for our analysis of individual differences.

The literature to be reviewed in this chapter is of four types: (a) reports describing rape in preliterate societies and attempts to compare and contrast rape across them, (b) descriptions of sexual behavior at different historical periods, (c) variations in rape among contemporary literate societies, and (d) rape and warfare. The review is based almost entirely on secondary sources. Historical and ethnographic data pertaining to rape are often fragmentary and sometimes anecdotal. Certainly, it is not primarily a literature of scientific inquiry, and it is seldom possible to use quantitative review techniques. Nevertheless, there are rich sources of information, and some of these provide compelling insights into the sexual politics of people far removed from us.

ETHNOGRAPHIC RECORD OF PRELITERATE SOCIETIES

Sexual behavior patterns vary widely over human cultures (e.g., Carstairs, 1964; Gadpaille, 1980). With respect to rape, there are great difficulties in obtaining incidence data over various cultures. First, one must depend on respondent reports rather than on frequency data; second, the term *rape* is socially defined, and this definition varies across cultures (Chappell, 1976). In addition, one cannot assume that the original writers, historians, or ethnographers always used the term *rape* to mean the same thing. In general, though, rape was used to mean *the forceful act of sexual intercourse against a person's will*. Unless otherwise noted, we use this definition in this chapter and the rest of this book, but we broaden it slightly to include any physical sexual contact performed with the use or threat of physical force. We use the term *sexual coercion* to refer to any physical sexual contact performed without a person's consent using any coercive methods (e.g., using a position of authority or verbal pressure).

Methodological and definitional difficulties notwithstanding, the prevalence of rape has been reported to vary markedly over cultures. For example, rape has been reported to be rare or absent among such disparate societies as the pygmies of the Ituri forest in Africa (Turnbull, 1961), the Ik of the African mountains (Turnbull, 1972), the aboriginals of the northeastern United States (Abler, 1992), and the Trobriand islanders of Oceania (Malinowski, 1929). In contrast, rape has been reported to be extremely common among certain societies and, in fact, LeVine (1959) reported that it was the most common form of sexual interaction among the Gusii of Kenya.

LeVine (1959) argued from his study of the Gusii that four factors are related to high rape frequency: (a) severe restrictions on nonmarital female sexual activity, (b) female sexual inhibition, (c) prolonged bachelorhood of men, and (d) an absence of physical segregation of the sexes. The proportion of bachelors in this polygynous population was determined by the bride price required to obtain a wife. Higher bride prices among the Gusii resulted in increased numbers of bachelors and an increase in the frequency of rape (Thornhill & Thornhill, 1983). A study of a single culture, however, can yield only hypotheses, and other interpretations of these data can be imagined.

Several interesting attempts have been made to examine differences in rape frequency among cultures in a systematic way, yielding somewhat comparable results. Broude and Greene (1976) examined cross-cultural data on sexual attitudes and behaviors from 200 societies contained in Murdock and White's (1969) Standard Cross-Cultural Sample. The Standard Sample contains data from the "ethnographic present" of societies from around the world selected to be geographically and linguistically isolated from each other. Broude and Greene discussed the limitations of the information available on sexual practices, including shyness on the part of the anthropologists or their informants, the nonquantitative nature of the observations, and the difficulty in interpreting whether a phenomenon is absent when it is never mentioned. The investigators coded 20 practices on which they independently agreed or agreed postdiscussion, although no interrater reliability calculations were computed. Broude and Greene coded rape as absent in 24% of the societies and rare in 35%. However, these data might be considered suspect by sexologists, given that homosexuality was coded as absent or rare in 59% of the societies. As we note in the study of other species, the absence of reports about sexual coercion cannot be interpreted as solid evidence that rape is absent.

Otterbein (1979) studied 135 nonliterate societies using data from the Human Relations Area Files; of these societies, there were data for 43 on rape frequency and for 32 on punishment for this crime. Rape frequency was coded on a 7-point scale ranging from 1 (*concept absent or rape reported not to occur*) to 7 (*all sexual relations viewed as aggressive*). Punishment severity was rated on a 7-point scale from *none* to *death*. Two other variables were coded. The first was the existence of fraternal interest groups, which are power groups of biologically related men who resort to aggression to defend their members' interests. The existence of fraternal interest groups was measured by patrilocality, a marital residence pattern in which the family lives with the groom's relatives, or by a residence pattern in which the males live together and apart from the family. The second variable was feuding, defined as blood revenge in response to a homicide.

Significantly higher rape frequencies were found in societies characterized by patrilocality and feuding. There was an inverse relationship between rape frequency and punishment severity. An interesting relationship among these two findings emerged: Punishment severity was negatively related to rape frequency only when there were no fraternal interest groups, and societies with no punishment for rape had high frequencies whether there were fraternal interest groups or not. That is, rape is common when the cost to rapists is low, but when men band together to aggressively promote their interests, high rates of rape apparently result even when punishment is severe.

Sanday (1981) examined 156 tribal societies from Murdock and White's (1969) Standard Cross-Cultural Sample. Interrater agreement on the 21 variables selected was high, and rape frequency data were found for 75 societies. Rape incidence was classified as (a) rare or absent, (b) present but there were no data on frequency or rape was said to be not atypical, or (c) rape prone (where used as punishment or as a threat against women, as part of a ceremony, or where rape was clearly of moderate to high frequency). Eighteen percent of the societies were classified as rape prone and 47% as rape free. Variables related to sexual repression (e.g., attitudes toward premarital sex and age of men at marriage) were not significantly related to rape frequency. However, four variables relating to interpersonal violence were correlated with rape frequency: (a) raiding other groups for wives, (b) degree of interpersonal violence, (c) ideology of male toughness, and (d) war. Similarly, five variables related to the ideology of male dominance correlated with rape frequency: (a) lack of female power and authority, (b) lack of female political decision making, (c) negative attitudes toward women as citizens, (d) the presence of special places for men, and (e) the presence of special places for women. The largest of these correlations, however, were found for degree of interpersonal violence and the ideology of male toughness.

The Yanomamo of South America offer a classic example of the link between interpersonal violence and rape (Chagnon, 1977). The Yanomamo prize male toughness, and rape frequency is very high. Fights within villages and wars between villages are very common, and male mortality due to warfare is high; both fights and wars are primarily over women. Dominant males and dominant villages possess more women than those less dominant. Symons (1979) concluded that warfare was very common among nonliterate groups before contact with state societies, that it was motivated by competition for women, and that it resulted in 25% of adult male mortality. One can conclude that rape among nonliterate societies must be viewed in the context of male competition for women. These observations make it appear that warfare among groups of men over women is among the best predictors of rape frequency. It is of interest that in other lowland Amazonian groups in which raiding for wives has not occurred for generations, such as the Tukanoans, gender antagonism and mythical stories involving rape as punishment for women and bride capture survive (J. E. Jackson, 1992).

Cross-gender antagonism has been extensively examined in the ethnographical literature (e.g., P. Brown, 1986; J. E. Jackson, 1992). It appears in widely separated societies, such as in various groups in New Guinea and the Amazon basin, and is related to the practice of obtaining wives from competing groups. That is, wives leave their own genetic kin and form a potential fifth column within the group they enter.[1] Under such circumstances, women seem especially unlikely to be trusted and prone to having their interests disregarded by men.

Schlegel and Barry (1986) examined the proportion of female contribution to subsistence in 186 nonindustrial societies in Murdock and White's (1969) sample. They concluded that

> rape is most likely to be absent where women make a high contribution and most likely to be common where their contribution is low. . . . Where men control women's subsistence, men also control their sexuality— licitly through an insistence on virginity, illicitly through rape. (p. 147)

---

[1]*Fifth column* is a phrase from the Spanish Civil War denoting a group of hostile combatants within one's own ranks or the ranks of one's opponent.

Palmer (1989a) examined the ethnographic evidence for the proposition that rape was nonexistent or rare in particular societies or that rape was unpunished. Contrary to what would be expected from earlier reviews, Palmer presented convincing evidence that in most, if not all, of the societies in which rape had been reported to be absent, rape in fact occurred and was punished. Palmer concluded that although the frequency of rape varies over cultures, it appears to be a cross-cultural universal. Rozée (1993) reached a similar conclusion from a survey of 35 randomly selected societies with a definition of rape that includes societally condoned but nonconsensual sexual contact with women.

In summary, although the measurement of rape in the ethnographic literature is weak, rape is probably universal across societies, but its frequency varies considerably. Rape is associated with male fraternal interest groups, warfare, gender antagonism, constraints on women's sexuality, and generally low status of women.[2]

HISTORICAL RECORD

In this section, we review a variety of historical sources from different parts of the world to provide a survey of views on rape in the past in several societies. We first discuss biblical texts that refer to rape, and then we review classical and medieval sources for other treatments of rape.

Biblical Sources

Deuteronomy 22:28–29 (probably written in the late 7th century B.C.E.) reads as follows:

> If a man meets a young woman, a virgin, who is not betrothed, and seizes her and lies with her, and they are found out, then the man who lay with her shall give to the father of the young woman fifty (shekels) of silver, and she shall become his wife, because he has violated her; he may not send her away all his days. (quoted in Hiebert, 1994, p. 204)

The later Mishnaic commentaries (final version, 3rd century C.E.) make a finer distinction:

> In Ketubot 3:4, it is stipulated that the seducer . . . must pay on the three counts of disgrace, deterioration in value, and a basic fine . . . specified in the Talmud as fifty shekels, whereas the rapist . . . must pay on the addi-

---

[2]The relationship between gender inequality (in socioeconomic success) and rape in contemporary America is not as clear. Using aggregate data, some researchers find no relationship, whereas others find a negative relationship—lesser inequality is associated with *higher* rape incidence (reviewed in Vieraitis & Williams, 2002).

tional count of compensation for bodily pain. (quoted in Hiebert, 1994, p. 214)

An Assyrian law of the second millennium B.C.E. is similar:

If a seignior took the virgin by force and ravished her, either in the midst of the city . . . or at a city festival, the father of the virgin shall take the wife of the virgin's ravisher and give her to be ravished; he shall not return her to her husband [but] take her; the father may give his daughter who was ravished to her ravisher in marriage. If he has no wife, the rav- isher shall give the [extra] third in silver to her father as the value of a virgin [and] her ravisher shall marry her [and] not cast her off. If the father does not [so] wish, he shall receive the [extra] third for the virgin in silver [and] give his daughter to whom he wishes. (quoted in Propp, 1993, p. 42)

In the King James Version of Genesis 34:1–35:1, Dinah, the young daughter of Jacob, is raped by a Hittite prince, Shechem, who "saw her, . . . took her, and lay with her, and defiled her." Shechem fell in love with Dinah, spoke kindly to her, and asked his father to "get me this damsel to wife." Shechem's father offered gifts and a dowry and told Jacob that the two peoples should live together, trade with each other, and intermarry. Jacob's sons an- swered deceitfully that the marriage could be arranged if the Hittite men all became circumcised. The Hittite men complied, and on the third day after the circumcision, when they were sore, Jacob's sons entered the Hittite city, killed all the men, stole all the livestock and goods, retrieved Dinah, and took the wives of the men they had slain. Jacob told his sons that they had made him "to stink among the inhabitants of the land . . . and I [being] few in number, they shall gather themselves together against me, and slay me; and I shall be destroyed, I and my house." The sons replied, "Should he deal with our sister as with an harlot?"

It is clear from this description that marriages were arranged between the guardians (fathers and brothers) of women. Women were paid for or ex- changed. Although Dinah was sexually assaulted, it is clear that Shechem wanted her for a wife. Dinah's views were not mentioned and presumably were not considered to be important. Rape was an affair between men (Propp, 1993). Although the narrator asserted that Dinah had been dishonored, Jacob considered the ensuing slaughter by the brothers to be an overreaction that would lead to feuding. We return to the story of Dinah when we consider attitudes toward sexual coercion in medieval Europe.

In these biblical accounts, the term *rape* is most accurately interpreted to mean "sex between a man and the female ward whose male guardians have not consented" (Propp, 1993). If the woman was unattached, the crime was viewed as relatively minor. However, if the woman was married or betrothed, the rapist was to be killed as an adulterer, as well as the woman, if complicit. Complicity was loosely interpreted—for example, if the woman was raped within a city, she was thought to have been able to summon aid (Propp, 1993).

Ancient Greece and Rome

Female perceptions of heterosexual relationships in ancient societies are difficult to reconstruct, because the written record comes almost exclusively from men. However, some inkling that it was understood that male and female interests diverged can be gleaned from DeBloois's (1997) interpretation of the Homeric *Hymn to Demeter* (7th or 6th century B.C.E.) as a rare presentation of both a male and a female view of the same event. The event is Hades's "marriage" to Persephone. In the hymn, the event is presented as both a traditional marriage, in which the father (Zeus) gives his daughter in marriage to another man (in this case, his brother, Hades), and a rape in which the mother (Demeter) must discover the "marriage" after the fact and in which the innocent and unsuspecting Persephone is forcibly seized by Hades and carried to the underworld. Hades is represented as a happy groom, in contrast to the miserable bride, who grieves for her mother.

Caesar Augustus (63 B.C.E.–14 C.E.) attempted to reform the morality of Rome with a view to increasing "family values" and the birth rate, with famous lack of success. In addition to tax incentives for marriage and children, the laws governing sexual behavior illustrate the flavor of his reforms: Those who committed or abetted adultery could be exiled to an island, subjected to loss of up to half of their property, or given corporal punishment. Similar penalties were applied to any man who had sex with another man or with a maiden or widow of respectable character (regardless of consent). A father who discovered his daughter committing adultery in her or her husband's home could kill both her and the adulterous partner. Similarly, a husband who caught his wife in adultery in his own house could kill the adulterer with impunity—if the adulterer was not a free man of respectable character (actors, gladiators, pimps, and convicted criminals were not), and provided that he divorced his wife immediately. A husband who failed to so punish adultery was himself punished as a pimp. For a description of these laws, see Lefkowitz and Fant (2004).

Ovid (43 B.C.E.–17 C.E.), who at age 50 was banished by Augustus, wrote popular and irreverent poems concerning mythology and the art of love. Some of his poems concerned rape. In particular, he described Jupiter's rape of Diana's companion, Callisto, twice, once in which the event is presented in a playful and sensual light and once in which the suffering of Callisto is forcefully brought home to the reader through a description of its consequences, including banishment from Diana, being turned into a bear by Jupiter's jealous consort Juno, and separation from the son conceived during the rape (W. R. Johnson, 1996).

It must be remembered that consent for sexual relations was not an issue for slaves. Slaves were the reproductive property of their masters. Not surprising, given the biological kinship involved, it was common for masters to free the children borne of these unions with an endowment (Betzig, 1992). That is, such children, though the offspring of slaves, were also the offspring of their owners and received benefits accordingly. Sex between masters and slaves, though certainly coercive and reflecting a great power imbalance, was understood at the time to be part of the normal range of male procreative activities.

Medieval Europe: England

From the time of St. Jerome (347–419), patristic interpretations of Dinah's rape in Genesis 34 emphasized Dinah's responsibility for her own defilement (Schroeder, 1997). In these later accounts, such as that of Bernard of Clairvaux (ca. 1124), Dinah should have stayed sequestered and away from the windows and doors of her father's home, not be off visiting other girls. Curiosity was a sin and a devil's snare. That is, Dinah's interests notwithstanding, she should have ensured that the interests of her male relatives (in her virginity) were protected. In contrast, as we shall see, secular sources viewed rape in somewhat more practical terms, and medieval literary sources were often more nuanced and sophisticated than ecclesiastical ones.

The first quasi-national English laws concerning rape are contained in Alfred the Great's DOMBOC, a codification of his own and earlier laws produced during the period 871 to 899 (Hough, 1997). Although not without some ambiguity, the statutes appear to specify compensation paid to the female victim as well as a fine payable to the king. The amount of the compensation and fine increased with the status of free women and the intrusiveness of the assault, but compensation was halved for nonvirgins. Interestingly, free women were allowed to give oaths as evidence. Alfred's statutes indicate that women's status in preconquest England was considerably higher than it was later to become and (as a likely consequence) that sexual assaults against women were considered to be more serious than they were considered to be later.

The statute of Westminster in 1285 proclaimed that rape of a virgin or married woman was a felony punishable by death and that the king could prosecute the offense. Until the end of the 13th century, the victim had been responsible for the prosecution of the perpetrator (J. M. Marshall, 1985). She had to show physical evidence of resistance and to repeat the charge in the royal court using exactly the same words as in the county court.

A statute of 1382 awarded fathers the right to accuse someone of rape (Post, 1980). These legal changes seemed designed to protect wealthy families from the threat to their property caused by eloping couples (Pistono, 1988; Post, 1980). In 1487, during the reign of Henry VII, parliament passed the "Acte agaynst taking awaye of Women agaynst theire Willes." This act made it a felony to abduct "women having substances" (Ives, 1978). Because the property of a woman passed to her husband upon marriage, it was thought necessary to protect propertied women from being abducted and forced to marry. It was, however, as earlier, more often the case that the "abduction" was collusive and the property being protected was the father's. Despite the intent, it is not clear that the 1487 act actually added anything of substance to earlier legislation (Ives, 1978).

Carter (1982) examined 97 records of rape hearings in rural and urban England from 1218 to 1276. None of the hearings involved aristocratic perpetrators and only one an aristocratic victim. There were many more rural than urban cases. Ecclesiastics were the largest group of accused rapists (28% of the total). Victim status (virgin or not) was not mentioned in these records. Roughly half of the cases resulted in the arrest of the complainant for false appeal (accusation), and in approximately a third, the alleged rapists were convicted. The most common punishment for the rapist was a fine, as has been found in other studies of this period (Marshall, 1985).

Hanawalt (1987) summarized the difficulties in obtaining information of interest to criminal justice specialists from 13th- and 14th-century records. Mostly, available records include court rolls of royal and local government; these often consist only of brief descriptions of the acts involved and the legal disposition. The lacunae in the historical records tempt us to examine fictional descriptions of rape to determine how it was viewed in medieval England. Geoffrey Chaucer (ca. 1343–1400) provided the most interesting of these treatments. In the "Wife of Bath's Tale" (C. W. Dunn, 1952), a lusty knight of King Arthur encounters a maid on his return from hawking. The knight seizes her and takes her maidenhead, despite her resistance. King Arthur sentences the knight to beheading, but the queen and her ladies request the king for grace. The fate of the knight is given over to the queen, and she states that she will grant him life if he can tell her what it is that women most desire. At length he gets the answer from a foul old woman—women desire to have sovereignty over both their husbands and their love.

The knight had to promise to marry the old hag in return for the answer but resists consummating the marriage. She tells him that in her current state, he need not fear being cuckolded because her filth and age are great keepers of chastity, but if he wishes, he can marry her as a beautiful but perhaps faithless woman. The knight, having learned his lesson, leaves the choice to her, and she gives him both beauty and faithfulness in return. They live happily ever after, and the moral is drawn that women will obey financially generous men who are willing to be overruled by their wives.

At the simplest level, this tale shows what elements of sexual behavior a medieval audience would think plausible. Rape, like other male sexual behavior, was seen to be differentially directed toward young, attractive, clean women. Male and female interests were seen to be divergent; men would be threatened with cuckoldry and women by rape. Execution of the perpetrator of an unambiguously resisted rape was seen as an appropriate societal response. To a modern audience, the most surprising aspect of the tale is King Arthur's decision to transfer consideration of the rape from a criminal court to a court of love. The latter courts were a chivalric innovation originating in Southern France in which senior noblewomen would pass judgment on problems and issues in the romantic affairs of the men and women in their entourage (Kelly, 1950). The decision, prompted by the queen, was to treat the rape as an affair of the heart, not a criminal offense.

Brown (1996) attempted to explicate both Chaucer's art and the deeper meaning of the tale. In her account, the lusty knight was led from an impulsive disregard of women's interests to a more thoughtful and empathic concern by the intervention of the Queen and her supernatural allies. The intervention primarily consisted in forcing the knight to engage in a lengthy effort to find out what it is that women really want. Not all modern readers would agree with this interpretation. Some, such as Barnett (1993), argued that Chaucer's tales primarily display callous male disregard for women, and some, such as Lee (1995), wondered whether the raped maid thought justice had been achieved by the knight's rehabilitation. Tigges (1992) made a convincing case, not dissimilar to Brown's, that the knight learned the important moral that women's views are important and ought to be considered, concluding with the interpretation that the Loathly Hag is a manifestation of the maid in the beginning of the story.

More generally, Vitz (1997) considered the meaning of rape in medieval literature and modern interpretations of it. She cautioned against reading contemporary concerns about the relations between the sexes into medieval literature. This literature was often designed to titillate and amuse both men and women, not necessarily to edify them. In Vitz's opinion, medieval men and women require no consciousness-raising efforts from modern scholars.

Medieval Europe: Italy

There is a surprising amount of documentation concerning crime and punishment in Venice in the 1300s (Ruggiero, 1980). People seem to have been killed for the same reasons they are now: trivial quarrels quickly escalating to murderous brawls, contract killings of business rivals, the murder of unfaithful wives or husbands, and the disposal of unwanted children. The nobility were a violent lot who were not punished very severely for any transgressions against the lower orders. Punishments were meted out in a politically sensitive manner. The stability of the state was the most important issue (vendettas among the nobility had to be suppressed, and the poor must not strike against the rich). In this connection, a great distinction was made between crimes of passion and premeditated crimes (the latter were punished more severely).

There were a substantial number of sex offenses. Rapes of children were punished severely. Rapes of postadolescent girls were not punished very severely, and rapes of married women were punished the most severely. Rape was not, however, seen as that important (there were problems of corroboration, potential blackmail of the rich by the poor, and so on). Physical injury and breaking into a house to commit the crime were viewed as more serious. In general, compared with today, property crimes were viewed as more serious than nonfatal crimes against the person.

Medieval Europe: Germany and France

Popular secular texts provide an important counterpoint to pronouncements on sexual conduct derived from medieval church and government sources. It must be remembered, particularly in dealing with church documents, that many of the clergy were breathtakingly naive about sexuality and the sometimes humorous light in which it was viewed. A striking example occurs in the *Malleus Maleficarum* (Kramer & Sprenger, 1486/1948). The learned Dominican monks, in describing an example of the evil that witches do in depriving men of their "members," unwittingly recounted what is certainly a childish joke about the size of a priest's penis:

> And what, then, is to be thought of those witches who in this way sometimes collect male organs in great numbers, as many as twenty or thirty members together, and put them in a bird's nest, or shut them up in a box, where they move themselves like living members, and eat oats and corn, as has been seen by many and is a matter of common report? It is to be said that it is all done by devil's work and illusion, for the senses of those who see them are deluded in the way we have said. For a certain man tells that, when he had lost his member, he approached a known witch to ask her to restore it to him. She told the afflicted man to climb a certain tree, and that he might take which he liked out of the nest in which there were several members. And when he tried to take a big one, the witch said: You must not take that one; adding, because it belongs to a parish priest. (p. 121)

The 12th-century French texts concerning Renart the Fox (Gravdal, 1991) are instructive in this regard: "The authors of the Renart trial scenes demonstrate with comic accuracy, the fallibility of oaths, the superstitious nature of ordeals, the dishonesty of the secular judiciary, and the impotence of feudal law enforcement" (p. 3). The subversive effects of this mockery show "a generous space for the legal protection of the rapist and the silencing of the most appropriate witness: the victim. The teeth of medieval misogyny are bared" (p. 4).

Luther (1483–1546) interpreted Dinah's rape differently than did St. Jerome and Bernard of Clairvaux (Schroeder, 1997). He approached her assault from the viewpoint of a grieved father. Luther was a great deal less naive than some of the Church fathers, having been married and raised children. Nevertheless, Luther agreed with St. Jerome that the windows and doors of houses were dangerous places for women and girls, they being "weak, irresponsible, foolish, and hence exposed to the snares of Satan" (p. 780, Schroeder, 1997). In Luther's view, Dinah's rape was a tribulation sent by God to test her father's faith. Rather than blame only Dinah's curiosity, Luther used the tale to warn parents to properly supervise their children lest they come to harm from the very real risk of abduction and rape. In Luther's view, Dinah's sins lay in her curiosity and disobedience to her parents by leaving the house, not in committing adultery, of which only Shechem was guilty.

MODERN PERIOD

In this section, we discuss rape as it has been viewed in modern times. Sources come from early modern Europe and Asia and more recent North America. The concept of rape in many societies has changed in the past 300 years, and it is informative to chart these changes, especially the more rapid changes that occurred in Western culture in the 20th century.

Early Modern Period in Europe

van der Heijden (2000) examined judicial records for 17th-century Holland and noted that women were more frequently punished for sexual offenses than men. These offenses included fornication, adultery, concubinage, and having illegitimate children. Rape of young (virginal) women was punished very severely, at least in part because these women were thought to have been dishonored. Rapes of married women were not harshly punished, and adult women were viewed with suspicion and often held jointly responsible with the perpetrator for the assault, on the grounds that they were sexually insatiable. Victims of incestuous rapes were treated inconsistently. The magistrates tended to take an "offense-centered" view of incest in which the victim was treated as an accomplice.

A statute of Elizabeth I of England (1533–1603) defined rape as "carnal knowledge of a woman forcibly and against her will" (p. 520, Conley, 1986). This definition remained unchanged through the 19th century (W. A. Davis, 1997). English courts construed "will" broadly to encompass meaningful consent; a sleeping or drugged woman who was sexually assaulted, for example, was considered to have been raped. This definition emphasized a woman's consent but made rape difficult to prove.

Capp (1999) investigated the double standard (in which men and women are held to different standards of conduct) in the early modern period (1500–1800) using the London Bridewell records and Old Bailey reports, supplemented by information from ecclesiastical and secular courts in the provinces. Women as well as men recognized that because of the double standard, sexual insults were more effectively used against women than men, explaining why women had more frequent recourse to defamation suits in church courts. Nevertheless, men in the middling classes prized a good reputation. The value of a good reputation provided women with opportunities both for redress of wrongs done to them and exploitation. As Capp summarized in the following:

> Fear of exposure or defamation could render respectable men vulnerable to wronged or calculating women and, while the sexes were never equally matched in the politics of sexual relations and reputation, it is wrong to see women as no more than passive and helpless victims. They were also agents: sometimes heroic, sometimes highly resourceful, at times cynical and shameless. (p. 74)

In particular, men of means and reputation were vulnerable to legal suit or blackmail for allegations of siring children, adultery, and rape. It is likely that out-of-court settlements were very common.

Conley (1986) documented the reluctance of English courts to convict men for rape using trial documents from Kent County between 1859 and 1880. Conviction and acquittal data provide an operational definition of rape as "a brutal act of violence usually committed in a public place on an apparently respectable woman who was previously unknown to her assailant and had done nothing even to acknowledge his presence" (p. 525). Judges always dismissed charges of rape if the woman's protector (father or husband) had accepted money as a settlement for the wrongdoing from the alleged perpetrator. More important, the perceived "respectability" of the alleged rapist was a powerful defense, and the working-class status of the alleged victim a powerful handicap, in the outcome of the prosecutory process.

Early Modern Period in Asia

Ng (1987) discussed sexuality and rape laws in Qing China (1644–1912), a straitlaced and sexually repressed society in which filial piety and female chastity were promoted by the government. The massive Qing legal code contained a section on "Sexual Violations" in which the criteria for establishing rape were delineated. The victim must provide evidence that she had struggled throughout the assault in the form of eyewitnesses, torn clothing, or physical marks of struggle. If initial violence resulted in submission, the crime was classified as "illicit intercourse by mutual consent" summed up by the phrase "forcible beginning, amicable ending." The stringency of this definition was part of a more general effort to reduce litigation in the population. In addition, the laws were designed to portray the government and its soldiers as disciplined and peaceful by discouraging disquieting allegations of rape against Qing soldiers.

The state sponsored a cult of chastity in which it was asserted, "It is a small matter to starve to death, but a serious matter to lose one's virtue" (p. 60). Widows were forbidden to remarry and encouraged to commit suicide upon the death of their husbands. Women were expected to defend their chastity against rapists until death. The few men who were convicted of rape (of chaste and innocent women) were strangled. Women who were found to have engaged in illicit intercourse by not resisting enough were given 80 blows with a heavy bamboo stick if unmarried and 90 if married.

19th- and Early 20th-Century North America

In a chapter concerning sexual conflict in Ontario (Canada) at the end of the 19th and beginning of the 20th century entitled "Maidenly Girls and Designing Women: Prosecutions for Consensual Sex," Dubinsky (1993) noted the following:

> The criminalization of voluntary sexual activities between women and men reveals something of the force of the double standard of sexual behavior, a cultural imperative of remarkable durability. But the sexual double standard was more than a powerful social prejudice. Legislation that made certain types of sex illegal (whether because sex was coerced, or because of the age or relationships of the individuals) was always framed to prevent men acting against women. Men do, of course, act against women's physical wishes, often. But the entire weight of Anglo legal tradition rests on the patriarchal assumption that as Rosalind Coward puts it, "only men have an active sexuality, therefore, only men can actively seek out and commit a sexual crime." (p. 65)

The assumptions Dubinsky (1993) noted remain alive and well in contemporary North America. This can be seen in the perceptions of sexual harassment, for example. Berryman-Fink and Riley (1997) found that having a "feminist orientation" was positively related to the perception of sexual harassment and that women perceived more behaviors to be sexually harassing than did men, although men and women agreed at the extremes (i.e., that some behaviors do not constitute sexual harassment and that others are clearly harassment or coercion). They tended to disagree about the sexually tinged but not overtly coercive behaviors. With respect to unambiguous sexual coercion, data from the National Crime Survey (Wolfgang, Figlio, Tracy, & Singer, 1985) show small differences between the sexes in the perception of crime severity for all crimes, including rape, although rape is perceived to be more serious by women than men.

Recent Trends in North America

The last decade of the 20th century saw a striking decrease in the number of rapes in the United States and Canada. Figure 2.1 shows the rate of

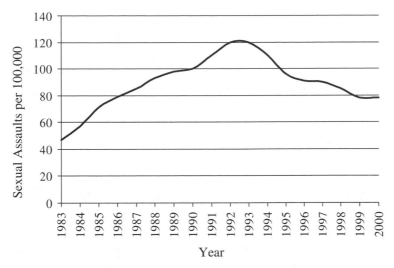

Figure 2.1. Sexual assault in Canada. Source: Statistics Canada.

sexual assault incidents reported to the police in Canada between 1983 and 2000. Yearly changes in these rates are affected by multiple factors, such as changes in reporting and recording behavior, along with real changes in the criminal behavior of interest (O'Brien, 2003). The rate more than doubled between 1983 and 1993 and then dropped by 35% over the following 7 years.

Figure 2.2 shows similar data for the United States. The rate of forcible rape incidents reported to the police declined by 26% from 1992 to 2001. An even more dramatic decline is revealed by U.S. victimization data (self-report data from the National Crime Victimization Survey), shown in Figure 2.3. The victimization rate in sexual assaults dropped by 68% from the peak of 1991 to 2002. As we will discuss in chapter 4, the decline in the number of rapes is not specific to this form of criminal behavior; the 1990s saw a decline in most criminal activities.

RAPE AND WAR

Old Testament accounts of warfare provide stark descriptions of rape, bride capture, and murder. The examples that follow are from the King James Version of the Bible:

> And the children of Israel took all the women of Midian captives, and their little ones, and took the spoil of all their cattle, and all their flocks, and all their goods. . . .
>
> And they brought the captives, and the prey, and the spoil, unto Moses, and Eleazar the priest, and unto the congregation of the children of Israel. . . .
>
> And Moses said unto them, Have ye saved all the women alive? . . .

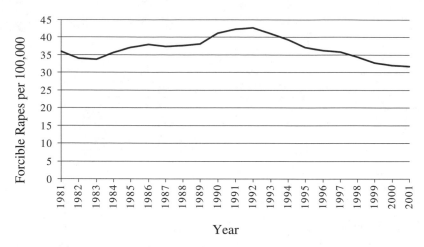

Figure 2.2. Forcible rape in the United States. Source: Uniform Crime Reports, Bureau of Justice Statistics.

> Now therefore kill every male among the little ones, and kill every woman that hath known man by lying with him.
>
> But all the women children, that have not known a man by lying with him, keep alive for yourselves. . . .
>
> And thirty and two thousand persons in all, of women that had not known man by lying with him. (Num. 31:9.9–Num. 31:35.10)

A similar practice is described in Deuteronomy (Deut. 20:13 & 14.3), Judges (Judg. 21:14.20), and Samuel (1 Sam. 30:1–30:2.5). However, sometimes not even the women were saved. For example, "And Nob, the city of the priests, smote he with the edge of the sword, both men and women, children and sucklings, and oxen, and asses, and sheep, with the edge of the sword" (1 Sam. 22:19.19). Particular forms of mutilation were favored, specifically ripping open women who were pregnant (e.g., 2 Kings 15:16.29; Amos 1:13.30).

In the Iliad (ca. 700 B.C.E.), Homer left no doubt about what was expected by a vanquished city in Priam's warning to Hector to retreat behind the walls of Troy:

> Zeus will destroy me in a wretched fate, after I have seen many evils, my sons killed and my daughters dragged away, and bedrooms ravaged and innocent children, thrown to earth in terrible warfare, and daughters-in-law dragged off at the hands of the Achaians, and me dogs will rend on the ground by the door. (quoted in King, 1987, pp. 26–27)

Because of divine intervention, King Agamemnon deprived Achilles of the beautiful Briseis, the prize he had been awarded from the spoils of a sacked city. Achilles, thus dishonored, said in a reply to Odysseus,

> He keeps my beloved wife. Let him enjoy sleeping with her. But why must the Argives fight with the Trojans? Why did Atreides gather and

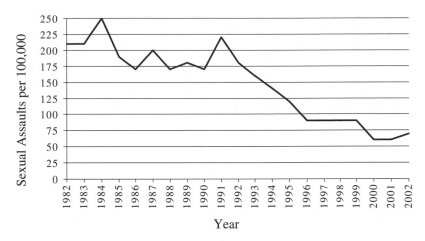

Figure 2.3. Rape victimization in the United States. Source: National Crime Victimization Survey, Bureau of Justice Statistics.

bring an army here? Was it not on account of fair-haired Helen? Are the Atreidai the only ones of mortal men who love their wives? Since any man who is good and sensible loves and cares for his own, as also I loved her from my heart, though she was won by my spear. (quoted in King, 1987, p. 33)

We need not take the Old Testament accounts or the accounts of the Iliad as statements of historical fact to believe that the audiences for whom these works were intended found the events and the motivations of the protagonists to be plausible. Indeed, the available archeological and historical evidence shows that events of the kind described did indeed occur. The ancient people of the Middle East and the Bronze Age Greeks appeared to behave very much like more recent nonindustrialized societies that raid other groups for wives.

In more modern times, the widespread rape of women by soldiers in occupied enemy territory has often been documented (e.g., Brownmiller, 1975; Epp, 1997; Lawson, 1989; Niarchos, 1995; Seifert, 1996). Although reports of rape have sometimes been exaggerated as part of nationalist propaganda, there can be no serious doubt that the practice is very common, involves very large numbers of incidents, and is not restricted to particular armies, countries, or political systems. Mass rape has been perpetrated by American soldiers in Vietnam, Pakistani soldiers in Bengal, German soldiers on the Eastern front in the Second World War, Soviet soldiers during the invasion of Germany, and so on. We provide some examples in the paragraphs that follow to give a taste of this gloomy literature.

The savage repression of the Scots by the English after the Culloden debacle in 1745 involved looting, kidnapping, laying waste the land, casual murder, starvation of the population, and rape:

Where the River Doe meets the Moriston in a black waterfall, Isolbel Macdonald was raped by five soldiers, and her husband, skulking high in the heather, watched this in agony. There were other women raped, too, and always before the doors of their burning homes. The soldiers marched on, shooting an old man and his son as they stood in their field, until the dark glen was burnt and despoiled from Loch Ness to Loch Cluanie. When Lockhart went away his soldiers left nothing of value behind them, and it took them a day to drive all the cattle back over the saddle to Fort Augustus. The women who had been ravished made pacts not to lie with their husbands until nine months had passed. "Which resolution," said the Laird of Glenmoriston, thinking of Isolbel Macdonald and one other, "the husbands agreed to. But they happened (luckily) not to fall with child by the ravishing, nor to contract any bad disease." (Prebble, 1967, p. 205)

In 1799, American General James Clinton instructed his men not to rape Indian women in the Ohio country because the Indians did not themselves rape women prisoners (Abler, 1992). The soldiers did not comply. An Onondaga chief later complained, "They put to death all the Women and Children, excepting some of the young Women that they carried away for the use of their Soldiers, and were put to death in a more shameful and Scandalous manner" (quoted in Abler, 1992, p. 15).

R. Harris (1993) examined the portrayal of French female victims of rape by German soldiers in 1914–1915. Despite greatly exaggerated British and later American propaganda concerning German sexual atrocities, particularly those in Belgium (Gullace, 1997), the rapes in France were carefully documented and appear not to be a figment of nationalist imagination. Nationalist and racist emotions were, however, part of the ensuing controversy over the "child of the barbarian":

> . . . The image of the child of the barbarian . . . raised the spectre of conquest made through the blood line. For those who called for abortion, this barbaric infiltration needed to be stopped at all costs. . . . Such a possibility implied the destruction of the French family. . . . In contrast, maternalism provided another, powerful set of national values to which those involved in the life-and-death struggle could cling. Its advocates argued that France must show herself morally pure and refuse to respond to the barbarian's crime with another "crime." (pp. 204–205)

As the war dragged on, the image of female sacrifice was supplemented by an opposite image of women cuckolding their husbands who were fighting at the front by cohabiting with the occupying German soldiers. The memory of the First World War, however, records only sacrifice and national solidarity. In contrast, after the Second World War, many women who had lived in Vichy France were accused of "horizontal collaboration" and publicly shamed.

The Japanese occupation of Nanking has been estimated to have produced 330,000 murders in 7 weeks (Chang, 1998; Yang, 1999). Japanese soldiers exerted every effort to round up all the young Chinese girls, whom they then raped and usually murdered. Estimates of the number of rapes in Nanking exceed 20,000 (Roland, 1997). The general in charge of the invading army had become severely ill shortly before the fall of Nanking. He had circulated orders prohibiting looting or abusing the population. One wonders whether it would have made a difference if he had been present but also what he knew that motivated him to write such a memo in the first place. It has been documented that there were many killings and about 10,000 rapes earlier when the Japanese army took Hong Kong (Roland, 1997), including a report that some Japanese soldiers were summarily executed for their participation. Although there is continuing controversy about the causes of the Nanking massacre, consensus among historians concerning its size and nature has increased over recent years (Yang, 1999). Elsewhere, the Japanese army forced large numbers of mostly Korean women into sexual slavery; these captives were euphemistically referred to as "comfort women."

The Russian invasion of Germany in 1945 resulted in rape on a truly massive scale. Reviewing the extensive documentation, Beevor (2002) concluded as follows

> The pattern, with soldiers flashing torches in the faces of women huddled in the bunkers to select their victims, appears to have been common to all the Soviet armies involved in the Berlin operation. This process of selection, as opposed to the immediate violence shown in East Prussia, indicates . . . [that] by this stage Soviet soldiers treated German women much more as sexual spoils of war than as substitutes for the Wehrmacht on which to vent their rage. . . . There is a dark area of male sexuality which can emerge all too easily, especially in war, when there are no social and disciplinary restraints. (pp. 326–327)

After the Second World War, attempts were made to make rape illegal in wartime. The 1949 Geneva Convention IV, Article 27, Part III, Section 1, states, "Women shall be especially protected against any attack on their honour, in particular against rape, enforced prostitution, or any form of indecent assault" (quoted in D. E. Buss, 1998, p. 181). Although laudable in intent, it is not clear that legal statutes have saved any women from wartime rape.

D. E. Buss (1998) described the rapes committed in Bosnia:

> Related to this policy of ethnic cleansing was the mass rape of women, principally Muslim women, as part of an officially condoned policy. Although all parties to the war in Bosnia are implicated in the rape of women as a policy of war, it appears that rape was primarily directed at Bosnian Muslim women by Bosnian Serbs. . . . The Warburton Commission concluded that the number of raped Muslim women ranged between 10,000 and 60,000, with 20,000 the likely figure. (p. 177)

Niarchos (1995) noted that virgins and young women between 13 and 35 were targeted for rape in Bosnia. As part of ethnic cleansing, one of the apparent goals was to force the birth of children of mixed "ethnic" descent in the Muslim group.

Modern history has rarely had respite from warfare somewhere on the globe, and the technological ability to make war has steadily increased. Despite the focus of the scholarly literature on rape (including this book) on the sexual coercion that occurs in relatively peaceful modern societies, it is clear that much rape takes place during wartime. In fact, on the basis of the many media accounts of mass rape during the continual warfare of the past century, one might think that at least as much rape is attributable to warfare as to the more ordinary circumstances that we concentrate on in this book. Unfortunately, it is unknown whether the individual differences in propensity to rape identified in this book are relevant to times of war, or whether rape is so common during such times that it becomes a near-universal activity that cuts across individual differences. We will return to the topic of rape and war in chapter 7.

RAPE OF MEN

There is very little evidence that rape of men by women occurs any more than as an oddity. As far as we have been able to determine, such rape is reported neither in the ethnographic literature nor in the historical literature. Modern North American surveys (e.g., Fiebert & Tucci, 1998) indicate that men very seldom report serious sexual coercion from women. In a German survey, 9% of women surveyed indicated that they had completed a sexual act with a man against his will at least once (Krahé, Waizenhöfer, & Möller, 2003). These acts were usually committed against ex-partners and never strangers, usually did not involve intercourse, and seldom used physical force (most often exploiting a man's intoxication or using verbal pressure). Similar results were obtained from a survey of men regarding their experiences of female sexual coercion (Krahé, Scheinberger-Olwig, & Bieneck, 2003); men described their reaction to female sexual coercion as "mildly upsetting."

However, rape of men by other men is mentioned in the historical literature. For example, Gade (1986) noted that homosexual behaviors were first prohibited in Scandinavia in an 1164 statute, where it was noted that "every man has the same right to compensation for carnal intercourse on behalf of his [male] thralls as on behalf of his bondwomen" (p. 136). In Norse literature, homosexual relations were ridiculed, but playing the passive role was particularly shameful (as in Greek and Roman societies). In modern North American societies, male homosexual rape is not infrequently a problem in prisons.

CONCLUSION

The historical and ethnographic literature suggests that rape frequency varies in an understandable fashion. Rape is differentially committed by young men (such as warriors and soldiers) and is most frequently directed at women of reproductive age. Rape is more common when there are few costs for the offenders, despite the high costs for victims. Rape is more frequent under certain and similar conditions across different cultures and time periods. It can reach epidemic proportions in wartime, when men are indifferent to the fates of enemy women or antagonistic toward them. War appears to create conditions that greatly facilitate rape, and rape and abduction of women in turn are often reasons for intergroup conflict and war. Rape in war is also frequently associated with brutal postcoital aggression and the killing of victims.

Rape is more common whenever men are indifferent to the interests of women in general or particular categories of women. Rape, therefore, is strongly related to social class in the historical record; high-status men were more likely to rape lower- than higher-status women. In the ethnographic literature, rape is more common when there are warlike fraternal interest groups. Although rape is less common in times of peace and social order, it is doubtful that there are or have been "rape-free" societies.

These conclusions are consistent with the notion that men and women have conflicting reproductive interests, a notion we return to later in this book. It is not that the reproductive interests of men and women always conflict, as implied by Brownmiller's (1975) famous remark that "rape is nothing more or less than a conscious process of intimidation by which *all men* keep *all women* in a state of fear" (p. 15). Men and women must cooperate as well as compete; their interests sometimes diverge but are overlapping. This is not only an obvious empirical fact but also a necessary consequence of our nature as a species. Humans are group-living animals in which men have female relatives (daughters, sisters, mothers, etc.) to whose destiny they cannot remain indifferent over evolutionary time. The same holds true for women and their inevitable interest in the fate of their sons, brothers, and fathers. Moreover, men, like women, compete with each other (e.g., for mates, reproductive opportunities, resources), making it difficult to maintain gender solidarity over time.

O. D. Jones (1999), drawing primarily on the work of Thornhill and his colleagues (e.g., Thornhill & Palmer, 2000; Thornhill & Thornhill, 1983), listed a number of predictions derived from an adaptationist view of rape, which asserts that rape may have been selected for throughout human evolution because of its positive effect on male reproduction. Among these predictions are the following: Rape will be overwhelmingly a male behavior; rapists will be disproportionately young adult males; rape will seldom result in harm sufficient to preclude conception and birth; and rape will be more common in some situations—those that produce fewer costs and more benefits in relation to alternative mating tactics. To these, we add the following: The environmental or situational factors associated with rape will be historically and culturally general.

None of these predictions demand that men have a psyche specifically adapted for coercive sex; all are compatible with the view that rape could be a by-product of men's strong motivation for having sex with reproductively competent partners (Palmer, 1991). Thornhill and Palmer (2000) listed psychological mechanisms that would constitute a rape-specific adaptation in men: mechanisms involved in evaluating potential victim vulnerability, motivations for men without resources to rape, differential evaluations of the sexual attractiveness of rape victims and consensual partners, differential sperm counts of ejaculates produced by interactions with rape victims and consensual partners, and differential arousal caused by depictions of rape and consensual copulations.

Many of O. D. Jones's (1999) predictions regarding the adaptationist view of rape are supported by the historical and ethnographic literature, especially that rape was committed by young men, has had little costs for the offender, and was differentially directed at fertile women. Rape is also more frequent under certain and similar conditions across cultures and time. One problematic aspect of the view that rape was specifically selected as part of the male reproductive strategy is that there were quite a few homicides and quite brutal treatment of rape victims likely to cause disability or death during wartime. This violence, which is problematic to the idea that rape is part of a male reproductive strategy, is not violence in the service of securing copulation, but rather gratuitous postcoital violence. However, the number of serious injuries and deaths following rape in the ethnographic and historical record cannot be easily quantified, and the number of rape-related pregnancies recorded during recent conflicts is substantial (e.g., Rwanda, Bosnia; reviewed in Swiss & Giller, 1993). We revisit these issues in subsequent chapters.

The historical and ethnographical literature suggests that rape be considered but one method in which men attempt to control women's sexual and reproductive choices. There are a wide variety of other methods by which this is accomplished, including marriage arrangements made by a woman's family, legal proscriptions concerning partner consanguinity and age, seclusion before and after marriage, and so forth. In some cases, the limitation of partner choice may be paternalistic but benignly intended, and in others the interest of the woman may be totally disregarded.

The dramatic short-term changes in the frequency of rape in contemporary societies suggest that some of the factors affecting the likelihood of rape can vary or change fairly quickly. As of this writing, however, there are no satisfying explanations for the recent decline in rape and other violent crimes. In chapter 4 we suggest and test an explanation of the recent decline in rape that is informed by our focus on individual differences.

3

FORCED COPULATION IN THE ANIMAL KINGDOM

Mating in the colorful summer duck or white-cheeked pintail (*Anas bahamensis*) can be quite violent. Some males attempt to force copulation on females by chasing them in flight or by diving after them; other females are waylaid by males hiding in the vegetation. Females try to avoid these aggressive males by staying out of sight. When discovered, they try to escape by diving and hiding under water or by taking flight, which sometimes prompts other males to get involved in the pursuit. Occasionally males manage to catch and mount females, even under water, and females are sometimes seriously injured as a result. Forced copulation is easily distinguished from unforced copulation in white-cheeked pintails by the absence of a courtship display, the grasping and mounting of a resisting female, and the absence of the typical prone posture of an unresisting female.

Sorenson's (1994a, 1994b) extensive field studies of the white-cheeked pintail showed that some individuals are more likely than others to be involved in forced copulation. As with many other ducks, almost all forced copulation involves a paired male and a fertile female other than his mate. In Sorenson's studies, fertile females experienced 0.8 forced copulation attempts per day, compared with 0.1 for unfertile females. This daily average is even

higher than the number of unforced copulations experienced by fertile females (0.5). Occasionally females are forced into copulation by their own
mates after another male has attempted forced copulation.

Perhaps surprisingly, female white-cheeked pintails paired with males
who engage in forced copulation (with other females) are less likely themselves to be the victims of forced copulation compared with females paired
with less aggressive males. That is, some males seem able to force copulations
on other females while also protecting their own mates from the same fate.
Other males both are unable to protect their mates and rarely attempt forced
copulations on other females.

The behavior of white-cheeked pintails illustrates many important points
that emerge from this chapter on forced copulation: Males can sometimes
overcome the resistance of females during mating, forced copulation is often
detrimental to females, certain conditions increase the likelihood of forced
copulation, certain male characteristics increase propensity for forced copulation, and forced copulation may be part of a male reproductive strategy. In
this chapter, we examine forceful male copulatory behavior in many different species. In keeping with the focus on individual differences, our main
goal is to uncover the reasons why some males and not others (within a species) engage in this behavior.

This chapter is divided into four sections. We first define the term *forced
copulation* and contrast it with other terms that have been used to describe
aggressive sexual interactions. We then discuss the ultimate reasons why
mating is often a source of conflict between the sexes. We explain how the
conflict between the sexes over mating can lead to the evolution of male
alternative mating strategies and tactics. Finally, we describe five strategies
that possibly underlie the use of forced copulation in the animal world and
provide examples of each from studies of insects, fish, reptiles, birds, and
mammals.

Before proceeding, it is important to remind the reader that our main
goal in this chapter is to provide a general scientific context to the study of
forced sex. Our lengthy discussion of forced copulation in nonhuman species
should not be taken as trivializing the experiences of human rape victims, as
excusing rapists or diminishing their responsibility because similar behaviors
are seen in other species, or as a shortcut to an easy explanation of the causes
of human rape. Elucidating the causes of human rape necessitates studies of
humans and considerations specific to our species, as we shall discuss in the
chapters that follow. At the same time, it would be scientifically imprudent
to ignore the fact that behaviors similar to rape occur in a wide variety of
nonhuman species, that these behaviors are not random aberrations, and
that much is known about the conditions that underlie their occurrence.
Some authors have postulated that forced sex and other forms of sexual coercion might represent a third form of sexual selection (along with male competition and female choice) that may have shaped the evolution of female

behavior and mating systems (e.g., Chavanne & Gallup, 1998; Smuts & Smuts, 1993).

DEFINING FORCED COPULATION

One of the most difficult aspects of the study of forced copulation in nonhuman species is defining and labeling sexual interactions. It is obvious that researchers cannot interview nonhuman animals about their preferred partners, willingness to mate, reactions to the event, and so forth. All these must be inferred from the behaviors that researchers can see. Labels and definitions used to characterize copulation by force vary a great deal, depending on the researchers and the species they study. Some biologists identify any aggressive sexual interaction as forced copulation. Others also attempt to determine whether the male is circumventing female choice.

In this review, the definitions used by the original researchers will be reported when possible. Readers can decide for themselves whether the behaviors described correspond to their own ideas about forced copulation and to the definition we offer. It is commonly argued that *rape* should be used only to describe relevant human conduct and that other terms should be used with other species (Estep & Bruce, 1981; D. F. J. Hilton, 1982). We follow this suggestion in this chapter.

The term *resisted mating* is commonly used in this field and usually applies to sexual interactions in which the female struggles and attempts to escape from the male in an obvious effort to avoid copulation. It is interesting that there are species in which essentially all matings are resisted; aggression, struggle, and escape are always observed when mating occurs. It is often suggested that females resist male mating attempts to select, directly or indirectly, the healthiest, most vigorous, or most dominant males as genetic fathers for their offspring (for a discussion of resisted mating as female choice, see Eberhard, 2002).

Another common term is *forced copulation* (or *forced mating*). Like resisted mating, forced copulation involves obvious female struggle and attempts to escape, but unlike *resisted mating, forced copulation* is generally used for species in which aggression and struggle are not part of the typical mating interactions. Thus, forced copulation occurs in species in which females sometimes mate without obvious physical resistance, choose the males with which they mate, or determine the start or end of copulation. The term *forced copulation,* as we use it in this chapter, does not apply to those situations just described in which females use resistance as a screening tool. Forced copulation involves the negation of female choice and, of course, requires knowledge of a species' customary courtship.

It is important to note that we do not include in this definition of forced copulation the effect of the behavior on the victim's reproductive success (or fitness). It would certainly be helpful to know whether females that have experienced forced copulation also experienced reduced reproductive success, because it would make it easier to conclude that female choice had been circumvented. Unfortunately, this crucial information is almost always unavailable.[1]

Exhibit 3.1 presents a few important concepts for readers less familiar with studies of animal behavior. Although the focus of this chapter is on forced copulation, we begin with an illustrative example of resisted mating and provide other examples in Exhibit 3.2. These examples show that it can be difficult to distinguish between forced copulation and resisted mating. More important, they reveal how very conflictual mating can be.

Water Striders in an Arms Race

Water striders are small carnivorous insects that skate on the surface of small bodies of water. In most of the 500 species of water striders, mating is quite aggressive. During the mating period, males—the smaller sex—search for females by detecting surface waves produced by moving females. When a male locates a female, he leaps on her and attaches himself to her back. The female inevitably responds by doing somersaults, which often result in the male being thrown upside down and under water. The male attempts to hold on by grasping the female's thorax with his forelegs and her legs with his midlegs. Despite the male's best efforts at holding on, few copulation attempts lead to genital contact. When genital contact does occur, however, the female stops struggling. After sperm transfer, the male rides passively on the back of the female for hours or even days, and the female resumes somersaulting.

Females appear to mate much more often then they need to. Indeed, females of the species *Gerris odontogaster* need only mate approximately every 10th day to fertilize all their eggs (females can store viable sperm for many days) but are sometimes observed to mate several times a day. Multiple mating does not increase viability or size of offspring, and the presence of males re-

---

[1]Other terms and definitions have been proposed. Palmer (1989b) defined *rape* as "copulation involving either the individual's resistance to the best of his/her ability, or the reasonable likelihood that such resistance would result in death or bodily harm to the victim or others whom he/she protects" (p. 358). Smuts and Smuts (1993) defined *sexual coercion* as the

> use by a male of force, or threat of force, that functions to increase the chances that a female will mate with him at a time when she is likely to be fertile, and to decrease the chances that she will mate with other males, at some costs to the female. (pp. 2–3)

This definition combines behavioral and functional elements and includes such nonsexual aggressive actions as infanticide and intimidation. Forced copulation, as defined here, is one of the many facets of sexual coercion as defined by Smuts and Smuts. See C. Crawford and Galdikas (1986) for more information on terms and definitions relevant to forced mating in nonhuman species. One final comment: It is possible, at least in principle, to observe species in which forced copulation characterizes all mating interactions; this could happen when males have a temporary evolutionary edge over females. In this chapter we focus on species in which forced copulation occurs in a proportion of the mating interactions observed.

EXHIBIT 3.1
Behavior, Intent, Purpose, and Reproduction

It is worth considering how we described the female behavior in the beginning of this chapter—that a female acts (in forcefully resisting mating) to achieve some end purpose (mating with the strongest and healthiest male). Do we really think that female beetles have a plan such as this implies? At the risk of being elementary for readers familiar with the animal literature, let us consider a well-known example of apparently planful and intentional behavior from the African savannah (Packer & Pusey, 1983a, 1983b).

Lions live in groups (prides) of several lionesses, who are usually close relatives, and their cubs, which are "headed" by two or three males (usually also related to each other), who are the fathers of all the young. From time to time, the dominant males' position is challenged by younger males in a fight. When these fights occur, the females disperse, and the cubs often hide. If the original dominant males win the fight—the usual outcome—the pride re-forms, and things return to normal. If the challengers win, the old dominant males leave, while the winners search the area and kill any cubs they find. The females do not fiercely defend the lives of their cubs, though they do protest and appear greatly distressed by these lethal actions. Soon after the takeover, the females come into estrous, mate with the new males, and become the mothers of their offspring.

This example points out one of the themes of this book—relations between the sexes invariably involve both mutual and conflicting interests. Informally, describing lions' behavior, we could say that the cubs hide to avoid being killed if challengers win the fight. We might say that a male kills the offspring of his predecessor so that all the pride's resources go into his own offspring. We might even say that the females mate with the murderers of their own cubs because that is the only choice available—not mating would mean not having babies at all. Of course, we do not really think that the hiding cubs "realize" the risks they face. After all, they are very unlikely to have witnessed previous takeovers. Similarly, does the male "understand" the relationship between ending suckling and the onset of estrous? Do the females actually evaluate their options and "decide" to make the best of a bad situation?

Obviously not, but what *do* we mean? Given typical adult male behavior, cubs who linger nearby face certain death after a successful challenge. Ancestral cubs that made themselves scarce, especially in the tallest, thickest grass, had some chance of surviving. Cubs with the inherited tendency to linger near male–male fights never lived to pass such a tendency on to descendants. Over many generations, all cubs then have come to possess the inherited tendency to take off whenever fights start, and any cub somehow born without such a tendency is unlikely to live long enough to pass it on. Similarly, dominant ancestral males who showed tolerance and solicitude toward the offspring of their predecessors saw fewer of their own offspring born and grow to maturity. And again, over many generations, the inherited tendency to seek out and kill cubs has prevailed, because males who lacked this tendency were less reproductively successful than males who possessed it. We leave it to the reader to draw out the natural selection argument for the behavior of the lionesses.

The important points we want to make with the lion story are these: First, the evolutionary way to describe the functions of purposeful behavior illustrated in the previous paragraph, though correct, is rather cumbersome. Thus, biologists often slip into the more informal descriptions illustrated in the paragraph before that. Biologists never forget that such language is a sort of shorthand, but they do sometimes forget to remind others. In the chapters that follow, we try to give such reminders, but we also trust readers to remember the story of the lions.

Our second point is that it is often easier to accept the evolution of physical traits (e.g., binocular vision or opposable thumbs) than that of behaviors, not to mention emotional tendencies. Nevertheless, the example of the lions clearly shows that natu-

continues

EXHIBIT 3.1
(Continued)

ral selection has profoundly affected all these things. Finally, we do not need to propose that the lions have foresight, plans, or insight to understand purposeful actions. The lions are undoubtedly conscious of something; the responses of the suddenly bereft lionesses clearly indicate strong emotional states. But we can explain the behavior without recourse to such things, and we shall do so in the chapters that follow.

---

duces female longevity (Arnqvist, 1989a). Males, however, benefit reproductively from mating with any female because their sperm may displace the sperm of previous males, the so-called *last-male advantage* (Arnqvist, 1988).

Researchers have observed that female water striders are always "reluctant" to mate and have speculated that females always resist mating (Arnqvist, 1988). One suggestion for explaining females' response to male mating attempts is that females struggle at the precopulatory phase to assess male vigor and struggle at the postcopulatory phase to avoid the costs of carrying a male. In G. *odontogaster* and other water strider species, females with males on their backs have reduced mobility, spend more energy, and are at greater risk of predation (Arnqvist, 1989a; Fairbairn, 1993; Watson, Arnqvist, & Stallmann, 1998).

Arnqvist (1992a, 1997) argued, however, that female precopulatory resistance involves a general female reluctance to mate due to the high cost of mating, rather than female testing of male quality. Nevertheless, subtle aspects of mate selection may occur directly or indirectly through female resistance. Indeed, through resistance, females may select better genetic fathers, because the most successful males are found to be better fed and freer of parasites (Arnqvist, 1992b). Also, and perhaps curiously, females who have never mated or females who have no sperm reserve still "put up a fight" (G. Arnqvist, personal communication, September 14, 2000).

The male of the species G. *odontogaster* has a grasping apparatus that is used exclusively, along with the forelegs, to secure females during mating. When the grasping apparatus is removed, male copulatory success drops dramatically. Males with naturally longer apparatus are more successful at mating (Arnqvist, 1989b) than males with naturally shorter apparatus. There is also stronger selection pressure on the size of the grasping apparatus when population density is low (i.e., when females are less numerous and thus harder to catch; Arnqvist, 1992b). It is quite likely that the grasping apparatus evolved to help males mate with reluctant females.[2]

---

[2]In many species (e.g., toads and frogs), males literally attach themselves to their mates to prevent other males from disrupting the copulation and taking over the female. Because takeover attempts are quite rare in water striders, the grasping apparatus probably did not evolve to prevent attempts by other males to interrupt copulation. It probably evolved to help males prevent subsequent mating with other males, because the last male to mate with a female has the best chance of fertilizing the most eggs. In some water striders, females already carrying a male are less often targeted for mating by other males than females not carrying a male (Rubenstein, 1984).

EXHIBIT 3.2
Examples of Resisted Mating

HOLDING ON TO A DUNG FLY

In the dung fly *Sepsis cynipsea,* males wait for females while patrolling a fresh patch of dung and mount them as they arrive. Males ride passively on the backs of females during egg laying, after which females leave the patch and attempt to remove the males by shaking vigorously. Males attempt genital contact only off the patch. To stay on, the males grab the wing base with modified forelegs that act as a clamp. About 40% of males successfully achieve mating; the others are shaken off. G. R. Allen and Simmons (1996) observed that the symmetry of the forelegs is related to male success (high body symmetry often reflects good genes or good health or both): Males who achieve mating are more symmetrical, on average, than other males. Female resistance thus seems to act as a filter to select the best males. The same seems true of certain beetles and crabs.

BEETLE BATTLES

Soldier beetles *(Chauliognathus pennsylvanicus)* mate on flowers, where they also feed. McCauley and Wade (1978; McCauley, 1981) reported that females always resist mating attempts by males by either struggling or fleeing and that most mating attempts are unsuccessful. Larger males are the most successful (McCauley & Wade, 1978; McLain, 1982). McCauley noted that female resistance may serve as a filter for male quality—the best males are the ones that are large, healthy, and strong enough to overcome female resistance.

CRAB KIDNAPS

Henmi, Koga, and Murai (1993) reported aggressive copulation in the sand bubbler crab *(Scopimera globosa)*. Courtship is absent in this species, and all copulations appear to be resisted by females. Sand bubbler crabs mate on the sand or in burrows, where females tend the eggs for a few days. The smallest males capture and mate with females on the surface of the sand, whereas larger males capture females, sequester them in a burrow, and mate with them there. The last male to mate has the reproductive edge. Henmi et al. proposed that forced mating can easily evolve and courtship disappear when members of the species live in very dense areas and when males can overcome female resistance. Males that spend time courting in dense areas lose to males that simply capture females.

SEAL OF DISAPPROVAL

Many mammals mate with much violence, and one of the most striking is the elephant seal *(Mirounga angustirostris)*. For a few weeks each year, female elephant seals gather on rock islands to deliver a single pup. Once pups are weaned, females mate again and then return to sea. Females usually mate with the harem holder, an older and very large male who keeps other males away. Sometimes other males sneak in and attempt to mate with females, who invariably emit loud cries in apparent protest. Males also attempt to mate when females leave the harem to return to sea. Males are so keen to mate they sometimes guard and mate with dead females.
Mating is quite aggressive:

continues

EXHIBIT 3.1
(Continued)

Male courtship is usually direct, aggressive and persistent. On land, where 95% of the copulations occur, a male moves directly to the side of a female, and without preliminaries, puts a foreflipper over her back, bites her on the neck, pulls her strongly to him with his foreflipper, and attempts intromission. (Le Boeuf & Mesnick, 1990, p. 145)

Males are about five times the size of females (harem holders can be 11 times larger) and can cause serious injuries to females and pups during mating and fighting with other males. In a study covering many years of observations, Cox and Le Boeuf (1977) examined the responses of females to mating. They distinguished among three responses. In the first, *total protest,* "the female issues threat vocalizations, whips her hindquarters from side to side, or tries to escape" (p. 321). In the second, *partial protest,* female resistance stops before the male achieves intromission. In the third, *no protest,* the female passively accepts mating, or she may merely try to move away. Of 1,478 mounting attempts observed, only 7% were not protested. Total protest or partial protest was the main response of females throughout the whole stay on the breeding island, except on the day of departure. It seems that females accept mounting attempts from males on the last day because it is the only safe way to leave the area and get to sea (Le Boeuf & Mesnick, 1990; Mesnick & Le Boeuf, 1991).

Why are females so reluctant to mate, even when in estrous? One likely explanation is that female protests initiate male–male competition. Indeed, female protests invariably provoke other males to approach and fight, and the winners of the fights are the ones who eventually get to mate. Protests may thus serve female reproductive interests by increasing the chances that she will mate with the strongest male. Although females often protest when mounted by harem holders, they do so less often and for a shorter period of time.*

HERDING IN DOLPHINS

Male bottlenose dolphins *(Tursiops sp.)* engage in a behavior called *herding,* in which two or more of them sequester a female for a few hours or even days. Connor, Smolker, and Richards (1992) described the aggressive behaviors of males toward the female: "Male aggression . . . included chasing, hitting with the tail, head-jerks . . . charging, biting, or slamming bodily into the female. Males enforced herding partly by making a 'popping' vocalization which induced the herded female to approach" (p. 987). Females were more likely to be herded when they were fertile. Herding ended when the female escaped. Males formed an alliance of two or three members to catch females or steal them from other males. They also formed super alliances (Connor, Heithaus, & Barre, 2001), in which two alliances join forces to steal a female from another alliance.

Virtually nothing is known about female choice in bottlenose dolphins (R. C. Connor, personal communication, December 4, 2001). The sexes sometimes engage in affiliative behavior, but noncoercive mating is very rarely observed (Connor, Richards, Smolker, & Mann, 1996).

---

*The mating behavior of the elephant seal illustrates that it can be difficult to distinguish between resisted mating and forced copulation. The same can be said for the Australian sea lion (*Neophoca cinerea;* Marlow, 1975), the Hawaiian monk seal (*Monachus schauinslandi;* Alcorn & Buelna, 1989), and the crabeater seal (*Lobodon carcinophagus;* Siniff, Stirling, Bengston, & Reichle, 1979). Campagna, Le Boeuf, and Cappozzo (1988) described organized and strategic raids of fertile females by bachelor Southern sea lions (*Otaria byronia).* Females vigorously resisted raiders, at least until the males became established residents.

Other body parts are helpful to males in overcoming female resistance. Males of the species *Aquarius remigis* have wider front legs than females, despite the fact that females are overall slightly bigger. Males with the widest legs have more successful mating attempts than other males (Weigensberg & Fairbairn, 1996), suggesting that they are better at overcoming female resistance. In addition, males with longer genital segments (independent of body size) also obtain greater mating success (Preziosi & Fairbairn, 1996).

One would expect that if males can evolve special body parts used to secure struggling females during mating, females might evolve special body parts to better resist males. Indeed, the female of the species *Gerris incognitos* has evolved spines to resist male grasping: "The modified female spines increase the posterior distance between the abdomens of the sexes during the premating struggle, impeding the male's critical genital grasp" (p. 124, Arnqvist & Rowe, 1995). Arnqvist and Rowe experimentally shortened or lengthened the female spines and observed that females with longer spines were more successful at throwing off males. Arnqvist, Thornhill, and Rowe (1997) observed that females with naturally longer abdominal spines mated less frequently (probably because they could better resist mating attempts).

Arnqvist and Rowe (2002) showed, in a study of 15 species of water striders, that males and females were in fact in an evolutionary arms race. Males evolve armament to secure females, whereas females evolve armaments to resist them. When one sex has an advantage over the other, the outcome of mating struggles favors that sex, at least for a while.

Other strider species have less conflictual copulations—at least sometimes. In some species, the male attracts females by defending an attractive territory. Females who visit the territory do not resist mating attempts. Some males, however, adopt an aggressive mating tactic under certain conditions, such as when they are small or when there are few suitable sites to deposit eggs (reviewed in Arnqvist, 1997). According to our definition, then, these males seem to be engaging in forced copulation.

Female resistance can serve as a screen to select the best males, either indirectly by inciting male–male competition or directly by mating with the strongest, healthiest male (the one that overcame female resistance). Although resisted mating is sometimes difficult to distinguish from forced copulation, there are species in which the behaviors observed clearly meet our definition of forced copulation. The orangutan is such a species.

Big and Small Orangutans

Orangutans (*Pongo pygmaeus*) are solitary, slow moving, long lived, arboreal, and very elusive. Fully mature adult males are about twice the size of mature females and are the most solitary (Rodman & Mitani, 1987). They announce their presence with calls heard over long distances and loud crashing of branches and trees. Mature males are spatially distributed but do not maintain a stable territory for very long. They ignore sexual invitations from adolescent females and are most attracted to mature females without infants.

Other sexually mature males are about the size of females. They follow adolescent and adult females around, even though adult females tend to ignore them. They carefully avoid big males and rarely tolerate the presence of other males their own size when females are around. They have none of the sexually dimorphic traits and behaviors of big males (long calls, big throat pouches, cheek pads, and long beards). A few have been seen to grow into big males in captivity (Maggioncalda & Sapolsky, 2002), and one was recently reported to do so in the wild (Utami, Goossens, Bruford, de Ruiter, & van Hooff, 2002). Females have fairly stable, small, and overlapping home ranges and are more social than males. Three or four females and a few small males may occupy the range of a big male at any one time. Most of the daily activities of orangutans consist of looking for and eating leaves, bark, and fruit.

Females form consortships principally with big males—exclusive pairings that last for periods of hours, days, or months. All unforced copulations occur in the context of consortships. Big males, but not small males, have a hard time keeping up with the females, and so consortships involving small males last longer but are invariably broken up when a big male appears.

Forced copulation and female resistance have been well described by field primatologists. For example, "males were generally aggressive, seizing apparently frightened females and clasping them round the thighs or waist with their feet. . . . In four aggressive attempts at copulation, males struck and bit struggling females" (MacKinnon, 1979, p. 261). Mitani (1985) observed that "achieving intromission with uncooperative females seemed difficult, and males had to grab, bite or slap females before they could copulate. While thrusting, males continue to restrain struggling females by grasping their arms, legs and bodies" (p. 396). Galdikas (1981) observed similar behavior:

> Rape occurred when a male attempted to copulate or copulated with a female who resisted his efforts to position her for intromission [insertion of penis]. A female's struggles ranged in intensity and duration all the way from brief tussles with squealing and some pushing and slapping at the male's hands to protracted violent fights in which the female struggled throughout the length of the copulation, emitted loud rape grunts, and bit the male whenever she could. (p. 288)

The rape grunt is a low, guttural sound emitted only on those occasions and only by adult females. Despite the violence of some of these events, female injuries have never been observed. Also, males are not aggressive toward females in other contexts.

Although both big and small males have been observed to engage in forced copulation in the wild, small males appear to do so much more frequently. Fertile females are the most common (if not the exclusive) targets of forced copulation[3] (Fox, 2002; Galdikas, 1979, 1981, 1985a, 1985b, 1985c; MacKinnon, 1979; Mitani, 1985; Rodman, 1979; Schürmann & van Hooff, 1986). Mitani calculated the ratio of the use of forced versus unforced copulation by individual males and found that it was inversely related to their dominance in relationship to other males (determined by observing the outcomes of male–male interactions). Thus, the most dominant male in Mitani's study (a big male) was the least likely to engage in forced copulation, and the least dominant (a small male) was the most likely (in fact, he engaged exclusively in forced copulations). This observation is somewhat intriguing, considering that females may not have witnessed dominance interactions between males. Females may prefer the company of big males because they prefer them as sexual partners but also perhaps because they receive protection from harassment from small males (Fox, 2002).

Big males defend territories that contain potentially fertile females and have mating access to them. They cannot herd females or control their whereabouts. Small males can enter these territories and locate fertile females faster than big males. Most researchers believe that small males are engaged in an alternative, low-cost reproductive strategy while waiting for their chance to become big males. In one study spanning 25 years, paternity analysis showed that small males had fathered 6 of the 10 offspring in the area (Utami et al., 2002), but it could not be determined whether those offspring were the result of forced or unforced copulations.

In a different line of studies, Nadler (1977) examined the sexual behavior of captive orangutan pairs placed in the same cage daily over a period of about 4 weeks. Females were generally unwilling to mate, but copulation occurred almost daily. Female resistance generally stopped once thrusting began. Females were more receptive and multiple copulations were more frequent at estrous. When females could control proximity to the male, copulatory frequency dropped dramatically and was highly correlated with estrous (Nadler & Collins, 1991).

In sum, females prefer large, mature males, and males prefer fertile, adult females. Small males are quite persistent when consorting with females, frequently attempt copulation with unwilling females, and frequently succeed (especially when no big males are around). Male dominance rank seems to determine the use of forceful tactics and female response to male copulation attempts. Big males and adult females generally engage in serial monogamy in the context of consortships. Most researchers believed that pregnancy almost exclusively results from consorts involving adult females and big males, but recent DNA fingerprinting data do not support this belief.

---

[3]Galdikas (1995) witnessed and described the rape of a woman by a human-habituated adult male orangutan.

Later in this chapter we present many other cases of forced copulation in different animal species. At this point we turn to the reasons why mating can be so conflictual in the animal world.

THE BATTLE BETWEEN THE SEXES

In many insect species, females are unreceptive after one mating. They have to defend themselves against persistent males by kicking their legs, moving their abdomens away, tightening their wings, flying or running away, or crashing into objects with a male on their backs. Repeated copulations have no benefit for females in terms of egg production but may have significant costs, such as increased predation risk and disruption of egg laying.

These behaviors reveal a fundamental conflict between males and females stemming from the fact that additional partners or copulations are likely to benefit males, in terms of reproductive success, but not necessarily females. A similar conflict arises with regard to duration of copulation in some species—a longer duration is often of benefit to males but not necessarily to females—and many other aspects of mating (W. D. Brown, Crespi, & Choe, 1997; Zuk & Simmons, 1997). As with water striders, females mate more often than is necessary for them to reproduce optimally (Arnqvist & Nilsson, 2000). Forced copulation is probably one reason why females mate more often than is optimal for them.

A general principle in biology helps explain reproductive conflict in insects and other animal groups. In most species, males have a larger potential reproductive rate than females. That is, the maximum number of offspring that can be produced in a given unit of time (e.g., a breeding season) is larger for males than for females (Clutton-Brock & Vincent, 1991). The reason for this sex difference is that in most species, females require more time and energy than males to produce offspring—they have a larger necessary parental investment (Trivers, 1972). The fruit fly is one example. After mating, the female lays eggs before mating again, whereas the male is almost immediately ready to mate again. The female is out of the pool of available mates for a while, whereas the male never leaves it. Thus, even though the sex ratio—the number of males relative to the number of females—might be fairly even, there are often more males than females available for mating, so the operational sex ratio is male biased. In mammals, the necessary female parental investment is even higher relative to that of males.

The sex difference in potential reproductive rate creates a situation in which male variance in reproductive success can exceed female variance. Because males are not as limited as females in the number of offspring they can produce, a few males can, in principle, obtain most mating opportunities and produce almost all the offspring (as in the case of elephant seals; see Exhibit 3.2), leaving the rest of males with very few or none. This phenomenon, called *polygyny*, tends to lead to fierce male–male competition for access to females and the evolution of male alternative mating strategies and tactics. It is important to note that in the few cases in which the necessary parental investment is higher in males than in females, as in pipefishes and some species of sandpipers, competition for mates is more intense among females (Daly & Wilson, 1983; Gwynne, 1991).

Thus, from the male's reproductive point of view (in all but a very few species), females are most of the time in short supply. From the female's point of view, there are too many males (and, often, too few good ones). Reproductive output is the bottom line in nature. Any behavior that increases it is selected and has greater representation in the next generations. The use of methods to seduce, persuade, coerce, or force females to copulate would be selected over generations when it has greater net reproductive benefit than cost for males. The use of methods to resist male seduction, persuasion, coercion, or force would be selected over generations when it has greater net reproductive benefit than cost for females.

It is not surprising, then, that the conflict between males and females over mating can lead to evolutionary arms races between the sexes, like that of the water strider. W. R. Rice (1996, 1998) directly observed such antagonistic coevolution in fruit flies by allowing males but not females to evolve over many generations. In Rice's studies, females could not evolve over successive generations because they always came from the original stock. He observed that males "adapted to the static female phenotype"[4] (Rice, 1996, p. 232) and were subsequently better at mating with already mated females. Male flies produced one peptide in their ejaculates that encouraged egg laying and diminished females' subsequent interest in mating and another that killed rival sperm (and was also toxic to females). After 40 generations, experimental males fathered more offspring, prevented competitors from siring progeny, and caused females to die young. When females were also allowed to evolve, however, they counteracted these effects.

The battle of the sexes can lead to creative female defenses. In some butterflies, females have solved the problem of males' relentless sexual attention in a unique way—by looking like males. Female African swallowtail butterflies (*Papilio dardanus*) come in three types (or morphs). In decreasing order of frequency, one mimics another toxic butterfly species, the second looks just like a colorful healthy male swallowtail (an andromorph), and the third mimics a faded old male swallowtail. Cook, Vernon, Bateson, and Guildford (1994) performed a mate choice experiment to determine what advantage the rarer but more vulnerable andromorphs get from their conspicuous appearance compared with the regular morph (the one that looks like a completely different species, one that is unappealing to predators).

---

[4]The phenotype represents the manifest characteristics of the organism. The genotype is the genetic constitution of the organism.

Although andromorphs may be more conspicuous to predators, they also seem to receive less male attention. A similar phenomenon has been observed in a damselfly, *Ischnura graellsii* (Cordero, 1992). Thus, instead of physical resistance, and despite the cost of conspicuousness, females in some species appear to have evolved andromorphy to avoid males' sexual attention.

ALTERNATIVE MALE STRATEGIES AND TACTICS

In evolutionary biology (and in this book), the term *strategy* refers to a genetically based decision rule that guides development and behavior. The term *tactic* refers to a phenotype (e.g., a preference, a behavior, a bodily structure) that results from a strategy. *Alternative strategies* are different strategies adopted by genetically different classes of males. For example, the bluegill sunfish *(Lepomis macrochirus)* grows either big or small and exhibits either a parental or a sneaky mating strategy, respectively, to match. The small–sneaky strategy works quite well, reproductively speaking, as long as there are not too many sneakers around. The reproductive success (or fitness) of the alternative strategies and genotypes are equal at a specific frequency equilibrium (frequency-dependent selection); if they were not, one strategy and genotype would supplant the other over evolutionary time. There are very few demonstrations of alternative strategies in the animal behavior literature, but they do exist (e.g., the ruff).

A more common type of strategy is called *conditional*. In conditional strategies, individuals are genetically the same but may adopt different (alternative) tactics, depending on conditions encountered during their lifetime. Alternative tactics, unlike alternative strategies, do not have the same fitness (except at the switch point between tactics). Biologists use the phrase "making the best of a bad job" to describe tactics that are not as successful as others, but that are used as a last resort to avoid reproductive oblivion.

Conditional strategies can be developmentally fixed or flexible. In developmentally fixed conditional strategies, once the organism is exposed to the relevant cues and adopts a given set of tactics, there is no further change. Developmentally fixed conditional strategies can produce individual differences in behavior, rates of maturation, or morphological features. For example, the presence of horns in the adult dung beetle *Onthophagus acuminatus* depends on food availability during larval development (D. J. Emlen, 1994). Males without horns cannot fight with other males for access to females and instead adopt a sneaky mating tactic. In developmentally flexible conditional strategies, the animal can switch back and forth from one tactic to the other as the situation or its status changes over time. There are many examples of such strategies in the animal world, and some are presented in the sections that follow. These concepts are extremely useful in understanding variations in individual development and in the use of particular behaviors, such as forced copulation (Alonzo & Warner, 2000; Dominey, 1984; Gross, 1996).

STRATEGIES POSSIBLY UNDERLYING FORCED COPULATION

A number of plausible strategies may lie behind forced copulation among animals. In this section we present the five main strategies that we identified as possibly underlying the use of forced copulation in the animal species studied so far, along with examples of each. The first four are conditional strategies, and the last is an alternative strategy.

The Circumstantial Opportunist

Circumstantial opportunists are males that generally court receptive females but switch to forceful tactics when females are unreceptive. Circumstantial opportunism is a conditional strategy in which all or most males use forced copulation only under this specific condition, and we use the term only with species that do not form pair bonds (opportunism in pair-bonded species is described in the following section as a separate strategy). This conditional strategy is most common in insects but has been seen in other species as well.

The apple maggot fly (Rhagoletis pomonella) is a good example. D. C. Smith and Prokopy (1980) observed that when females are on leaves, males tend to approach them from the front, and females accept mating attempts. When females move to fruit to lay eggs, however, males approaching from the front are rebuffed. All successful matings on fruit occur when a male surprises a female from behind. Smith and Prokopy noted that males can use both approaches and that mating with nonvirgin females (those on fruit) sometimes leads to fertilization. Most mating on fruit "may be forced mating with unreceptive females" (p. 585).

The Lake Eyre dragon (Ctenophorus maculosus) is a tiny reptile living in an arid part of Australia. At the end of the receptive period, the female's belly becomes bright red. The bright belly is exposed when females flip over to reject males and is never exposed at other times. In a study of a semicaptive group of dragons, Olsson (1995) observed that males continued to target and copulate with red-bellied and unwilling females. Sexually aggressive males do not engage in courtship; instead, they rush the females, grasp their napes, roll them onto their sides, and attempt copulation. Females, sometimes injured in these attacks, defend themselves by running away, threatening, or flipping over. Larger males are more successful at overcoming resistance.

It is not clear why male Lake Eyre dragons sometimes target postreceptive females (perhaps they can store sperm) or why females are so reluctant to mate. Females also reject some males during their receptive period. Females' bright undersides may serve to distract males or may simply function to attract heat from the ground during incubation (Mitchell, 1973). Coercive mating has been reported in other lizard species as well (e.g., D. I. Werner, 1978) and in snakes (Shine, Langkilde, & Mason, 2003).

In sum, circumstantial opportunists are males of species that do not form pair bonds who use forced copulation opportunistically and conditionally. Males compete for access to receptive females, and they attempt forced copulation when females are unreceptive. Coercive males do not appear to be at a competitive disadvantage. Other examples are provided in the Appendix at the end of the book.

The Opportunistic Spouse

Opportunistic spouses are males who have attracted a mate but who also obtain additional matings by forcing copulation on other females. This conditional strategy has been observed in some pair-bonded bird species where forced copulation is used only by some of the males and only under specific conditions.

Many of the scientific studies of forced copulation involve ducks, especially mallards (Anas platyrhynchos). Ducks have an intromittent organ (penislike structure) that may facilitate forced copulation (Briskie & Mongomerie, 1997). Forced copulation in mallards has been reported throughout the century and as early as 1910 (reviewed in Burns, Cheng, & McKinney, 1980). In a study of a crowded population in Manitoba, Titman and Lowther (1975) observed many examples of what they called "rape attempts," which involved no courtship display, female resistance, and mating on land rather than on water. These attempts tended to attract other males, who sometimes joined in. An average of just under four males were involved in each rape attempt. If he was present, the mate of the female under attack usually tried to defend her. Females suffered serious injuries in these assaults, and few led to intromission. The authors wondered whether the crowded conditions were responsible for this and other "behavioral abnormalities" (p. 1281).

Two years later, Barash (1977) reported 83 rape attempts in a small population of mallards (rape was defined as involving obvious female resistance and escape and no courtship display). Sixty-four of these incidents involved multiple attackers with an average, again, of roughly four per incident. The mate of the victim tried to defend her, especially when there was only one attacker.

Later work showed that forced copulation in mallards is directed at fertile females and can produce offspring. Cheng, Burns, and McKinney (1982) observed that forced copulations (those that seemingly resulted in intromission) in mallards were most likely during the egg-laying period: "Males were sensitive to the laying status of the females and were making determined [forced copulation] attempts on days when they were most likely to fertilize eggs" (p. 698). Burns et al. (1980) introduced 16 young males and 11 young females to a captive area prior to the mating period. Half of the males carried a rare recessive gene affecting the color of the plumage. Progeny produced by males without the rare gene could not show the unusual plumage. Nevertheless, among females paired with males without the rare gene, 8% of the progeny showed the unusual plumage, indicating that females sometimes copulated with males other than their mates. Burns et al. observed 58 forced copulations and 309 forced copulation attempts (in which intromission was unlikely), and most of the females with progeny with unusual plumage had experienced forced copulation prior to egg laying.

Insemination through forced copulation probably leads to production of offspring in the wild as well. In a genetic study of wild mallards, Evarts and Williams (1987) found that almost one brood in five involved multiple paternity. Multiple paternity is unlikely to be the result of unforced extra-pair copulations or of egg dumping, because these are extremely rare events in mallards.

Forced copulation has been observed in other ducks.[5] Bailey, Seymour, and Stewart (1978; see also Stewart & Titman, 1980) observed eight "attempted rapes" by paired and unpaired male blue-winged teals (Anas discors) but noted that the unpaired males were more likely to use courtship displays and their forced mounting attempts were rarely successful. Brewer (1997) observed 800 forced copulation attempts in a captive population of chiloe widgeon (Anas sibilatrix), all by paired males. Females successfully thwarted most attempts.

McKinney and Stolen (1982) introduced eight wild-caught pairs of green-winged teals (Anas crecca carolinensis) into two flight pens and observed their mating behaviors over a 9-week period. The pairs maintained their bonds during the study period, but all males attempted forced copulation on other females when egg laying began. Males achieved copulation by pursuing, grasping, and generally overpowering females. Chases and hiding were commonplace, turning the study area into a battlefield. All males defended their mates but also engaged in forced copulations on their own mates when unsuccessful in their defense. Females vigorously resisted forced copulation.

In an ambitious 4-year study of 649 individually marked lesser scaup (Aythya affinis) in their natural habitat, Afton (1985) found that copulations "in spite of female resistance" (p. 147) were more often directed at the most fertile females (i.e., in the prelaying and laying period), even though these same females were much better protected by their mates than less fertile

---

[5]McKinney (1985) noted that forced copulation has been observed in 21 of the 37 species of "dabbling" ducks (Anatini). He later increased the number to 55 species in 17 genera of waterfowl (McKinney & Evarts, 1997).

females. Paired males were more likely than unpaired males to engage in forced copulation; in fact, forced copulation attempts by unpaired males were extremely rare.

In sum, the mating behavior of many dabbling ducks appears to involve a primary tactic of courtship and pair bonding, which includes protection of the mate from other males and from predators (Titman, 1983), and a secondary tactic involving courting other females and attempting copulation with them whether they are willing or not (Bossema & Roemers, 1985). The loose territoriality in some species sets the stage for this conditional strategy (Gauthier, 1988). Unpaired males court females and rarely engage in forced copulation even when they have no access to unpaired females (Goodburn, 1984). Forced copulation is therefore not the result of lack of access to mates (McKinney, 1985). In fact, males who have the best pairing success are the most likely to use forced copulation and the most adept at protecting their mates against the same fate (E. S. Davis, 2002a). These conclusions also apply to other species of birds, including geese (see the Appendix for a detailed account of forced copulation in geese and other bird species). M. J. L. Magrath and Komdeur (2003) discussed the factors that affect the perennial trade-off between parental care and mating effort and noted that high-quality males may not need to reduce the first for the latter because of their lesser investment in somatic maintenance.

In birds, forced copulation is almost always a special kind of extra-pair copulation, in that perpetrators and victims already have a mate. When forced copulation occurs between paired birds, it is usually due to suspected (another male is hanging around) or observed extra-pair copulation by the female member of the pair (more on this in the next section). Thus, understanding forced copulation in birds requires understanding extra-pair copulation.

Westneat, Sherman, and Morton (1990) documented a number of well-accepted facts about avian extra-pair copulation: It is common, it occurs when females are fertile, it sometimes results in fertilization and offspring, it is probably a male tactic of increased mating effort stimulated by certain conditions, and it is rarely solicited by females and is often actively resisted.[6] The reproductive benefits of extra-pair copulations are fairly obvious for males. Extra-pair copulations can augment the number of offspring. Although one might expect the costs to include risk of cuckoldry and less paternal investment, males who succeed in extra-pair copulation are actually also successful in guarding their mates.

Females may benefit from extra-pair copulations by ensuring fertilization, by mating with a male of higher quality than their own mate, or by promoting genetic diversity in the brood. (Foerster, Delhey, Johnsen, Lifjeld,

---

[6]Female solicitation of extra-pair mates has been observed in the red-winged blackbird (*Agelaius phoeniceus*; E. M. Gray, 1996), the chaffinch (*Fringilla coelebs*; Sheldon, 1994), and the razorbill (*Alca torda*; Wagner, 1991), as well as other species.

& Kempenaers, 2003, reported evidence for the latter.) Costs could include aggressive retaliation from their mates, mating with a male of lower quality than their own mates, loss of paternal care, increased within-brood competition due to lesser genetic relatedness, risk of predation due to vulnerability during mating, and risk of receiving parasites. These considerations are complicated by female resistance, which could increase both benefits (stronger, healthier males will overcome resistance and thus eliminate the risk of mating with a low-quality male) and costs (injury). Little is known about the reproductive consequences of female resistance to extra-pair copulation. The extent of resistance in waterfowl strongly suggests that forced copulation has negative consequences for females.[7]

Not everyone agrees that forced copulation has reproductive benefits for males. Gowaty and Buschhaus (1998) proposed that the anatomy of the female cloaca (genital opening in birds) makes it unlikely that forced copulation leads to successful insemination in species lacking an intromittent organ. Indeed, they argued, females could prevent the entry, eject, or kill sperm from coercive males. They developed an alternative to the idea that males increase reproductive success through forced copulation. They suggested that male aggression toward females (including sexual aggression) creates a dangerous environment for females, leading them to pair bond with protective males. In other words, males benefit from aggression by later being chosen by females who desire protection.

There are two reasons why this notion is probably incorrect. First, most predictions derived from this theory are not confirmed (e.g., that unpaired males should be the most aggressive and that aggressive copulation attempts should occur outside the fertile period). Second, even though females might in principle be able to reject the sperm of coercive males, there may be little selection pressure for them to do so. Indeed, even though females may have been selected to resist extra-pair copulation attempts, after forced copulation has happened, there may be little to gain by rejecting the sperm. And females might even have something to gain by not rejecting it—obtaining genes from skilled, strong, and successful males. In support of this idea, in Japanese quails (*Coturnix japonica*) the fertilization success of forced copulations equals that of unforced copulations, even though males do not have an intromittent organ and females are able to expel sperm from their cloacae (Adkins-Regan, 1995).[8]

Gowaty and Buschhaus (1998) mentioned that their theory does not apply to species with intromittent organs. Only 3% of birds have an intro-

---

[7]Female mallards have even been observed to avoid forced copulation by perching on trees, a very uncommon behavior for mallards (Bingman, 1980).

[8]Mesnick (1997) developed a similar but more promising proposal, the *bodyguard hypothesis*, which says that throughout evolution, sexual aggression by males has created a selection pressure in some species for females to affiliate and bond with males for protection. Wilson and Mesnick (1997) tested this hypothesis with humans and observed that being married greatly decreases the risk of sexual coercion from men other than spouses or boyfriends.

mittent organ, but many of the species discussed in this chapter do have one. Briskie and Montgomerie (1997; Briskie, 1998) suggested that the intromittent organ might have "evolved primarily as a result of the selective advantages accruing to males that force copulation" (p. 84; see also McKinney & Evarts, 1997).[9]

The Cuckold

The cuckold attempts forced copulation on his own mate when he suspects that she has engaged in extra-pair copulation (forced or not). It is a conditional strategy used by males under that specific circumstance. In the American black duck (*Anas rupribes*), forced copulation may occur even when the male simply finds another male swimming near his mate upon his return to the nest area (Seymour & Titman, 1979). Male mallards that fail to defend their mates against forced copulation are often seen attempting forced copulation on them about 10 minutes after the incident (Barash, 1977). Intra-pair forced copulation is a frequent response of male shrikes (*Lanius minor*) after the absence of their mates, but only during the fertile period (Valera, Hoi, & Kristin, 2003).

Interesting studies of forced copulation and mate guarding have been conducted with the zebra finch (*Taeniopygia guttata*), revealing that particular males are more likely to be cuckolded. Zebra finches are monogamous, and both parents care for the nestlings, but extra-pair copulations are observed frequently (Birkhead & Fletcher, 1995; Birkhead, Hunter, & Pellatt, 1989). In one set of experiments, pairs with particular plumage color combinations were introduced in an aviary and their mating behaviors recorded. Males carefully guarded their mates, and pairs copulated frequently when females were fertile. Males also courted other females and sometimes engaged in extra-pair copulations without female resistance. Some males, however, actively disrupted intra-pair copulations and forced copulation on the female. Extra-pair forced copulations were also observed when females were left alone (because the paired male either left or was removed). Similar behaviors are observed in the wild (Birkhead, Clarkson, & Zann, 1988).

Males who saw their mates engage in extra-pair copulation were aggressive toward them and sometimes forced copulation. Intra-pair forced copulation was never observed in any other context. Last sperm precedence is estimated to be about 80% in zebra finches. A significant number of offspring were the result of extra-pair copulations, but the authors could not determine the reproductive success of forced extra-pair copulation or the reproductive success of males' aggressive response to their mates' extra-pair copulations.

---

[9]It is interesting that the testes, sperm number, and cloacal size of birds increase at the arrival of the breeding season and, in some species, increase only if the birds are paired, which might explain why unpaired males are rarely involved in forced copulation.

In an ingenious experiment, color bands were added to the legs of the males to increase (red band) or decrease (green band) attractiveness to females[10] (Burley, Enstrom, & Chitwood, 1994). Eighty percent of the 906 observed extra-pair copulations were forced ("when a female resisted male mounting attempt(s) by pecking the male and/or attempting to flee by flying and/or hopping away rapidly"; p. 1034). Attractive males were more often involved than unattractive males in unforced extra-pair mating (in which females did not resist) but were just as often involved in forced extra-pair mating. Of particular interest, females mated to green-banded males were more often the recipients of both forced and, especially, unforced extra-pair mating attempts than females mated to the more attractive red-banded males.[11] Females mated to more attractive males were the most successful in thwarting copulation attempts by other males. Despite their lowered attractiveness, both to their mates and to other females, green-banded males did not show any particular tendency to engage in extra-pair forced copulation.

In some birds, the mate can be quite aggressive, but not necessarily in a sexual way, toward a female that has copulated or just consorted with another male. For example, in the ring dove (*Streptopelia risoria*), males are able to determine if a female has recently consorted with a male, probably by observing her nesting behavior, and consequently are quite aggressive toward her (Erickson & Zenone, 1976; Zenone, Sims, & Erickson, 1979). In some species, males simply reduce the amount of investment they provide to the chicks when extra-pair copulations are suspected, whereas in others, males seem to ignore the extra-pair copulation and continue to invest in offspring.

There are a few other examples, some mentioned in the Appendix, of forced copulation by cuckolds. The forceful behavior of the cuckold likely serves his reproductive interests through sperm competition. *Sperm competition* refers to a form of male–male competition that takes place after mating and inside the female reproductive tract (Birkhead, 2000). The reproductive outcome of forced copulation by cuckolds, however, is unknown. It is also possible that forced copulation serves to "punish" females and therefore prevents future extra-pair copulations (these are sometimes called *retaliatory copulations*)—although, if this were the case, nonsexual aggression would achieve the same goal.

The Competitively Disadvantaged

Some males are more attractive than others, either because they are healthier, older, or more dominant or because they possess resources impor-

---

[10]The greater attractiveness of red-banded zebra finch males has been demonstrated in many different ways, and these males achieve greater reproductive success.
[11]As a result, green-banded males are more likely to tend genetically unrelated offspring (Burley, Parker, & Lundy, 1996).

tant to females (e.g., food, good territory, desirable nest site). Sometimes females let the males fight and simply pick the victor. In all these situations, there are some males who cannot attract or have access to mating partners using "conventional" approaches. To achieve some mating success, they have to resort to alternative, second-rate, last-resort tactics. The use of forced copulation as a result of competitive disadvantage, another conditional strategy, characterizes many species. Again, the reproductive success of alternative, "best of a bad job" tactics does not need to be high for these tactics to evolve. It only has to be greater than zero and higher than the opportunity costs in forgone reproductive success through other tactics. In the following paragraphs we present examples of this strategy in insects, birds, and mammals.

A clear case of forced copulation as a result of competitive disadvantage can be seen in the migratory grasshopper *Melanoplus sanguinipes*. Belovsky, Slade, and Chase (1996) performed ingenious mate choice experiments and found that females prefer the best foragers, even if males are deprived of foraging opportunities prior to mating. This suggests that females attend to some phenotypic characteristics that signal, perhaps among other things, foraging abilities. These characteristics are likely to be visual and may involve behavior, because blind females chose males at random and immobilized males were ignored.[12]

When males were allowed to compete for females, the worst foragers engaged in forced copulation. In grasshoppers, forced copulation is difficult to distinguish from ordinary copulation because both involve the male leaping on the female, but Belovsky et al. (1996) carefully noted that "When a male displayed prior to attempting copulation, females responded with femoral vibrations and body swaying. When a male stalked a female and tried to copulate without first displaying, the female reacted by leaping, flipping over, and prying at the male with her hind legs" (p. 439).

Forced copulation attempts were less successful than copulation attempts preceded by a display. Larger males were more successful at forced copulation than smaller males, but male body size did not affect the success of displays. In repeated trials, males were found to adjust their mating behavior (stalking vs. display) as a function of the foraging ability of other males in the experimental box. Forced copulation had costs for females in preventing successful copulation with better foragers. Forced copulation in grasshoppers seems to be a conditional mating tactic used by (relatively) low-quality males to secure mating opportunities with reluctant females.

Another good example of condition dependence is provided by the scorpion fly. Thanks to the work of entomologist Randy Thornhill, scorpion flies (*Panorpa*) are by far the best-studied species, insect or otherwise, with regard to forced copulation. Male scorpion flies hunt for dead insects, sometimes ending their lives in spider webs. After having located and defended a dead

_____

[12]Not surprisingly, males were less selective and attempted copulation with female dummies.

insect, males of many scorpion fly species secrete a pheromone to attract females, who eat the dead insect while copulating. Sometimes males secrete a salivary mass that is also defended from other males and readily accepted as food by females. Some males are unable to capture an insect or have eaten too long ago to produce a salivary mass. Such males do not produce pheromones, are avoided by females, and attempt forced copulation:

> A rape attempt involves a male without a nuptial offering . . . rushing toward a passing female and lashing out his mobile abdomen at her. On the end of the abdomen is a large, muscular genital bulb with a terminal pair of genital claspers. If the male successfully grabs a leg or wing of the female with his genital claspers, he slowly attempts to re-position the female. He then secures the anterior edge of the female's right forewing with the notal organ . . . a clamp-like structure formed from parts of the dorsum. . . . Females fight vigorously to escape. When the female's wings are secured, the male attempts to grasp the genitalia of the female with his genital claspers. The female attempts to keep her abdominal tip away from the male's probing claspers. The male retains hold of the female's wing with the notal organ during copulation, which may last a few hours in some species. (Thornhill, 1980, p. 53)

The notal organ is used in both forced and unforced copulation, but experiments show that the notal organ is particularly helpful in achieving or prolonging copulation with unreceptive females (Thornhill, 1980). When the notal organ of one male scorpion fly species is covered by warm beeswax, males without nuptial offerings are rarely seen copulating. When the notal organ is covered by warm water (which does not interfere with its use), males without nuptial offerings do manage to copulate. The notal organ thus seems to have evolved to help males secure unwilling females.

Thornhill's research suggests that males are capable of using all three tactics. Their first tactical choice is to capture a dead insect, offer it to the female, and copulate with her. When dead insects are unavailable, they move to the second-choice tactic, the salivary mass. When they cannot produce a salivary mass, they resort to the third choice, forced copulation. The first two tactics have a very high rate of copulation and fertilization; the third is much less effective: Males manage to copulate in only 15% of forced mating attempts, and only 50% of those copulations result in insemination. Unforced copulations have much higher fertilization success. Female resistance probably causes the low rate of fertilization by forced copulation, but perhaps males who have difficulty finding food have fewer sperm.

Several factors influence males' choice of tactics. First is the availability of dead insects. Males who force sex on females switch to nuptial offerings when insects become available and switch back to forcing copulation when insects are scarce. Body size, which is associated with success in male–male competition and access to food, has also been shown to influence the choice of tactics (Thornhill, 1987). In some species at least, males who lose in competition for insects have less symmetrical forewings, and they mate less often (Thornhill, 1992).

Female scorpion flies show clear mate preferences. They prefer males with large insect offerings, then males with small insects, and then males with salivary masses. They strongly avoid males without offerings. Thus, "the directions of preference of alternatives adopted by males and of preference of males by females are identical" (Thornhill, 1981, p. 381). Because of this symmetry of preferences, conflict between the sexes arises only when males are unable to provide nutrients to the females.[13]

In other scorpion fly species, males offer salivary masses during copulation and do not appear to attempt to force copulation when they have nothing to offer. Instead, males aggressively attempt to increase the duration of copulation even after the salivary mass is gone. It is to the advantage of the male to copulate for a long time, because copulation duration is related to probability of fertilization. From the female viewpoint, a long copulation prevents her from feeding.

Thornhill and Sauer (1991) studied the notal organ in these species under a number of conditions. Some males had their notal organ rendered inoperative with adhesive; other males had adhesive placed near but not covering the notal organ. They also varied the feeding history of males and females and observed the duration of copulations. Length of copulation was directly related to the number of salivary masses a male could produce. Also, the notal organ allowed males to greatly extend the duration of copulation. Thus, the notal organ allows these males to coerce females into longer copulations.

In the birds examined already in this chapter, males and females form pair bonds. This is not the case for orange- or yellow-rumped honeyguides (*Indicator xanthonotus*). Honeyguides eat honey, larvae, and beeswax, and they get their name from their habit of "leading" animals and people to beehives. Male honeyguides mate via one of two routes. A few defend areas around a beehive and receive visits from hungry females. These territorial males court and copulate with almost all visiting females. Other males, called *peripherals* or *satellites*, loiter around occupied territories and attempt to copulate with visiting females by force. Females always avoid these males. When the territorial male is removed, a peripheral male takes his place and females willingly copulate with him (Cronin & Sherman, 1976). It thus appears that these males use forced copulation conditionally when they do not have access to the resources females seek.

Female bighorn (mountain) sheep (*Ovis canadensis canadensis*) are receptive for only a few days each year and copulate frequently during that

---

[13]In another related species, *Harpobittacus nigriceps* (hanging flies), males do not coerce females when they do not have a nuptial offering. The mating conflict manifests itself differently: Males hang from branches with their offerings, and females eat the dead insect while copulating. Sometimes females prematurely end the copulation when they are done eating. Females may even fight with small males, steal the insect, and fly away without copulating at all (Thornhill, 1983).

THE CAUSES OF RAPE

period. Males, the bigger sex, fight with one another for dominance and access to females. Dominant males achieve most copulations by tending and defending a single female at a time. Ewes prefer dominant rams and congregate where dominant rams will find them. Subordinate rams try to mate with an ewe in estrous by blocking her access to the main rutting area and keeping her away from other rams. Other subordinate rams engage in what Hogg (1984, 1987) called *coursing*—fighting dominant males or sneaking past their defenses. Some of these attempts are successful due to exhaustion or injury to the dominant ram or the sheer number of coursers.

Ewes are unreceptive to coursers: "Ewes resist rams attempting coursing copulations by (a) accelerating, dodging, or whirling as a coursing ram rises to mount, (b) perching on ledges that are difficult to approach, (c) standing under rock overhangs or deadfalls, and (d) winding through aspen groves or other vegetation that limits male maneuvers" (Hogg & Forbes, 1997, p. 34). These behaviors are not observed in courtship involving dominant males.[14] Almost 80% of coursing copulations were followed by copulations without courtship by a dominant male within 10 minutes (Hogg, 1984). Coursers obtain a large number of copulations concentrated on the last day of a female's estrous, suggesting that coursing may be a reproductively viable tactic (Hogg, 1988).

Hogg and Forbes (1997) studied the reproductive consequences of the three male bighorn tactics. Rams can use all three tactics (depending on their dominance rank), but the researchers were able to link the identities of copulating rams and conceptions. On the basis of genetic data, behavioral observations, and mathematical modeling, they found that almost half of conceptions resulted from coursing. Coursing seems to be a successful mating tactic by mature rams without consorts of their own. The relative number of coursers is fairly constant across years, suggesting it is a frequency-dependent tactic (Hogg, 1987).[15]

Forced copulation as a result of competitive disadvantage is well documented in orangutans, as we described earlier in this chapter. Small males, who typically are rejected by fertile females, frequently engage in forced copulation. Field researchers have noted that forced copulation is quite rare in other primates.[16] In a recent book on primate sexuality (Dixson, 1998), only

---

[14]The interactions between coursers and ewes meet our definition of forced copulation, whereas the interactions between blockers and ewes meet Smuts and Smuts's (1993) definition of sexual coercion.
[15]In contrast, forced copulation does not occur among the less sexually dimorphic pronghorn (*Antilocapra americana*). Pronghorn males form harems, and a few males get most of the copulations. During a given season, most males do not copulate. Female pronghorns actively select males and mate only once. They travel from harem to harem until they settle at estrous on one male. Females also incite male fighting by moving away from the harem holder to peripheral males. After the fights, they refuse all males except the winner (J. A. Byers, Moodie, & Hall, 1994). Pronghorns show that lack of access to females is not sufficient for the evolution of forceful copulatory tactics.
[16]Monkeys have been extensively studied in the wild and in the laboratory, but very few instances of forced copulation have ever been reported. C. B. Jones (1985) reported forced copulation attempts in mantled howler monkeys (*Alouatta palliata*), but females were able to repel all of them. Milton (1985)

one page of text is devoted to coercive mating. In the 40 chapters of the edited book *Primate Societies* (Smuts, Cheney, Seyfarth, Wrangham, & Struhsaker, 1987), only a few pages are devoted to forced copulation, in a chapter on orangutans. Forced copulation has been observed, however, in laboratory tests under certain conditions (see Appendix).

Opportunists, cuckolds, and competitively disadvantaged males use forced copulation as an alternative tactic under those conditions that favor it. The tactic is likely part of a single strategy shared by all males of the species. Forced copulation is proximally caused by particular cues (which vary by species). There is one other very different type of strategy—the morph.

The Morph

In a few species, males that use forced copulation (or sneaky fertilization in oviparous fish) are genetically different from males that do not; forceful or sneaky tactics are part of an alternative strategy.

A single genetic polymorphism[17] on the Y chromosome controls the size of male swordtails *(Xiphophorus nigrensis)* such that some mature early and remain small whereas others mature late and grow large. Large males almost always court females, whereas small males sometimes attempt forced copulation, depending, among other things, on the presence of large males (Zimmerer & Kallman, 1989). Females prefer large males (Ryan & Causey, 1989). Ryan, Pease, and Morris's (1992) study of fecundity, age at first reproduction, and death rate suggests that the reproductive success of the two male morphs are roughly equal.

Similarly, in the bluegill sunfish *(Lepomis macrochirus)*, there are two types of males. Parental or territorial males are large and mature late at 7 or 8 years old. They defend a nest, attract females, and protect the eggs. Cuckolders are smaller males that mature at 2 years. Small cuckolders attempt to sneak past parental males to mate with spawning females. Larger cuckolders mimic spawning females to enter a parental male's territory (Gross & Charnov, 1980). Cuckolders have a much larger testis-to-body-weight ratio than parental males (Dominey, 1980) and win in sperm competition with parental males (Fu, Neff, & Gross, 2001). They do not live as long as parental males but account for a large proportion of the population.

---

reported that male woolly spider monkeys *(Brachyteles arachnoides)* may successfully attempt copulation with a female right after a copulating pair breaks off, but females' resistance was equivocal: "This reluctance on the female may be feigned because, when males lost sexual interest, the female actively solicited copulation" (p. 56). Bercovitch, Sladky, Roy, and Goy (1987) studied adult rhesus macaques *(Macaca mulatta)* in captivity. Although young males were particularly likely to attack older females, few of the attacks led to copulation. In fact, copulation was more likely when both partners were not aggressive. Attacks by young males seemed to be an effort to assert dominance rather than to force copulation. Soltis, Mitsunaga, Shimizu, Yanagihara, and Nozaki (1997) studied captive Japanese macaques *(Macaca fuscata)* and concluded that "forced copulation is not known to occur in Japanese macaques" (p. 734).

[17]A genetic polymorphism refers to a gene having different "versions" or alleles.

Some authors believe that the two bluegill sunfish morphs represent true alternative strategies maintained by frequency-dependent selection. Gross (1991a) tested this idea by analyzing the effect of population density on the pairing success of the two morphs at four natural spawning sites. Pairing success was defined as the frequency of sperm released with females as they dip to the bottom to release eggs. The relationship between density of cuckolders and pairing success varied by site, mostly because of differences in the amount of cover or hiding places used by the cuckolders. The general pattern, however, was of a peak pairing success for cuckolders at a certain density, followed by a decline as the number of cuckolders increased: "Each colony thus has an optimum cuckolder density, dependent on cover, at which cuckolder pairing success is maximized" (Gross, 1991a, p. 64). Later studies using DNA tests of paternity showed that the reproductive success of sneakers was about equal to their proportion in the population (Neff, 2001).

CONCLUSION

It is clear that forced copulation occurs in a wide variety of species. It has even been suggested that some plants engage in forceful mating—the male plant tries anything possible to get its pollen around females' barriers, and females erect ever more effective barriers (Janzen, 1977). Yet despite the many examples reviewed in this chapter and in the Appendix, our reading of the literature left us with the impression that much remains to be discovered.

The lack of systematic studies of forced copulation in most species does not allow a precise identification of the characteristics of species that engage in forced copulation or the conditions under which it could be expected to evolve. There are some promising candidates, as suggested by the notion of conflict between the sexes and the empirical data on species that use forced copulation: sexual size dimorphism favoring males (i.e., males can physically overpower females), polygynous mating system (i.e., some males obtain more mating partners than others), male-biased operational sex ratio (i.e., there are more males than females available to mate), asynchronous breeding (i.e., not all females copulate and breed at the same time), group living or breeding (i.e., a male has easy access to more than one female), and lesser male than female parental investment (i.e., larger sex difference in maximum reproductive rates). Many of these characteristics co-occur. Most, but not all, of the species reviewed in this chapter have these characteristics, but many species have these characteristics and do not, as far as we know, engage in forced copulation. All of these characteristics are present in *Homo sapiens*.

Despite major gaps in the literature, a number of regularities are apparent. First, forced copulation is something males do to females. Although females in some species can be quite assertive when it comes to mating, we have not encountered a single instance of a female forcing sex on a male.[18] Second, forced copulation does not appear to be an anomalous behavior generated by such unusual conditions as overcrowding, captivity, or poor health. Third, males tend to target fertile females. Fourth, forced copulation sometimes leads to insemination, fertilization, and offspring. Fifth, males in most species do not engage exclusively in forced copulation; males that engage in forced copulation are generally also seen courting females at other times. Sixth and finally, some males are more likely than others to engage in forced copulation, and some are more successful at it than others.

These regularities lead to the general conclusion that forced copulation (and sneak fertilization in oviparous fish) is a tactic used by some males under some conditions to increase reproduction. The use of DNA fingerprinting will help better determine the reproductive consequences of forced copulation in different species. In this review we propose five strategies that underlie the use of forced copulation. Apart from one rare strategy (the morph), forced copulation is used conditionally, based on particular individual and situational characteristics.[19]

As suggested by the notion of an evolutionary arms race, the threat of forced copulation has probably been a strong selection pressure for female mating behavior toward males. The bowerbird provides a fascinating example of the effect of the threat of forced copulation on the exercise of female choice and the evolution of courtship. Male bowerbirds build elaborate structures to attract females. Females carefully inspect these structures and their owners and settle on one male to mate with. Studies by Borgia (1995) have elucidated the origin of bower building. It seems that females use the structure to protect themselves against the possibility of forced copulation. Indeed, because males have to run around a wall or a pole to get to the female, females can safely inspect the male and can leave the area unmolested if they wish. The bower was (and probably still is) a way for the male to indicate to the female that she will be able to exercise mate choice.

---

[18]Clearly, morphological constraints might prevent females from successfully forcing sex on males in most species. Paul Vasey has observed female Japanese macaques (*Macaca fuscata*) harassing unresponsive males until they copulated (personal communication, January 27, 2004). Hatziolos and Caldwell (1983) reported female sexual harassment of males in the crustacean *Pseudosquilla ciliata*, a species in which males are quite choosy.

[19]We caution that it is possible that some species have been incorrectly assigned, because we sometimes had to rely on incomplete information; it is also possible that forced copulation is not part of a reproductive strategy in some of the species we reviewed, but rather a by-product of general male aggressive tendencies or (in rare cases) of abnormal environmental or social conditions.

II

IDENTIFYING AND MAKING SENSE OF INDIVIDUAL DIFFERENCES

4

ANTISOCIALITY AND MATING EFFORT

Not all men are inclined to rape. If this statement were false, there would be no reason for the focus of this book, and rape could be understood, at least proximally, by analyzing the transient and immediate circumstances (e.g., opportunities) that promote rape. Even if it was found that most men rape in some circumstances (e.g., when a group of men invades enemy territory and comes across young defenseless women), one would still need to explain why only a proportion of these men rape in other circumstances. What is it about the characteristics of some men, and the interaction of these characteristics with certain contexts, that increases the likelihood of rape?

We thus turn our attention to individual differences in men's propensity to rape. We closely investigate the roles of antisociality, mating effort, sexual preferences, and different psychopathologies in rape and then discuss the roles of various situational and contextual factors. We also examine the sources of those individual differences that are reliably associated with propensity to rape. In doing so, we use many of the concepts introduced in the previous section, in particular the notions of reproductive variance, conflict between the sexes, and conditional versus alternative strategies. We begin

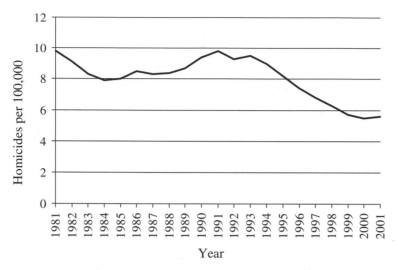

Figure 4.1. Homicide victimization in the United States. Source: Uniform Crime Reports, Bureau of Justice Statistics.

this section of the book with an examination of the role of antisociality and mating effort.

Aggregate statistics suggest that many of the factors that influence men's propensity to commit rape also influence men's propensity to commit crimes more generally. For instance, young men are overrepresented among persons charged or convicted of rape (see W. M. Shields & Shields, 1983; Thornhill & Thornhill, 1983), just as they are more likely than anyone else to commit other violent crimes, such as homicide and assault, as well as such nonviolent crimes as theft (Ellis & Walsh, 2000).

Another indication of the link between rape and general criminality at the aggregate level is that rates of rape tend to parallel rates of other crimes over time and places. For example, as we mentioned in chapter 2, victimization and official statistics in the United States and Canada show a decline in rape in the 1990s (Figures 2.1 and 2.2) that closely parallels a general decline in such other crimes (Figures 4.1 and 4.2) as homicide, assault, sexual and physical abuse of children, the victimization of women by their partners, and robberies (Blumstein & Wallman, 2000; Finkelhor & Jones, 2004; L. M. Jones & Finkelhor, 2001; Lykken, 2001; Ouimet, 2002). Also, there is a very strong and positive correlation between the prevalence of rape and the prevalence of murder and assault across different societies (Barber, 2000).

The first goal of this chapter is to investigate the link between rape and antisocial tendencies at the individual (rather than aggregate) level. Is rape part of a general antisocial lifestyle? Are rapists crime specialists or generalists? The second goal of this chapter is to examine the sexual behavior, or *mating effort,* of rapists. Are there links between the propensity to rape and the tendency to engage in other sexual behaviors? Are rapists

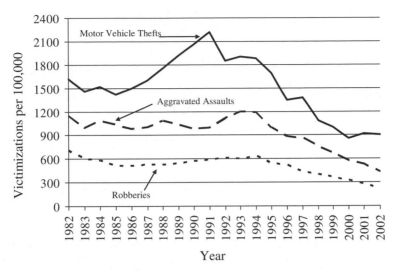

Figure 4.2. Crime victimization in the United States. Source: National Crime Victimization Survey, Bureau of Justice Statistics.

similar to other offenders with regard to mating effort? Do they have access to consenting sexual partners, or are they, as is often postulated, deprived of sexual opportunities?

The concepts of antisociality and mating effort are closely linked, both theoretically and empirically, and thus we consider them together in one chapter. As we shall discuss, these concepts have a large role to play in an understanding of men's propensity for rape and sexual coercion. In Exhibit 4.1, we briefly discuss the concept and the origins of individual differences, and in Exhibit 4.2 we discuss methods used to search for meaningful differences among men in their propensity to rape.

MATING EFFORT AND PARENTAL INVESTMENT

The concept of mating effort is best understood when contrasted with the concept of parental investment. *Mating effort* refers to energy expended in acquiring and keeping sexual partners, whereas *parental investment* refers to energy expended in the care and protection of the mate and especially offspring. Mating effort necessarily precedes (and often accompanies) parental investment, but it is not necessarily followed or accompanied by parental investment.

The sex difference in the necessary or minimum amount of parental investment needed for reproduction and the associated sex difference in potential reproductive rate discussed in chapter 3 imply that there may have been a stronger selection pressure on men than on women to seek and be open to sexual opportunities. An increase in number of sexual partners is

EXHIBIT 4.1
Individual Differences

Individual differences are those characteristics that vary among people but are stable over time and circumstances within a person. The sources of individual differences can be classified, using a developmental arrow, into four major areas: genes, prenatal environment, family environment, and the larger social environment.

Humans share many of the same genes, but a small proportion come in different versions (polymorphic genes). Psychological characteristics are about 50% heritable— about half of the observed variation among people (in most traits, including antisociality) is attributable to genetic differences among people. The other half of this variation is due to exposure to different environments (Plomin & Daniels, 1987). This is a well-accepted fact, and researchers have turned to the role that particular genetic units play in development. Although the developmental arrow starts with genes, genes do not stop work at birth; they affect behavior throughout the life span (Johnston & Edwards, 2002).

The second source of individual differences is the prenatal environment. Fetuses are exposed to different uterine environments because they have different mothers and because the uterus changes with each pregnancy. Even identical twins are exposed to different uterine environments (of which the other twin is an important part), explaining why twins have different fingerprint patterns. Events occurring before birth greatly influence development, including later antisocial behavior.

The third source of individual differences is the family. Families vary in resources, number of parents, amount of conflict, degree of intellectual or athletic stimulation, and so on. Even within the family, children are exposed to different environments. A first-born child has a different social environment than younger siblings. Parents do not treat children identically. Between- and within-family variation is related to development, including antisocial behavior.

Fourth, the larger social environment might produce or accentuate individual differences. Neighborhood characteristics, peers, and local educational and economic resources are related to development throughout life and also to the development of antisocial behavior.

As mentioned above, about 50% of observed variation in psychological traits is due to environmental influences, of which there are two types—shared environment and nonshared influences. Shared environmental influences make siblings alike (in addition to genes) and make siblings from one family differ from those of other families. Nonshared influences make siblings differ from one another. Shared influences are things to which siblings are more or less similarly exposed (e.g., parents' education, number of books in the home), whereas nonshared influences are things to which siblings are not equally exposed (e.g., the uterine environment, accidents, differential parental treatment). Studies have shown that most of the environmental effect on psychological traits is of the nonshared variety. What differs *between* families is much less important than what differs *within* families. There may even be within-family processes accentuating sibling differences (Lalumière, Quinsey, & Craig, 1996). Antisocial behavior is heavily influenced by nonshared factors, but aspects of the shared environment are also important (Carey & Goldman, 1997).

People are not randomly or passively exposed to the environment, however. Children at greatest genetic and neurobiological risk for later serious antisocial behavior are also more often exposed to adverse environments. People seek different environments based on initial characteristics, and their environments in turn affect them. This active synergy between genetic tendencies and the environment is probably responsible for the finding that measures of trait heritability tend to increase with age (Plomin, 1989).

There are two general types of developmental program. The first is executed regardless of normal variations in the environment. For example, within a very wide

continues

range, variation in the uterine environment has no influence on the number of eyes or fingers. The environment is important—nutrients are necessary, for example—but outside extreme perturbations of the uterine environment, babies are born with 10 fingers and binocular vision. People readily develop a fear of heights (or at least a strong feeling of discomfort standing next to a cliff), a tendency to seek food when hungry, and a preference for symmetrical features, irrespective of variations in the environment. These are examples of outcomes of *obligate* programs, in contrast with *facultative* or *conditional* programs.

In conditional programs, development is guided by environmental cues that, over evolutionary history, have been relevant to the development of the feature in question. Examples are the ability of the skin (in most people) to darken because of sun exposure and children's ability to acquire the language spoken by people around them. In chapter 3, we saw examples of conditional programs underlying male use of forced copulation. Throughout this book we discuss sources of individual differences in men's use of sexually coercive tactics, sometimes referring to these concepts. Recent reviews of individual differences in antisocial behavior can be found in Quinsey et al. (2004) and D. C. Rowe (2002).

---

more likely to have produced an increase in reproductive success for men than women over human evolutionary history. Indeed, research has confirmed that men and women have different mating strategies and aspirations and that men spend more energy on mating effort than women (reviewed in D. M. Buss, 1999; Low, 2000; Mealey, 2000; for cross-cultural evidence, see Schmitt, 2003).

But there are important intrasex differences in the amount of energy devoted to mating effort and parental investment (D. M. Buss & Schmitt, 1993; Gangestad & Simpson, 2000; Haselton & Buss, 2001; Landolt, Lalumière, & Quinsey, 1995; Simpson & Gangestad, 1991). Some men commit to one partner and devote all their energies to their families, whereas, at the other extreme, some men never commit to one partner and spend all their energy courting new partners. Women, also, show variation in their allocation of mating and parenting effort (reviewed in Gangestad & Simpson, 2000). As we will discuss, this variation is closely linked to variation in antisociality in both sexes.

ANTISOCIALITY

Antisociality is a broad construct referring to antisocial conduct and to personal characteristics associated with or promoting antisocial conduct. *Antisocial conduct* is any criminal, delinquent, or violent behavior in which the interest of one person is disregarded for the benefit of the actor. It is the opposite of the cooperative behaviors that form the basis of formal and informal social contracts. Antisociality is strongly related to age and gender, with young men being the most antisocial across cultures and historical periods (reviewed in Ellis & Walsh, 2000; Quinsey, Skilling, Lalumière, & Craig, 2004). But beyond age and sex differences, there are important individual

EXHIBIT 4.2
A Methodological Caution

Psychologists and other social scientists commonly use two different methods when searching for useful variables related to men's tendency to rape. The first is the *hidden groups* approach. In such a method, questionnaires are given to a sample of men—volunteers answering an advertisement or college undergraduates, for example. Among the questionnaires is one that asks men whether they have ever (or how many times they have) engaged in a number of increasingly coercive sexual behaviors, ranging from subtle verbal pressure to forceful rape using a weapon (e.g., Koss & Gaines, 1993). Some researchers (e.g., Malamuth & Ceniti, 1986) have asked men whether, if they knew they would not be caught and no one would ever know, they would rape someone. By adopting a cutoff, researchers then classify the participants as sexually coercive or not. Researchers could also ignore cutoffs and treat participants as varying in their amount (or severity) of sexual coercion, but this is rarely done.

Also among the questionnaires are those touching on the researchers' theoretical interests—opinions about women's liberation, attitudes about delinquent behavior, feelings of loneliness or anger, and so on. Differences in these opinions, attitudes, or feelings as a function of the sexually coercive distinction from the other questionnaire are used to test hypotheses about the causes of sexual coercion.

At first glance, this makes sense. It stands to reason that participants know better than anyone else what they have done (or might do) in the way of sexual coercion. As well, it seems sensible to assume that an anonymous questionnaire would elicit honest reports of these things, as well as sincere answers about opinions, attitudes, and feelings. Why would participants lie in an anonymous survey? However, what stands to reason might not be true. Unfortunately for the scientific investigation of the propensity to rape, people's anonymous reports of what they have done, let alone what they would do in a hypothetical situation, are quite poor. Self-reports are affected by things they should not be and unaffected by things that should exert an influence. For example, in a study of teenagers' anonymous reports of aggression (including sexual aggression), randomly selected participants reported approximately the same number of violent incidents *in the last month* as did other randomly selected participants *in the last year* (N. Z. Hilton, Harris, & Rice, 1998). Conversely, in studies of representative samples from one population, men reported committing many fewer acts of violence toward women than women reported experiencing by men—something that also could not be true. Moreover, people do not have special knowledge (i.e., over and above what could be predicted by a third party) about what they will do in a hypothetical situation (e.g., Ross & Nisbett, 1991). Common sense aside, self-report is an imprecise way to study much of human behavior.

The second research strategy is the *known groups* method: Men charged or convicted of rape (or sexual assault), usually tested in prison or psychiatric hospitals, are compared with other men. Sometimes this comparison group consists of criminals with no known history of rape, but it is also common for the controls to be nonoffenders recruited from the community. During intake assessment or assessment before beginning treatment, paper-and-pencil questionnaires are administered. One key issue with the known groups method concerns the composition of the control group. It is not obvious whom such a group should contain. To illustrate, consider a hypothetical study: A researcher hypothesizes that rape occurs when men feel shame. Shame might be the result of harsh parenting or sexual abuse or might occur when a man experiences failure at work or in social life as an adult.* To test this hypothesis, the researcher constructs a paper-and-pencil test of shame that asks people to agree or disagree (on a 7-point scale) with "I could never visit a nudist camp" or "I am disgusted with myself." Assuming that these items do a good job of measuring shame, what

continues

control group should be used? Nonoffenders from the community might be correct if the hypothesis were about crime in general. But this hypothesis—that rape occurs when men have been made to feel shame—says nothing about whether other antisocial behavior or violence are also due to shame. If the hypothesis were about violent crime in general, how should the community volunteers be chosen? College undergraduates are different from imprisoned rapists in many ways (e.g., socioeconomic status, education, age) not directly related to violent crime. Researchers' hypotheses are often unclear about the specificity of causation, making the choice of a suitable control group problematic.

But assume that the hypothesis is very specific: Only rape occurs when men feel shame, and rape occurs only when men feel shame. First, men who have committed violent crimes other than rape should not give high scores on the shame scale. Thus, a group of violent offenders (e.g., kidnappers, murderers, bank robbers) from the same institution would be a good control group. But that is only half the story. On the basis of the very specific hypothesis, the researcher needs to seek other men who have high shame scores. According to the specific hypothesis, it should be very difficult to find men with high shame scores who have not committed rape. If there were many men living peacefully (i.e., no hint of sexual aggression) in the community with high shame scores, the hypothesis about a unique and specific relationship between shame and rape would be invalid. Researchers in this area rarely test the second part of this hypothesis by trying to recruit men with high shame scores and evaluating whether they have committed rape.

Before leaving our hypothesis about shame and rape (and hidden and known groups methods), there is another matter. Even if rape and shame were uniquely related, the shame–rape hypothesis is unproved. If shame caused rape, shame and rape would certainly be related—men high on shame must, on average, be more likely to be rapists than men low on shame, and rapists must, on average, be higher on shame than other men. But many things are related without one causing the other. Most obviously, an association between shame and rape could just as easily mean that rape caused shame. Perhaps being arrested, tried, convicted, and sentenced for a sex crime (or simply committing a sex crime) causes shame. Such shame could be greater than that caused by all other tribulations, even arrest, trial, and conviction for other crimes. Even if shame and rape were uniquely related, it is just as plausible that rape causes shame.

And there is another possibility: Two things can be related without either one causing the other when both are caused by a third factor. Perhaps social failure independently causes both shame and rape. Thus, if shame and rape were actually caused by a third factor, shame and rape would be associated in most known and hidden groups studies, despite the fact that neither caused the other.

Our illustration about control groups and the error called *post hoc ergo propter hoc* underlines two concerns about research on human problems and rape especially. First, hypotheses are often not clearly specified. Our hypothesis that rape occurs when men feel shame seemed clear at first, but we soon saw that it failed to say whether shame uniquely caused rape. Researchers rarely make their hypotheses sufficiently specific that they can be clearly tested—they often fail to make truly falsifiable hypotheses. Second, finding simple associations can be seductive (even for experienced researchers), especially when confirming one's hypotheses. Newspapers are replete with examples: Associations between corporal punishment of children and later crime, regular exercise and subjective well-being, and marriage and longevity all seem like solid evidence on which to base one's actions (even better, proof that the course already chosen was the right one all along). These ubiquitous reports prove little, however. Regular exercise might cause people to feel better, but it is just as possible that feeling well makes exercise more likely. The tendency to infer cause from correlation is subtle yet often irresistible. Readers might suspect us of

continues

EXHIBIT 4.2
(Continued)

falling into the trap in this book's first paragraph, for example. We try to be alert for this through what follows, but readers should take the results reported in this book with a healthy dose of causal salt.

---

*Although this example sounds a bit fanciful, some writers have indeed proposed that shame may underlie human violence in general (e.g., Coleman, 1985) and sexual offending in particular (S. G. Price, 1999; Proeve & Howells, 2002): "This shame is the result of multiple kinds of abuse, and the offending behavior itself may be an attempt to gain mastery over the shaming event(s)" (S. G. Price, 1999, p. 1.11).

---

differences in antisociality that have been found repeatedly in cross-sectional and longitudinal studies of children and adults. These individual differences can be documented with a wide variety of intercorrelated measures (e.g., Bonta, Law, & Hanson, 1998; Quinsey, Harris, Rice, & Cormier, 1998) that all successfully predict antisocial outcomes.

The fact that a wide variety of measures of antisociality correlate with each other is highly reminiscent of the literature on the measurement of intelligence, where this phenomenon is referred to as the *indifference of the indicator*. Measures such as mazes, vocabulary tests, simple reaction times, and so forth all correlate with each other and predict outcomes like job performance and grade point average (Jensen, 1998). The correlations among these disparate measures are represented by *g* in statistical studies of the correlations among tests (technically, *g* emerges as a superfactor in factor analytic studies[1]). Outcomes are better predicted by intelligence tests to the extent that the outcomes tap *g*. For example, intelligence tests predict the quality of performance regardless of the job, but the correlations are higher for such occupations as computer programming that demand mental ability. As with psychological tests, occupations are more or less correlated (saturated) with *g*.

By analogy, D. C. Rowe and Rodgers (1989) called the superfactor in antisociality *d* (for deviance or delinquency). Given the many intercorrelations among measures of delinquency, one might expect the same indifference of the indicator to characterize *d*. An instrument's accuracy in measuring and predicting antisocial tendencies and behaviors is, therefore, affected by technical psychometric issues involving the instrument itself and the characteristics of the particular sample selected, as well as, substantively, its saturation with *d*. As an illustration, there are a variety of actuarial scales, each significantly saturated with *d*, that predict criminal violence in offender populations at very similar levels of accuracy (e.g., Barbaree, Seto, Langton, & Peacock, 2001; G. T. Harris et al., 2003; Kroner & Mills, 2001).

---

[1]The idea of *g* underlying intelligence test scores has been seen as controversial (Sternberg & Grigorenko, 1997), but the hypothesis that there is a superfactor is all that is required to follow the logic presented here.

Most of the time, psychological constructs are thought of as lying on a continuum—people vary in a fairly continuous way in cleverness, musical talent, and shyness, for example. Furthermore, the continuum usually looks like the familiar bell-shaped curve, so that most people cluster (in cleverness, musical talent, or shyness) around the middle of the range, with many fewer as one approaches the extremes—extremely shy or clever people are pretty rare. Not many people have enough talent to make a living as musicians. This continuity in most human traits arises partly out of the ways the traits are measured, but it is quite clear that most of the continuity is real. There are some traits that exist in a (pretty much) all-or-nothing fashion, however. These traits are called *natural classes* or *taxa* (singular *taxon*).

Biological sex is a good example. It is clear that just about everyone is either male or female (i.e., has the XX or XY chromosomal endowment). It is easy to detect this natural class anatomically, but other natural classes are harder to detect because there are no perfect all-or-nothing measurements. Instead, there are imperfect indicators or continuous scales that might indicate the likelihood that an individual is a member of the taxon. The statistical tools developed by Meehl and his colleagues rely on more subtle inferences to detect a natural class (Meehl & Golden, 1982). The logic behind all these tools is simple, however.

To take a homespun example, imagine that one wished to detect a sex taxon among a group of male and female 6-year-olds. But the task is made more difficult because one cannot see or talk to the children. Instead, all one has is a few indirectly informative facts about each child—hair length, favorite toy, favorite television show, preferred clothing color, and so on. One would expect that among a group of girls, toy choice, hair length, and how often the child wears pink would be uncorrelated (or they would have low intercorrelations). In a group of boys, similar low intercorrelations among indicators would be expected. On the other hand, in a group composed equally of boys and girls, hair length, toy choice, and clothing color indicators should be much more highly intercorrelated, because they are effects of (or are correlated with) a common cause, the sex taxon. If this pattern of results can be observed, there is evidence for an underlying natural class.

Unlike g, the physical nature of d has not been investigated very much, although there is now overwhelming evidence that individual differences in antisociality are heritable to a substantial degree, especially among young children and adults (reviewed in Quinsey et al., 2004). Although measures of antisociality are distributed continuously, a substantial part of individual variation in antisociality appears to reflect a discrete difference in kind among individuals—that is, a small minority of men form a qualitatively distinct subgroup of the population. Taxometric analyses among adult offenders (G. T. Harris, Rice, & Quinsey, 1994; Skilling, Harris, Rice, & Quinsey, 2002) and an unselected group of elementary school boys (Skilling, Quinsey, & Craig, 2001) showed strong evidence of the existence of a small, qualitatively distinct subgroup (see Exhibit 4.3 for a discussion of taxometrics).

Many indicators can identify members of this distinct subgroup. Among adult offenders, these characteristics include impulsivity, callousness, irresponsibility, lack of remorse, being conning and manipulative, shallow affect, early behavior problems, violent adult behavior, lying, parasitic lifestyle, sexual promiscuity, elementary school maladjustment, criminal history, separation from biological parents under age 16, and a history of running away from home. Interestingly, several of these characteristics refer to early childhood adjustment. Among elementary school boys, characteristics that detected members of the discrete group include criminal versatility (i.e., variety of types of offending), having stolen while confronting a victim, having stolen without confronting a victim, need for stimulation and proneness to boredom, frequent lying, frequent bullying, use of threats and intimidation, suspension or expulsion from school, destruction of others' property, physical cruelty to people, being conning and manipulative, poor behavioral controls, and being irresponsible.

The taxometric finding is consistent with Moffitt's (1993; Moffitt & Caspi, 2001) theoretical taxonomy that there are two types of delinquents, those who begin their aggressive and antisocial behavior early in childhood and persist throughout their lifetime (the smallest group, which she called *life-course-persistent*) and those who limit their antisocial activities to adolescence and early adulthood (the largest group, which she called *adolescence-limited*). Moffitt's life-course-persistent group very likely comprises in fact two subgroups, a group of offenders who have experienced early neurodevelopmental perturbations (subtle or not-so-subtle damage to the developing nervous system caused by prenatal toxicity, malnutrition, injury, and so on) along with significant social adversity and a group of offenders who show little evidence of neurodevelopmental perturbations and who seem much less affected by their social environment (Quinsey et al., 2004). The latter group includes psychopaths (Hare, 1991). We will return to this three-group taxonomy later in this chapter.

LINK BETWEEN ANTISOCIALITY AND MATING EFFORT

Aggressive and antisocial behavior and poor psychosocial adjustment in both boys and girls are associated with early sexual intercourse (Bingham & Crockett, 1996; Jessor, Costa, Jessor, & Donovan, 1983). Middle-adolescence risk taking is among the best predictors of adolescent pregnancy involvement for both male and female young adults (L. V. Scaramella, Conger, Simons, & Whitbeck, 1998). Thus, in both sexes, there is a relationship between antisociality, mating effort, and its occasional consequence, reproduction. In this section, we explore this relationship.

Serbin et al. (1998) found that mothers' aggression measured in childhood predicted teen motherhood and close spacing of births in a large longitudinal study of the intergenerational transfer of psychosocial risk between mothers and children. East and Jacobson (2001) studied the younger sisters of teenage mothers and concluded,

> Relative to other youths, the sisters of parenting teens exhibited a sharp increase in drug and alcohol use and partying behavior across time and

had the highest pregnancy rate [18 months later] (15%). The siblings of parenting teens spent 10 hr a week caring for their sisters' children, and, for girls, many hours of childcare was associated with negative outcomes including permissive sexual behavior. Findings suggest that the younger sisters of parenting teens are at very high risk of early pregnancy and that this risk becomes increasingly pronounced across time. (p. 254)

Stouthamer-Loeber and Wei (1998) found, in a longitudinal study of inner-city public schools in Pittsburgh, that 12% of 506 young men fathered a child before age 19. These fathers were over 200% more likely than other men in the sample to have committed serious crimes. Delinquency did not decrease after fatherhood. Fagot, Pears, Capaldi, Crosby, and Leve (1998) followed 206 9- and 10-year-old boys in the Oregon Youth Study sample. The 35 boys who became fathers by age 20 were different from those who did not as early as 6th grade. The adolescent fathers were characterized by low socioeconomic status of origin, parental antisocial behavior, poor parental discipline, deviant peer group membership, academic failure, and antisocial behavior. They had more substance abuse problems and arrests than boys who had not become fathers. Antisocial behavior was a better predictor of age at first intercourse than it was a predictor of early pregnancy. By age 2, 40% of the offspring had no contact with their adolescent fathers. The at-risk fathers showed more negative reactions when their children worked on a puzzle task than control fathers.

Personality measures related to antisociality are also associated with sexual behavior. For example, hypermasculinity and machismo (reflecting a person's need to be dominant and callous in social interactions), machiavellianism (reflecting a tendency to manipulate others), and sensation seeking—three constructs closely linked with antisociality—were associated with an index of potential conception in a general sample (Linton & Wiener, 2002). *Potential conception* refers to the probable number of conceptions based on frequency of intercourse and number of partners if there were no contraception. The relationship was stronger for men not involved in a relationship at the time of testing, suggesting that number of partners is more critically related to these constructs than frequency of intercourse.

The link between delinquency (or antisociality) and sexual activity (or mating effort) seems so obvious to researchers that there are not very many studies specifically designed to address this issue. Instead, precocious and promiscuous sex is often part of the very definition of delinquency. D. C. Rowe and Rodgers's (1989) concept of *d* is in fact meant to explain the strong association between delinquency and precocious and varied sexual behavior. Other researchers have demonstrated, through factor analyses, that one factor underlies propensity for "problem behavior," a factor that includes violent behavior and precocious and varied sexual activities. Jessor and his colleagues labeled this factor *unconventionality* (e.g., Donovan, Jessor, & Costa,

1988).[2] Ellis (1987; Ellis & Walsh, 2000) identified studies documenting the link between early onset of sexual activities or number of sexual partners and criminality, drug use, and sensation seeking. There is also overlap, in longitudinal studies, between the predictors of delinquency and the predictors of precocious sex (Felson & Hayne, 2002; French & Dishion, 2003).

The relationship between measures of antisociality and mating effort, however, is not always straightforward. We recently conducted a factor analysis—with a factor extraction that allowed factors to correlate—of measures of aggression (e.g., scales of the Buss–Perry Aggression Questionnaire; A. H. Buss & Perry, 1992), antisociality (e.g., Childhood and Adolescence Taxon Self-Report Scale; Quinsey et al., 1998), and mating effort (e.g., age at first intercourse, number of sexual partners per sexually active year) among a large sample of young men recruited from two communities and one university campus (Quinsey, Book, & Lalumière, 2001). Aggression and Antisociality emerged as two separate factors and were significantly and positively correlated, as expected. Age at First Intercourse loaded on Antisociality, but the other sexual variables (self-perceived mating success, number of sexual partners per sexually active year, preference for partner variety and casual sex) loaded on a third factor we labeled Mating Success. Mating Success was uncorrelated with the other two factors. Although antisociality may be associated with variables indexing early mating effort, it may not be necessarily associated with mating success, particularly in later adolescence and young adulthood.

ANTISOCIALITY, MATING EFFORT, AND RAPE

We now turn to the association between measures of antisociality and mating effort and rape and sexual coercion. Research addressing this association typically has used two research strategies. Most commonly, data are obtained from self-reports of volunteers from colleges, universities, or the general community (the hidden groups approach). Less commonly, data are obtained from self-reports and institutional files of men accused or found guilty of charges of rape or sexual assault (the known groups approach).

Community Samples

The Sexual Experiences Survey is probably the most frequently used instrument in the study of self-reported sexual coercion in nonoffender samples (Koss, 1988; Koss & Dinero, 1988; Koss & Leonard, 1984; Koss & Oros, 1982). Koss and Dinero reported that of a national sample of 2,972 male

---

[2]In an interesting study of siblings, D. C. Rowe, Rodgers, Meseck-Bushey, and St. John (1989) observed that knowledge of one sibling's delinquency predicted the other sibling's sexual behavior, and vice versa, for both sexes.

American college students, 4% reported that they had raped, 3% had attempted rape, 7% had been sexually coercive (using a position of authority or verbal pressure to obtain sexual intercourse), and another 10% had made unwanted sexual contacts (using a position of authority or threats of force for sex play). Malamuth (1988a) and Rapaport and Burkhart (1984) reported similar figures. Another measure of sexual coercion used frequently with nonoffender samples is the Likelihood of Forcing Sex Scale (Malamuth, 1988a). This scale asks about the individual's likelihood of forcing sex or raping in a hypothetical detection- and punishment-free situation.

Several studies have examined the antisocial attitudes of sexually coercive men as defined by the Sexual Experiences Survey. In these studies, the identified group of sexually coercive men generally includes anyone who reported having engaged in rape, attempted rape, sexual coercion, or unwanted sexual contacts as defined in the preceding paragraph. Compared with other men, sexually coercive men hold stronger "pro-rape" attitudes, stronger adversarial sexual beliefs (e.g., "A woman will only respect a man who will lay down the law to her"), and more pronounced sex-role stereotypes (e.g., "A woman should be a virgin when she marries"); are more accepting of interpersonal violence (e.g., "A man is never justified in hitting his wife"— reverse scored); have more hostile attitudes toward women (e.g., "When it really comes down to it, a lot of women are deceitful"); are more likely to associate dominance and sexual activity; and are more domineering in their social interactions with women. The effect size for the relationship between such measures of "masculine ideology" or "hostile masculinity" and sexual coercion is small to moderate on the basis of a meta-analysis by Murnen, Wright, and Kaluzny (2002).

Many studies have also reported that sexually coercive men are less empathic, more callous, and more aggressive; espouse more conservative sex roles; and, importantly, are more likely to engage in other (nonsexual) antisocial activities than other men (Burt, 1980; Feild, 1978; Greendlinger & Byrne, 1987; Koss & Dinero, 1988; Koss, Leonard, Beezley, & Oros, 1985; Kosson, Kelly, & White, 1997; Lisak & Ivan, 1995; E. R. Mahoney, Shively, & Traw, 1986; Malamuth, 1988a; Malamuth, Heavey, & Linz, 1993; Malamuth & Thornhill, 1994; Muehlenhard & Linton, 1987; Petty & Dawson, 1989; Porter, Critelli, & Tang, 1992; Rapaport & Burkhart, 1984; Sarwer, Kalichman, Johnson, Early, & Ali, 1993; Spence, Losoff, & Robbins, 1991; W. D. Walker, Rowe, & Quinsey, 1993; Wheeler, George, & Dahl, 2002). Lisak and Miller (2002) found that some self-reported rapists had committed many rapes and other violent behaviors (e.g., battery, child abuse).

Studies of sexually coercive men have also investigated their sexual experiences along with their antisocial tendencies and behaviors. In a study of university freshmen, Dean and Malamuth (1997) found that the likelihood of reporting past sexual coercion was associated with above-median scores on five measures: (a) a combination of Acceptance of Interpersonal

Violence (Burt, 1980) and Rape Myth Acceptance (Burt, 1980), (b) a combination of Sexual Dominance (Nelson, 1979) and Hostility Toward Women (Check, Malamuth, Elias, & Barton, 1985), (c) Family Violence (Bardis, 1973), (d) Nonconformity (Rapaport, 1984), and (e) Sexual Experience (Bentler, 1968). Men who were high on these five measures were more likely to report sexual coercion if they were also self-centered as opposed to nurturant.

In a similar study, Christopher, Owens, and Strecker (1993) found that self-reported premarital sexual coercion (broadly defined) was associated with violent attitudes, sexual promiscuity, and negative relationship experiences. Calhoun, Bernat, Clum, and Frame (1997) replicated the association between self-reported delinquency and broadly defined sexual coercion in a sample of rural, relatively sexually inexperienced men. They did not find a correlation between promiscuity and sexual coercion, perhaps because of restriction of range in sexual experience in this sample.

Lalumière and Quinsey (1996) studied the relationships among mating effort, antisociality, and self-reported sexual coercion in a sample of 99 heterosexual men recruited from a university and the local community. Mating effort was measured by a Sexual Experience Scale (Lalumière, Chalmers, Quinsey, & Seto, 1996) that contains items concerning age at first intercourse, number of sex partners, and number of casual sexual relationships; the Preference for Partner Variety and Casual Sex Scale (Lalumière, Chalmers, et al., 1996) designed to measure interest in uncommitted sexuality; and the Sociosexual Orientation Inventory (Simpson & Gangestad, 1991), a measure of propensity for unrestricted (impersonal and varied) sexuality. Also included was the Self-Perceived Mating Success Scale, which describes one's self-assessed attractiveness to others as a potential sexual partner (Landolt et al., 1995) and a measure of general self-esteem (Rosenberg, 1979). Antisociality was measured with the Childhood and Adolescent Psychopathy Taxon Self Report Scale (G. T. Harris, Rice, & Quinsey, 1994; Seto, Khattar, Lalumière, & Quinsey, 1997) consisting of items related to early behavioral problems; the Psychopathy Scale (Levenson, Kiehl, & Fitzpatrick, 1995) describing antisocial acts and attitudes; the Sensation Seeking Scale (Zuckerman, 1979) measuring thrill seeking, experience seeking, disinhibition, and susceptibility to boredom; and a number of measures related to attitudes toward women and sex.

Indicators of antisociality and mating effort were associated with one another and with Koss's measure (Koss & Oros, 1982) of self-reported sexually coercive behaviors. The strongest indicators of past sexual coercion were antisociality (as assessed by the Childhood and Adolescence Taxon Scale), sensation seeking, positive self-perceived mating success, and an extensive history of uncommitted sexual relationships. Lalumière, Chalmers, et al. (1996) obtained similar results in a study of 156 university students. In both studies, men who reported sexually coercive acts that would be considered rape in most legal jurisdictions were fairly similar to men who reported less serious coercive acts.

The many variables included in Lalumière and Quinsey's (1996) study were submitted to factor analysis, and the factor scores were used to "predict" the past use of sexually coercive behaviors. Similarly to the findings of Quinsey et al. (2001), three factors emerged. The first was a mix of antisociality and mating effort variables. Interestingly, this factor also included a measure of frequency of use of mating tactics that are rated by women as ineffective (e.g., flexing muscles, showing ability to drink a lot, flashing money). The second factor reflected hostility and aggression. The third factor reflected mating success (sexual experience, self-esteem, self-perceived mating success, and the use of mating tactics rated as more effective, such as displaying a good sense of humor or showing sympathy). Factor scores were entered in a simultaneous multiple regression, and all three had positive relationships with past sexual coercion (the first factor was statistically significant, and the third approached significance).

The relationship between sexual experience and sexual coercion has also been observed among noncollege, older samples. For example, in a rare study using a random sample of 195 community men (25% response rate, mean age of 41 years), Senn, Desmarais, Verberg, and Wood (2000) found that the number of sexual partners in adolescence was one of the best predictors of self-reported sexual coercion.

Although sexually coercive men tend to report a great amount of sexual experience with many partners (see also E. S. Byers & Eno, 1991; Gold & Clegg; 1990, Koss & Dinero, 1988; Koss et al., 1985; E. R. Mahoney et al., 1986), they seem unsatisfied with the amount of sex they report. Kanin (1983, 1985) studied undetected rapists and nonrapists and found the usual difference favoring rapists in self-reported number of sexual partners, but rapists also reported higher sexual "aspirations" and were often sexually frustrated despite their greater involvement in sex. It seems safe to conclude that sexually coercive men engage in high mating effort.

In summary, studies of community and student samples consistently show that antisociality and mating effort are related and are themselves important correlates of sexual coercion and rape. Antisocial men tend to engage in high mating effort (i.e., they try to have sex early in a relationship, prefer and seek multiple partners, and avoid long-term relationships) and probably use sexual coercion as part of this effort. The fusion of antisociality and high mating effort is well captured by the Greek term *ludus*, a type of approach to romantic relationships (or love style) characterized by little emotional involvement, manipulation of partners, desire for multiple sexual relationships, and a game-playing approach to romance. Compared with other men, sexually coercive men score higher on a scale specifically designed to assess *ludus*. They also score lower on a scale assessing *agape*, a term that refers to unconditional love (Russell & Oswald, 2002; Sarwer et al., 1993).

This literature provides no support for the often-proposed idea that men who do not have access to consensual sexual partners are more likely than other men to engage in rape: Sexually coercive men, as a group, appear to be more, rather than less, sexually experienced than other men. Sexually coercive men are not just more sexually experienced; they also seek greater partner variety and more casual sex than other men. Indeed, Lalumière, Chalmers, et al. (1996) found that a measure of preference for partner variety and casual sex was related to a history of sexual coercion even when a composite measure of sexual experience was statistically controlled.

One way of interpreting at least part of the influence of antisociality and mating effort on sexual coercion is that such tendencies and traits lower the experienced psychological cost of coercion for the perpetrator. If this interpretation is correct, other attitudes and traits that lower this cost should also be related to sexual coercion. We have already discussed some evidence for this; men who believe that sexual aggression is justified or who are hostile to women as a group might be expected to incur lower perceived costs for sexual aggression. W. D. Walker et al. (1993) examined one such constellation of beliefs, encapsulated by the authoritarian personality dimension.

The Right Wing Authoritarianism (RWA) Scale (Altemeyer, 1988) contains three covarying attitudinal clusters: authoritarian submission, or submission to perceived legitimate societal authorities; authoritarian aggression, or aggressiveness toward groups of individuals that is perceived to be sanctioned by established authorities; and conventionalism, or a high degree of adherence to social conventions perceived to be endorsed by society's established authorities. Altemeyer (1981, 1988, 1996) has amassed extensive psychometric support and external validity data for the RWA Scale. High scores on the scale are related to attitudes and beliefs relevant to authoritarianism, including preference for right-wing political parties, tolerance of government injustices such as wiretaps of union leaders or illegal drug raids, harsher sentences for low- versus high-status criminals, and fundamentalist religious beliefs. Closely related to authoritarianism are beliefs concerning women's "proper" place in society. The Sex Role Ideology Scale is designed to measure these prescriptive beliefs about the behaviors and roles appropriate for the two sexes (Kalin & Tilby, 1978).

In two studies of men recruited from the community and university undergraduates, W. D. Walker et al. (1993) used the RWA, Sex Role Ideology, Hostility Towards Women, Acceptance of Interpersonal Violence, Adversarial Sexual Beliefs, and Rape Myth Acceptance scales, as well as measures of past sexually coercive behavior and likelihood of future sexual coercion. Authoritarianism and sex role ideology were as closely related to self-reported past and potential future sexually coercive behavior as were the specifically sexual and aggression-related predictors (Hostility Towards Women, Acceptance of Interpersonal Violence, Adversarial Sexual Beliefs, and Rape Myth Acceptance scales). Thus, attitudes implying that women's interests should generally be subordinated to those of men and generally advocating coercive social control accounted for self-reported sexual coercion. The relationship of authoritarianism and sexual coercion was larger in community than in university samples in both studies. In chapter 7, we return to the role of the sociopolitical environment in causing rape.

Strengths and Weaknesses of Studies of Community Samples

How much confidence should be placed in the results of studies of self-reported sexual coercion among university and community samples? This literature has many strengths. Large samples of men are typically studied. There is little ascertainment bias (i.e., the samples are not selected because they are high risk or special in a way relevant to sexual aggression, as found in clinical and offender samples), many of the studies use sophisticated data analytic and modeling techniques, and the results obtained are generally replicated over studies. Although it can be argued that the findings pertain primarily to North American college freshmen, this population is large enough to be of interest in itself, and some similar findings have been obtained in noncollege samples and in data obtained outside of North America (e.g., Patton & Mannison, 1995a, 1995b).

There are weaknesses and ambiguities in this literature as well. The first involves the exclusive use of self-report measures. As we mentioned, self-report is well known to inaccurately reflect the frequencies of particular behaviors and when they occurred (N. Z. Hilton et al., 1998). Second, there are serious problems of shared method variance—the same source of information is used for most variables of interest. Third, the dependent measures are usually defined very broadly to include behaviors like "continually asking for sex" or reporting some low likelihood of forcing someone to have sex if one was guaranteed not to be caught. Some of the behaviors that are studied in this literature would not meet legal definitions of rape. These behaviors are important to study, but their correlates might not always apply to behaviors more customarily defined as rape. Fourth, the nonsexual antisocial behaviors of sexually coercive and noncoercive young men are rarely studied, so it is difficult to determine whether the correlates of sexual coercion are specific to such coercion or whether they are general to most criminal activities.

Malamuth, Linz, Heavey, Barnes, and Acker (1995) addressed some of the limitations in this literature by performing a 10-year follow-up of previously assessed men, most of whom were initially assessed as undergraduates as part of a research project. The results of this study support the centrality of antisociality and high mating effort in increasing the likelihood of sexual coercion. Of 423 men in the original studies, follow-up data were available for 132, and of the latter, videotapes of couples engaged in a problem-solving task were obtained for 47 men and their female partners. Men's initial self-reports of sexual coercion were correlated with both their report of sexual coercion at follow-up ($r = .41$) and their partners' reports of relationship distress and both sexual (.38) and nonsexual aggression (.55) directed toward them by their partner. The initial reports of sexual coercion correlated with videotape observers' ratings of hostility and domineeringness at follow-up. Initial responses on the Hostility Toward Women Scale were significantly related to videotape ratings of hostility and dominance. Sexual coercion at follow-up was predicted by impersonal sex and general hostility at initial assessment, but nonsexual verbal or physical aggression was not.

Malamuth et al.'s (1995) longitudinal study was motivated by the confluence model of sexual aggression, which implicates two main factors associated with self-reported sexually coercive behavior: sexual promiscuity or impersonal sex (which we would consider part of mating effort) and hostile masculinity (which we would consider part of antisociality). These two factors tend to correlate, and high scores on both best predict self-reported sexual coercion in community samples. Malamuth (2003) recently argued that general antisociality is an important correlate of sexual coercion but that more specific measures of antisociality having to do with women and sex are even stronger correlates.

Offender Samples

It is likely that most of the sexually coercive young men studied in community and college samples are adolescence-limited offenders, as defined by Moffitt (1993). In contrast, offender samples are typically much older, and many of these offenders would be classified as offenders.

Beyond important differences in the nature of the samples studied, there are several methodological differences between studies of offenders and studies of community samples. For instance, the classification of men as rapists versus nonrapists is often based, in offender samples, on a legal finding rather than on an admission on a self-report questionnaire. Also, the variables studied are often based on file data (which often include collateral information) rather than on self-report alone. Sexual offenders are often compared not only to nonoffenders but to other types of offenders as well.

There are also limitations. The self-reports of institutionalized sex offenders, when used as part of a study, are less likely to be reliable for a number of obvious reasons (e.g., lesser perceived or actual anonymity). Also, researchers are often limited in the choice of variables by what is available in the files. Despite these limitations and methodological differences, the offender literature has produced findings that are strikingly consistent with the literature just reviewed.

Compared with nonoffenders, rapists recruited from correctional and psychiatric institutions are more antisocial, more hostile, and less empathic;

have more favorable perceptions of rape; and have more conservative attitudes toward women and sexuality (Armentrout & Hauer, 1978; Feild, 1978; Langevin, Paitich, & Russon, 1985; Quinsey, Arnold, & Pruesse, 1980; Raider, 1977; M. E. Rice, Chaplin, Harris, & Coutts, 1994; R. L. Scott & Tetreault, 1987; Seto & Barbaree, 1993). However, these differences usually disappear when rapists are compared with other offenders recruited from the same institutions. Indeed, rapists are quite similar to other types of violent offenders with regard to most measures of antisocial traits and behaviors.

Another way to examine the link between rape and antisocial tendencies is to examine the criminal history of known rapists. Many incarcerated rapists have an extensive criminal history involving nonsexual crimes. In a study of the clinical files of more than 100 rapists (Bard et al., 1987), 93% of rapists had committed a victimless nonsexual crime (e.g., breaking and entering), and 45% had committed a nonsexual crime directly involving a victim (e.g., assault). In another study, this time looking at the official criminal records of more than 200 rapists (Barbaree & Seto, 1998), the mean number of previous nonviolent, nonsexual offenses was 13, and the mean number of violent nonsexual offenses was 2.

Studies using self-reports also reveal extensive criminal histories among convicted offenders. Weinrott and Saylor (1991) used a computerized self-report measure to investigate the criminal behavior of 37 convicted rapists in the 12 months preceding their incarceration. The rapists reported more than 19,000 nonsexual crimes, with a median of 136 per offender. The most common offenses were public drunkenness (median = 20), stealing less than $100 (4), using hard drugs (4), and hitting a woman (2). Antisociality among rapists most likely involves a general antisocial tendency found among most serious offenders rather than a specific antisocial tendency in the sexual domain.

The antisocial tendencies and criminal histories of incarcerated rapists may be similar to those of other offenders, but they do differ from those of other sex offenders, in particular child molesters. M. E. Rice and Harris (1997) compared the criminal backgrounds of 88 rapists and 142 child molesters who were all subsequently followed up after release. Compared with child molesters, rapists had more extensive violent and nonviolent criminal histories and higher scores on the Psychopathy Checklist—Revised[3] (PCL–R; Hare, 1991), a measure of persistent antisociality. Once released, rapists committed new nonsexual crimes faster than child molesters, but child molesters committed new sexual crimes faster than rapists. Other investigators obtained

---

[3]The PCL–R contains 20 items: glibness/superficial charm, grandiose sense of self-worth, need for stimulation/proneness to boredom, pathological lying, conning/manipulative, lack of remorse or guilt, shallow affect, callous/lack of empathy, parasitic lifestyle, poor behavioral controls, promiscuous sexual behavior, early behavior problems, lack of realistic long-term goals, impulsivity, irresponsibility, failure to accept responsibility for own actions, many short-term marital relationships, juvenile delinquency, revocation of conditional release, and criminal versatility.

similar results with other populations of incarcerated sex offenders (e.g., Bard et al., 1987; Serin, Mailloux, & Malcolm, 2001; Seto & Barbaree, 1999; Weinrott & Saylor, 1991). In a recent meta-analysis, juvenile sex offenders against peers scored higher than juvenile sex offenders against children on various measures of conduct problems (Seto & Lalumière, in press).

Rapists also seem to have a more antisocial "interpersonal style" than child molesters. For example, D. Anderson (2002) found that rapists rated themselves higher than child molesters on such traits as cold-heartedness, assured–dominant, arrogant–calculating, and aloof–introverted and lower on warm–agreeable. These findings relating rape to general antisociality are not new: Many years ago Gebhard, Gagnon, Pomeroy, and Christenson (1965) noted, from an extensive study of sex offenders, that "the majority of [rapists] may be succinctly described as criminally inclined men who take what they want, whether money, material, or women, and their sex offenses are by-products of their general criminality" (p. 205).

Studies investigating the predictors of continued offending (or recidivism) are also relevant to this discussion. Criminal history and PCL–R scores are the best predictors of sexual reoffending among institutionalized rapists (R. K. Hanson & Bussière, 1998; G. T. Harris et al., 2003; Quinsey, Lalumière, Rice, & Harris, 1995; Quinsey, Rice, & Harris, 1995). Thus, even among men who have already committed at least one rape, measures of antisociality still predict their future perpetration of sexual crimes. The predictive ability of measures of mating effort has not been investigated to date.

With regard to mating effort, there are unfortunately very few studies of the sexual behavior and aspirations of incarcerated rapists. We investigated rapists' responses to questionnaires assessing their self-perceived mating success, their preference for partner variety and casual sex, and their general sexual experience before incarceration. Compared with a group of offenders who had committed nonsexual offenses against persons, rapists reported earlier age at first intercourse and more sexual partners since puberty; had higher scores on the Sociosexuality Inventory, indicating a tendency for short-term, uncommitted sexual relationships; and had higher self-perceived mating success (Lalumière & Quinsey, 1998a).

Langevin, Paitich, et al. (1985) compared the sexual histories of rapists and other violent men and found much similarity. Both groups showed an earlier age of sexual activity onset and a greater number of consenting partners (including affairs with married women) than another group of sex offenders (mostly exhibitionists and voyeurs) and a group of men recruited from the community. Finally, Gebhard et al. (1965) compared different groups of sex offenders and observed that rapists had above-average heterosexual adjustment (in terms of consenting sexual partners) prior to their offenses. These results suggest, again, that rapists do not lack access to sexual partners and may be particularly interested in partner variety and casual sex (see also McDonald & Paitich, 1983).

In sum, studies of known groups of rapists have so far produced results similar to studies of hidden groups. Rapists engage in much nonsexual criminal and generally antisocial activities and may score high on measures of mating effort. With regard to most measures studied to date, rapists are quite similar to other violent offenders. The similarity of rapists and other violent offenders led Langevin, Paitich, et al. (1985) to "wonder why the sexual aggressives raped and common assaulters did not" (pp. 33–34). We offer an answer to this question in chapter 5.

SPECIALIZATION AND ESCALATION

We have noted that antisocial characteristics are related to early initiation of and varied sexual activities, early reproduction, and relatively little parental investment. Moreover, antisocial characteristics are associated with rape and sexual coercion among men. These findings raise the question of whether antisociality is a sufficient explanation for individual variations in men's propensity to rape. One aspect of this fundamental empirical issue concerning rapists is the extent to which they specialize in sexual coercion and rape. The question is fundamental because it strongly constrains the kinds of explanations that can account for the behavior.

One possibility is that rapists are generalists and that rape is simply one of a variety of antisocial behaviors exhibited by any single individual (as suggested by findings reviewed in the previous section). This sort of explanation is consistent with Gottfredson and Hirschi's (1990) general theory of crime that asserts that all criminal behaviors occur when the perceived rewards associated with a criminal opportunity outweigh the anticipated costs. One expects from this theory that a man convicted of rape is no more likely to commit a further rape than a man convicted of any other sort of crime and that there will be no pattern, such as escalation, within a series of offenses.

Soothill, Francis, Sanderson, and Ackerley (2000) argued from conviction data that there are both specialists and generalists among sex offenders, with some subgroups, such as offenders against male victims, showing more evidence of specialization. In their study, offenders against female victims tended to also have convictions for nonsexual offenses such as violence against the person and theft. However, given the vagaries of the criminal justice system, particularly the tenuous relationship between the actual criminal behavior and the nature of the charge for which an offender is convicted, as well as the number of offenses that occur for which no one is convicted, questions concerning specialization and escalation may better be addressed with a combination of self-report and official information.

W. D. Walker (1997; W. D. Walker & Quinsey, 1998) examined these questions using official conviction, file information, and self-report data obtained from 409 convicted Canadian sex offenders. To measure escalation,

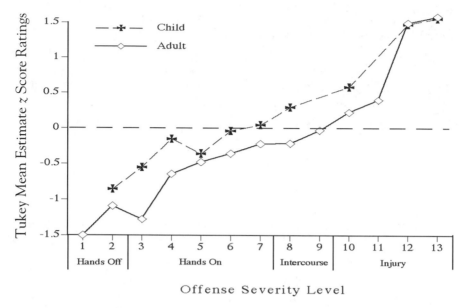

Figure 4.3. Rated offense severity for a variety of sexual offenses. The data are from *Patterns in Sexual Offending* (Figure 2), by W. D. Walker, 1997, unpublished doctoral dissertation, Queen's University, Kingston, Ontario, Canada.

Walker had 45 men and 45 women, all experienced in working with sex offenders or child protection agencies, rate the seriousness of 54 sex offenses and 4 nonsexual violent offenses (the latter taken from Wolfgang, Figlio, Tracy, & Singer, 1985) using a magnitude estimation procedure. There was strong consensus among the raters, and the procedure produced a linear ordering of the offenses along a seriousness continuum, shown in Figure 4.3.

Log-linear analyses for matched categorical data (Agresti, 1996; Britt, 1996) showed strong evidence of escalation in offense severity to the level of intercourse without physical injury from first to last offense by those who had committed five or more sexual offenses. As shown in Figure 4.4, offenders whose first offense involved physical contact with the victim moved toward intercourse over offenses; if their first offense involved intercourse, they stayed at that level of severity. If their first offense involved both intercourse and physical injury, they tended to de-escalate to intercourse. As shown in Figure 4.5, a similar pattern was found among men who committed five or more offenses against the same victim (primarily incestuous child molesters). These men moved from less intrusive sexual behaviors toward intercourse over offenses against the same victim, and when they offended against a new victim, the same pattern reoccurred. These results strongly suggest that sexual aggression, like consenting sexual activities, is fundamentally a reproductive behavior.

Official records revealed no evidence for sex offense specialization among groups of offenders defined with respect to victim age, sex, or relationship

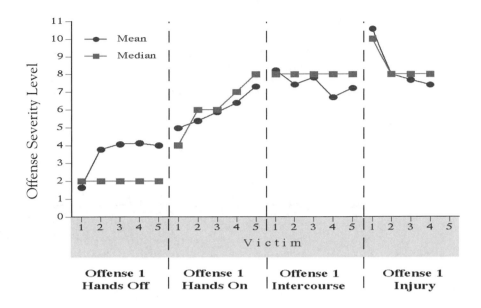

Figure 4.4. Changes in offense severity for multiple victims and with different starting severity value. The data are from *Patterns in Sexual Offending* (Table 14), by W. D. Walker, 1997, unpublished doctoral dissertation, Queen's University, Kingston, Ontario, Canada.

with the offender. In contrast, file and self-report data indicated that men who committed sexual offenses against victims less than 16 years of age, male victims, and any family member specialized in sex offenses. Offenders against adults, only female victims, and only extrafamilial victims did not specialize in sex crimes. Some rapists, however, were quite persistent. Among the 120 men who had committed a hands-on sexual offense against at least one woman (W. D. Walker, personal communication, 1998), one hundred and ten men committed a second sexual assault, and fewer than 60 committed more than two. In the combined self-report and official record data, if a man committed two sexual assaults, the probability that he would commit at least one more was slightly more than .50. If he had committed three assaults, however, the likelihood that he would commit at least one more rose to about .80. Across successive sexual assaults, the likelihood of committing at least one more remained constant until the seventh, where the few rapists who had committed eight or more had probabilities of around .90 of committing at least one more sexual assault.

Another way to address the question of specialization is to examine the antisocial antecedents of men who report engaging (or were found to have engaged) in sexual coercion. Cross-sectional research by Malamuth and his colleagues (e.g., Malamuth et al., 1993) consistently showed that general juvenile delinquency is associated with the use of sexually coercive tactics among young adults. Antisocial behavior as a juvenile is also a strong precur-

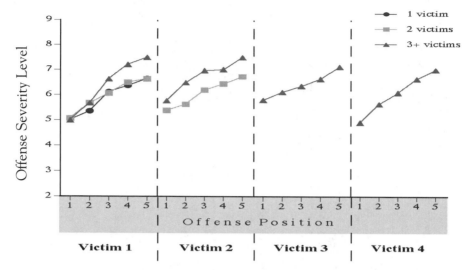

Figure 4.5. Changes in offense severity for multiple victims and multiple offenses for the same victim. The data are from *Patterns in Sexual Offending* (Table 14), by W. D. Walker, 1997, unpublished doctoral dissertation, Queen's University, Kingston, Ontario, Canada.

sor of sexual coercion among offenders (Knight & Sims-Knight, in press). Of course, early delinquency is also a strong precursor of adult criminality in general.

Similar results have been obtained in longitudinal studies. Elliott's study of the National Youth Survey, a longitudinal self-report survey that revealed much higher rates of serious offending than official data suggest (Elliott, Huizinga, & Morse, 1987), confirmed that rape is most often part of a general criminal career (Elliott, 1994). It also revealed the antisocial trajectory underlying rape: Minor delinquency, alcohol use, and marijuana use preceded involvement in serious crime, and aggravated assault and robbery preceded rape. In order words, most rapists had prior nonviolent or violent crimes, but not all delinquents engaged in rape. Taken together, these results suggest that most rapists do not specialize in rape.

Lack of specialization among the majority of rapists makes it unlikely that studies will observe developmental antecedents specific to them. However, because men who have committed several rapes are much more likely than other offenders to commit subsequent rapes, there are likely to be specific developmental antecedents for this small proportion of repetitive rapists.

ORIGINS OF ANTISOCIALITY

Because of the strong connection between antisociality and rape, much can be learned about men's propensity to rape by examining the causes of antisocial tendencies. As we mentioned earlier in this chapter, there are likely three general courses in the development and manifestation of antisociality (Quinsey et al., 2004). The first involves the initiation and termination of antisocial activities during adolescence and early adulthood. Moffitt (1993) made a good case that this adolescence-limited delinquency is largely responsible for the steep peak in criminality observed at this age. Most adolescents and young adults report engaging in some delinquent behavior at one time or another. In fact, engaging in delinquent activities in adolescence appears normative. Those who abstain from any delinquent activities may even be less well adjusted as adolescents. In one study, adolescent abstainers were overcontrolled, timid, socially awkward, and sexually inexperienced; they were, however, well adjusted and well educated as young adults (Moffitt, Caspi, Harrington, & Milne, 2002).

The second developmental course involves individuals who begin their antisocial and aggressive behaviors early in childhood (they are difficult, aggressive, hyperactive, and so on), are delinquent during adolescence, and do not desist from their antisocial and criminal behavior in adulthood. Moffitt (1993) called this small group *life-course-persistent offenders*. These offenders typically show signs that they have experienced neurodevelopmental perturbations early in life, along with continued and significant social maladjustment. There is much empirical evidence to support the distinction between adolescence-limited and life-course-persistent delinquency and for the dual and interactive role of neurodevelopmental sensitivities and social maladjustment in the genesis of life-course-persistent offending (Brennan, Hall, Bor, Najman, & Williams, 2003).

The third group is also persistent throughout the life span but does not appear to have experienced perturbations in neurodevelopment, and variations in the quality of the environment seem to have little impact on their problem behavior. They seem well adjusted for a life of defection, cheating, manipulation, aggression, and mating effort (Mealey, 1995). We call these individuals *psychopaths*. This three-prong developmental taxonomy offers a good framework for understanding men's propensity toward sexual coercion. In the following section we examine this taxonomy and its relevance to rape.

Young Male Syndrome

The incidence of rape, like most crimes, peaks in late adolescence and early adulthood[4] (e.g., Greenfeld, 1997). Why should this be so? M. Wilson and Daly (1985) described what they called the *young male syndrome*, a phenomenon in which young men are willing to accept risk to compete for (his-

---

[4]Although many rapists are young men, rape perpetrators may be, as a group, slightly older than perpetrators of other violent crimes. Also, there is some evidence that age of rapists is positively related to degree of acquaintanceship, such that rapists who target intimates are the oldest (e.g., Muir & MacLeod, 2003).

torically) reproductively relevant goals—status, resources, and mates. Many antisocial and criminal acts, together with other dangerous activities young men tend to engage in, appear to be manifestations of this taste for risk. From a selectionist point of view, young men are more risk accepting than women and more risk accepting than other men because the reproductive stakes for them have always been particularly high throughout hominid evolution. Indeed, the sex difference in potential reproductive rates creates a situation in which competition and risk acceptance were more likely to have paid off for men than for women and more likely to have paid off at times and circumstances when the gains (and the variance in gains) were particularly high. Of course, the statistical link between particular behavioral tendencies and reproductive success (or fitness) may or may not be observed in current novel environments; adaptive responses to one's situation in life are legacies of humans' evolutionary past (Daly & Wilson, 1999).

Both M. Wilson and Daly (1985) and Moffitt (1993) suggested that important life events in adulthood lead to a subsequent reduction in risk taking and desistence from antisocial activities. Daly and Wilson (1999) focused on events having to do with the acquisition of the things teenagers and young adults compete for, whereas Moffitt focused on events having to do with the acquisition of adult roles; these are completely compatible views. As men get older, obtain marketable skills or a degree (status) and employment (resources), and marry (a mate), they switch from a risky, competitive, high-mating-effort mode to a less risky, high-parental-effort mode. Variation in allocation of time and effort to mating versus parenting as a function of current circumstances is a common feature of biparental species.

The switch from mating effort to parenting effort is fairly well documented. Getting married is associated with reduced criminal behavior, even after controlling for individual differences predisposing to marriage (e.g., Laub, Nagin, & Sampson, 1998; Sampson & Laub, 1993; Warr, 1998), and not being involved in a stable mateship is consistently one of the best predictors of continuity of offending among adult offenders (e.g., Bonta et al., 1998). Marriage (and impending fatherhood) reduces testosterone, a hormone associated with mating effort, risk taking, aggression, and crime (Book, Starzyk, & Quinsey, 2001; Ellis & Walsh, 2000; Gray, Kahlenberg, Barrett, Lipson, & Ellison, 2002; Mazur & Booth, 1998; Storey, Walsh, Quinton, & Wynne-Edwards, 2000).[5] Employment likely leads to desistence from crime for adolescence-limited offenders (Rutter, Giller, & Hagell, 1997; Sampson & Laub, 1993; E. E. Werner, 1989).[6] Even major personality traits change as a function of age in a manner consistent with a change from mating effort to paren-

---

[5]Men who subsequently divorce experience an increase in testosterone.
[6]However, the same factors that predict adult criminality also predict adult unemployment (Caspi, Moffitt, Entner Wright, & Silva, 1998), suggesting that failure to obtain a job (at least during periods of economic stability) may be a marker of underlying predisposition to crime rather than a causal factor for crime.

tal investment (McCrae et al., 2000). Thus, the young male syndrome looks very much like a facultative, situationally and contextually dependent phenomenon. To use terms from chapter 3, it is likely part of a conditional strategy. The low heritability of antisocial behavior among adolescents is consistent with this view.[7]

Females, too, compete among themselves for reproductively relevant goals (a good mate, a good reputation, and so on) and are also more likely to engage in aggressive and delinquent behavior during adolescence, albeit in a less violent and less direct form. As predicted by the sex difference in reproductive variance, female competition is less physically risky. Campbell (1995) provided a cogent account of female delinquency as an outcome of female intrasexual competition.

Determinants of Risk Acceptance

The level of risk acceptance during adolescence and early adulthood should be commensurate with the intensity of the competition, but perhaps also with the degree of success in attaining reproductively relevant goals (resources, status and reputation, and mates) and with perception of future prospects. High intensity of competition, low success, and perception of poor future prospects raise the stakes and should lead to even more risky and dangerous activities. M. Wilson and Daly (1997) provided compelling evidence linking indicators of competitive disadvantage (e.g., income inequality) and poor prospects (e.g., low life expectancy) to rates of homicides using aggregate data (see also Daly & Wilson, 2001; Daly, Wilson, & Vasdev, 2001). Pezza Leith and Baumeister (1996) provided experimental evidence for a proximal cause of risk taking. They showed that intense negative emotion causes a shift toward higher risk choices (i.e., greater likelihood of choosing a lottery option of a low probability of a high gain rather than one with a high probability of a small gain). Because of the particular focus of their study, however, the experimental manipulations did not involve risk choices of equal expected value. Future work may reveal that events that generate negative emotions (and perhaps especially those involving competitive failures) increase risk taking, even in choices of equal expected outcome. Negative moods are frequently noted among released offenders (including rapists) just before their relapse (e.g., Zamble & Quinsey, 1997).

Risk taking, rebelliousness, and delinquency, however, may also be ways to exhibit competitive abilities, to display qualities that are hard to fake.

---

[7]Moffitt (1993) explained adolescence-limited delinquency with the *maturity gap*, a fairly novel phenomenon in which adolescents have the maturity to adopt adult roles but are unable to do so. Delinquent activities are ways to obtain things that adolescents desire (money, sexual experiences, autonomy) but cannot obtain legitimately. As they get older, adult roles become available to them, and antisocial activity stops paying off. In support of that theory, the size of the adolescent peak in delinquency has increased over the century, as has the length of the maturity gap because of earlier puberty and longer education. This theory, which involves a proximate explanation, is quite consistent with our discussion; a longer maturity gap intensifies competition.

Zahavi and Zahavi (1997) called these hard-to-fake displays *honest signaling*. Willingness to fight may reflect bravery and physical strength. Leading a gang may show dominance and leadership qualities. Stealing and robbery similarly require certain skills and demonstrate a willingness to incur risks to attain goals. Not following authority displays autonomy and independence. Of course, there are other, socially accepted ways to display these qualities, such as team sports, leadership of social clubs, and certain occupations; young men are attracted to these activities as well. But perhaps there is something special about dangerous and rebellious activities that reveals qualities that cannot be feigned. In Exhibit 4.4 we address the controversial topic of female resistance as a test of certain male qualities.

Competition, Mating Effort, and Rape

Dominance, risk taking, fearlessness, and physical prowess are characteristics associated with high mating effort and mating success. For instance, gang leaders (Palmer & Tilley, 1995) and young men rated as dominant (Mazur, Halpern, & Udry, 1994) have more sexual partners. Risk acceptance and attraction to dangerous activities have consistently been associated with early sexual intercourse and high number of sex partners (e.g., Seto, Lalumière, & Quinsey, 1995, and references therein). Degree of body symmetry, an index of physical quality and health, is associated with success in mating effort and with social dominance, physicality (robustness and vigor), and body mass (Gangestad & Simpson, 2000). And, as we discussed earlier in this chapter, antisociality, risk taking, and mating effort are characteristics of men who engage in sexual coercion and rape.

Young men are particularly likely to engage in rape and sexual coercion, and men who score higher on measures of antisociality, risk taking, and mating effort are particularly likely to report rape and sexual coercion compared with men who score lower. It is not difficult to imagine that men who are focused on mating effort and willing to take risks are less likely to attend to their partners' wishes. High mating effort requires a measure of antisociality, because it involves an unwillingness to compromise with women's preferred mating strategy, which frequently involves emotional attachment and commitment. Sexually coercive tactics may not be the preferred tactics used by men engaged in a higher-risk, high-mating-effort approach, but they may be part of a panoply of mating tactics—such as charm, display of prowess, and false promises—used to obtain sexual relationships. The cost of sexual coercion—for instance, not being able to date that person ever again—are often not very high for these men, especially in contexts in which the perception of costs is altered (e.g., alcohol intoxication) or low (e.g., when reports of sexual coercion to authorities are unlikely).

As men get older, begin a career, and begin investing in a long-term relationship, the balance of the costs and benefits of risk taking, mating effort, and the use of antisocial mating tactics changes dramatically. This view

EXHIBIT 4.4
Resistance as a Tool of Selection?

Elsewhere (Lalumière & Quinsey, 2000), we suggested that female resistance to sexual advances may serve as a test of certain male qualities, such as physical strength, dominance, willingness to pursue sexual activities, and so on. As we discussed in chapter 3, females in some nonhuman species use resistance as a tool of mate selection developed these ideas in her *sexy son* account of forced mating. According to this account, female resistance to sexual advances could act as a filter for the selection of reproductively successful characteristics that are passed on to their sons (who would be likely to be reproductively successful). In support of this hypothesis, Mealey reviewed studies indicating that some women reported that they sometimes said no when they meant yes and that victims of date rape often continue to date their assailants afterwards, and are more likely to do so if the rape is completed rather than uncompleted.

The idea that female resistance may act as a tool of selection of particular characteristics and that date rape may not always involve the negation of female choice may be somewhat disquieting but is empirically refutable. For example, men who are willing to be sexually coercive in the context of dating, who are more likely to complete date rapes, and who continue to date their victims afterward should show more signs of good genes and good health (e.g., more attractiveness, less fluctuating asymmetry, greater physical strength). Women who resist these men should have lesser trauma from the event. Work by Gangestad and Simpson (2000) suggested that men who engage in high mating effort show many of those signs of "good genes."

It is also important to point out in this context that the idea that female resistance may be a form of testing to select sexual partners of high reproductive fitness implies nothing about awareness or conscious planning. Although such selectionist hypotheses are often expressed as though the behavior were explicitly or deliberately goal directed, this is a kind of descriptive shorthand (recall the example of infanticide in lions described in Exhibit 3.1). The more correct but cumbersome expression of the hypothesis would be to say that the behavioral and psychological female tendency to resist mating was at least partially heritable; compared with other women, those who preferentially mated with men who exhibited the ability to overcome some degree of female resistance had more offspring, who also had more offspring, than other women; and therefore the tendency for women to "test" their potential sexual partners became widespread in the population. The hypothesis really says little about the subjective feelings of women when doing this testing. Finally, even if this testing sometimes occurs, it remains absolutely appropriate for society to legally and morally proscribe the use of sexual coercion and force by men.

---

of antisociality, risk taking, and mating effort and of its link with sexual coercion can help explain why a whole category of people (young men) is more at risk of sexual coercion and why some young men are more at risk than other young men (those who have more to gain—or less to lose—by using risky tactics of competition).

Starks and Blackie (2000) documented a link between intensity of competition and rape. They reviewed data showing that men are more likely than women to remarry following divorce and that the age difference between the partners increases as men remarry. This finding means that even in the context of an equal sex ratio, a high divorce rate creates a situation in which there are fewer desirable marriage partners for young men (a male-biased operational sex ratio). The authors showed that increases in divorce

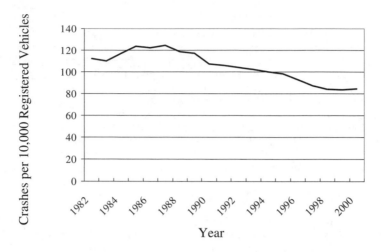

Figure 4.6. Car crashes in Canada. Source: Transport Canada.

rates over time and greater divorce rates in some states than in others are associated with higher rates of reported rapes. Although there might be other explanations for these findings,[8] the link between divorce rates (as a proxy for the intensity of competition) and rape provides support for the view that intensity of competition among men is associated with higher risk taking, including risky sexual tactics. We discuss sexual coercion directed at spouses in chapter 7.

It is quite likely that future studies examining factors that affect intensity of competition, personal and situational features associated with competitive success, and cues to long-term prospects will provide important insights into the causes of rape and criminal behavior. In the next section we return to the issue of the decline in the incidence of rape and other crimes throughout the 1990s and examine whether it may be related to changes in risk tolerance.

Risk Tolerance and the Crime Drop

We mentioned already that the incidence of rape and most other crimes has decreased during the last decade. Many hypotheses have been offered to explain this dramatic crime drop, most of them reviewed in a recent book (Blumstein & Wallman, 2000). These hypotheses include an increase in the number of incarcerated men, an increase in policing resources, a smaller relative number of young men, a decline in the use and selling of hard drugs, reduced availability of handguns, and changes in the abortion law (i.e., po-

---

[8]For example, high mating effort and low parental investment, two factors associated with rape, may lead to divorce. The authors' conclusion would be stronger if they showed that the men who do rape are more likely to be unmarried young men (other studies suggest that they are).

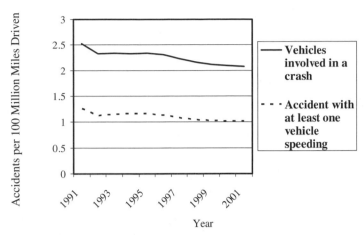

Figure 4.7. Vehicle accidents in the United States. Source: Bureau of Transportation Statistics.

tentially at-risk offspring are more likely to be aborted; see Donohue & Levitt, 2001). Most of these hypotheses fare well in the United States but fail to account for similar crime drops in other countries. For example, Canada experienced a significant crime drop without a concomitant increase in incarceration or resources allocated to policing (Ouimet, 2002). Demographic changes (e.g., an older population and fewer young men) very likely account for a significant proportion of the decline, but the decline in crime has been observed for all age groups examined so far.

As we mentioned in this chapter, risk acceptance should vary not only as a function of sex and age but according to context as well. Situations in which the cost–benefit ratio of risk taking is favorable (such as when long-term prospects are poor) should lead to greater risk acceptance. Because of the strong link between risk taking and crime, is it reasonable to postulate that the significant decline in criminal behavior in the 1990s is due in part to social, economic, or other changes (e.g., the decrease in the population prevalence of age-peer competitors) that improved perceptions of long-term prospects and thus decreased willingness to take risks. One way to test this idea is to examine changes in risk-taking activities that have occurred in the last decade.

Figures 4.6 to 4.13 show statistics for several risk-taking activities or activities associated with risk taking. As can be seen, the rate of car crashes has dropped since the late 1980s in Canada and since the mid-1990s in the United States. The rate of workplace injuries has dropped steadily since the early 1990s in both countries. Adolescent risk taking has also been on the decline since the early 1990s. Figures 4.9 to 4.13 are based on data from a U.S. nationwide survey of 5,000 to 15,000 teenagers in grades 9 to 12 conducted every 2 years since 1991 as part of the Youth Risk Behavior Surveillance System. The figures show a clear decline in what most people would

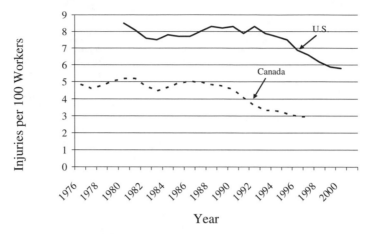

Figure 4.8. Workplace injuries in Canada and the United States. Sources: Association of Workers' Compensation Boards of Canada; Bureau of Labor Statistics.

consider to be risk-taking activities. Figure 4.14, from the same survey, shows that teenagers are not simply engaging in fewer behaviors.

One could legitimately argue that the decline in behaviors and outcomes shown in the figures is due to the proliferation of prevention programs targeting these behaviors. It is intriguing, however, that the decline in crime and risk-related activities began at about the same time. It would be worthwhile to investigate the possibility that there have been changes in the cues that people use (probably unconsciously) to modulate their risk acceptance. On the basis of the theoretical considerations we propose in this chapter, perhaps people's perceptions of their long-term prospects changed during the late 1980s and throughout the 1990s, decreasing their risk acceptance and increasing their investment in the future. These cues could involve (for self and for others) good health, few accidental injuries and accidents, other cues to higher life expectancy (e.g., grandparents still living), reliable employment, and improvement in economic circumstances. They could also involve improvement in social stability, little risk taking and crime in members of one's social group (a positive feedback loop), less economic inequality, and so on. There are data to support positive changes in most of these cues (with the notable exception of economic inequality, which increased slightly in the 1990s). Needless to say, solving this puzzle could lead to a better understanding of the causes of rape. We now turn to the second developmental pathway underlying antisocial propensities.

Life-Course-Persistent Delinquency and Competitive Disadvantage

Moffitt's (1993) life-course-persistent delinquents are a small group of men (and women, although they appear to be extremely rare; Moffitt & Caspi, 2001) who are difficult children, antisocial adolescents, and unremitting adult

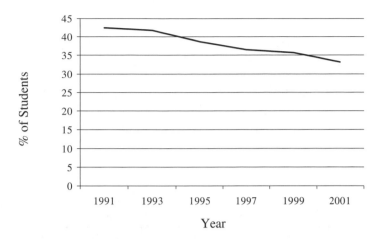

Figure 4.9. Percentage of students involved in at least one physical fight in the past 12 months. Source: National Center for Chronic Disease Prevention and Health Promotion, Youth Risk Behavior Surveillance System.

offenders. Many boys who display aggressive and antisocial behavior in childhood and early adolescence begin life with neurodevelopmental insults and are raised in disadvantaged environments. There are a multitude of factors that can produce neurodevelopmental perturbations, and many have been empirically related to persistent delinquency. These factors include heritable vulnerabilities, maternal smoking during pregnancy, obstetrical complications, exposure to environmental toxins, malnutrition, and brain injuries (reviewed in G. T. Harris, Rice, & Lalumière, 2001; Quinsey et al., 2004).

Similarly, there are several social factors that are empirically related to delinquency, such as single parenthood, poverty, chaotic neighborhoods, physical abuse, inconsistent discipline, large number of siblings, poor parental monitoring, and parental psychopathology (reviewed in G. T. Harris, Rice, & Lalumière, 2001; Quinsey et al., 2004; Rutter et al., 1997). Recent research has placed particular emphasis on the interaction of neurodevelopmental vulnerabilities and poor social environment, despite the fact that the statistical power to detect these interactions is typically very low. For example, Arsenault, Tremblay, Boulerice, and Saucier (2002) found that an index of obstetrical complications interacted with an index of family adversity at age 6 to predict teacher-rated aggression at age 6, serious self-reported delinquency at age 17, and, importantly, the continuity of early aggression to adolescent delinquency.

The common interpretation of these findings is that personal and social vulnerabilities decrease intellectual abilities (especially verbal abilities), promote impulsive thinking and actions, decrease the effectiveness of punishment, reduce the presence of effective socializing agents, impair abilities to develop prosocial skills, decrease the chances of success at school and at

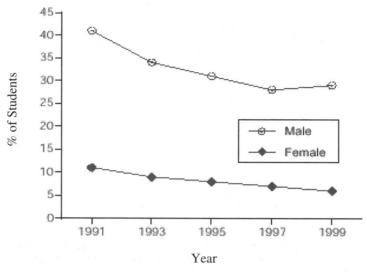

Figure 4.10. Percentage of students who carried a weapon in the past 12 months. Source: National Center for Chronic Disease Prevention and Health Promotion, Youth Risk Behavior Surveillance System.

work, and decrease the likelihood of success in establishing stable relationships with nondelinquent peers and prosocial mates. Early neurodevelopmental deficits combine with poor social support and lack of success in dealing with the tasks of life, creating ever-increasing adjustment problems (a snowball effect) and leading to persistent conduct problems. Men are more susceptible than women to this process, because they are more vulnerable to early neurodevelopmental insults (Gualtieri & Hicks, 1985).

This interpretation asserts that persistent antisocial tendencies reflect a failure of socialization mechanisms due to poor personal and social conditions. It is a pathological outcome of pathological processes. There is little doubt that pathological processes are involved in the ontogeny of some life-course-persistent delinquency (e.g., exposure to teratogens). Whether antisocial behavior is a pathological end product of this process, however, is not so clear.

The men described by Moffitt (1993) and others as life-course-persistent offenders are at a significant competitive disadvantage compared with other men. Their poor neurodevelopmental histories and their adverse social environments make them unlikely to succeed in competition for status, resources, and desirable mates. To use a term from human behavioral ecology, they have low embodied capital (Bock, 2002). *Embodied capital* refers to the stock of personal attributes (e.g., health, attractiveness, education, possession of specialized skills) that facilitates the acquisition of resources and mates, the formation of alliances, the effective rearing of children, and so on. Low embodied capital changes the cost–benefit ratio of antisocial activities, such that illicitly acquiring goods, establishing dominance through

94   THE CAUSES OF RAPE

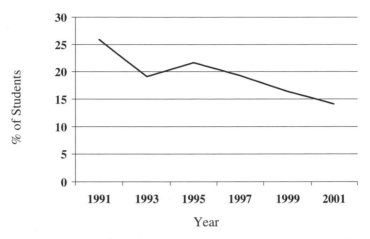

Figure 4.11. Percentage of students who never or rarely wear a seat belt. Source: National Center for Chronic Disease Prevention and Health Promotion, Youth Risk Behavior Surveillance System.

fighting, forcefully obtaining sex, and so on become "reasonable" activities. The long-term prospects of these men are bleak. Discounting of the future, high risk tolerance, and early reproduction may be reproductively adaptive responses to their disadvantageous circumstances. Desistence from antisocial activities is unlikely for these men, because they cannot adopt the roles or acquire the things that normally lead to desistence among young men (e.g., stable and profitable job, good reputation, good mate). Using the terms of chapter 3, life-course-persistent antisociality among these men resembles a conditional (and probably developmentally fixed) social strategy. There are good reasons to believe that neurodevelopmental problems and social adversity have been recurrent circumstances of human history and thus provided selection pressures for the evolution of such alternative responses.

As we mentioned before, there is research supporting the connection between competitive disadvantage, poor prospects, and criminality. Daly et al. (2001) found a very strong relationship between an index of economic inequality and the homicide rate in American and Canadian state and provincial aggregate data. Economic inequality as measured by the Gini index (which assumes a value of 0 when all households have equal income and a value of 1 when all income accrues to one household) was much more closely related to homicide rates than were measures of economic prosperity.[9]

M. Wilson and Daly (1997) also examined the relationships among average male life expectancy, economic inequality, reproductive timing, and homicide in aggregate data from 77 Chicago neighborhoods. Male life expectancy (with the effects of homicide removed) was very strongly negatively related to the homicide rate. The addition of economic inequality sig-

---

[9]This relationship held both in Canada, where economic inequality and prosperity are positively correlated, and in the United States, where they are negatively correlated.

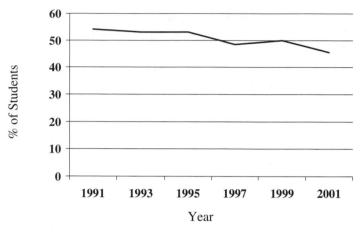

Figure 4.12. Percentage of students who have had sexual intercourse. Source: National Center for Chronic Disease Prevention and Health Promotion, Youth Risk Behavior Surveillance System.

nificantly improved the prediction of homicide rate, but adding median income did not. There was also an inverse relationship between age at first motherhood and the homicide rate. Taken together, these data suggest that competitive disadvantage, as assayed by economic inequality, increases risk taking and violence. Perceptions of longevity (i.e., short- vs. long-term horizons) influence risk taking among men and reproductive strategies among women. We expect similar relationships between indexes of competitive disadvantage and sexual coercion.[10]

Earlier we noted the reliable link between mating effort—as indexed principally by age of initiation of sexual activities, number of sexual partners, and preference for partner variety and casual sex—and sexual coercion. This link suggests at first glance that competitive disadvantage and low embodied capital would be a rare cause of sexual coercion, because sexually coercive men are typically more sexually experienced (successful) than other men. What we suggest, however, is that low embodied capital changes the costs and benefits of mating effort and of the transition to parental investment. High and continuous mating effort is more likely to pay off for these men compared with the alternatives (for a similar view, see Shields & Shields, 1983).

Moffitt et al. (2002) recently reported on the follow-up of their Dunedin cohort of children, 26 years old at follow-up, showing the connection between competitive disadvantage, crime, and early reproduction. Those classified as life-course-persistent delinquents were more likely than adolescence-limited delinquents to be later convicted of violence against women (rape or assault; 11% vs. 1%), more likely to have fathered children (45% vs. 23%),

[10]T. Gottschall (2003) recently reported a significant positive relationship between the Gini index and rape rates across New York counties.

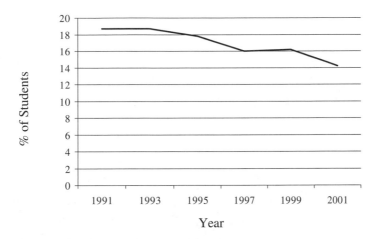

Figure 4.13. Percentage of students who have had sexual intercourse with four or more partners. Source: National Center for Chronic Disease Prevention and Health Promotion, Youth Risk Behavior Surveillance System.

more likely to have fathered multiple children (29% vs. 9%), less likely to have completed their education, more likely to be supported by public benefits, and less likely to have high occupational status. They also had less positive (but not statistically significantly so) expectations about the future. Even though life-course-persistent offenders accounted for only 8% of the cohort, they had fathered 27% of the children. They also had a significant number of mental health problems (e.g., depression).

A cautionary note is in order. The causal role of social disadvantage and neurodevelopmental perturbations on life-course-persistent antisociality is based almost entirely on correlational findings. Although it is plausible that neurodevelopmental problems or social disadvantage causes antisociality, it is just as possible that the deficits associated with low embodied capital and antisociality share a common cause. The most obvious candidate, of course, consists of the heritable tendencies toward antisociality in parents. That is, antisocial parents are more likely to neglect and abuse their children and to expose them to disadvantageous environments, and they are also more likely to pass on to them the heritable psychological traits that form the basis for life-course-persistent antisociality (G. T. Harris, Rice, & Lalumière, 2001). Twin studies of antisocial behavior, however, consistently find that environmental differences (which include pre- and postnatal influences) are an important source of individual differences in antisociality independent of genetic differences (reviewed in D. C. Rowe, 2002).

Psychopathy

The third pathway to antisociality is psychopathy. Psychopaths are impulsive, deceitful, selfish, aggressive, promiscuous, irresponsible individuals

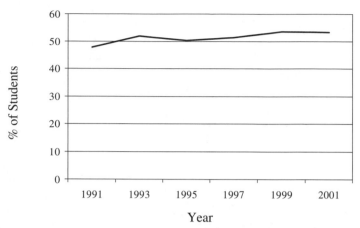

Figure 4.14. Percentage of students who exercised three or more of the past seven days. Source: National Center for Chronic Disease Prevention and Health Promotion, Youth Risk Behavior Surveillance System.

who have very little remorse or guilt for their misbehaviors and little concern for the welfare of others. They are the quintessential life-course-persistent offenders in terms of their early onset and perseverance, but they appear to differ in fundamental ways from other adult offenders with regard to their antisocial history, their affective and physiological characteristics, their interpersonal relations, and, importantly, they show no signs of early neurodevelopmental perturbations.

Compared with nonpsychopathic adult offenders, psychopathic offenders have more extensive and versatile criminal histories, are more prone to instrumental than reactive violence, are more likely to use weapons in their offenses, are more likely to select men and strangers as victims, and are more likely to cause serious injury to their victims. They are much more likely to fail their parole or commit new crimes once they are released from an institution, and some institutional treatment programs are associated with increased recidivism among psychopaths (reviewed in Gacono, 2000; Hare, 1991; Hare, Clark, Grann, & Thornton, 2000; G. T. Harris, Rice, & Cormier, 1994; G. T. Harris, Rice, & Lalumière, 2001; G. T. Harris, Skilling, & Rice, 2001; Lalumière, Harris, & Rice, 2001; Quinsey et al., 2004).

In the laboratory, psychopaths show little tolerance of delay, more perseverance when punished, less control over dominant (highly probable) responses, and are generally less affected by the consequences of their actions (Howard, Payamal, & Neo, 1997; Howland, Kosson, Patterson, & Newman, 1993; Lykken, 1957; Newman & Kosson, 1986; Newman, Kosson, & Patterson, 1992; Newman, Patterson, & Kosson, 1987). Psychopaths are less physiologically reactive when exposed to cues of distress or to aversive or unexpected stimuli like loud sounds and less reactive when anticipating some aversive stimuli (Hare, 1978; Ogloff & Wong, 1990; Patrick, 1994; Schmauk,

1970). Psychopaths appear to process emotionally charged information very differently: In contrast to nonpsychopaths, psychopaths do not show different behavioral and electrocortical reactions to emotional and neutral verbal information (Williamson, Harpur, & Hare, 1991). Also, psychopaths show less cerebral lateralization (i.e., the brain's cerebral hemispheres show less specialization) than nonpsychopaths and differ on contemporaneous measures of cerebral activity when processing verbal information (Day & Wong, 1996; Hare & McPherson, 1984; Intrator et al., 1997; Kiehl, Hare, Little, & McDonald, 1999; Raine, O'Brien, Smiley, Scerbo, & Chan, 1990). Results of neuropsychological and neuroimaging tests have shown functional and structural differences between psychopaths and other offenders but no evidence of lesions or brain damage (Hare, 1984; Hart, Forth, & Hare, 1990; Laakso et al., 2001; Raine, Lencz, Bihrle, LaCasse, & Colletti, 2000).

The uniqueness of psychopaths observed in many studies is consistent with the finding that psychopathy represents a discrete statistical entity. G. T. Harris, Rice, and Quinsey (1994) and Skilling et al. (2001) found, using Meehl's taxometric methods (Meehl & Golden, 1982), that a score on a measure of psychopathy represents a *probability* of the person assessed belonging to the psychopathy class rather than a *degree* of psychopathy. This empirical finding has been obtained with samples of adult male psychiatric patients, adult male prisoners, and grade-school boys. The discrete nature of psychopathy suggests that its development may differ from that of other offenders.

Much theorizing on the origins of psychopathy is based on the assumption that psychopathy is a result of perturbations in brain development, perhaps from deleterious genes, prenatal insults, postnatal brain injuries, severe physical abuse, or other factors affecting brain development. Following from this view, the observed differences between psychopaths and other men are described as "deficits" or "abnormalities." For example, Patrick (1994) concluded that "the absence of normal startle potentiation in psychopaths during exposure to aversive pictures or warning cues signifies a *deficit* in the capacity for defensive response modulation, which is the essence of fear" (p. 327, italics added).

Differences between groups are not necessarily caused by abnormal development—for example, men and women show fundamental differences in brain structure and organization. But more important, research has so far provided no support for a pathological origin of psychopathy or for the labeling of psychopaths' unique features as deficits or abnormalities. As mentioned above, neuropsychological and neurological studies of psychopathy have observed some subtle differences between psychopaths and other men but have not discovered, at least so far, signs of brain pathology or neurodevelopmental perturbations. Other studies using a different approach have also observed that psychopaths appear in fact neurodevelopmentally healthy.

Obstetrical problems and high morphological asymmetry are known correlates of many different neurodevelopmental problems (e.g., schizophrenia, low IQ) and of poor health. Lalumière et al. (2001) compared the obstetrical histories (from file information) and the morphological asymmetry (from direct measurement of 10 body parts, such as length of fingers on each hand) of a group of psychopaths and a group of other violent offenders, both recruited from a maximum-security psychiatric institution. Psychopaths had fewer obstetrical problems and were more symmetrical than other offenders. The men most likely to be psychopaths (i.e., those with the highest scores on the revised version of the Hare Psychopathy Checklist) were just as symmetrical as a group of nonoffenders. Coid (1993) reported that indicators of neuropsychological abnormality (perinatal trauma, developmental delay, and history of seizures) did not correlate with a diagnosis of Antisocial Personality Disorder according to the *Diagnostic and Statistical Manual of Mental Disorders* (American Psychiatric Association, 1994) but did correlate with schizotypal and schizoid personalities (the Antisocial Personality Disorder diagnosis is strongly correlated with the Psychopathy Checklist; Skilling et al., 2002). Schulsinger (1972) reported that psychopaths (defined in his study as men with a consistent pattern of "impulse-ridden, or acting-out behavior" without psychosis or neurosis) did not differ from matched control participants with no mental disorder on a composite measure of obstetrical complications.

G. T. Harris, Rice, and Lalumière (2001) investigated the pathways to persistent violence using structural equation modeling among more than 800 offenders. A latent factor representing possible early neurodevelopmental problems—indicated by obstetrical complications, low academic status, learning disorders, infancy problems, and low IQ—was related to persistent violence. Another latent factor representing psychopathy was also, but even more strongly, related to persistent violence. Of relevance for this discussion, these two latent factors were themselves unrelated. These results strongly suggest that neurodevelopmental problems, at least as assessed in these studies, cannot be causes of psychopathy.

Evolutionists have long argued that a strategy of social defection and cheating could evolve under certain conditions. From this point of view, the behavioral, emotional, cognitive, and neurological uniqueness of psychopaths would not be deficits or impairments; instead, they would be part of a set of organized, functional, and specialized phenotypic features that formed an alternative social strategy, one that was reproductively viable during human evolution.

Harpending and Sobus (1987) used the concepts and results of game theory research to demonstrate that a cheater (or "nonreciprocator") could achieve Darwinian success under certain conditions: Cheaters are successful when they are difficult to detect, highly mobile, verbally skilled, and especially skilled at persuading females to mate. Mealey (1995) extended and documented these ideas and suggested that psychopathy—what she called *primary sociopathy*—might be an evolutionarily stable strategy maintained by frequency-dependent selection. By this account, psychopaths are genetically different from other antisocial individuals and from everyone else, their geno-type strongly predisposing them to a lifetime of antisociality: "Without love to 'commit' them to cooperation, anxiety to prevent 'defection,' or guilt to inspire repentance, they will remain free to continually play for the short-term benefit in the Prisoner's Dilemma".[11]

A "cheater" or "defector" model of psychopathy would require the fol-lowing minimal conditions during human evolution: (a) most members of human social groups were strongly inclined to cooperate, (b) it was possible to move from one group to another, and (c) detecting defectors entailed costs. A fairly evenly mixed group of cooperators and defectors would have resulted in many fruitless interactions between defectors and in greater vigi-lance for defection by cooperators. Lack of mobility would have resulted in gaining a reputation as a defector and eventual ostracism. Cost-free detec-tion would have excluded defectors from all interactions.

These ideas suggest that the defining features of psychopaths (manipu-lative, charming, glib, deceptive, parasitic, irresponsible, selfish, callous, pro-miscuous, impulsive, antisocial, aggressive) and their performance in labora-tory tests (fearlessness, intolerance of delay of gratification, perseveration despite punishment, superficial processing of emotional material, lesser reac-tivity to cues of others' distress and fear) are not pathological outcomes of impaired development, but rather features of a Darwinian adaptation de-signed to thrive in an interpersonal environment dominated by social coop-erators (G. T. Harris, Skilling, & Rice, 2001).

This model of psychopathy is highly reminiscent of the alternative strat-egy (the morph) used by the swordtail and the bluegill sunfish (discussed in chap. 3). It remains possible, however, that the development of psychopathy is condition dependent—that it develops only when certain cues are present (e.g., an adverse environment). We believe that condition dependence is less likely, because serious criminal behavior is highly heritable (the herita-bility of psychopathy as assessed with the PCL–R is as yet unknown[12]), psy-chopathic-like children can be identified quite early, and environmental cues that seem correlated with the development of other children are unrelated to the development of psychopathic children.[13] Although this evolutionary model of psychopathy has survived empirical tests (e.g., Lalumière et al.,

---

[11]The prisoner's dilemma is a game in which players have to decide whether to cooperate with another player or defect. The payoff matrix is set to reward cooperators when they interact with each other and to reward defectors even more when they interact with cooperators. In this game, cooperation pays off in the long run (when players have repeated interactions), but defection pays off in the short run.

[12]Blonigen, Carlson, Krueger, and Patrick (2003) reported on the heritability of psychopathic personality traits among a nonoffender twin sample. Heritability was high but mostly nonadditive. There was also an effect of nonshared environment. It is unknown whether these findings are relevant to the genetics of psychopathy per se.

[13]Wootton, Frick, Shelton, and Silverthorn (1997) reported that children ages 6 to 13 classified as callous and unemotional (features linked to psychopathy by Frick, O'Brien, Wootton, & McBurnett, 1994) differed from other children with regard to the impact of ineffective parenting on their conduct problems. Specifically, the number of conduct problems was not linked to the effectiveness of

2001), much more research is required to refine and further test it. A more detailed discussion and test of this model of psychopathy can be found in Quinsey et al. (2004).

High mating effort is a crucial feature of psychopathy. The life-history model of psychopathy suggests that psychopaths should begin their sexual activities quite early, should be particularly interested in partner variety and casual sex, should particularly focus their effort toward reproductively viable partners, and should be willing to use coercive tactics to obtain reproductive opportunities. In this view, psychopaths are behaving just like young men (with respect to sexual behavior), except that they start earlier and do not eventually desist. There are data to support some of the predictions regarding the sexual proclivities of psychopaths. As we mentioned earlier in this chapter, sex offenders who target adult women score higher on the PCL–R than sex offenders who target male or female children. We predict that psychopathic sex offenders should predominantly target young (fertile) women as victims.

Thus, we propose that

- whereas some men adopt a mixture of mating and parenting effort tactics according to circumstances, a small group of men adopt a high mating effort strategy that they pursue in most contexts; their mating strategy is part of a generally antisocial lifestyle and is entirely driven by the acquisition of a large number of partners with little investment in mates and offspring;
- sexual coercion is only one of the tactics (along with charm, false promises, and deception) used by psychopaths to acquire multiple partners; and
- sexually coercive tactics are probably used when less coercive tactics are not successful with a particular woman or whenever the costs of coercion are not too high.

The use of a high-mating-effort strategy among psychopaths is not due to an inability to compete in prosocial ways for resources and status, but rather is part of an alternative strategy of social competition (see Lalumière & Quinsey, 1999).

CONCLUSION

A comparison of the historical literature and the findings on individual differences provide some theoretical clues into the nature of rape. The his-

---

parenting among callous/unemotional children, whereas it was negatively linked among other children. In fact, there was a nonsignificant tendency for callous/unemotional children to have more conduct problems when parenting was more effective.

torical literature describes circumstances that rape is related to but offer little insight into how these relate to the different characteristics of individuals. Nevertheless, similar conclusions emerge: History shows that rape is more common when the women to be raped are devalued and the perceived costs of rape are low—for example, when the women are of markedly lower social status or part of an enemy group in wartime. The study of individual differences shows that men who are more likely to devalue women and who incur or perceive lower costs for exhibiting sexual coercion are more likely to rape. Antisociality and high mating effort probably cause men to be relatively indifferent to the preferred mating strategies and the best interests of women.

Rape and sexual coercion appear to be part of a general antisocial tendency. Rapists are not sexually deprived, in terms of access to sexual partners, and appear to seek short-term and frequent sexual relationships to a greater extent than nonsexually coercive men (which may make them *feel* deprived). This is true of undetected sexually coercive men and perhaps also of incarcerated rapists. The use of sexually coercive tactics is likely part of a host of other mating and antisocial tactics used by antisocial men to create sexual opportunities and increase their number of sexual partners.

There are likely three pathways to the development and expression of antisociality and high mating effort. Mating effort and intrasex competition rise during late adolescence and early adulthood for men in general, increasing the likelihood of rape and other risky activities during that period and therefore accounting for adolescence-limited offending. M. Wilson and Daly (1985) aptly labeled this phenomenon the *young male syndrome*. Correspondingly, the constellation of high mating effort and generally high-risk and antisocial behavior characterizes two small groups of men during their whole lifetimes. In the first group, it may be the result of competitive disadvantage, and in the second it may be part of a lifelong alternative social strategy (psychopathy).

The distinctions among adolescence-limited offenders, offenders with low embodied capital, and psychopaths have not been used in studies of sexually coercive men. One can argue, however, that studies of college students and community samples include mostly offenders who limit their antisocial activities to adolescence and young adulthood, whereas studies of incarcerated samples include mostly life-course-persistent offenders (psychopaths and those with low embodied capital). We expect that these distinctions will greatly improve understanding of the link between antisociality, mating effort, and sexually coercive behavior and a general understanding of the causes of rape.

5

SEXUAL INTEREST IN RAPE

One of the most controversial topics in the study of rape over the past two decades has been the idea that some form of sexual disorder might underlie men's propensity to rape. To some, the idea is somewhat disturbing because it appears to excuse rapists by allowing that their reprehensible conduct is due to a disorder, perhaps beyond their control. The very idea of rape as a sexual act is often viewed as anathema. Indeed, many commentators have speculated that rape is simply an act of male aggression against women—essentially a nonsexual act whose function is to keep women, in general, subjugated to men, in general.[1]

---

[1]For example, Brownmiller (1975) wrote,

> For if the first rape was an unexpected battle founded on the first woman's refusal, the second rape was indubitably planned. Indeed, one of the earliest forms of male bonding must have been the gang rape of one woman by a band of marauding men. This accomplished, rape became not only a male prerogative, but man's basic weapon of force against woman, the principal agent of his will and her fear. His forcible entry into her body, despite her physical protestations and struggle, became the vehicle of his victorious conquest over her being, the ultimate test of his superior strength, the triumph of his manhood.
>
> Man's discovery that his genitalia could serve as a weapon to generate fear must rank as one of the most important discoveries of prehistoric times, along with the use of fire and the first crude stone axe. From prehistoric times to the present, I believe rape has played a critical function. It is nothing more or less than a conscious process of intimidation by which *all* men keep *all* women in a state of fear. (p. 15)

In the first part of this chapter we review what is known about a particular class of sexual disorders known as *paraphilias*. Paraphilias are distinguished from such other dysfunctional conditions as premature ejaculation or vaginismus, called *sexual dysfunctions*. Paraphilias involve intense, recurrent sexual fantasies, urges, or actions focusing on objects (a fetish), on activities with persons who do not or cannot consent (as in child molestation), or on activities involving humiliation and suffering of someone (as in sadism or masochism). The first snag we shall encounter here is the lack of scientific consensus on the meaning of *disorder*.

Second, we review the empirical literature on the sexual interest of men assessed by health professionals after having been accused of coercive sexual offenses against women. In tackling this topic we discuss a laboratory method often used to study the sexual interests of sex offenders. Finally, we examine the differences between rapists and other men with respect to their sexual interests and try to determine the meaning and the sources of those differences.

WHAT IS A SEXUAL DISORDER?

In this era of Viagra and prime-time television commercials about erectile dysfunction, one might think that men's sexual disorders had recently seen a scientific revolution. In truth, very little scientific work is conducted on the topic. In many scientific quarters, the study of sex among humans is still regarded with suspicion. What is a sexual disorder, especially a paraphilic sexual disorder? Homosexuality used to be considered a paraphilic disorder by professionals but is no longer so. This is not an accomplishment such as that achieved over smallpox, where the combination of vaccination and cure eradicated the disease from all human populations. Homosexuality disappeared as a disorder because experts changed their minds about it being a disorder in the first place. Our purpose here is not to dispute this change, but to highlight the problem raised by the very definition of disorders in general and sexual disorders in particular.

One of the most influential documents in the general area of unusual, deviant, or troublesome human conduct is the *Diagnostic and Statistical Manual of Mental Disorders*, 4th edition (*DSM–IV*) published by the American Psychiatric Association (1994). Although conceding that they could not provide a "consistent operational definition that covers all situations" (p. xxi), the authors stated that a *disorder* "is a clinically significant behavioral or psychological syndrome or pattern . . . associated with present distress . . . or disability . . . or with a significantly increased risk of suffering death, pain, disability, or an important loss of freedom" (p. xxi). Thus, *paraphilias* are described as a particular class of sexual disorders characterized by persistent and intense sexual fantasies, urges, or behaviors that interfere with successful occupational or social functioning, including being subject to arrest or incarceration.

Pedophilia is, therefore, classified as a paraphilic sexual disorder involving sexual attraction to prepubescent children and characterized by arousing sexual fantasies, urges, or behaviors that cause distress and impairment. We spend some time in the next section describing pedophilia, because an understanding of the scientific approach to that condition helps illuminate the issue when we turn to the possibility that a paraphilic sexual disorder might underlie men's propensity to rape.

PEDOPHILIA

There is not much doubt that pedophilia is a sexual disorder based on the *DSM–IV* definition. In modern Western society, sexual molestation of children (people who have not begun puberty) is a relatively frequent crime, despite strong social condemnation and occasionally severe punishment. Men who commit sexual offenses against children often rationalize their behavior and deny any sexual interest in children, but it appears that many of these men experience strong sexual urges toward children.

There is good evidence that when first apprehended, many offenders against children have had many sexual contacts with children. Unlike most criminals, offenders against children often exhibit a considerable degree of specialization, such that sexual crimes against children form their only serious antisocial conduct. It has proved to be remarkably difficult to change child molesters' sexual interests or otherwise cause them to desist through treatment (Furby, Weinrott, & Blackshaw, 1989; G. T. Harris, Rice, & Quinsey, 1998; Quinsey, Harris, Rice, & Lalumière, 1993; M. E. Rice & Harris, 1999, 2003a; M. E. Rice, Harris, & Quinsey, 2001).

It is clear that many sexual offenses against children occur because some men have an enduring powerful sexual attraction to children. This condition seems "disordered" in that men are rarely sexually attracted to children—men are predominantly and most frequently attracted to adults or at least sexually mature individuals. Certainty about what is normal in this regard is so clear that one takes it for granted—it doesn't take a scholar of human culture or history to recognize the ubiquity and function of typical adult male sexual interests, at least as far as the age of prospective partners is concerned. Indeed, if ancestral men had been exclusively sexually attracted to prepubescent individuals, no one would be here today to wonder about it.[2]

The best source of information about men's sexual attractions comes from phallometry. Phallometry is a set of laboratory techniques used to study

---

[2]Indeed, such a consideration might have been a basis for homosexuality's prior status as a disorder. Of course, moral condemnation was probably the primary basis.

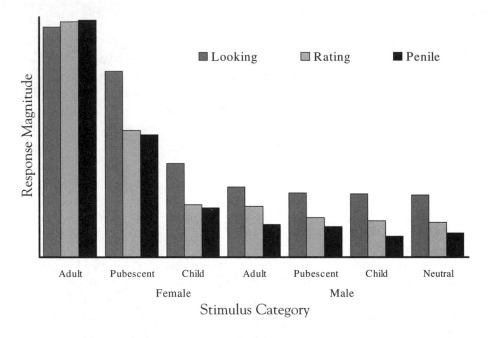

Figure 5.1. Looking times, ratings of sexual attractiveness, and penile responses among normal men (*n* = 25). Data are from "Viewing Time as a Measure of Sexual Interest Among Child Molesters and Normal Heterosexual Men," by G. T. Harris, M. E. Rice, V. L. Quinsey, and T. C. Chaplin, 1996, *Behavioural Research and Therapy, 34,* p. 392, Figure 1.

men's sexual interests without relying on verbal report. Under many circumstances, men's reports of their sexual interests are quite valid (G. T. Harris & Rice, 1996; G. T. Harris, Rice, Quinsey, & Chaplin, 1996), but when studying disorders, especially those that involve condemned and criminal targets or activities, psychophysiological assessment is preferred. *Phallometry* is the monitoring of erectile responses while presenting controlled stimuli in the form of pictures or recorded stories. Altering characteristics of the stimuli allows researchers to test hypotheses about how men's sexual interests vary and how those variations might be related to their sexual behavior outside the laboratory.[3]

Consider Figure 5.1, which shows the typical phallometric responses of "normal" heterosexual men to each of several categories of pictures (from G. T. Harris et al., 1996). These heterosexual men are typically called *normal* because they are volunteers from the local community who have no record of criminal conduct and state that their sexual experience and interest are confined to adults. It is not surprising that the greatest penile response is to pictures of young adult women, and there is little or no response to pictures

---

[3]For general and user-friendly reviews of phallometry, see G. T. Harris and Rice (1996), Lalumière and Harris (1998), Quinsey and Lalumière (2001), and Seto (2001).

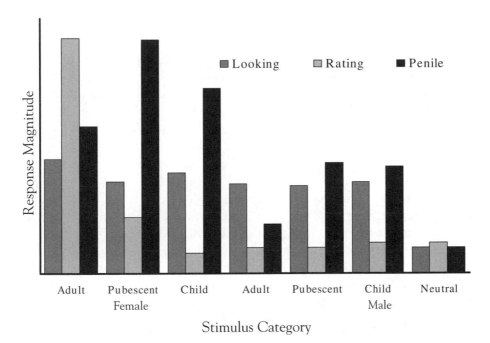

Figure 5.2. Looking times, ratings of sexual attractiveness, and penile responses among child molesters (*n* = 26). Data are from "Viewing Time as a Measure of Sexual Interest Among Child Molesters and Normal Heterosexual Men," by G. T. Harris, M. E. Rice, V. L. Quinsey, and T. C. Chaplin, 1996, *Behavioural Research and Therapy, 34,* p. 392, Figure 1.

of men, boys, or sexually neutral stimuli (e.g., landscape photographs). Perhaps more surprising is the fact that these men exhibit intermediate amounts of erection to pictures of pubescent and even prepubescent girls. That is, men show graded preferences—a maximal response to one category and lesser responding to others to the extent that stimuli are similar to the preferred category. Also shown in Figure 5.1 are the men's ratings of sexual attractiveness, as well as unobtrusively recorded looking times for the same categories of pictures recorded in a separate session. Thus, among normal men, phallometric measurement converges with sexual history, self-reported interest, and other ways of assessing sexual interest.

Now consider Figure 5.2, which shows the average penile responses, looking times, and ratings of sexual attractiveness given by a group of sex offenders against children; these offenders were referred to our laboratory after having been apprehended by the authorities for "hands-on" sexual offenses against children under the age of 14 (also from G. T. Harris et al., 1996). Several things are immediately apparent. First, the offenders' ratings of sexual attractiveness were very similar to those of the normal men in Figure 5.1; the offenders reported that they were maximally attracted to female adults. Second, the phallometric responses converged not with self-report of attraction, but with the men's officially recorded sexual histories. That is, the offenders' average responses to some categories of pictures of children were greater than their responses to adults. These phallometric responses indicate pedophilia. Despite what they say, many offenders against children are sexually attracted to children. Of course, this does not by itself prove that the pedophilic preference caused the sexual offenses. The relationship might be more complicated; perhaps sexual experiences with children (initiated because of influences other than sexual preferences) can cause men's sexual preferences to change.

There are several reasons why this kind of reverse causal effect is unlikely. Sexual attraction to particular categories of persons tends to precede sexual activities: Heterosexual men are sexually attracted or interested in postpubertal women before their first heterosexual experiences, and the same goes for homosexual men (reviewed in Herdt & McClintock, 2000). Also, although researchers and clinicians have made many efforts to do so, it is extremely difficult to change men's phallometrically measured sexual preferences in significant ways (Lalumière & Quinsey, 1998b), other than by showing them how to fake deliberately. It seems unlikely that such major changes occur very often in the natural world as a result of experiences. Among those who admit their sexual behaviors and preferences, child molesters commonly report that their pedophilic sexual interests long preceded their first sexual activity with children (Freund & Kuban, 1993). We cannot recall a single child molester who acknowledged pedophilic sexual preferences and said he had normal sexual interests before his first sexual experiences with children. For some child molesters, at least, pedophilic sexual interests are longstanding.

There are a few more things to note regarding the data shown in Figures 5.1 and 5.2. First, not much can be learned about sexual interests by considering only the responses of the sex offenders; some comparison with data from normal men is required. That is, we can draw conclusions about what is abnormal or atypical only by comparing the child molesters' responses to those of men who do not commit sexual offenses against children. Specifically, child molesters' rather large responses to pictures of pubescent girls might seem remarkable, but Figure 5.1 implies that many normal men also exhibit fairly large responses to that age and gender category.

Second, it is desirable to manage the data[4] so as to best reveal whatever differences are actually there (G. T. Harris & Rice, 1996; G. T. Harris, Rice, Quinsey, Chaplin, & Earls, 1992). Thus, in the figures, child molesters' aver-

---

[4]This issue of managing the data raises another statistical matter. Readers might be curious about the variability of the results shown in these figures. Phallometric responses (i.e., the average increase in penile size associated with each stimulus category) often exhibit much greater variance than ratings or viewing times, especially for preferred categories. Most of this variance is scientifically uninteresting, however. As with other psychophysiological measures, validity is enhanced by statistical corrections (e.g., converting all responses to standard scores) that remove irrelevant between-participant variability in overall magnitude of the erectile response (Earls, Quinsey, & Castonguay, 1987; G. T. Harris et al., 1992). After such a transformation, phallometric responses are less variable than ratings and viewing times.

age responses to prepubescent girls are higher than those of normal men, and conversely, normal men's average responses to young adult women are somewhat higher than those of the child molesters. But using those two facts simultaneously makes the group difference even clearer. Even further, calculating, for each man, a relative response score (e.g., largest prepubescent category minus largest adult category) yields one number that captures his preference. Such individual relative response scores produce even better discrimination between the groups than is apparent from Figures 5.1 and 5.2. This relative method of computing individual preferences will be important when we turn to men's sexual interest in rape.

It might surprise some to know that phallometric assessment works in the first place. It is remarkable that a sterile laboratory where a man is shown somewhat grainy pictures can produce data so consistent with his sexual history. But it does work. Any competent researcher can obtain differences similar to those shown in the figures. Indeed, the general patterns reported in this section have been replicated so many times that if a researcher were to report failure, everyone in the field would examine the methods in a search for what must have been done wrong.

Moreover, phallometric assessment predicts future behavior. Child molesters who exhibit pedophilic interests are more likely to commit new sexual offenses when released (Hanson & Bussière, 1998; M. E. Rice, Quinsey, & Harris, 1991). That fact, together with the consistent between-group discrimination (G. T. Harris & Rice, 1996), means that the phallometric assessment of pedophilia among child molesters has good discriminative and predictive validity. Of course, nothing is perfect. There is evidence, for example, that men can learn (especially if specifically taught) to fake their sexual attraction, usually by inhibiting their responses to preferred categories (Lalumière & Earls, 1992; Quinsey & Chaplin, 1988b). Nevertheless, phallometric research with child molesters has been of great value. Researchers have a way to study pedophilia fairly directly, and clinicians have a means to help assess risk and identify a target in therapy.

Earlier we discussed how obvious it must be that a strong sexual interest in children (i.e., pedophilia) is a paraphilic sexual disorder. There are those (e.g., Lilienfeld & Marino, 1999) who assert that *disorder* has no useful scientific meaning. That is, one can infer some patterns of meaning from examining how the term is used, but a coherent definition is impossible. It is quite obvious that if we agreed with that reasoning, we would not belabor this issue. We think Wakefield (1992, 1999) has provided a conceptually and practically useful definition of *disorder*.

According to Wakefield, a phenomenon should be called a disorder when it is a "harmful dysfunction." To be a harmful dysfunction, two criteria must be met: First, a structure or a process does not function as designed by natural selection, and second, the dysfunction results in suffering, distress, or social impairment. The harm need not necessarily be only to the person who has the disorder (Wakefield, 1993). Thus, pedophilia seems to be the result of disrupted sexual development, and it also results in harm and socially undesirable outcomes, such as imprisonment and the sexual coercion and exploitation of children. Thus, according to this definition, pedophilia is a sexual disorder.[5] Certainly, Wakefield's definition does not make everything easy. What is distressing, socially impaired, or harmful can change and will also vary from group to group, which is why Wakefield called it the *value criterion*. Such decisions are political, social, and emotional and not simply a matter of scientific inquiry. As well, it is definitely not an easy matter to know what a particular feature of human psychology or physiology was designed for or, indeed, whether it was designed by natural selection at all.

There is less uncertainty, however, about what sexual behavior was designed for or that sex is the product of natural selection (Quinsey & Lalumière, 1995; Ridley, 1994). Sexual interests in prepubescent children appear to represent something not functioning in accordance with design by natural selection, because it seems impossible that a sexual preference for nonreproductively viable persons could ever evolve. And when it comes to sexual aggression and exploitation, there is nearly universal agreement about what is abhorrent or harmful.

Using our discussion of pedophilia as a guide, let us now examine the possibility that a sexual disorder causes rape. We must address two questions: First, are rapists sexually different from men who do not commit rape? Rape can be attributed to a sexual disorder only in men who are somehow sexually different from men who do not commit rape. That is, are there reliable individual differences in sexual interest among men that are related to their likelihood of engaging in sexual coercion? Second, what is the meaning of any such rape-related differences in sexuality among men? Quite obviously, people can be different, even in very fundamental ways, without there being a disorder involved. To take an obvious example, men and women are different physically and psychologically, but no one would suggest, except in jest, that maleness is a disorder. Thus, are these differences in sexuality among men that are related to rape due to the failure of a structure or process to function as designed by natural selection?

PHALLOMETRIC ASSESSMENT OF RAPISTS

Phallometry with offenders against children usually uses pictures of males and females of differing ages. It has been shown, however, that pictures are not necessary. Some phallometric assessments of child molesters have used stories. The stories are recorded and played back using a tape recorder so that

---

[5]For a recent debate on this question, see the special section on pedophilia in *Archives of Sexual Behavior*, 31 (2002).

the stimulus is exactly the same each time it is presented. For a given assessment, the stories are standardized so that they all have the same structure. Just like the pictures, stories are designed in clear-cut categories: neutral stories (e.g., a trip to the laundromat), stories about mutually consenting and satisfying sexual intercourse between a man and a woman, and stories about a sexual assault of a child by a man. Phallometric assessments using such stories show the same kinds of differences between offenders against children and normal men as do assessments using pictures (e.g., Barsetti, Earls, Lalumière, & Bélanger, 1998; Quinsey & Chaplin, 1988a). In fact, although not many studies have yet been done, assessments using stories appear to achieve even better between-group discrimination than pictures, especially if the child is described, in some stories, as being physically brutalized as well as sexually violated. That is, child molesters and non–sex offenders are most different from each other in their phallometric responses when the suffering of victims is emphasized (e.g., Chaplin, Rice, & Harris, 1995).

This finding leads to clear expectations when it comes to rape. Perhaps rape occurs because some men's sexuality is plagued by sexual attraction to force and coercion, characterized by persistent and intrusive arousing sexual thoughts, fantasies, and urges about rape such that mutually consensual sex is not preferred. Of course, this would be a difference in preference not for type of partner (like pedophilia) but for type of activity. If this were so, then one would predict that rapists tested in the laboratory would show a pattern of responses consistent with their sexual history and, of course, different from that shown by normal men.

Researchers have developed phallometric assessments using stories of consenting sex, rape, nonsexual violence, and neutral stories to determine if rapists and nonrapists differ in their sexual interests (the seminal work can be found in Abel, Barlow, Blanchard, & Guild, 1977; Barbaree, Marshall, & Lanthier, 1979; Quinsey & Chaplin, 1982, 1984; Quinsey, Chaplin, & Upfold, 1984; Quinsey, Chaplin, & Varney, 1981). Rapists have usually been defined as men who have been arrested for committing sexual assaults against adult women. Men in the comparison group are usually men from the community or volunteers from the same institution without a criminal sexual history.

Let us consider one study in which we observed a very large group difference (M. E. Rice, Chaplin, Harris, & Coutts, 1994). Although our laboratory is located in a maximum-security psychiatric hospital, none of the rapists were psychotic, and almost all of them were (after their assessment in our hospital) convicted and sentenced to prison. We used stories designed to emphasize the victim's perspective. Thus, we had stories in which a woman's voice was heard describing, in the first person, a brutal rape in which she suffered great pain, terror, and humiliation. There were also first-person stories in which a woman described mutually consenting and satisfying sexual intercourse and another described a terrible beating without any sexual con-

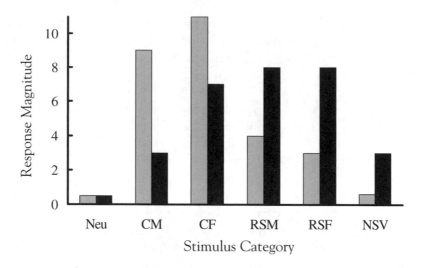

Figure 5.3. The phallometric responses of rapists (black bars, *n* = 14 and nonrapists (gray bars, *n* = 14) to different audiotaped stories. Neu = neutral; C = consenting; RS = rape (with much suffering); NSV = nonsexual violence; M or F = male or female perspective. Data are from "Empathy for the Victim and Sexual Arousal Among Rapists and Nonrapists," by M. E. Rice, T. C. Chaplin, G. T. Harris, and J. Coutts, 1994, *Violence and Victims, 8,* p. 143, Figure 1.

tent. As well, there were stories told in a man's voice in the first person and neutral stories. Stories of nonsexual violence are presented to determine the extent to which rapists are attracted to violence per se.

The results of this study are summarized in Figure 5.3. First, participants showed greater responses to consenting sex stories told from the woman's perspective; it seems that stories that emphasized the other person's experience yielded greater arousal. Second, control group men showed a strong overall preference for consenting sex stories. Third, rapists showed a small overall preference for rape stories. Finally, rapists yielded slightly greater responses to stories describing brutal nonsexual beatings then did the other men.

Much greater between-group discrimination occurs when, within individuals, responses to rape stories are compared with responses to consenting sex stories. This discrimination was greatest when the rape stories considered were those in which a suffering victim described the events from her own perspective—that was the rape category that produced the lowest responding from the nonrapists. Participant-by-participant relative scores (average response to all rape stories minus average response to all consenting sex stories) yielded almost no overlap between the scores of rapists and nonrapists.

We recently used some of the stories from the M. E. Rice et al. (1994) study to investigate, among other things, whether men who have been assaultive toward women (either spouses or other relatives, or strangers), but not in a sexual way, show sexual interests that resemble those of rapists or

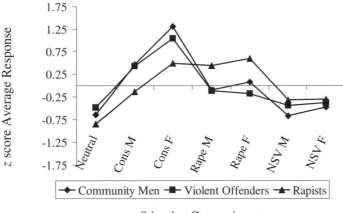

Figure 5.4. Phallometric profiles of rapists (*n* = 24), community normal participants (*n* =19), and nonsexually violent offenders against women (*n* = 11). Cons = consenting; NSV = nonsexual violence; M or F = male or female point of view. Data are from "Are Rapists Differentially Aroused by Coercive Sex in Phallometric Assessments?" by M. L. Lalumière, V. L. Quinsey, G. T. Harris, M. E. Rice, and C. Trautrimas (2003), in *Sexually Coercive Behavior: Understanding and Management* (Volume 989, p. 218, Figure 2), edited by R. Prentky, E. Janus, and M. C. Seto, New York: Annals of the New York Academy of Sciences.

those of nonoffenders (normal men). Assaultive men of female victims are an interesting group to study because, like rapists, they have been violent against a woman, and like normal men, they have not committed a sexual assault. In addition, rapists and nonsexually violent offenders are quite similar with regard to their criminal history, personality, psychopathology, sexual history (apart from sexual assaults, of course), and so on. The comparison of these two offender groups provides the strongest test of the possibility that rapists might have unique sexual interests.

The results from that study are shown in Figure 5.4. Just as M. E. Rice et al. (1994) found, the rapists showed stronger overall responses to the rape stories than to the consenting sex stories. The men recruited from the community showed a clear preference for consenting sex (especially when told from the female point of view). The assaultive men produced a pattern of response that was virtually indistinguishable from that of the community men. It seems clear from these two studies that rapists show different sexual interests than nonrapists.

Among sex offenders against children, the finding of consistent and theoretically meaningful phallometric differences is well established, but those who have studied rapists have not always been able to detect such group differences. In several studies by our research group, rapists consistently showed statistically different patterns of sexual arousal compared with men who were not rapists (Quinsey & Chaplin, 1984; Quinsey et al., 1981, 1984; M. E. Rice et al., 1994). Other researchers have reported similar differences (Abel et al.,

1977; Barbaree et al., 1979; D. A. Crawford, 1979; Earls & Proulx, 1986; Fedora et al., 1992; Freund, Scher, Racansky, Campbell, & Heasman, 1986; Miner, West, & Day, 1995; Wydra, Marshall, Earls, & Barbaree, 1983) in samples drawn from forensic psychiatric facilities and prisons. It is interesting that Malamuth (1986; Malamuth & Check, 1983), in a sample primarily of college undergraduates, reported that phallometric responses to rape stories were the best discriminator between men who reported past sexual coercion and men who did not (see also Bernat, Calhoun, & Adams, 1999; Lohr, Adams, & Davis, 1997).

Although positive results are more numerous, there are several reports of failures to obtain statistically significant differences (e.g., Baxter, Marshall, Barbaree, Davidson, & Malcolm, 1984; Murphy, Krisak, Stalgaitis, & Anderson, 1984; Seto & Barbaree, 1993).[6] Faced with these kinds of equivocal results, commentators traditionally review the studies and derive a box score to summarize the situation. This is usually accompanied by speculation about the possible sources of apparent conflict (e.g., Blader & Marshall, 1989).

There is, however, a much better way to resolve apparent inconsistencies in research findings. Meta-analysis is a set of statistical techniques that allows research results from many studies to be combined, permitting a statement about the likelihood that a group difference or relationship actually exists, how big it is, and why some studies find it and some do not. The study of rapists' sexual responses is a particularly fruitful area for meta-analysis for several reasons. Many studies in this area use fairly small samples—statistically significant differences might not be found because of low statistical power. There are differences among studies in the kinds of stimuli used (e.g., rape stories vary greatly in how much violence is depicted); the number of stimuli per category (having several stimuli per category usually improves reliability); and the procedures for recording, scoring, and summarizing erectile responses (statistically significant differences might not be found because of the failure to use optimal laboratory techniques or scoring). Meta-analysis overcomes the problems of small sample size and can test hypotheses about the sources of differences in findings reported.

Two meta-analyses of the phallometric assessment of rapists have been published (Hall, Shondrick, & Hirschman, 1993b; Lalumière & Quinsey, 1994). These meta-analyses show that the overall phallometric difference between rapists and nonrapists was moderate to large. The size of this difference was significantly related to whether rapists were compared with other sex offenders or to non–sex offenders (Hall et al., 1993b) and to the particular set of stories used (Lalumière & Quinsey, 1994). Rapists and nonrapists were better differentiated to the extent that the stories used emphasized brutality and victim suffering.

---

[6]There is also one study in which the authors concluded that there was no difference between rapists and nonrapists, even though they reported descriptive data (Table 2, p. 518) that showed a statistically significant difference (Baxter, Barbaree, & Marshall, 1986).

It is important to distinguish between overall levels of arousal and discrimination. It need not be the case that rapists, as a group, respond more to brutality than to less violent material. The point is that the difference between rapists and nonrapists is greatest when very violent material is used. The difference is also larger when participants have not been previously tested and methods to prevent dissimulation are used (G. T. Harris, Rice, Chaplin, & Quinsey, 1999).

When using optimal procedures, about 60% of rapists tested in the laboratory show equal or greater arousal to rape stories than to consenting sex stories. The comparable value for nonrapists (or at least men who have no criminal history for rape and who deny having committed rape) is about 10% (Lalumière & Quinsey, 1993; Lalumière, Quinsey, Harris, Rice, & Trautrimas, 2003). The available evidence strongly supports the conclusion that rapists, as a group (at least those detected by the criminal justice system, and perhaps undetected rapists as well), are sexually different from men who do not commit rape and that this difference is large and consistent when appropriate laboratory techniques are used (for a recent review of this literature, see Lalumière et al., 2003).[7]

As was the case with child molesters, the phallometric responses of rapists predict future behavior, although there are just a few studies on this topic. M. E. Rice, Harris, and Quinsey (1990) studied 87 rapists and found that arousal to rape stories (relative to arousal to consenting sex stories) was nonsignificantly but positively related to the commission of a subsequent sexual offenses. Also, an index of relative arousal to nonsexual stories (in which a woman is assaulted by a man, but there is no sexual content in the story) was positively and significantly associated with sexual recidivism in the same study. It is interesting that arousal to rape stories may predict sexual aggression even among offenders who have not committed rapes. Rabinowitz Greenberg, Firestone, Bradford, and Greenberg (2002) reported that an index of relative arousal to rape stories predicted the commission of hands-on sexual offenses among 41 men who had been assessed because of their exhibitionistic ("hands-off") behaviors. It thus seems that phallometric assessment of rapists' sexual interest has discriminative and predictive validity, although much more work is needed on predictive validity. We now turn to the more difficult question of whether rapists' unique sexual interest in rape represents a sexual disorder.

SEXUAL AROUSAL TO RAPE AS A SEXUAL DISORDER

There is no doubt that there is something different about at least some rapists' phallometric responses in the laboratory. This finding is both impor-

---

[7]On the basis of the empirical data, one would think that this conclusion reflects a general consensus in the field, but this is not the case (e.g., Marshall & Fernandez, 2000).

tant and puzzling, because it is probably the only variable that reliably distinguishes rapists from other antisocial men (at least so far). Sexual interest in violent and coercive sex may provide part of the answer to Langevin, Paitich, et al.'s (1985) bewilderment about "why the sexual aggressives raped and common assaulters did not" (pp. 33–34).

As mentioned before, about 60% of rapists show phallometric arousal in the laboratory to scenarios depicting the rape of a woman by a man that equals or even surpasses their arousal to scenarios depicting mutually consenting sexual activities (Lalumière et al., 2003). Rapists sometimes even show sexual arousal to stories in which a man violently beats up a woman (but not when the victim is a man). Nonrapists typically show much stronger sexual arousal to consenting scenarios than to rape scenarios and show no arousal to nonsexual violence. Because of the possibility of faking (especially for men who have been charged with rape), the 60% value may be an underestimate. Whether this unique arousal pattern represents a sexual disorder, however, is unclear.

Rape Proneness as a Sexual Disorder

An intriguing line of research in the area of sexual deviance and sexual offending was initiated by forensic sexologist Kurt Freund, who coined the term *courtship disorder* (Freund was also responsible for the invention of phallometry). Freund's use of the term *courtship* has nothing to do with romance; it is similar to the way it would be used by a naturalist or an ethologist observing a species in the wild. Freund observed that human sexual behavior follows a species-typical sequential pattern. Stripped of any romantic connotations and in scientific jargon, he labeled the four primary phases of human courtship as partner location, pretactile interaction, tactile interaction, and genital union (Freund, 1988, 1990; Freund, Scher, & Hucker, 1983).

Freund's insight was that several paraphilias seem to constitute an exaggerated or distorted form of normal male responses for a particular phase. Thus, voyeurism is a disruption at the partner location phase; exhibitionism and telephone scatologia (making obscene phone calls) are disruptions of pretactile interaction; frotteurism (touching and rubbing nonconsenting victims) is disrupted tactile interaction; and rape proneness, masochism, and sadism are disruptions at the genital union phase.

In support of this way of thinking, Freund reported that these particular courtship paraphilias tend to co-occur (in medical terms, "are comorbid") and that phallometric responses to stimuli depicting different disordered courtship behaviors tend to be associated (Freund et al., 1983, 1986; Freund & Seto, 1998; Freund, Seto, & Kuban, 1997; Freund & Watson, 1993). On the other hand, these courtship paraphilias also tend to be associated with paraphilias that seem to have nothing to do with the phases of normal courtship and intercourse. Because courtship disorders, especially rape proneness, as Freund called it, are also comorbid with pedophilia (Freund, 1990) and transvestic fetishism (Freund & Watson, 1993), it is unclear how specific one can be about the nature of the sexual disorder that might underlie rape. Freund's work, however, has led to the notion that different paraphilias may have similar causes.

Sadism

It has sometimes been suggested that rapists' sexual arousal, as observed in the phallometric laboratory, is indicative of sadism. Sexual sadism is a paraphilia described in the *DSM–IV* (American Psychiatric Association, 1994) as intense sexual arousal to the mental or physical suffering of another. Men who rape may be motivated to do so because they find the fusion of sex, violence, and humiliation of the victim to be most arousing, and the rape scenarios used in phallometric testing certainly capture all of these elements (in addition to the element of nonconsent).

A condition characterized by the irresistible urge to physically injure one's sexual partners would clearly meet Wakefield's (1992, 1999) harm criterion. As to the functional criterion, it seems certain that a preferential tendency to maim one's sexual partners cannot have contributed to reproductive success in humans' evolutionary past. One could argue that a condition in which a man has a sexual preference for seriously physically injuring his sexual partners *must* be due to the failure of some mechanism to perform as it was designed by natural selection.

There is some support for the view that the sexual arousal of rapists to rape stories may represent, at least in part, a sadistic interest. The largest differences between rapists and nonrapists in phallometric assessments occur when the rape scenarios are extremely salient—that is, when they are described from the female point of view and include extreme brutality, humiliation of the victim, and graphic violence (e.g., Proulx, Aubut, McKibben, & Côté, 1994; Lalumière & Quinsey, 1994; M. E. Rice et al., 1994). Also, as mentioned, at least some rapists respond sexually to stimuli depicting nonsexual violence, but only when the victim is a woman (Quinsey et al., 1984). Finally, there is a small but significant and positive relationship between the rape index—a measure of relative interest in rape scenarios versus consenting scenarios—and the amount and nature of injuries suffered by the actual victims of the rapists assessed (Quinsey & Chaplin, 1982; Quinsey et al., 1984; but see Lalumière et al., 2003).

There is also evidence against the view that sadism explains the differences in the arousal patterns of rapists and other men. Studies classifying rapists into sadistic versus nonsadistic subgroups based on clinical criteria do not observe consistent phallometric differences between these two groups. If the sexual arousal of rapists to rape scenarios represents, even just in part, a sadistic interest, then one would expect that rapists who are classified as sadists would show the greatest arousal to rape stories. Langevin, Ben-Aron, et al. (1985) compared seven sadistic rapists and nine nonsadistic rapists and observed a nonsignificantly lower average rape index among the sadists. Seto and Kuban (1995) obtained similar results in a comparison of seven sadistic rapists and 14 nonsadistic rapists. Marshall, Kennedy, and Yates (2002) compared 41 sex offenders (almost all of them rapists) diagnosed as sadists and 18 rapists who received other psychiatric diagnoses. A larger number of nonsadists than sadists showed their largest arousal to rape or to nonsexual violence. In the Seto and Kuban study, men who admitted sadistic fantasies involving sexual violence or rape showed a preference for rape stimuli over consenting stimuli (as expected), but their responses diminished when the rape stories were particularly violent. The only result that came close to the expected pattern was that of Barbaree, Seto, Serin, Amos, and Preston (1994), in which a small group of sadistic rapists ($n = 8$) had a higher (but not quite significant) rape index than a small group of nonsadistic rapists ($n = 15$). Of course, it is possible that the failure to find the predicted differences in the pattern of arousal of sadists and other rapists is due to poor reliability or poor validity in the clinical diagnosis of sadism (see Marshall, Kennedy, Yates, & Serran, 2002).[8] Also, perhaps sadists' sexual interests are very idiosyncratic and are not appropriately tapped in standardized phallometric assessments.

Another prediction is that if a sadistic interest is driving rapists' arousal to rape stories, rapists should differ from nonrapists in their arousal to stories describing sadistic or sadomasochistic activities involving consenting partners. Quinsey et al. (1984) found that rapists did not respond significantly more to these scenarios than nonrapists. This was not a strong test of the hypothesis, however, because the sadistic stories involved only bondage and spanking and were very mild in comparison to the rape scenarios, where the rapists responded much more than the nonrapists.

Most clinicians working with rapists can easily recall many cases that would fit anyone's definition of sadism. We are not arguing here that sadism does not exist, only that sadism appears, at least for the moment, to be an unsatisfactory explanation for the difference between rapists and other men in their sexual arousal to scenarios describing rape. It remains possible that some of the observed differences between rapists and nonrapists are due to some rapists having sadistic interests, but this interest has been difficult to

---

[8]One might think that it would be easy for researchers to identify sexual sadists in any sample of rapists, at least on the basis of the injuries caused to victims. It turns out, however, that rape victims are sometimes injured or killed not because the perpetrator was aroused by causing pain and suffering, but because the rapist used considerable force to subdue the victim or because he wished to eliminate her as a possible witness (Quinsey & Upfold, 1985). Researchers and clinicians in this field have so far found it difficult to do a convincing and reliable job of classifying rapists as sadistic or nonsadistic on the basis of victim injury and other criteria (Marshall, Kennedy, Yates, & Serran, 2002).

assess and would probably not account for the fact that a large number of rapists show a pattern of arousal that differs from that of nonrapists.

If the explanation of arousal to rape in terms of sadism is unsatisfactory, the problem may lie in the conceptualization and measurement of sadism. We know that rapists are differentially sexually responsive to descriptions of extremely brutal rapes. The question is how to characterize this responsiveness. The concept of sadism is probably heterogeneous. In some sadistic sexual practices among consenting partners the sadist often appears to be acting in the service of the masochist's sexual enjoyment. This is the opposite of what is captured by the rape scenarios used in phallometric assessment. Perhaps some rapists do have a paraphilia, but one that is better described by phrases such as *hyperdominance*. That is, such a paraphilia would be characterized by intense sexual interest in the exercise of power, physical control, and physical and emotional dominance (rather than the inflicting of pain and injury itself). In a sense, such a hyperdominance paraphilia may be an extreme version of typical male sexual behavior in which males more frequently adopt an initiating and dominant role in courtship (men are overrepresented among recreational sadists, whereas women are overrepresented among recreational masochists). Hyperdominant rapists would be expected to cause more injury, to be sexually preoccupied with coercive fantasies, and to have more victims. Following Wakefield (1992, 1999) again, such a condition would be sensibly classified as a paraphilic disorder to the extent that men who had it suffered from lowered reproductive fitness in ancestral environments.

SEXUAL AROUSAL TO RAPE AS A BY-PRODUCT OF ANTISOCIALITY

It has been hypothesized that normal men are aroused by the sexual elements of the rape stories in phallometric assessment but that arousal is greatly reduced (or inhibited) by the brutal violence depicted (Barbaree, 1990). Normal men, as part of a more or less cooperative (or at least compromising) approach to relationships, are generally designed to be responsive and sensitive to the feelings and interests of their partners. Therefore, their arousal to consenting stories is greater than their arousal to rape stories. Indeed, experimental studies have shown that the introduction of coercion in a sexual story that began as mutually consenting reduces normal men's penile arousal (Bernat et al., 1999; Lohr et al., 1997). Also, experimental studies have shown that it is possible to *disinhibit* normal men—for example by intoxicating them, by inducing anger at a woman, or by exposing them to pornography prior to testing—so that their relative arousal to rape stimuli is increased (see review in Barbaree, 1990).

Rapists, on the other hand, as part of a general antisocial lifestyle, are relatively insensitive to the feelings and interests of others, especially in a sexual context (e.g., M. E. Rice et al., 1994). Because of this insensitivity, it has been hypothesized that rapists fail to be inhibited by the violence and expression of refusal portrayed in rape scenarios presented during phallometric assessments. The sexual elements are arousing, and the violence and brutality do nothing to interfere with arousal. In accord with this idea, the introduction of coercive elements in a sexual story that began as mutually consenting does not appear to inhibit the arousal of sexually coercive men (Bernat et al., 1999; Lohr et al., 1997). The fact that the largest differences between rapists and nonrapists in phallometric assessments occur when the rape scenarios are described from the female point of view and include extreme brutality, humiliation of the victim, and graphic violence may be a manifestation of the sensitivity of nonrapists and the lack thereof of rapists, rather than a manifestation of sadism.

Callousness, low empathy, lack of remorse, selfishness, and sexual promiscuity are all indicators of antisociality, especially life-course-persistent antisociality. It is to be expected that the three groups of antisocial men described earlier (young men, low embodied capital men, and psychopaths) would care little for the feelings of others. It could be that rape, together with being unaffected by the suffering portrayed in a phallometric assessment, is a reflection of a general insensitivity to others' interests. It could also be that this insensitivity is especially revealed in sexual situations. In any case, one would expect that men who score very high on measures of antisociality would exhibit relatively little decrement in penile erection to sexually explicit material, even when considerable suffering of a nonconsenting victim is simultaneously described. By the same token, the impulsivity, callousness, selfishness, and lack of concern for rules would lead some men to commit a disproportionate amount of rape. There is a substantial amount of evidence in support of the latter expectation. But what about the idea that antisociality and sexual arousal to violence and suffering (as measured by phallometry) are related?

We assessed the self-reported empathy of the participants in the study of rapists' sexual responses described earlier (M. E. Rice et al., 1994). Deviant sexual responses (for both nonsexual violence and rape) were associated with lower self-reported empathy (the negative relationship was significant for the whole group of 28 rapists and nonrapists and non-significant within each group). We did not, however, have a good measure of antisociality in that study. In another study we assessed psychopathy with the Psychopathy Checklist—Revised (PCL–R) and correlated the scores with the rape index among 11 rapists, obtaining a correlation of .23 (Lalumière et al., 2003). Serin, Malcolm, Khanna, and Barbaree (1994) reported a statistically significant association between phallometric deviance and psychopathy (assessed with the PCL–R) in a mixed group of 65 child molesters and rapists; the correlation for the rapist group alone (n = 33) approached significance. In that study, however, all forms of phallometric deviance (including pedophilic responses) were lumped together. Although the insensitivity hypothesis leads us to expect an association between psychopathy and phallometric responding to rape, we have no reason to expect such an association for psychopathy and pedophilia. Psychopathy may increase the probability of child molestation among pedophilic men, but there is no reason to expect that psychopathy should be related to a sexual preference for children.

In one study, the PCL–R scores of sex offenders ($n = 63$) were significantly correlated with relative phallometric responses to sexual coercion, and there was no association between PCL–R scores and relative phallometric responses to prepubescent children (G. T. Harris, 1998). As well, PCL–R scores were positively related to the number of female or adult rape victims the offenders had and negatively related to the number of male or child victims. In another study, Firestone, Bradford, Greenberg, and Serran (2000) reported a significant correlation between a phallometric rape index and PCL–R scores among 369 sex offenders, and the correlation for the phallometric pedophilia index was not significant.

Looking at community samples, Malamuth (1988b) reported an association between a phallometric rape index and laboratory aggression (delivering a noise contingent on errors during a task), but only if the target was a woman. Other significant predictors of laboratory aggression toward women in that study included dominance as a motive for sex, Eysenck's psychoticism (psychopathy), acceptance of interpersonal violence, and sex role stereotyping. Men who reported being sexually coercive with women tended to deliver a louder noise to both female and male confederates. In another study, Malamuth (1986) found that relative arousal to a rape story was positively associated with dominance (in a sexual context) and hostility toward women. Lalumière and Quinsey (1996), however, did not find positive associations between measures of antisociality and phallometric interest for rape in a study of 99 male volunteers.[9]

There is some evidence, therefore, that part of the difference between the arousal of rapists and nonrapists in the laboratory could be accounted for by antisociality. It is important to point out, however, that if rapists responded significantly more to rape scenarios than consenting scenarios, one would have to add some additional explanation or conclude that a preference for sexual coercion was an inherent aspect of antisociality. The hypothesis that arousal to rape is a by-product of antisociality suggests that it is not indicative of a pathology in the Wakefield (1992, 1999) sense to the extent that it did not interfere with men's reproductive outcomes in ancestral environments.

---

[9]In a small study, Plaud and Bigwood (1997) found that the degree of arousal to a sexual scenario in which the woman said no was positively related to having had sexual intercourse with a stranger, having had sex with more than one person at a time, having been part of an orgy, having looked at people having sex, having had sex with a much younger person, and having looked at obscene pictures and films.

SEXUAL AROUSAL TO RAPE AS A DESIGN
FEATURE OF ANTISOCIALITY

Young men who exhibit high risk taking, offenders with low embodied capital, and psychopaths are all prone to using antisocial tactics and to exhibit high mating effort as part of their social and reproductive strategies. Young men are involved in intense competition, competitively disadvantaged offenders are trying to make the best of a bad deal, and psychopaths are pursuing a finely tuned alternative strategy of defection and aggression. One could hypothesize that arousal to coercive sex is a fundamental component of these strategies in that it supports the proximal goal of acquiring sexual partners. The idea is that mating requires one of two largely incompatible sets of behavior—either investing time in finding someone who is likely to be interested, getting to know that person, building a relationship, and finally (sometimes) sexual contact, or attempting deception and sometimes forcing sex on someone. Whereas most men are designed to prefer the former set of tactics, antisocial men may be designed to prefer the latter. In this sense, arousal to rape would not be a pathology or even an unhappy by-product of their antisociality, but instead a design feature of the reproductive strategy associated with antisociality.

A sexual interest in nonconsensual sexual activities is detectable in a substantial proportion of rapists when using optimal laboratory procedures. However, whether such interests are a by-product or a fundamental component of antisociality (and mating effort) is not easy to answer with available studies of rapists. For some rapists, coercive sex is preferred over consensual sex, suggesting that the by-product hypothesis is insufficient. The side effect model suggests that such interests do not serve particular functions but rather are simply the by-product of the general insensitivity associated with antisociality and mating effort. By contrast, the fundamental component model suggests that such sexual interests serve the pursuit of reproductive goals that are associated with high antisociality and mating effort.

Both the side effect and the fundamental component views make the novel prediction that relative arousal to coercive sex should change with age. In a general population, young men as a whole should show the greatest interest in such scenarios, with a significant decline with age. Those who become persistent offenders should not exhibit changes in interest with age, however. Another novel prediction is that persistently antisocial men, whether they are of low embodied capital or psychopaths, should show elevated arousal to sexual coercion stimuli (compared with nonoffenders), even if they have never been apprehended for sexually coercive behaviors. Readers may remember, however, that the phallometric studies described in this chapter show that offenders who are not rapists exhibit phallometric profiles identical to non-offenders. In fact, few studies of rapists' phallometric responses have used offenders as comparison participants. In the few that have, it is not clear how many of the controls were life-course-persistent offenders. Certainly, the idea that phallometrically measured responses to sexual coercion are linked to antisociality and mating effort means that it should be very difficult or impossible to find men who score high on the Psychopathy Checklist—Revised, for example, who do not also show sexual interest in rape in the laboratory, whether or not they have an officially recorded history of rape. Available data do not permit an evaluation of these predictions.

What is needed is research in which rapists are compared with other offenders with similar scores on measures that indicate life-course-persistent antisociality and research linking variation in antisociality and arousal to rape in different groups of offenders and nonoffenders. Another powerful test of these predictions could come from a longitudinal study of adolescent men that tested whether phallometric responses to rape stimuli changed over time and were correlated with other antisocial conduct in the ways predicted by these hypotheses. Another promising avenue of research is to examine the development of sexual interests in boys at risk to become life-course-persistent offenders. For example, van Goozen, Cohen-Kettenis, Matthys, and van Engeland (2002) reported that 8- to 12-year-old children with behavioral problems (conduct disorder or oppositional defiant disorder) spent more time looking at pictures depicting aggressive (a man shooting a gun) and sexual (a woman with naked breasts) content than did control group children.

DEVELOPMENTAL SOURCES OF SEXUAL AROUSAL TO SEXUAL VIOLENCE

As the preceding discussion suggests, the meaning of the difference observed in phallometric assessment between rapists and other men remains to be elucidated. Another interesting question is the developmental source of this difference. What developmental factors increase a man's sexual interest in violent sex? Perhaps because few researchers and clinicians have accepted that rapists do indeed show a unique pattern of sexual interest, there are few studies on that question. One interesting line of research comes from studies of birth order.

One of the most intriguing scientific findings in the entire field of sexology and anomalous sexuality is that birth order is related to sexual orientation in men. Men born later in their siblingships are statistically more likely to be homosexual than men born earlier (Blanchard et al., 2000; Ellis & Blanchard, 2001; Purcell, Blanchard, & Zucker, 2000). Sulloway (1996) provided a cogent and persuasive account of the effects of birth order on personality and temperament suggesting that later-born people are less likely to be conventional in all kinds of ways, including their sexuality. Sulloway suggested that natural selection has given humans a tendency to respond to their birth position in the family. Briefly, later-borns tend to be less conventional because throughout evolutionary history, such a strategy has been more successful than trying to occupy the exact same social niche already occupied by a more experienced older brother or sister.

But the findings about birth order and homosexuality seem to be about something quite different. In many independent data sets, R. Blanchard and colleagues (Blanchard, 2001; Purcell et al., 2000) have shown that birth order is related to homosexuality in a very particular way. A man's likelihood of being gay increases only with his number of older brothers. His number of older sisters or younger siblings is irrelevant. Also, birth order is not related to female homosexuality. It is hard to see how this very particular result can be the same phenomenon as that described by Sulloway (1996).

Blanchard and Klassen (1997; Blanchard, 2001) suggested a different explanation, one based on the fact that a male fetus has a tendency to engage a mother's immune responses. We already know that fetuses sometimes do engage maternal immunoreactivity; the Rh phenomenon is a well-known example. If something about a male fetus is antigenic to the mother (a blood factor linked to the Y chromosome, for example), the more boys a mother has already had, the more likely it would be that an immune response between mother and fetus would occur. If this antigenic response disrupted psychosexual development, homosexuality would be related to the number of older brothers but not the number of older sisters (because a mother and female fetus are more immune compatible). And, of course, the number of younger siblings cannot matter, because their pregnancies happen later (Ellis & Blanchard, 2001).

Is it possible that other variations in sexual interest are associated with birth order, in particular birth order among brothers? Sexual interest in children (pedophilia) does not seem to be associated with the number of older brothers a person has.[10] What about sexual arousal to rape? In one study (Lalumière, Harris, Quinsey, & Rice, 1998), phallometric deviance among rapists was positively associated with the number of older brothers but not older sisters or younger siblings. As well, in a subsequent and more detailed study, the older brother effect was observed only for sexual preferences involving violence (Côté, Earls, & Lalumière, 2002), regardless of the age of the victim. Thus, among a mixed group of child molesters and rapists, the larger the number of older brothers, the greater the relative response to stimuli depicting violent sex with female adults or children of both sexes. Finally, in another study, a group of rapists recruited from secure institutions and from the community had a larger number of older brothers than a group of

---

[10]There is a fraternal birth order effect for sexual orientation among pedophiles, but not for pedophilia (Blanchard et al., 2000; Bogaert, Bezeau, Kuban, & Blanchard, 1997). For a review of the neurohormonal theory of pedophilia, see Quinsey (2003).

nonrapists recruited from the community, even after controlling for number of other types of siblings (Lalumière et al., 2000).

Although much more work remains to be done on this question, these studies suggest that the sexual attraction of some rapists to violent sexual activity may be due to a maternal immune response that affected neurodevelopment. If so, what are the implications of this finding in the context of our previous discussion of the reasons for rapists' sexual arousal to violence? One obvious possibility is that some rapists' relative arousal to violence is a result of perturbations in neurodevelopment in which sex and violence are somehow fused. Another, less obvious possibility is that later birth order among brothers has consistently been a context of competitive disadvantage because of either lowered embodied capital due to lower neurological health or lesser parental solicitude toward later-born sons (e.g., primogeniture). For example, lower IQ appears to be related to later birth order (Zajonc, 2001). Thus, later birth order among men might be a cue of forthcoming competitive disadvantage (or correlated with such a cue) for the development of alternative social strategies, such as antisociality. This would suggest that later birth order among brothers should be associated with antisociability. The possible connection between birth order among brothers and two male sexual interests (homosexuality and sexual arousal to violence) that themselves seem completely unconnected provides a considerable challenge to explain.

CONCLUSION

Rapists are characterized by high mating effort and antisociality. Are individual differences in propensity to rape also related to a paraphilic (or other) sexual disorder? There is strong phallometric evidence that many rapists are sexually different from men who do not commit rape. The meaning of this difference is as yet unclear. In this chapter we discussed the possibility that rapists' unique sexual arousal may represent sadism and thus a pathology. The evidence for this is meager, and the very notion of sadism may need to be re-examined. We also discussed the possibilities that rapists' sexual arousal to rape is not pathological but rather a by-product of their general antisocial tendencies, or even a fundamental component (design feature) of the different antisocial strategies discussed in chapter 4. There seems to be a relationship between arousal to rape and measures of antisociality among rapists, but much more work remains to be done to further test these possibilities.

From a Darwinian perspective, the function of the male sexual preference system is to direct male sexual behaviors toward reproductively capable females. Thus, Wakefield's (1992, 1999) definition suggests that pedophilic preference is pathological because it would be expected to decrease fitness in ancestral environments. On the other hand, preferences for coercive sexual activity could well increase male fitness, because rapes may result in a man fathering more children than he would have otherwise under some conditions. The fitness benefits depend on the costs to the rapist (as caused, for example, by revenge exacted by the woman's relatives or the damage to the man's reputation) and the likelihood of the woman becoming pregnant and the child surviving to adulthood. The latter likelihood depends in part on the rape victim herself surviving, remaining in good health, and being able to secure sufficient resources to raise the child. Wakefield's definition leaves unresolved the question of whether preferences for coercive sexual activities are pathological, because the fitness implications of these preferences are unknown. All that we know is that rape is very rarely associated with life-threatening injury in peacetime and sometimes results in pregnancies (see chap. 9).

It has been argued that rape cannot be reproductively viable because rape victims are sometimes physically injured or murdered. Indeed, there are a small number of sexual predators who kill their victims as part of sadistic assaults, and as we have noted, soldiers who occupy enemy territory sometimes rape and subsequently murder large numbers of victims. These two disparate phenomena are best considered separately.

Considering serial sexual killers first, it seems clear that many, if not all, of these rare individuals find their sadistic acts, including murder, to be intensely sexually arousing (Ressler, Burgess, & Douglas, 1988). Because sadistic and masochistic sexual interests, including bondage and the infliction of pain and humiliation, are not uncommon (e.g., Alison, Santtila, Sandnabba, & Nordling, 2001; Baumeister, 1988, Langevin, 1983; Leitenberg & Henning, 1995), it is possible to conceptualize dominance and submissiveness, at least in muted form, as a normal part of sexual behavior. If this idea is correct, then a sexual interest in coercive sexual behavior can be seen as an exaggeration of this component of sexual desire, culminating in the sadistic fantasies and behaviors of sexual murderers. Thus, an interest in sexual domination may lie on a continuum, one end of which is anchored in normal sexual behavior and the other in a pathological exaggeration.

In contrast to serial sexual homicide, the phenomenon of rape and murder in wartime illustrates the idea that men are adaptation executors and not fitness maximizers. That is, under many circumstances, men pursue mating opportunities when the cost of doing so is low, reproductive consequences notwithstanding. Under many conditions, then, men are motivated for sex but not reproduction. Thus, under circumstances favoring the killing of enemies, rape in the context of warfare could reflect adaptive male mating effort and intergroup aggression without being a pathology or an adaptation in itself.

6

PSYCHOPATHOLOGY

The notion that rapists have some kind of mental disorder has a long history. In this chapter, we consider the evidence that men who commit rape are driven to do so at least in part because of some form of psychopathology other than a specifically sexual disorder. First, we review studies that have examined known rapists and comment on the prevalence of various psychopathologies. Next, we examine several specific psychopathologies that have been postulated as causal factors in rape. We remind readers about the definition of *disorder* we rely on: A difference between men who rape and those who do not is a disorder only if it is due to something not functioning as designed by natural selection and causes harm. Thus, if propensity to rape were caused by head injury or other forms of brain damage, it could be said that rape was the result, at least in part, of some type of psychopathology. Clearly, the most relevant group comparisons would involve rapists and other offenders, because our interest is whether a difference is associated specifically with rape, as opposed to criminal conduct in general.

STUDIES OF PSYCHOPATHOLOGY AMONG RAPISTS

There have been many attempts to examine whether rapists exhibit any specific form of psychopathology. Many studies have compared adjudicated rapists with other groups of offenders using objective psychopathology tests such as the Minnesota Multiphasic Personality Inventory (MMPI; Hathaway & McKinley, 1967) or the Millon Clinical Multiaxial Personality Inventory (MCMI or MCMI–II; Millon, 1977). Although some MMPI studies found that rapists had elevations on Schizophrenia, Psychopathic Deviate, or Mania scales or two-point profiles involving combinations of these scales, the majority of studies, and all three of the most methodologically sound studies, found no difference between rapists and various other offenders (reviewed in Marshall & Hall, 1995).

Attempts to compare rapists with other groups on derived scales from the MMPI have either produced inconsistent results or found no differences between rapists and other offenders (Marshall & Hall, 1995). Chantry and Craig (1994) compared the responses of child molesters, rapists, and nonsexually aggressive felons on the MCMI. Similar to the MMPI results, the rapists were more like nonsexual offenders than were the child molesters, although they showed some small differences from nonsexual offenders.

Apart from paraphilias and antisocial personality, which we discussed in earlier chapters, the only main diagnostic categories rapists fall into with any regularity are those having to do with drug and alcohol abuse, which we will discuss further later in this chapter. Rapists who have psychotic disorders rarely exceed 15% of samples, even among those in psychiatric hospitals or prisons (Groth, 1979; Henn, Herjanic, & Vanderpearl, 1976; Seghorn, Prentky, & Boucher, 1987; Sturgeon & Taylor, 1980). There have been some similarities noted between obsessive–compulsive disorders (OCDs) and sexually compulsive behaviors (that can include rape), and there has been some suggestion that paraphilias and compulsive sexual behavior should be included in the OCD spectrum disorders (Balyk, 1997; Bradford, 1999, 2001). However, at present, there is little empirical basis for the idea that rapists in general have an obsessive–compulsive disorder. In addition, there is little reason to believe that, except for antisocial personality disorder, rapists differ from other offenders in the prevalence of any mental disorder (Hudson & Ward, 1997).

SPECIFIC OR GENERAL BRAIN DAMAGE

Mark and Ervin (1970) described an "episodic dyscontrol syndrome" associated with impulsive sexual behavior, including rape. The syndrome is characterized by hyperaggressivity, pathological intoxication, and other forms of compulsive behavior such as reckless driving. According to Mark and Ervin, the syndrome is the result of limbic system dysfunction in which the cortical structures of the limbic system fail to inhibit impulses. Similarly, Money (1995) considered paraphilic serial rape to be a brain disease. However, no empirical evidence has been adduced to support either of these possibilities.

There is some evidence of poor performance by rapists in comparison to normative samples on neuropsychological tests and other measures of brain function (e.g., Graber, Hartmann, Coffman, Huey, & Golden, 1982; Stone & Thompson, 2001). However, few studies have compared rapists to other types of sex offenders or other types of offenders. One study (M. L. Scott, Cole, McKay, Golden, & Liggett, 1984) examined 36 mentally disordered sex offenders in a maximum security psychiatric hospital and compared their performance on the Luria–Nebraska Neuropsychological Battery (Golden, 1979) with the performance of a group of normal control participants. They found that although some of the rapists obtained scores in the brain damaged range, when age and education were controlled they performed no worse than comparison participants and, in fact, showed a tendency for better scores. By contrast, the child molesters performed worse than the rapists on all scales.

Another study (Hucker, Langevin, Wortzman, et al., 1988) compared computed tomography (CT) scans of 22 sadistic rapists, 21 nonsadistic rapists, and 36 nonviolent nonsex offenders and found that sadistic rapists showed evidence of right-sided temporal lobe abnormality more often than nonsadistic rapists. Specifically, they found that the sadistic rapists were more likely to show an enlarged right lateral ventricle in the area of the temporal horn. Also, nonsadistic rapists showed more global impairment on the Luria–Nebraska Neuropsychological Test Battery than other participants. Another study by the same group of researchers examined bilateral sites in the brain at the level of the temporal horns and failed to find overall differences in brain density between 34 rapists and 12 nonviolent nonsexual offenders. The study also included pedophiles and incest offenders, and on average the brains of sex offenders were relatively smaller in the left hemisphere than the brains of control participants. Rapists, specifically, had more right and bilateral temporal horn dilation (Wright, Nobrega, Langevin, & Wortzman, 1990). Another study of 108 rapists, as well as control participants and other sex offenders, found evidence of deficits only for pedophiles (Langevin, Wright, & Handy, 1989). It is unclear how much overlap there was among the participants in the studies this group of investigators reported.

Finally, another recent study used magnetic resonance imaging to examine whether violent offenders showed brain abnormalities (Aigner et al., 2000). Fifty of the 96 participants, all of whom were said to be mentally ill and held in a high-security prison, were sex offenders. The offenders were divided into those who had committed physical violence and those who had not. Among the whole sample, and among the sex offenders specifically, those who had committed physically violent acts were reported to show more abnormalities on the magnetic resonance imaging reports compiled by examiners blind as to offenders' histories. It is interesting that the investigators noted temporal horn abnormalities exclusively for the sexual sadists ($n = 3$).

In summary, there is no conclusive evidence at this time that rapists as a group show any higher incidence of neurological deficits, whether in general or at any specific site, than other nonsex offenders or nonoffenders. There is evidence that they show a lower incidence of neurological deficits than pedophilic offenders. There is also some suggestion that sadistic rapists may have impaired neurological functions, with the temporal horn being especially implicated. This research is generally methodologically poor. Also, neurological differences among participants are not easy to interpret. Certainly, gross lesions and clear signs of brain damage would meet our definition of disorder, but the meaning of more subtle differences is not so clear. For instance, we would expect neuropsychological and even neuroanatomical differences between psychopaths and other offenders. According to the etiological model of psychopathy presented in chapter 4, such differences may reflect adaptive design rather than deficit or disorder.

There is not much doubt that gross damage to some brain structures (e.g., some temporal and frontal areas) can cause defective impulse control, which could include sexual aggression (Simpson, Tate, Ferry, Hodgkinson, & Blaszczynski, 2001). There is, as yet, no evidence about brain structures specific to sexual aggression. In addition, of course, unusual cases in which clearly established brain damage led to rape really tell us little about the role of brain damage in causing a propensity to rape.

TESTOSTERONE AND OTHER HORMONAL IMBALANCES

Testosterone is the most abundant of the androgens, or sex hormones, that are found in considerably higher concentrations in men than in women. One of the most consistent findings in the area of sexual aggression is that offenders are almost exclusively men. Of course, at least until fairly recently, the offense of rape was defined in such a way that the perpetrator had to be male and the victim female. However, the fact that women are still extremely rare as perpetrators, even since rape has been included in broader sexual assault laws, leads to the idea that male hormones (or any other male-specific or male-dominant features) are implicated in rape.

It is often mentioned that the pubertal rise in androgens among young men and the simultaneous rise in crime and risk taking are not a coincidence (Ellis & Coontz, 1990). Part of the reason why it has been difficult to establish a clear relationship between androgens and aggressive behavior, however, is that there are neurological effects of androgens before and just after birth that are just as important as postpubertal androgens in affecting aggression. Ellis and Coontz postulated that androgen exposure promotes aggressive behavior by affecting three patterns of brain functioning: First, exposure to androgens contributes to a lowering of neurological arousability, inclining those with higher exposure to seek more intense stimulation and to be able or willing to tolerate more punishment as they pursue that stimulation. Second, increasing androgen exposure lowers the brain's seizuring threshold, thus increasing emotional volatility and impulsive behavior. Third, androgen exposure causes a shift toward the right hemisphere in neocortical functioning, which decreases prosocial emotional expression and increases antisocial emotional expression.

There is evidence that aggression in humans is positively but modestly correlated with levels of testosterone (reviewed in Book, Starzyk, & Quinsey, 2001; Dabbs & Dabbs, 2000; J. A. Harris, 1999; see also Olweus, Mattsson, Schalling, & Löw, 1988; Pope, Kouri, & Hudson, 2000; T. J. Scaramella & Brown, 1978). However, there is little evidence that testosterone or other androgens are related to human sexual aggression (Bain, Langevin, Dickey, & Ben-Aron, 1987; Thiessen, 1990).

Christiansen and Knussmann (1987) measured salivary testosterone, along with serum concentrations of total testosterone and 5 dihydrotestosterone, in 117 healthy young men and compared these levels with a measure of interest in both general and sexual aggression. Although all three were correlated with interest in general aggression, none was correlated with interest in sexual aggression. Rada, Laws, and Kellner (1976) investigated the testosterone levels of incarcerated rapists who had brutalized their victims and of those who had not physically injured their victims and found higher levels among the former group. They also found that the plasma testosterone levels of the entire group of rapists were within normal limits. In a subsequent study (Rada, Laws, Kellner, Stivastava, & Peake, 1983), it was hypothesized that rapists would have higher testosterone levels than child molesters and that offenders in both groups who committed higher levels of violence during their offenses would have higher levels of testosterone than other offenders. The results did not confirm the hypotheses, although there were trends that supported a relationship between testosterone and the amount of violence in the offence. Bradford and McLean (1984) hypothesized, but failed to find, a correlation between plasma testosterone and sexual violence among 50 male sex offenders (including rapists as well as various other offenders) referred for pretrial assessments.

More recently, one study found higher testosterone levels among rapists than among control participants (Giotakos, Markianos, Vaidakis, & Christodoulou, 2003). In that study, 57 men convicted of rape and imprisoned in Greece were compared with 25 men recruited from the staff of a nearby hospital. The samples were matched on age and body mass index. Circulating levels of androgens (total testosterone, dihydrotestosterone, and free-androgen index) were all significantly higher among the rapists than among the control participants. In addition, the rapists showed increased levels of luteinizing hormone. Together with the increased androgen levels, these results suggested an overactive hypothalamic–pituitary–gonadal axis among the rapists. Another result of this study was the finding of lower levels of the serotonin metabolite 5HIAA (5-hydroxyindolacetic acid) in the urine samples of the rapists than among the control participants. It is interesting that 5HIAA levels were also significantly correlated with self-reported lifetime history of aggression.

Another body of evidence that bears on the question of the role of androgens in rape is the literature on surgical or chemical castration for the control of sexual aggression. The literature on surgical castration, despite thousands of such procedures, is unfortunately very weak because there have been no controlled studies. Nevertheless, the data are at least consistent with the hypothesis that surgical castration reduces both sexual and nonsexual aggression (Bremer, 1959; Heim, 1981; Heim & Hursch, 1979; Thiessen, 1990; see chap. 8). There is evidence, however, that sexual behavior and sexual responsiveness can continue after surgical castration, albeit at a reduced frequency, even without hormone replacement (Cooper, 1987; Heim & Hursch, 1979). With respect to rapists in particular, Heim (1981) noted that they remained more sexually active following surgical castration than pedophiles or homosexuals, although their frequencies of intercourse, masturbation, and sexual fantasies were reduced. Furthermore, Raboch, Cerna, and Zemek (1987) reported a rapist who committed a very brutal murder and attempted rape several years following surgical castration. Although only a case study, the authors concluded that surgical castration is not a guaranteed method of preventing sexual assault.

Chemical agents that have been used to counteract the effects of endogenous androgens include cyproterone acetate (CA), medroxyprogesterone acetate (MPA), and leuteinizing hormone-releasing hormone agonist (LHRH). We have summarized the literature on the treatment of sex offenders using methods of chemical castration elsewhere (G. T. Harris, Rice, & Quinsey, 1998; M. E. Rice & Harris, 1999; see chap. 8). Briefly, studies using these agents have the same deficiencies as those using surgical castration, largely because many sex offenders refuse these treatments. As is the case with surgical castration, chemical castration probably does decrease sexual activity among those men who voluntarily take the drugs. However, just as with surgical castration, prescribing antiandrogens is no guarantee that sexual recidivism will be eliminated. In one study (R. K. Hanson & Harris, 2000), sex offenders prescribed antiandrogens were more likely to commit a new sex offense than other sex offenders (presumably because higher-risk offenders were selected for drug treatment).

In summary, then, despite evidence of a positive relationship between androgens and aggression in general, the relationship in men between androgens (especially testosterone) and sexual aggression remains weak. The fact that rape is an almost exclusively male behavior and that the peak in criminal activities (including sexual aggression) coincides with the peak of testosterone in adolescence implicates a role for testosterone and other masculinizing agents. On the other hand, there is little research showing that rape can be linked to either interindividual or intraindividual variation in androgens.

CHILDHOOD SEXUAL ABUSE

A popular explanation for sex offenses is the *cycle of abuse* notion, according to which sex offenders commit their offenses because they were sexually abused themselves (R. K. Hanson & Slater, 1988). In fact, many authors have attempted to explain much or all of adult psychopathology (and other undesirable outcomes) as the result of child sexual abuse, with posttraumatic stress disorder, depression, and dissociative disorders as the most common psychopathologies (Becker, Kaplan, Tenke, & Tartaglini, 1991; Friedrich et al., 2001; Rind, Tromovitch, & Bauserman, 1998). Indeed, there are many reports in the literature that support a relationship between being sexually abused as a child and later perpetration of sexual offenses (Bagley & Shewchuk-Dann, 1991; Groth, 1979; R. K. Hanson & Slater, 1988; Langevin et al., 1989; M. Rubinstein, Yeager, Goodstein, & Lewis, 1993; Zgourides, Monto, & Harris, 1997). In a study of serial rapists, for example, three quarters of the 41 participants reported experiencing childhood sexual abuse, compared with only 16% reported among the general male population (McCormack, Rokous, Hazelwood, & Burgess, 1992). Moreover, among rapists who reported being victims of abuse, the abuser was more likely to have been a family member than among non-rapist victims (Burgess, Hazelwood, Roukas, Hartman, & Burgess, 1987).

Unfortunately, most studies on the subject of the cycle of abuse are methodologically very weak. Because of an overdependence on self-report and retrospective data, as well as other problems, Kaufman and Zigler (1987) concluded that the evidence for the cycle of abuse hypothesis was inconclusive and that although being maltreated as a child was a risk factor for becoming abusive, the path from abused child to abusive adult was far from direct or inevitable. Methodological problems aside, one problem with the cycle of abuse hypothesis, especially as it applies to sexual aggression, is its failure to account for the fact that almost all perpetrators are male, whereas most child victims are female (Widom, 1999). Most of the research, at least until very recently, on the effects of child sexual abuse pertains to its effects on female victims (Browne & Finkelhor, 1986). Furthermore, in most studies, the majority of sex offenders do not report having been victims of sexual abuse as a child. And most victims, even most male victims, do not become adult perpetrators (Finkelhor, 1986; Langevin et al., 1989).

A few recent studies have used methodologically stronger, prospective designs and have compared self-reports with officially documented sources. Widom and Morris (1997) studied 1,196 young adults for whom documentation existed of sexual abuse when they were children. In-depth interviews when they were young adults about their past sexual abuse experiences revealed some support for the validity of the self-reports, especially for women. However, only 16% of the men with documented histories of sexual abuse considered their childhood experiences to have constituted sexual abuse. The authors suggested that men's early socialization experiences may have resulted in them viewing these behaviors as nonpredatory and nonabusive and more as part of a learning process for adult sexual activity. The authors also suggested that social pressures may have resulted in more reluctance among the men than among the women to report sexual abuse.

The problems with retrospective self-reports as a measure of abuse are especially significant among apprehended offenders. Offenders' reports may be especially susceptible to overreporting compared with nonoffenders because they have more reason to look into their past for something that explains or excuses their offending (R. K. Hanson & Slater, 1988). They also might be motivated to make false or exaggerated claims to get a more positive court report or be recommended for treatment rather than prison.

A few studies deserve special mention because they have attempted to overcome some of the methodological problems common to this field of research. Worling (1995) made an attempt to corroborate offenders' reports of victimization. Participants were 87 adolescent male sex offenders, all of whom acknowledged having committed hands-on sexual offenses against children ($n = 60$) or exclusively against female peers or adults ($n = 27$). In all but seven cases, reports of sexual victimization gathered by therapists during clinical interactions with the adolescents were corroborated by reports from child welfare or probation agencies. Overall, 43% of the offenders reported sexual victimization. The rate was no different among offenders against peer or adult females (26%) than among those who offended against only female children (24%). However, the rates for these two groups were significantly lower than among those offenders who had at least one male victim (75%). Thus, although there was evidence that offenders with male victims were highly likely to have been sexually abused as a child, the same was not true for offenders with female victims.

Another study (Langevin et al., 1989) used a database of sex offenders and community control participants that was collected between 1967 and 1973, before the cycle of abuse hypothesis became popular. As part of their assessment, the participants were asked whether they had ever engaged in "sex play" of any sort with older boys or girls (4 or 5 years older than themselves) or with adult men or women. Over half of the 479 men reported no sexual contacts. The sex offenders were much more likely to report "sex play" than the community control participants. The medical records of a sample of 70 of the "abused" men were searched for further details about their "victimization." In only 21% of these cases was there sufficient detail in the clinical file to determine the nature of the physical contact. In all cases in which the sex of the perpetrators could be determined, a male perpetrator was involved (two of the 15 cases also involved a female perpetrator). In over half the cases where the relationship of the perpetrator could be determined, the perpetrator was a male relative. In the entire sample of sex offenders ($n = 425$), a comparison was made of those who reported "abuse" versus those who did not. Members of the "abused" group more often perpetrated rape than members of the nonabused group, and they were more likely to have engaged in a variety of anomalous sexual activities. The home environments of the abused sex offenders were more often characterized by parental alcohol abuse and criminality and father–son aggression.

A third study (Seghorn et al., 1987) had the common methodological problems of retrospective self-report and lack of a non-sex offender comparison group. However, we report on it because it included a fairly large number of incarcerated rapists (n = 97) and compared their reports to those of a group of 54 child molesters also incarcerated in a treatment center for sexually dangerous persons. They reported that the child molesters were twice as likely as the rapists to report experiencing sexual abuse but that the abused rapists were three times as likely as the abused child molesters to have been abused by a family member (most often by the father). Furthermore, they reported that when the offender was sexually assaulted as a child, the assault was generally associated with many other indexes of family turmoil and instability. Among the rapists, the childhood abuse most often also included physical and sexual abuse of female family members by the father. The authors speculated that as children, these men learned to identify with the aggressor (their father), to project blame onto female victims, and to connect aggression and sexuality. It is also possible, however, that many of the abusive fathers were highly antisocial individuals who passed along to their sons genes associated with antisocial propensities.

Malamuth, Sockloskie, Koss, and Tanaka (1991) used structural equation modeling to test a causal model of sexual and nonsexual coercion against women among 2,652 college men. According to their model, being sexually abused as a child, particularly if combined with physical abuse, contributes to juvenile delinquency, which contributes to sexual promiscuity and attitudes supporting violence, which eventually contribute to coercion against women. They obtained considerable support for their model. Although the model was built on cross-sectional retrospective data, the results are consistent with a small contribution of a combination of sexual and physical abuse as a child to later sexually and physically coercive behavior toward women.

There is other evidence that being physically abused as a child is related to later becoming a perpetrator of rape. Fagan and Wexler (1988) studied 34 juvenile sex offenders and 208 other violent juvenile offenders. Forcible rape was the most frequent sex offense. Information about sexual and physical abuse victimization was gathered using self-report and also by examining official reports of protective services agencies. Although the frequency of abuse reports was much lower using official reports, the trends using self-reports and official reports were the same. Sex offenders were more likely to have been victims of sexual abuse than other violent offenders and also more likely to have been victims of physical abuse from their parents.

Widom and Ames (1994) used a prospective design to assess the long-term criminal consequences of sexual and physical abuse. They examined the official criminal histories of 908 men and women who were, according to court records, physically or sexually abused or neglected before the age of 12. When other relevant variables were controlled, men who had been physically abused as children were significantly more likely to be arrested as adults for rape or sodomy than men who had been neglected or sexually abused.

In summary, despite methodological shortcomings, there appears to be a correlation between being a rapist and reporting childhood abuse. As Gelles (1982) pointed out, the effects of sexual abuse must be understood in the context of physical abuse and neglect and general family disintegration that frequently accompanies the sexual abuse experience. A recent meta-analysis that reviewed many studies, both prospective and retrospective, among nonoffender populations concluded that the negative effects of child–adult sexual contact are typically quite minor, especially among men, and that the effects of child sexual abuse were nonsignificant when family environment was statistically controlled (Rind et al., 1998).

As mentioned earlier in this section, it is possible that the correlation between childhood abuse and rape is due to the effect of common inheritance. That is, generally antisocial fathers would engage in abusive and negligent parenting (and contribute in other ways to a chaotic family environment), and sons of such fathers would be antisocial (and sexually coercive) in part because of heritable factors. In a recent study of the paths leading to persistent criminal violence (G. T. Harris, Rice, & Lalumière, 2001), we showed that antisocial parenting is linked to both neurodevelopmental problems and psychopathy (despite the fact that these two constructs were not linked to one another). The mechanisms for these links are probably different. Antisocial and abusive parenting could contribute to the development of persistent antisociality and competitive disadvantage by creating or accentuating early perturbations in neurodevelopment and creating unsupportive environments. With regard to psychopathy, and referring back to our discussion of conditional and alternative strategies in chapters 3 and 4, abusive parenting could provide the signal for its development (if the psychopathic strategy is conditional) or could simply reflect common inheritance (if it is inherited and obligate).

ALCOHOLISM AND OTHER SUBSTANCE ABUSE

A consistent relationship has been found between alcohol problems, drug problems, and a mixture of the two with crime in general and with aggression of all types (Anglin, 1982; White, 1997). Similarly, there is evidence that substance abuse, particularly alcohol abuse, is associated with sexual offending in general and rape in particular (Henn et al., 1976; Langevin & Lang, 1990; Lightfoot & Barbaree, 1993; Rada, 1975; Yarvis, 1995).

For example, Langevin and Lang (1990) studied the histories of alcohol and drug use using the Michigan Alcoholism Screening Test (MAST; Pokorny, Miller, & Kaplan, 1972) and the Drug Abuse Screening Test (DAST; Skinner, 1982), both self-report measures, among 461 male sex offenders. More than half of the participants qualified as alcoholics on the MAST, but fewer than 20% obtained scores indicating a drug abuse problem. Rada (1975), using data collected from detailed autobiographies of 77 convicted rapists, found that 35% were alcoholics.

Abracen, Looman, and Anderson (2000) compared self-reported alcohol and drug abuse among 72 rapists, 34 child molesters, and 24 personality-disordered violent offenders with no known history of sexual offending. Rapists were most likely to have severe alcohol abuse scores (46%) and violent nonsex offenders the least likely (4%). Rapists had the highest scores on the MAST, with scores significantly higher than those of the nonsex offenders. The mean score for the rapists was just below the severe alcohol abuse cutoff. By contrast, the nonsex offenders scored significantly higher than the child molesters on the DAST, with the rapists scoring in between. The mean DAST score for the rapists was at the top of the mild range.

Allnutt, Bradford, Greenberg, and Curry (1996) also used the MAST to examine alcohol abuse among a sample of 728 sex offenders. The mean score of the rapists was in the alcoholic range, although the distribution of scores was skewed and only 32% scored in the alcoholic range. Many rapists were classified as sexual sadists, and more than half of the sadists scored in the alcoholic range. There were no significant differences between rapists and other sex offender groups in their mean scores on the MAST (except that the scores were significantly lower than for the group they labeled sadists, nearly half of whom had committed rape).

In another study (Ouimette, 1997), alcohol and drug abuse diagnoses were found to be more common among 47 nonincarcerated men who self-reported rape or attempted rape compared with 56 nonincarcerated men who denied perpetrating sexual aggression. Frequency and amount of alcohol use are reliable correlates of self-reported sexual coercion among college men (e.g., Koss & Gaines, 1993; Schwartz, DeKeseredy, Tait, & Alvi, 2001; A. E. Wilson, Calhoun, & McNair, 2002).

The research on alcohol and drug use among rapists is plagued by a strong reliance on self-report. Rapists may be more likely to report higher levels of alcohol abuse than other participants to minimize responsibility for the offense. It has been suggested that the same might be expected for drug abuse, but the evidence suggests that rapists are, if anything, less likely to report drug abuse than nonsex offenders in some studies. Abracen et al. (2000) argued that the fact that rapists do not report more drug abuse than nonsex offenders is evidence that the self-reports regarding alcohol abuse are likely to be valid. One could argue, however, that because drug abuse is a criminal activity, it might not be perceived by sex offenders as minimizing their responsibility to the same extent that alcohol abuse does.

In a review of the physiological and biological effects of alcohol on sexual functioning, J. A. Price and Price (1983) concluded that alcoholism in men generally leads to decreased levels of testosterone and increased levels of estrogens, which can lead to feminization and reduced sexual functioning. Moreover, even among men without physical dependence on alcohol, Price and Price concluded that the general consensus among researchers is that alcohol depresses sexual behavior even at low concentrations. They also concluded that although it is commonly thought that alcohol is a disinhibitor in sexual and other behavioral domains, the evidence suggests that the circumstances under which the alcohol is ingested and other psychological factors are just as important in affecting sexual behavior as the alcohol itself.

In summary, alcohol abuse is an extremely common problem among rapists, but drug abuse is much less common. Chronic substance abuse might plausibly interfere with decision making in many facets of life, and it is just as plausible that chronic substance abuse would particularly interfere with sexual behavior. The evidence regarding acute substance use as a situational and facilitating factor in rape will be discussed in the next chapter.

RAPE AS AN ADDICTION

In addition to the various pathologies referred to in earlier sections, there have been some reports suggesting that paraphilias, and perhaps also fantasizing about and committing rape, are addictions. Paraphilic sexual fantasies can sometimes lead to significant impairment or distress. Many sex offenders report an escalation of their deviant sexual behaviors over time, analogous to the phenomenon of tolerance exhibited by true addictions. As is the case with substance abuse, many sex offenders have multiple paraphilias or deviant sexual behaviors (e.g., Abel et al., 1987; Freund, 1990).

The idea that deviant sexual behaviors are similar to substance addictions has led to the development of 12-step models of treatment programs fashioned after Alcoholics Anonymous (e.g., Tays, Earle, Wells, Murray, & Garret, 1999). On the other hand, other than cravings perhaps, paraphilic disorders (and rape) lack the physiological qualities of withdrawal that characterize substance addictions. Noffsinger and Resnick (2000) argued that paraphilias (and rape) are better classified as sexual compulsions rather than sexual addictions. Nevertheless, there is little evidence at the present time to support either of these ideas.

CONCLUSION

In summary, there is little evidence that rapists are particularly affected by mental disorders or brain damage. There is evidence suggestive of more abuse victimization in the childhood histories of rapists than nonrapists and of more alcohol abuse among rapists than nonrapists. The interpretation of these findings is as yet unclear. Thinking back to the three-group model of antisociality and sexual coercion presented in chapter 4, the lack of neuro-pathologies suggests that most rapists should fall into the adolescence-limited and psychopathy pathways, at least as far as recognized psychiatric disorders are concerned. This said, however, there is very little good neurological and neuropsychological research involving rapists, especially research involving subtle neuropathology of the kind that initiates life-course-persistent antisociality, so our conclusions should be considered provisional.

7

CONTEXTUAL AND SITUATIONAL FACTORS

In the previous three chapters we examined whether there were individual differences that could explain men's propensity to engage in rape and other sexually coercive behavior. In this chapter we turn our attention to more immediate, circumstantial elements, sometimes called *contextual* or *situational factors*. These factors include such things as the characteristics of the victims, the emotional and cognitive state of the offender, the features of settings in which rape takes place, and so on. We attempt, when possible, to address the link between individual differences and contextual factors.

CHARACTERISTICS OF RAPE VICTIMS

The vast majority of the empirical research on rape has focused on characteristics of men who are apprehended for rape or report committing coercive sexual acts in surveys. There has been only a small amount of work on how women who become rape victims differ from women who do not. This is a controversial topic, because some people believe that the discovery of victim characteristics may lead to the blaming of victims. This belief is of course

Figure 7.1. Age distribution of two groups of victims of sexual coercion. The two groups are (a) married and (b) unmarried Canadian women in the population at large who reported in 1993 either sexual assault or unwanted sexual touching in the past year by men other than husbands or dates or boyfriends; data are from a national survey of women age 18 and over. From "An Empirical Test of the Body Guard Hypothesis," by M. Wilson and S. L. Mesnick, Eds, in *Feminism and Evolutionary Biology* (p. 509), 1997, New York: Chapman Hall. Adapted with permission.

fallacious, unless one is willing to blame the victims of (say) robberies because they own desirable things.

As illustrated in Figure 7.1, young unmarried women are overwhelmingly the most common victims of rape (B. S. Fisher, Cullen, & Turner, 2000; Langan, Schmitt, & Durose, 2003; Marx, van Wie, & Gross, 1996; M. Wilson, Daly, & Scheib, 1997; M. Wilson & Mesnick, 1997; see also reviews by Shields & Shields, 1983; Thornhill & Palmer, 2000; Thornhill & Thornhill, 1983). Of course, most rapists are young, too, but even rapists in their late 30s tend to have victims in their early 20s (Lim, Gwee, Woo, & Parker, 2001; see also Greenfeld, 1997). The risk to young unmarried women may be partly due to their increased vulnerability—they may be more likely to associate with young men and to frequent bars and other "risky" venues (sometimes referred as the *routine activity hypothesis*)—but there seem to be other factors involved besides vulnerability. In one study, victims of robberies were more likely to also be raped if they were young than if they were old (Felson & Krohn, 1990). In other studies, sexual-related homicides primarily involved young perpetrators and young victims, but theft-related homicides primarily involved young perpetrators and much older victims (Shackelford, 2002a, 2002b; M. Wilson et al., 1997).

As well, rape victims as a group have earlier and more experience with consensual sex with a greater number of partners (especially casual partners) than do women who do not report having been raped (Harned, 2002; T. L. Jackson, 1996; Marx et al., 1996; Testa & Dermen, 1999). Rape victims also have been reported to be less assertive, to score higher in sensation seeking, to use more alcohol, to expect that alcohol will increase the likelihood of sexual intercourse, to exhibit lower self-esteem, to have experienced prior sexual victimization, to have been raised in single-parent homes, and to hold more liberal sexual attitudes (e.g., B. S. Fisher et al., 2000; Gidycz, Nelson Coble, Latham, & Layman, 1993; Himelein, 1995; Testa & Dermen, 1999).

Some of these characteristics may be the result of having been the victim of rape. The few longitudinal prospective studies suggest, however, that such characteristics as number of consensual partners, frequency of alcohol use, risk taking, and liberal sexual attitudes *precede* victimization (Combs-Lane & Smith, 2002; Himelein, 1995; Zweig, Sayer, Crockett, & Vicary, 2002). Alcohol seems particularly important. In one study, the frequency of alcohol use assessed at one point in time was the best predictor of sexual victimization occurring during the following 6 months (Combs-Lane & Smith, 2002).

IS THERE A "RAPE-PRONE" ENVIRONMENT?

Over the past several decades, there have been attempts to elucidate features of the cultural, social, neighborhood, or interpersonal environment that contribute to the occurrence of crime or violent crime, or sexual offenses or rape in particular. Almost nothing is known, however, about any features of the physical or interpersonal environment that are uniquely associated with the occurrence of rape. For example, there is persuasive evidence that rape exhibits "seasonality"—rape is relatively prevalent in hot weather (C. G. Anderson & Anderson, 1998; Michael & Zumpe, 1983). This must be a relative phenomenon, in that temperatures associated with low prevalence in southern latitudes are simultaneously associated with high prevalence in northern locations. In any case, it appears that the seasonality of rape is merely one aspect of a general trend toward seasonality in all forms of human aggression (C. G. Anderson & Anderson, 1998; Rotton & Cohn, 2003). Whether the seasonality of aggression is a biophysiological effect or merely due to the relative proximity of perpetrators and victims is as yet unclear.

Other investigators have attempted to study whether aspects of the sociopolitical environment are associated with the prevalence of rape using aggregate data. For example, Baron, Straus, and Jaffee (1988) developed an assessment of the degree to which states engage in "legitimate violence"—government use of violence, violence in the mass media, legal and social approval of violence—and showed that this index was related to the prevalence of rape, as well as of other measures (e.g., divorce rate, marriage rate, and racial composition). As another example, Austin and Kim (2000) reported a positive association between nations' sexual equality and rates of rape (see also Vieraitis & Williams, 2002). Of course, it is quite possible that sexual equality is accompanied by the devotion of more criminal justice to the detection and prosecution of rapists.

PORNOGRAPHY

Centerwall (1992) asserted that "epidemiological evidence indicates that if, hypothetically, television technology had never been developed, there would today be 10,000 fewer homicides each year in the United States, 70,000 fewer rapes, and 700,000 fewer injurious assaults" (p. 3061). What is the evidence for the assertion that portrayals of sexual aggression cause rape? Probably the most studied sociocultural factor associated with rape has been the availability and use of pornography.

The role of pornography in sexual aggression has been subject to several large-scale public inquiries going back to at least 1970 and the U.S. Presidential Commission on Obscenity and Pornography. After a careful review of the scientific data available at the time and after commissioning some research specifically to help them in their deliberations, the commission concluded that a link between pornography and rape could not be demonstrated. Another commission in 1986 headed by U.S. Attorney General Edwin Meese (1986) found, in contrast, that "substantial exposure to sexually violent materials . . . bears a causal relationship to antisocial acts of sexual violence" (p. 326). Unlike the first commission, however, the Meese Commission members were primarily nonscientists, and no research was done by the commission itself.

In Canada, the Fraser Committee in 1985 examined the evidence and concluded that it was insufficient. The British (Williams) Committee on Obscenity and Film Censorship (Home Office, 1979) reported that "from everything we . . . have learnt in the course of our enquiries, our belief can only be that the role of pornography in influencing the state of society is a minor one" (p. 95).

Over the past 15 years, has anything changed to alter the equivocal evidence of a link between pornography and rape? In our consideration of this question, we rely heavily on two recent and comprehensive reviews of the literature on the topic (Malamuth, Addison, & Koss, 2000; Seto, Maric, & Barbaree, 2001) and conclude that the answer is yes. It is also important to note that there is still a highly cited contrary view asserting that currently available evidence has failed to confirm any association between violent pornography and sexual aggression (W. Fisher & Grenier, 1994). The evidence against this contrary view is discussed in both of the above-mentioned reviews.

It is clear that the pornography industry has been growing rapidly, and thus, if there is a causal link between pornography and rape, there is grave cause for concern. A 1997 survey of sales and rentals of adult videos found a doubling in 5 years, with annual revenues of $4.2 billion (Adult Video News, 1998, reported in Seto et al., 2001). At the same time, the increasing availability of access to the Internet has undoubtedly made additional sources of pornography more readily available. Some Internet pornography companies are listed on the NASDAQ stock exchange, and pornography was reported in *Forbes* magazine as a $56 billion global industry (Morais, 1999, reported in Malamuth et al., 2000).

Many types of studies have addressed the question of whether pornography influences the rate of sexual violence. Most are correlational. One type of correlational study is the population or aggregate-level study that examines the correlation between the availability of pornography and the prevalence of sex crimes (especially rape). Despite earlier studies supporting a relationship between the availability of pornography and sex crime rates (Court, 1976; Jaffee & Straus, 1987), more recent studies have either failed to find such a link or have found the opposite relationship. Kutchinsky (1991) examined the prevalence of sex crimes in Denmark, West Germany, Sweden, and the United States in relationship to the availability of pornography. Between 1964 and 1984, pornography laws in all those countries became less restrictive, yet rape rates did not increase relative to rates of other types of violent crime in any of those countries. Diamond and Uchiyama (1999) found that rape rates decreased in Japan significantly relative to murder and nonsexual crimes as the availability of pornography increased. Similarly, Kimmel and Linders (1996) examined the relationship between pornography consumption and rape rates in six U.S. cities matched on socioeconomic variables. They found that as censorship led to a decline in consumption of printed pornography, rape rates increased. Of course, among the problems with these population-level studies, as pointed out by Seto et al. (2001), is that they cannot examine whether sexually aggressive men actually consume more pornography, and they have not distinguished among different types of pornography. Most have examined only the availability of sexually explicit magazines rather the more violent printed, video, or Internet materials.

Several meta-analyses of the pornography literature have appeared, and their findings have generally been consistent with each other (Malamuth et al., 2000). Thus, we will briefly describe the most rigorous of the meta-analyses. M. Allen, D'Alessio, and Brezgel (1995) examined the findings of studies on the effects of pornography exposure on aggression exhibited in the laboratory under rigorous experimental conditions (especially random assignment) that allow cause-and-effect conclusions to be made. Their meta-analysis included 33 studies with a total of 2,040 participants. The overall effect (r = .13) shows that pornography exposure caused an increase in laboratory aggression (not sexual aggression, but rather mild forms of verbal or physical aggression). However, subsequent analyses of moderating variables showed that viewing nudity alone *reduced* aggression, whereas exposure to nonviolent but coercive or violent pornography *increased* aggression.

Allen, D'Alessio, and Emmers-Sommer (2000) conducted a meta-analysis on the use of pornography among convicted sex offenders in comparison to noncriminals. Among the measures (all were retrospective self-reports) they examined were the frequency of pornography use, the age at first exposure, and the degree to which pornography exposure was related to sexual acts including masturbation, consensual sex, and forced sex. Across 13 studies and all of the measures used in the study, there was a small, nonsignificant association between criminality and pornography ($r = .06$). Offenders reported slightly (but not significantly) less exposure to pornography ($r = -.05$) than did nonoffenders. Also, sex offenders reported being exposed to pornography at a slightly (but not significantly) earlier age than noncriminal control participants. However, sex offenders reported being significantly more likely than noncriminals to perform a sexual act after pornography exposure ($r = .23$).

Malamuth et al. (2000) also reviewed the few naturalistic studies (too few for a meta-analysis) among noncriminals that examined the relationship between self-reported pornography use and self-reported sexual aggression. They concluded that there was strong evidence that the use of pornography depicting rape or other sexual violence was positively correlated with self-report measures of sexually coercive behavior. There was no evidence that exposure to soft-core pornography (i.e., magazines such as *Playboy*, *Penthouse*, and *Hustler*) was positively related to self-report measures of sexually coercive behavior.

In addition to the literature reviewed in this section, there is also a considerable body of literature that has examined (and found modest support for) a relationship between exposure to violent pornography and both attitudes supporting sexual aggression and attraction to sexual aggression (reviewed in Malamuth et al., 2000). Considering the literature overall, we agree with the conclusions of Malamuth et al. and Seto et al. (2001) that there is an association between exposure to violent pornography and aggression and sexual aggression toward women. At the same time, there is little evidence for a direct causal link. It seems that those individuals who are already predisposed to sexually offend or who are heavy users are those who show the strongest association.

Informed by the results of their extensive review, Malamuth et al. (2000) used structural equation modeling to examine the role that pornography exposure plays in nonsexual and sexual aggression toward women in a nationally representative sample of 1,500 U.S. college men. The data had all been gathered as part of an earlier study (Koss, Gidycz, & Wisniewski, 1987). All measures were self-report, and pornography use was limited to use of nine currently popular sexually explicit magazines. The structural model they used as a starting point was the confluence model developed by Malamuth, Sockloskie, Koss, and Tanaka (1991) and described in chapter 4. The model identifies the confluence of two constellations of variables that they labeled *sexual promiscuity* (mating effort) and *hostile masculinity* (antisociality) and that, taken together, predict self-reported sexual aggression.

The initial model without pornography use gave a good fit to the data, was successfully replicated in two randomly split halves of the sample, and accounted for 78% of the variance in the construct of Coercion Against Women. This construct included both sexual and nonsexual aggression. In the analyses reported in their 2000 study, Malamuth et al. first added only an association between sexual promiscuity and pornography use. The data suggested a strong association but also suggested some remaining association between pornography use and Coercion Against Women that needed to be accounted for by further model development. Further analyses were consistent with the hypothesis that pornography is a contributing cause of aggression but also with the reverse hypothesis, that aggression is a cause of interest in pornography. On the basis of their analyses, then, it was not possible to conclude whether pornography use was a cause or a result of sexually aggressive tendencies (or both).

Regression analyses showed that after controlling for other factors predicting sexual aggression (family violence, delinquency, attitudes, promiscuity, and hostile masculinity), pornography use still added significantly to the equation. Furthermore, additional subsequent analyses revealed that interactions among hostile masculinity, sexual promiscuity, and pornography use also predicted sexual aggression. Analyses investigating these interactions revealed that high pornography use in itself was not necessarily indicative of high risk for sexual aggression. However, among men who were already at high risk for sexual aggression (based on the risk factors of hostile masculinity and sexual promiscuity), those who were also high consumers of pornography were much more likely to admit to sexually aggressive behavior than their high-risk counterparts who did not report such frequent use of pornography.

In summary, the currently available data support a relationship between the use of violent and sexually coercive pornography and sexual aggression. It is plausible that very heavy exposure to violent pornography could induce some shift in men's sexual strategies by, for example, making women seem antagonistic and making rape seem enjoyable and unlikely to result in punishment (just as nonviolent pornography may provide the false cue that many women are willing to engage in sex with little or no courtship). It is also plausible that sexual preferences for rape might be conditioned via repeated exposure to violent pornography paired with sexual arousal. However, some independent factors would have to be adduced to explain why some men choose to expose themselves to such heavy doses of violent pornography but most do not. The current data do not allow us to determine which (of pornography and sexual coercion) is the cause and which is the effect, or whether the causality is bidirectional. The relationship also seems to be confined to those men who are high on other risk factors.

DATE RAPE AND MISCOMMUNICATION

Although rape has long been recognized as a crime, it has also been recognized that many rapes occur without coming to the notice of anyone other than the two people involved. As early as the 1950s, researchers have surveyed college students about coercive sexual experiences. Kanin (1957) reported that young women who grew up with older brothers were statistically less likely to become the victims of rape. In the past 20 years, studies asking college students about their experiences have become common.

This work has revealed that young women of high school and college age report that they experience a lot of unwanted sexual contact, and a sizeable minority (about 20% to 25%) report that they have had sexual intercourse when they did not want to because of physical force applied by a man (e.g., Aizenman & Kelley, 1988; Baier, Rosenzweig, & Whipple, 1991; Hilton, Harris, & Rice, 2003; Schwartz, DeKeseredy, Tait, & Alvi, 2001). Some studies have referred to incidents that have occurred in the context of a dating relationship as "date rapes." It is unclear from the methods described, however, how many respondents were reporting about ongoing, established relationships (e.g., T. L. Jackson, 1996). It would be more accurate perhaps to refer to this research as "acquaintance rape among young unmarried North Americans."

It is not surprising that acquaintance rapes (compared with rapes perpetrated by strangers) are more likely to occur in a vehicle or home and less likely to occur outdoors (Stermac, DuMont, & Kalemba, 1995). As well, such sexual assaults are characterized by less physical force and more use of threats than rapes committed by strangers (Bownes, O'Gorman, & Sayers, 1991). The risk of acquaintance rape in the context of a date appears to be statistically increased when the man initiated the date, provided transportation, and spent money (Muehlenhard & Linton, 1987). It has been suggested that sexual assaults between acquaintances are more likely to occur after some amount of mutually consenting sexual activity, such as kissing and fondling, has occurred (Bownes et al., 1991; Marx et al., 1996; Muehlenhard & Linton, 1987).

These findings have led to the suggestion that acquaintance rape might be due, in part, to misperception of sexual cues by young men (Marx et al., 1996) or miscommunication about sexual behavior between partners (Byers & Lewis, 1988). There is evidence that young men in general are much more likely to infer sexual interest on the part of women than the same women say they have (Haselton & Buss, 2000). Making the situation even more complicated, some young women report using "token resistance" when intending to have sexual intercourse by pretending to resist so as not to appear promiscuous (Marx et al., 1996). Consistent with the idea that acquaintance rape is, at least partly, due to miscommunication and misperception between young men and women about sex is the frequent finding that alcohol use is associated with reports of acquaintance rape and rape in general (Canterbury, Grossman, & Lloyd, 1993; Copenhaver & Grauerholz, 1991; Ginn et al., 1998; S. D. Johnson, Gibson, & Linden, 1978; Marx et al., 1996; Muehlenhard & Linton, 1987; Testa & Dermen, 1999). That is, alcohol (perhaps combined with the expectation that alcohol consumption leads to disinhibition of sexual behavior) results in cognitive impairment, thereby worsening the already much-less-than-perfect communication about sexual matters between young men and women (Abbey, McAuslan, & Ross, 1998; Abbey, Ross, McDuffie, & McCauslan, 1996; Marx, Gross, & Adams, 1999; Testa & Parks, 1996).

On the other hand, things might not be that simple. First, given the importance of sex and its consequences for young men and women, how could it be so fraught with miscommunication and misperception that young men "accidentally" commit rape (and young women "accidentally" are raped)? This level of proneness to error demands more of an explanation. Haselton and Buss (2000) provided an account of male "misperception," essentially arguing that throughout human evolution, there has been a selective advantage for men who make errors of this type. Specifically, they argued that there was little cost (and some reproductive advantage) to ancestral men who "overestimated" the sexual interest of female peers and engaged in some efforts to obtain sexual intercourse, true female sexual interest notwithstanding.

Second, some of the research on acquaintance rape makes the phenomenon appear a little less "accidental." As we mentioned, the risk for this form of sexual coercion appears to be increased by male expenditure of resources in one form or another. As well, men who perpetrate acquaintance rape have more sexual experience, and became sexually active younger than men who do not commit this type of sexual coercion (T. L. Jackson, 1996; Kanin, 1983; Lalumière, Chalmers, Quinsey, & Seto, 1996; Lalumière & Quinsey, 1996). These findings suggest that acquaintance rape might be an aspect of mating effort. Sexually coercive men are more likely than noncoercive men to misread women's cues and overestimate their sexual interest (Craig Shea, 1993; Lipton, McDonel, & McFall, 1987; Malamuth & Brown, 1994; McDonel & McFall, 1991). Viewed in this light, the association between alcohol use and acquaintance rape might reflect a somewhat more deliberate male tactic aimed at lowering female resistance, as opposed to the simple consequence of "accidental" loss of decision-making ability (Abbey,

McAuslan, Zawacki, Clinton, & Buck, 2001; Brecklin & Ullman, 2001; D. M. Buss & Malamuth, 1996; Ullman, Karabatsos, & Koss, 1999).

ALCOHOL INTOXICATION

Alcohol intoxication is a frequent feature of sexual crimes. Brecklin and Ullman (2001) found, using National Criminal Victimization Survey data, that 61% of offenders used alcohol prior to sexual assaults (based on victims' reports). In a study of rape within the military (Sadler, Booth, Cook, & Doebbeling, 2003), 52% of perpetrators were under the influence of alcohol or other drugs at the time of the offense (again, based on victims' reports). In this section we examine the causal role of alcohol intoxication in the commission of rape.

Certainly, the relationship between alcohol use and rape, and alcohol use and sexual behavior or aggression in general, is murky at best (Seto & Barbaree, 1995). It seems safe to conclude that alcohol use contributes to human aggression (Bushman & Cooper, 1990). It is somewhat unclear, however, how much of that causal effect is due strictly to alcohol's pharmacological properties, as opposed to people's expectancies about its effects. In one recent study of college men using a hidden group design, alcohol expectancies moderated the effect of alcohol consumption on sexual coercion. In other words, young men who reported sexually coercive behaviors reported greater alcohol consumption *and* expected that alcohol would have an effect on sexual behaviors and feelings (A. E. Wilson, Calhoun, & McNair, 2002). The available data do not imply a specific association between alcohol and rape, however. Men who are more likely to engage in sexually coercive behaviors might also be more likely to use or abuse alcohol (Testa, 2002).

Clearly, chronic and heavy alcohol use is generally incompatible with sexual activities in general (J. A. Price & Price, 1983). Whether alcohol intoxication facilitates or inhibits male sexual arousal appears to be a fairly complicated function of expectancy (whether the man believes alcohol enhances or diminishes sexual arousal), experience with alcohol and sex, and the actual alcohol dose (Crowe & George, 1989; J. A. Price & Price, 1983). Some research suggests that the effects of alcohol on male sexual arousal (measured phallometrically) are due entirely to the drug itself, with no effect of expectancy (G. T. Wilson, Lawson, & Abrams, 1978; G. T. Wilson & Niaura, 1984). Conversely, other research suggests that the effects are due entirely to participants' expectancies about alcohol's effects on arousal, with no direct effect of alcohol itself (Lansky & Wilson, 1981). George and Marlatt (1986) reported that alcohol use increased viewing times (an index of sexual interest) of sexually violent material. Alcohol appears to facilitate phallometric responding to sexual aggression cues (Seto & Barbaree, 1995), but other researchers have failed to obtain this finding (Barbaree, Marshall,

Yates, & Lightfoot, 1983). The phenomenon of alcohol abuse in general was reviewed in the previous chapter. The general link between sexual coercion and alcohol use was extensively reviewed by Testa (2002).

One finding is consistent: Alcohol use is a reliable and moderately strong correlate of sexual coercion and rape, even in competition with other correlates for outcome variance. This correlation might result from the fact that young men frequently use the tactic of alcohol intoxication to try to obtain sex from potentially reluctant women (e.g., Kanin, 1984). As mentioned above, intoxication undoubtedly interferes with a woman's successfully warding off an attempted sexual assault.

MALE FRATERNITIES

Consistent with the suggestion that acquaintance rape is related to male variation in mating effort and increased competition in late adolescence and early adulthood, there is intriguing research on the association between sexual coercion and male membership in certain sports teams and college fraternities (Copenhaver & Grauerholz, 1991; Humphrey & Kahn, 2000; T. L. Jackson, 1996; Koss & Gaines, 1993; P. Y. Martin & Hummer, 1998; see also Boswell & Spade, 1996). It appears that such all-male groups or organizations share certain characteristics—strong loyalty to the group, secrecy, intergroup competitiveness, emphasis on dominance and stereotyped masculinity, and a general attitude of male superiority and antagonism toward women. Men who report sexual aggression are more likely to report that they have friends who support physical violence against women and who have been sexually aggressive toward women than men who do not report sexual aggression (Schwartz et al., 2001). Of course, given the available data, it is difficult to make causal inferences here. That is, it is possible that such group norms cause young men to believe that women's interests sharply diverge from men's and to disregard the interests of their female peers, making them more likely to commit rape. At least equally possible, however, is that such groups and organizations differentially attract young men who already have these characteristics (and are already differentially likely to perpetrate acquaintance rape). Nevertheless, these rape-prone group characteristics are reminiscent of some stereotypical military qualities and might be related to the high prevalence of rape perpetrated by gangs (Sanday, 1990) and armies.

WAR

As discussed in chapter 2, rape and warfare have co-occurred throughout human history. Indeed, one of the primordial reasons for war was probably bride capture (Ghiglieri, 1999). Certainly there is good evidence that even in modern times, rape is widespread during military conflicts (e.g., Mezey, 1994; Rosenman, 2000). Although forbidden by international law in the 20th century, rape has also been used as official military policy (D. E. Buss, 1998). The ubiquity of rape during warfare suggests that a very high proportion of men (perhaps the majority) commit rape when there are few consensual heterosexual outlets, high immediate social support for rape, antagonistic attitudes toward the victims' group, and little perceived likelihood of punishment or retaliation (Smuts, 1996). Indeed, although there is little good research on the topic, it appears that heterosexual outlets can be scarce enough and the social support for rape strong enough (and the likelihood of punishment and retaliation low enough) that heterosexual men will rape other men in prison (Nacci & Kane, 1984). Of course, prisons contain a very disproportionate number of life-course-persistent antisocial men with high rates of mating effort and lack of concern for the interests of others. As discussed in previous chapters, however, it seems that rape is due to sexual deprivation only in the most extreme and unusual circumstances. The most obvious support for that conclusion comes from the fact that rapists, as a group, experience no fewer sexual opportunities than other men and generally have had more sexual partners. Some rapists are married or involved in a long-term relationship (i.e., have available and presumably consenting sexual partners).

SPOUSAL RAPE

Many women are raped by their own spouses (Kilpatrick, Best, Saunders, & Veronen, 1988). Victims of marital rape have been reported to experience (perhaps to a greater degree than other rape victims) serious and long-lasting psychological and physical consequences (DeMaris, 1997; Goodman, Koss, & Russo, 1993; Kilpatrick et al., 1988).

The phenomenon of spousal rape presents somewhat of a puzzle. By definition, marital rape cannot be part of a male strategy to increase the number and variety of sexual partners. One possibility is that marital rapists have a preference for violent and coercive sex, as discussed in chapter 5. A man who sexually preferred coercion and violence would, in theory, be likely to be sexually violent even if the spouse agreed to sexual intercourse. Warren and Hazelwood (2002) interviewed 20 partners of extremely sadistic men (seven of whom had murdered extrafamilial victims) and concluded that the men's sadistic fantasies became the organizing principle in the behavior of their female partners. The female partners were subjected to increasingly sadistic assaults over time, and many came to collude in the sadistic assaults of other women. Despite these extreme cases, the limited amount of available data implies that this sexual preference hypothesis can account for only a small minority (perhaps 5%) of marital rapists (Monson & Langhinrichsen-Rohling, 1998). There is no empirical work, however, on the phallometrically measured sexual interest of marital rapists.

Another possibility is that spousal rapists are generally antisocial men who are willing to use aggressive and coercive tactics even against the people with whom they live. In support of this view, spousal rape is strongly associated with nonsexual violence directed toward spouses (DeMaris, 1997; Kilpatrick et al., 1988; Monson & Langhinrichsen-Rohling, 1998; Resnick, Kilpatrick, Walsh, & Veronen, 1991). Monson and Langhinrichsen-Rohling estimated that such generally antisocial men represent over half of marital rapists.

In addition to the personality features of men who assault their wives, there are certain marital contexts that increase the likelihood of violence. Both sexual and nonsexual spousal violence appears to be occasioned by the same precursors—sexual jealousy and impending marital separation (Groth, 1979; P. Mahoney & Williams, 1998; see also Figueredo, Sales, Russell, Becker, & Kaplan, 2000). Indeed, male sexual proprietariness is a common source of spousal conflict, and sexual jealousy is the most common motive for men assaulting and even killing their wives (Daly & Wilson, 1988).

Spousal rape and spousal violence might be, in part, aspects of a male sexual strategy designed to prevent or counter cuckoldry. We saw in chapter 3 that forced intra-pair copulations in many bird species that form pair bonds almost exclusively follow suspected or actual extra-pair copulation by the female mate. Human sexual and nonsexual violence has been hypothesized to be means whereby men control the sexual behavior of their partners by making women afraid to leave the relationship and even afraid to be in the company of other men (N. Z. Hilton, Harris, & Rice, 2000; Smuts, 1995, 1996). Also, men who suspect their partners of sexual infidelity might demand sex (and use coercion and violence if refused) to increase their chances of paternity through sperm competition.[1] N. M. Shields and Hanneke (1983) found, in a study of spousal violence, that marital rape was more likely when the victims reported they had engaged in extramarital sex. Burch and Gallup (2000) studied a group of domestic assaulters and found that those who had nonbiological children were more violent toward their spouses, and those who perceived less physical resemblance between their putatively biological children and themselves were less solicitous toward their children and inflicted worse injuries on their spouses.

Violence and battering might even serve to terminate pregnancies. Goodman et al. (1993) reviewed evidence that pregnant women are more

---

[1]Of course, the proximate cause of spousal rape and violence, if this hypothesis is correct, is jealousy. Occasional loss of paternity through extra-pair copulation by mates is the selective (ultimate) cause for the emotion of jealousy.

likely than nonpregnant women to be the targets of violence by husbands, that the abdomen is more often directly targeted when the spouse is pregnant, and that battering of pregnant spouses sometimes results in miscarriage and stillbirths. One could predict that such targeted violence is more likely when the man expects that infidelity has occurred.

CONCLUSION

Research on nonhuman species suggests many contextual or situational factors associated with a greater likelihood of forced copulation. Depending on the species, forced copulation is more likely when there is a shortage of receptive females, when successfully mated males have opportunities to mate with additional and easily accessible fertile females, when males are unsuccessful in competition for fertile females, and when a mate is suspected of copulating or has copulated with other males.

Strangely, perhaps, we know much less about the circumstances that promote or facilitate rape in *Homo sapiens*. Research reviewed in this chapter allows us, however, to make some suggestions. Rape appears more likely when the target is of reproductive age (i.e., young adults), when young women are sexually available (i.e., unmarried, dating, and sexually active), when the protagonists have a less-than-optimal understanding of the costs and benefits of different behaviors (such as when intoxicated), when there are cues of male competition or exclusively male social groups (e.g., fraternities), when men expect sex (e.g., after expenditure of resources), when men perceive possible targets as vulnerable (e.g., when intoxicated or unprotected by male relatives or during war) or as enemies, and when there are cues of infidelity.

Is there a causal relationship, however, between the contextual and situational factors reviewed in this chapter and rape? It is plausible that exposure to pornography, alcohol use, misperception of sexual cues, and membership in stereotypical male organizations (to take a few examples) all contribute to causing rape. There is little doubt that some aspects of the context contribute to rape—social support and the low likelihood of punishment must, for example, be part of the explanation for the high incidence of rape during war. Certainly, young women experience risks of being raped over and above that conferred by opportunity alone. It is unfortunate that the available data do not permit us to go much further for many factors. There is some evidence to support the idea that many of the statistical relationships reported in this chapter are due to the operation of other factors. That is, men who are high in mating effort and antisociality may simultaneously abuse alcohol, hang out with men who hold unsympathetic attitudes toward other people (and especially women), use violence to control the behavior of their sexual partners, infer sexual interest, enjoy violent pornography, and engage in sexual coercion. One can hypothesize that much of the statistical association between contextual factors and rape is underlain by the same causal individual differences in personality in general, and sexual strategies in particular, that we discussed in the previous chapters. Nevertheless, future research may reveal interesting interplays between the individual differences identified in this book and the contextual factors associated with increased likelihood of rape.

III

IMPLICATIONS

8

CLINICAL ASSESSMENT AND TREATMENT OF RAPISTS

Over the past 20 or 30 years, mental health professionals have been tackling the problem of rape. Rape has long been viewed as a crime, but it has been only relatively recently that rape has been addressed as a mental health matter. As we demonstrated in earlier chapters, it seems quite clear that not much rape can be attributed to known psychiatric disorders. Despite many well-established individual differences associated with rape, the only exception to this conclusion is psychopathy. There is little doubt that rape is disproportionately committed by psychopaths. As discussed in chapter 4, however, there are good reasons to doubt that psychopathy is a disorder (in the sense provided by Wakefield, 1992, 1999). Nevertheless, an intervention that decreased the antisocial and aggressive behavior of psychopaths would definitely lower the incidence of rape. It is safe to conclude, however, that despite several attempts, no effective treatment for psychopathy has yet been identified. Unfortunately, it appears that some established treatments actually increase the risk posed by psychopaths (Hare, Clark, Grann, & Thornton, 2000; G. T. Harris, Rice, & Cormier, 2002).

The absence of other psychiatric disorders notwithstanding, and inspired by the evidence for the effective treatment for criminal offenders in

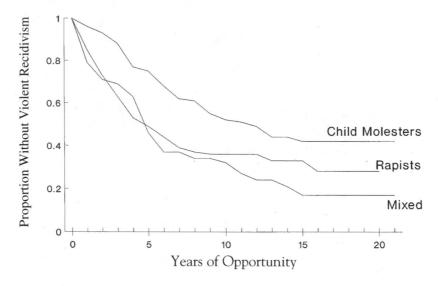

Figure 8.1. Kaplan–Meier survival curves for violent recidivism for three groups of sex offenders: those with a history of offense (a) against children, (b) against adult women, or (c) against both. From "Cross-Validation and Extension of the Violence Risk Appraisal Guide for Child Molesters and Rapists," by M. E. Rice and G. T. Harris, 1997, *Law and Human Behavior, 21*, Figure 1A. Copyright 1997 by Springer. Reprinted with permission.

general (e.g., Braukmann & Morris, 1987; Gendreau & Ross, 1979; Lipsey, 1992), mental health professionals have developed therapeutic programs especially for sex offenders. The most promising of such programs are informed by the characteristics of effective treatment gleaned from the evidence from criminal offenders in general (Andrews et al., 1990). Because a treatment for rapists usually instantiates (implicitly or explicitly) an explanation of rape in the first place, we review the evidence for the effectiveness of treatments for sex offenders in this chapter. We review assessment and treatment questions that are of concern to clinicians, lawyers, institutional administrators, policy makers, and others. First, however, we review what is known about the assessment of risk among rapists based on some recent empirical developments in assessments designed to evaluate the risk of recidivism posed by sex offenders. Although not an explanation of rape, an assessment approach that rendered an accurate prediction about which rapists were most likely to commit new offenses would surely have implications for theories about why some men rape.

CAN THE RECIDIVISM OF SEX OFFENDERS BE PREDICTED?

Consider the data presented in Figures 8.1 and 8.2. These figures are survival curves that show the number of people out of the original sample who have "survived" at different points in time. In this case, *survival* means not having been rearrested or reconvicted for a sexual or violent offense once released from secure institutions. Figure 8.1 illustrates the long-term follow-

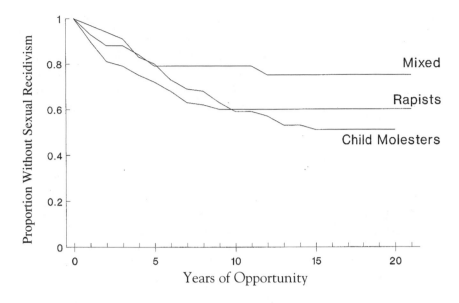

Figure 8.2. Kaplan–Meier survival curves for sexual recidivism for three groups of sex offenders: those with a history of offense (a) against children, (b) against adult women, or (c) against both. From "Cross-validation and Extension of the Violence Risk Appraisal Guide for Child Molesters and Rapists," by M. E. Rice and G. T. Harris, 1997, *Law and Human Behavior, 21,* Figure 2A. Copyright 1997 by Springer. Reprinted with permission.

up of sex offenders from some of our earlier studies (Quinsey, Rice, & Harris, 1995; M. E. Rice & Harris, 1997) with respect to violent recidivism (any offense against the person, including contact sexual offenses). The figure shows the cumulative proportion of participants who remain free of arrest for a violent offense as a function of the duration of opportunity to reoffend. The three lines refer to three different groups of offenders. The top line shows the survival curve for 142 sex offenders who had committed an offense against a child under the age of 14. The middle line shows the survival of the 88 sex offenders who had committed an offense against a woman at least 14 years old. The bottom line illustrates the survival curve for the 58 men in our study who had at least one victim in both of those categories.

In Figure 8.1 the functions steadily drop for at least 15 years—that is, the risk represented by these sex offenders persists for a very long time. The mixed group of offenders (those with both adult and child victims) exhibits extremely high recidivism; the survival function approaches asymptote below 20%. With regard to violence in general, child molesters exhibited the lowest risk (although at 15 years the cumulative recidivism rate was greater than 50%). Figure 8.2 shows that the reverse pattern was obtained for sexual recidivism (arrest for a clearly sexual offense): Mixed offenders exhibited the lowest recidivism rate, whereas the rapists' rate was higher. Child molesters showed the highest rate; by 15 years, the recidivism rate was greater than 50%. In fact, for child molesters only, the two survival curves are almost identical. Thus, for sex offenders whose victims are exclusively children, it is clear that if violent recidivism occurs, it is likely to include sexual offending. On the other hand, it is clear that although rapists are more dangerous (i.e., more likely to exhibit violent recidivism) overall, much of that violence does not appear to be sexual, at least as far as can be ascertained from official records (consistent with the information presented on the lack of specialization among rapists in chap. 4; see also Langan, Schmitt, & Durose, 2003).

The Outcome to Be Predicted

At first glance, it might seem that the most relevant outcome for sex offenders is a repetition of the sex offense for which the offender was originally convicted—most probably another sex offense. *Sexual recidivism* has variously been defined as any new arrest, conviction, or, less often, hospital readmission for a sexual offense. Often official criminal records constitute the only available information. Of course, all official records are an underestimate of the actual rates of reoffending. In the case of sexual offenses, there is additional cause for concern because of the tendency for the "sexual" component of the offense to be eliminated from the arrest or conviction offense (e.g., sexual assault becomes simply "assault") either because of a lack of sufficiently hard evidence of the sexual component or through a plea bargaining agreement. Another outcome measure used for predicting recidivism among sex offenders, one that we have used in our research, has been an arrest, conviction, or readmission to hospital for any violent offense (defined as offenses ranging from assault or armed robbery to murder and including all contact sexual offenses). Although overinclusive, violent recidivism is likely to capture significantly more sexual reoffenses than the more commonly used sexual recidivism definition. In fact, we have found that when we have had the resources to obtain more comprehensive information concerning recidivism offenses, many repeat offenses of sex offenders that appear on the criminal record to be nonsexual violent offenses actually have a sexual component or sexual motivation. For example, sexually motivated homicides or attempted homicides are often recorded on the criminal record as "murder" or "attempted murder," and it is sometimes hard to tell that the offense was sexually motivated.

Nevertheless, many sex offenders, especially rapists, do not confine their recidivism offenses to clearly sexual crimes. For example, we have found that whereas child molesters who reoffend are much more likely to be convicted of a new sex offense than of another violent offense, rapists are just about as likely to be convicted of a nonsexual violent offense as of a sexual one. Both groups are also at risk for nonviolent, nonsexual offenses. Most members of the public at large are concerned not just about new sexual offenses by rapists and other sex offenders, but about all new offenses, especially violent ones. We believe that the outcome of greatest relevance for the appraisal of risk among sex offenders, as it is among other offenders, is violent—including sexual—recidivism. And even if one is interested only in new sexually violent offenses, it may be argued, for the reasons we have outlined, that violent recidivism is a more valid outcome measure for evaluating prediction accuracy than is sexual recidivism as usually defined.

Predictors of Recidivism

Reviews of the prediction of recidivism among sex offenders before 1990 noted a lack of progress in the area. Although there were a number of follow-up studies (e.g., Frisbie & Dondis, 1965; Gibbens, Soothill, & Way, 1981; Radzinowicz, 1957; Soothill, Jack, & Gibbens, 1976), the differences in the proportions of recidivists among studies were dramatic, and Quinsey (1984) concluded in a review of research on rape that "by selectively contemplating the various studies one can conclude anything one wants" (p. 101). Nevertheless, it was clear from the studies that there were some groups of offenders who were at significant risk of committing new acts of sexual violence upon release. Frisbie and Dondis followed 70 men who had committed sexual acts accompanied by threats or force on women 18 years of age or older and found that 36% of the men committed a new sexual offense within 5 years of their release from Atascadero, where they had been judged on admission as sexually dangerous. This was a very high rate of recidivism for studies of this era.

Throughout the 1990s, several studies of the prediction of recidivism among sex offenders have found more consistent patterns than had been observed earlier. M. E. Rice, Harris, and Quinsey (1990) examined the sexual and violent recidivism of a group of 54 rapists assessed in a forensic hospital and released (usually after serving time in prison). The follow-up period averaged 46 months. The predictors included those found to be related to violent reoffending among offenders in general (psychopathy, past criminal history, age, and marital status), those known from the previous research literature to be important for the prediction of sexual offenses (especially those having to do with past sexual offending), and those known to discriminate between rapists and nonoffenders (phallometric arousal to violence). Given the relatively short follow-up period, the violent recidivism rate of 43% was high (28% were convicted of a new sexual offense). As a group, then, these men constituted a high-risk sample. For the prediction of new sexual offense convictions specifically, the best predictors included previous convictions for violent offenses, previous sexual offenses, and phallometric arousal. It is interesting that predictions of later violent or sexual offenses or both could be made just as well from only two variables (phallometric arousal and psychopathy) as from a larger set of predictors. The data from this study supported an account of rape as an act of sexual violence differentially committed by men who exhibit a criminal lifestyle and an exploitative approach to social relationships.

R. K. Hanson and Bussière (1998) examined the predictors of sexual recidivism among sex offenders in a meta-analysis of studies available by the end of 1995. They found 87 articles based on 61 data sets, and half of the reports had been produced since 1989. The median sample size was 198, and the median follow-up period was 4 years. In total, 28,972 sexual offenders were included. The offenders included child molesters, rapists, and men who had committed other sex offenses such as exhibitionism, frotteurism, indecent exposure, or voyeurism. Their results were consistent with those of M. E. Rice et al. (1990) in showing the importance of deviant sexual preferences and antisociality. The strongest predictor of sexual recidivism in their meta-analysis was deviant sexual preferences measured phallometrically. However, the effect was due to preferences for children and not to preferences for rape. As discussed in an earlier chapter, stimulus sets that included more brutal and graphic stimuli have demonstrated that relative arousal to sexual or nonsexual violence is a good predictor of sexual recidivism among rapists (M. E. Rice et al., 1990), and few of the studies Hanson and Bussière included used those types of stimuli.

Other important predictors included prior sexual offenses and early onset of sexual offending. In addition, other important predictors (also commonly found to be important predictors of general recidivism among offenders) were young age and never having been married. Because there were so many sex offenders included in this meta-analysis, it was also possible to identify some factors that were not related to sexual recidivism. Having a history of being sexually abused as a child, substance abuse, and general psychological problems (including anxiety, low self-esteem, and depression) were unrelated to sexual recidivism. There was no evidence that treatment reduced sexual recidivism. All these conclusions were supported by a recent update of this meta-analysis (R. K. Hanson, Morton, & Harris, 2003). In addition, this meta-analysis also indicated that actuarial risk assessment was significantly superior in accuracy to unstructured clinical judgment and "empirically guided" or structured professional discretion.

Prediction Tools

Follow-up studies have identified characteristics of sex offenders that could be used to reduce uncertainty about who will commit further violent offenses. Some follow-up studies go on to identify the smallest set of variables that, when combined statistically, produces the most accurate prediction of recidivism. Such variable sets are called *actuarial prediction tools*. More commonly, however, assessment of the risk posed by sexual aggressors is accomplished with clinical judgment—a clinician (e.g., mental health professional, parole official, judge) applies experience, clinical training, theory, and intuition to render a statement about the likelihood of recidivism. In hundreds of comparisons over many domains, including the prediction of recidivism, clinical judgment has never been found to be superior to actuarial methods, whereas the converse has most often been demonstrated (Grove & Meehl, 1996; G. T. Harris et al., 2002; Mossman, 1994). Some studies have shown better-than-chance performance by clinicians (i.e., they outperformed blind guesswork), but many have not. Clinicians' judgments are not more accurate than those of laypersons (Quinsey & Ambtman, 1979).

G. T. Harris, Rice, and Quinsey (1993) developed an actuarial instrument called the Violence Risk Appraisal Guide (VRAG) for the prediction of violent recidivism among offenders with mental disorders and without mental disorders. The instrument was developed with a sample of 618 offenders, of whom 28% were men whose criminal history included at least one offense that was sexually motivated. In its development, several steps were taken to ensure that the resulting instrument would generalize to a new sample. For example, although multiple regression procedures were used to select the best combination of variables to include in the instrument, the weighting procedure did not rely on those obtained from the multiple regression analyses but instead used a much simpler method based on the strength of the univariate relationships of the variables with violent recidivism.

The VRAG was found to yield a correlation with violent recidivism of .44 in a 7-year follow-up. The instrument also performed well by comparison to predictive tools in other fields. A statistic called *area under the receiver operating characteristic curve*, or AUC, is a number between .50 and 1. The higher the number, the better the predictive accuracy (see M. E. Rice & Harris, 1995a; Swets, Dawes, & Monahan, 2000). The AUC for the VRAG was .76. According to commonly accepted standards (Rice & Harris, 2004), this is a large effect size. In another study (M. E. Rice & Harris, 1995a) that included the original offenders plus additional offenders for a total sample size of 799 (288 of whom were sex offenders), it was found that the prediction instrument was robust with respect both to the length of the prediction interval (it worked equally well across follow-up intervals from 3.5 to 10 years) and to the severity of the offense being predicted (i.e., it predicted the most serious violent offenses just as well as all violent offenses). Scores on the VRAG are positively related to the seriousness of the recidivistic violence (when it occurs) and to the speed with which violent recidivism occurs (Quinsey, Harris, Rice, & Cormier, 1998).

Furthermore, the VRAG instrument was cross-validated by testing how well it predicted violent and sexual recidivism in a sample of 159 sex offenders not included in the original construction of the instrument. The follow-up averaged 10 years, and the violent recidivism rate was 58%. It was found that the VRAG predicted violent recidivism at least as well in the sex offender sample as it had in the original construction sample. Not surprising, the instrument did not perform nearly as well in predicting sexual recidivism exclusively, yielding a correlation of .20 and an AUC of .62. In the same report, an instrument that had been developed for the prediction of sexual recidivism among sex offenders (Quinsey, Rice, et al., 1995) on a sample of 178 sex offenders was also tested on cross-validation with a new sample of sex offenders. Although the instrument had yielded a correlation with sexual recidivism of .45 on the construction sample, its correlation with sexual recidivism on the validation sample was poorer than that of the VRAG.

Several studies on other populations of sex offenders have confirmed the accuracy of the VRAG and other actuarial instrument in predicting recidivism (Barbaree, Seto, Langton, & Peacock, 2001; Bélanger & Earls, 1996; G. T. Harris et al., 2003; Quinsey, Book, & Skilling, in press; Sjöstedt & Långström, 2002), with AUCs up to .84 under favorable conditions (i.e., no missing data, constant follow-up period).

A Special Method for Sex Offenders?

Studies of sex offenders are consistent in finding groups of variables (such as psychopathy, criminal history, and marital status) that predict violent and sexual recidivism and groups of other variables (such as prior sexual offenses and phallometrically measured sexual deviance) that predict specifically sexual offenses (e.g., R. K. Hanson & Bussière, 1998; Prentky, Knight, & Lee, 1997). Among sex offenders, victim injury has been positively related to the probability of violent and sexual recidivism, whereas it is inversely related among offenders in general. Also, whereas having a female victim is negatively related to the risk of violent recidivism among offenders in general, for sex offenders the negative relationship holds only for child victims. It appears, then, that there may be a need for a special instrument to predict recidivism among sex offenders. We have attempted to construct such a special sex offender instrument—the Sex Offender Risk Appraisal Guide (SORAG; Quinsey, Harris, et al., 1998). The SORAG was constructed by incorporating variables (such as deviant sexual preferences and history of sex offenses) shown to be important for sex offenders. Scoring instructions and normative data are provided in Quinsey, Harris, et al. (1998). The SORAG has 14 items, 10 of which are identical to VRAG items, and thus the SORAG is highly correlated with the VRAG (e.g., Barbaree et al., 2001, reported a correlation of .90). The SORAG, like the VRAG, was developed to predict new arrests or convictions for violent (including sexual) offenses. Several studies with sex offenders have shown it to have high accuracy in the prediction of violent (including sexual) recidivism and moderate accuracy in predicting offenses known to be sexual (Barbaree et al., 2001; Dempster, Hart, & Boer, 2001; G. T. Harris et al., 2003; Nunes, Firestone, Bradford, Greenberg, & Broom, 2002; M. E. Rice & Harris, 2002).

Another instrument for the prediction of recidivism among sex offenders is the Rapid Risk Assessment for Sex Offender Recidivism (RRASOR; K. Hanson, 1997). It was developed using an initial item pool of seven easily scored variables found to predict sex offense recidivism in R. K. Hanson and

Bussière's (1998) meta-analysis. Using multiple regression and examining intercorrelations among the variables in each of seven different data sets, the number of variables was reduced to four, and a weighting system was determined. Several studies have shown the RRASOR to be a good predictor of sexual recidivism and violent (including sexual) recidivism among sex offenders (Barbaree et al., 2001; Dempster et al., 2001; Sjöstedt & Långström, 2002; see also R. K. Hanson & Harris, 2000).

The Static-99 was constructed by combining the RRASOR and an unpublished nonactuarial instrument (R. K. Hanson & Thornton, 2000). The scale was tested on four samples of sex offenders (the same offenders used to derive the RRASOR) and showed moderate to high accuracy in the prediction of both sexual and violent recidivism. Subsequent research has reported significant correlations between recidivism and scores on the Static-99 (Barbaree et al., 2001; Nunes et al., 2002).

Actuarial instruments are in principle atheoretical because the estimates of the likelihood of recidivism they provide are obtained empirically from follow-up research. Nevertheless, it is clear that these instruments work in the case of sex offenders because the predictors they use are characteristics of persistently antisocial offenders or related to sexually deviant preferences. Currently available actuarial instruments use historical predictors to estimate the likelihood of at least one instance of recidivism of a particular kind over a long period of opportunity to reoffend. Actuarial instruments can serve the important purpose of risk assessment in the context of dispositional decisions in the criminal justice and psychiatric systems and determination of the intensity of supervision and treatment that are appropriate for individual offenders. The risk principle asserts that the amount of investment in treatment and supervision should be proportionate to an offender's level of risk (Andrews & Bonta, 2003). However, variables pertaining to the provision of treatment or progress in treatment are not currently included in actuarial instruments. Treatment-related variables must be shown to increase the accuracy of prediction to be included in future actuarial instruments. The next section examines the likelihood of this desirable prospect occurring in the foreseeable future.

DOES TREATMENT REDUCE RECIDIVISM?

In this section, we review research on the treatment of men who have committed rape. In most cases, rapists have been treated using the same methods as other sex offenders, especially child molesters. Often, rapists and child molesters are treated together in the same groups. In fact, few treatment programs have been designed for rapists only. Thus, our review includes programs that included rapists but that also included other sex offenders (primarily child molesters). Although it might seem that there would be good reasons to treat rapists and child molesters separately, most treatment programs have included both, and often other sex offenders as well. As we saw earlier in this chapter, there are men who have offended against both children and adults.

We have reviewed the treatment of sex offenders in greater depth—in fact, some would say we have reviewed the topic to death—elsewhere (G. T. Harris, Rice, & Quinsey, 1998; Quinsey, Harris, Rice, & Lalumière, 1993; M. E. Rice & Harris, 2003a, 2003b). In this section we briefly review some of the most influential and methodologically rigorous studies to give the reader a flavor of the treatment approaches that have been tried and the success to date of those approaches. But first we discuss how one can tell whether a particular treatment program was effective.

There are some generally agreed-on standards for conducting research in general and treatment evaluation in particular. Most commonly, evaluating treatment entails two stages (Streiner, 2002). The first stage, *establishing efficacy*, involves rigorous research designs (random assignment, double-blind placebo, multiple outcome measures) and maximizing treatment effects (homogeneous groups, manualized therapy, treatment process measures). The second stage, *establishing effectiveness*, involves studying the smaller treatment effects achieved in ordinary practice in which such thorough control of therapeutic efforts is usually not possible. In the field of psychological treatment for sex offenders, the question of efficacy (Can treatment work?) has not been settled. Most investigators in the field have skipped to the effectiveness question (Does treatment work?) because of its greater relevance to public policy.

Measuring Treatment Effectiveness

Investigators generally agree that it is desirable to eliminate or control possible sources of measurement bias and that useful evaluation comes from studies in which a treated group is contrasted with a comparable group that receives no treatment (or a clearly different treatment). Differences among experts arise in matters of degree. No study can be free from all threats to internal validity, and so the crucial question concerns how tightly designed a study must be before it can be informative. The gold standard is a random assignment study, but even random assignment to treatment does not guarantee that groups are comparable—random assignment merely guarantees that differences are randomly distributed. Most experts would agree that something can be learned from imperfect research (after all, no study is perfect). There is less agreement about how much can be learned from studies of lesser methodological quality and about what standards should define minimally useful evaluation research.

Our view is that relatively high quality research (closer to efficacy evaluation) is required before conclusions are warranted because we believe that the acceptance of low standards entails an unacceptable risk of credulous acceptance of findings. A famous example is the Cambridge Somerville Youth Study (McCord, 1978). In this study, several hundred boys from disadvantaged neighborhoods were randomly assigned to either a treatment or a control group. The families of boys in the treatment group received services for an average of 5 years including family counseling, extra tutoring, summer camp, Boy Scouts, the YMCA, and other community programs. Thirty years later, weak inference, or subjective evaluations of the program by those who received it, suggested it had very positive effects. However, more rigorous evaluation comparing the treatment and control groups indicated that the program had adverse effects on criminal behavior, death, disease, occupational status, and job satisfaction.

So what are our criteria for evaluating treatment efficacy or effectiveness for sex offenders? First, it is necessary to compare the outcomes of treated offenders against those of untreated offenders or of offenders given a different treatment (McConaghy, 1999; Quinsey et al., 1993). Otherwise, there is no way to determine that change in offending following treatment is due to the specific effects of the target treatment rather than to such other factors as passage of time, increased age of the offender, or offender expectancy. The presence of a control group is the most important methodological feature of a treatment evaluation; consequently, we consider only controlled studies.

Second, because the ultimate goal of treatment for rapists is the reduction of recidivism, some measure of that is the primary yardstick for evaluating treatment. But what measure of recidivism—general, violent, sexual, or specific offenses such as rape or sexual murder? Obviously, the more specific the measure, the lower the recidivism rate will be. Ought we to use self-reported recidivism or official arrest and conviction data? Unfortunately, the validity of self-reports has rarely been evaluated in treatment outcome studies. Among rapists and sex offenders specifically, denial, distortion, and minimization are extremely common (Abel, Mittelman, Becker, Rathner, & Rouleau, 1988; Pollock & Hashmall, 1991). Without special steps to ensure and evaluate their validity, offenders' self-reported recidivism cannot be trusted. Arrest and conviction data from police rap sheets are frequently used as outcome measures. Both have the advantage of being "hard" in the sense that it is unlikely that an arrest or, especially, a conviction will be recorded if nothing happened. On the other hand, both are conservative, because many offenses do not result in an arrest or conviction. Moreover, because of plea bargaining, many men arrested for sex offenses are subsequently convicted of nonsexual offenses. Despite the fact that they underestimate offending, officially recorded sexual or violent reoffending (including sexual) are probably the best available measures to evaluate comparative recidivism rates among treated and untreated groups because they are the least subject to bias related to treatment participation.

Risk of violent and sexual recidivism among rapists and child molesters has been shown to persist over decades (G. T. Harris et al., 1998; M. E. Rice

& Harris, 1997), so longer follow-ups will lead to higher cumulative rates of recidivism. Although official recidivism is the most important outcome measure, pre- and posttreatment changes on measures relevant to specific treatment components are also important. If pre–post changes on these measures are correlated with lower recidivism, then there is strong evidence that the treatment component is effective.

Treatment effectiveness will be grossly overestimated if treatment refusers and dropouts are ignored. This happens when, for example, persons who refuse treatment are excluded from the treatment group, but persons who would have refused treatment, had it been offered, are included in the comparison group. Similarly, counting as "treated" only those who remained in treatment until completion and ignoring the outcomes of dropouts (or even worse, putting those who dropped out or refused into a control group) grossly inflates estimates of treatment effectiveness. Attrition is best handled by analyses in which all individuals initially assigned to each group are included—the "intent to treat" design (Chambless & Hollon, 1998; Flick, 1988). In other words, there are general effects of treatment participation—a treatment regimen selects relatively compliant and motivated individuals. The important social policy questions pertain to the specific effects of treatment: Does the treatment itself cause a reduction in offending? Consequently, the widely accepted practice standards (e.g., randomized control, unbiased outcome measures, double-blind administration, monitoring attrition) for evaluating any treatment are designed to measure its specific, causal effects.

In addition to these methodological issues, narrative reviews of treatment effectiveness experience other difficulties. For example, when positive effects are found in some studies and not in others, there is no quantitative way to evaluate whether the different results are due simply to sampling error or whether variables related to outcome (called *moderator variables*) such as client characteristics, setting, or treatment characteristics account for the differences. Meta-analysis allows data from many studies to be combined to determine the average effect and evaluates whether moderator variables can account for the disparate results. Although meta-analyses cannot make up for all the inadequacies of individual studies, they do permit a more definitive conclusion about treatment efficacy. Unless there are enough high-quality studies, however, meta-analysis is not dependable (Chambless & Hollon, 1998). Unfortunately, as we see later in this section, we believe that there are too few well-controlled studies of sex offender treatment to conduct an informative meta-analysis.

Nonbehavioral Psychotherapy

Until recently, the most common treatment for rapists and other sex offenders has been group or individual psychotherapy (Quinsey, 1977, 1984). Unfortunately, the treatment is seldom well described, usually seems to have been unstructured, and has rarely been evaluated in a controlled fashion. The few controlled evaluations that exist have provided no evidence that nonbehavioral psychotherapy reduces the likelihood of reoffending. Frisbie (1969) and Frisbie and Dondis (1965) studied treatment of "sexual psychopaths" in a humanistic, peer-led program in a maximum security psychiatric hospital and compared their outcomes with those of untreated sex offenders. The treated and untreated groups were neither matched nor randomly assigned. The rate of new sexual offenses was higher among the treated men. Sturgeon and Taylor (1980) followed a later cohort of 260 men treated in the same institution. Sexual and nonsexual violent reoffending was compared with that of a group of 122 untreated sex offenders released from prison the same year. The untreated group, which included more rapists, were younger, had spent longer incarcerated, and had more serious violent and nonviolent criminal histories (but less serious histories of sexual offenses). The treated men subsequently had fewer reconvictions for sex offenses, but there were no differences for nonsexual violent offenses.

Romero and Williams (1983) conducted what is undoubtedly the best controlled of the treatment outcome studies for psychotherapy. Probationers (over 80% of whom were rapists or child molesters) were randomly assigned to either intensive probation or psychodynamic group therapy plus probation. Those assigned to psychotherapy had higher rates of rearrest for sex offenses (though not significantly) than those assigned to intensive supervision alone. Moreover, among those men who completed over 40 weeks of treatment, treated participants were significantly more likely to be rearrested for a sex offense. Thus, similar to findings for offenders in general (Andrews et al., 1990), humanistic and psychodynamic treatments do not reduce offending by rapists or other sex offenders. They might even increase recidivism.

Castration and Pharmacological Treatments

Although its use is rare today, castration (surgical removal of the gonads) was used extensively in Europe to reduce sex drive and sexual recidivism. Castration might also reduce aggression more generally. Most human studies of castration have been completely uncontrolled, and many included men who now are not considered to be sex offenders (e.g., gay men with adult partners). Freund (1980) reviewed uncontrolled and partially controlled studies of castration and concluded that sexual recidivism rates among castrated offenders were very low, even though offenders considered for castration were at high risk. In one partially controlled study, Cornu (1973; reported in Freund, 1980) compared the postcastration recidivism of 121 male sex offenders in Switzerland with 50 men who were also recommended for the procedure but refused. In a 5- to 30-year follow-up, 7% of the castrated men and 52% of the uncastrated men committed another sex offense. Although the difference in outcome was striking, those who were recommended but refused may have been at higher risk than those who agreed. For example, they may have been less likely to admit that they had a problem. In another study (Wille & Beier, 1989), 104 voluntarily castrated sex offenders were compared with 53 men, most of whom withdrew their consent before surgery. The sexual recidivism rate for the castrated men was 3% compared with 46% for the comparison sample.

In another partially controlled study of castration, Stürup (1968) studied the outcomes of 38 men who had offended against either adult women or female children and had been treated in a social therapy program. Eighteen men were castrated prior to release; another 18 were not (two were never released). Over a follow-up lasting up to 25 years, one of the castrated and three of the noncastrated men were charged with additional sex crimes. There was no evidence that those considered for the procedure had worse sexual offense histories, but the uncastrated men had more psychiatric symptoms. Although Stürup reported that he considered the results of castration to be very positive, it would be difficult to recommend the procedure on the basis of these results.

It seems beyond doubt that castration reduces sex drive and could reduce the risk of sexual reoffending among offenders whose offenses are limited to sexual ones and who freely consent. The issue of consent has practical as well as legal and ethical implications, especially for incarcerated offenders or offenders who are given a choice between castration and incarceration (Alexander, Gunn, Taylor, & Finch, 1993). Offenders who are castrated under coercion might, for example, illicitly obtain testosterone or other anabolic steroids and thereby reverse the effects of castration. Although this has not been much of a problem to date, anabolic steroids are now easily available from the illicit market and are commonly used by body builders and other athletes (Brower, 1993). In any event, professionals have argued that castration is not appropriate for the large proportion of sex offenders (especially rapists and incarcerated offenders) who have histories of diverse nonsexual offenses (see Eastman, 1993).

Pharmacological treatments are more popular than castration, especially in North America. Several drugs have been used to reduce deviant sexual behavior, including various serotonergic medications, but most common are drugs called antiandrogens (including cyproterone acetate, gonadotropin-releasing hormone analog, leuprolide acetate, and medroxyprogesterone acetate, or MPA) that reduce or block testosterone. Only MPA has been subjected to controlled outcome evaluations. Antiandrogens achieve the sex-drive-reducing effects of surgical castration with fewer ethical problems because their effects are completely reversible upon withdrawal. However, they have unpleasant side effects, and most men strongly dislike taking them (Langevin, Wright, & Handy, 1988). Common complaints include weight gain, fatigue, headaches, reduced body hair, depression, and gastrointestinal problems. As an example of the unpopularity of antiandrogens, Hucker, Langevin, and Bain (1988) studied child molesters randomly assigned to either MPA treatment or placebo. Of 100 offenders approached to participate, 48 agreed to complete the initial assessment, and 18 agreed to take part in the study. Only 11 completed a 3-month trial, 5 MPA participants and 6 control participants. Although there was evidence that MPA reduced testosterone levels, there was no evidence that MPA changed sexual behavior.

Emory, Cole, and Meyer (1992) compared 40 men treated with MPA with 21 men who refused. Most were child molesters; the remainder were rapists, exhibitionists, and voyeurs. Both groups received outpatient psychotherapy, and all admitted to their offenses and to having overwhelming deviant fantasies. Men who admitted their offenses but blamed alcohol or drugs were excluded, as were men who had histories of serious antisocial behavior. Twenty-nine of the 40 men started on MPA dropped out of the drug treatment, and 10 of these later reoffended. Also, 7 reoffended while taking the drug. Although only 18% of the men started on MPA reoffended while on the drug, 43% of the men started on MPA reoffended before the end of the study. By comparison, 12 of 21 or 58% of the men who refused MPA treatment reoffended. The recidivism rates (which included self-reported and official arrests for sex offenses) were not significantly different, and recidivism rates were surprisingly high considering that the men were relatively low risk and highly motivated. Similar findings showing no differences in recidivism between the MPA and comparison groups were obtained by other researchers (Maletzky, 1991; McConaghy, Blaszczynski, & Kidson, 1988).

In summary, it appears that very few sex offenders will voluntarily accept currently available drugs to reduce testosterone, and fewer still continue to take the drugs for extended periods. The available evidence suggests that reoffense rates are low among those few offenders who stay in treatment that includes such drugs. There is as yet no convincing reason to believe that the drugs cause reductions in reoffending. The small proportion of sex offenders who remain in drug treatment might be especially highly motivated.

As a cautionary note, R. K. Hanson and Harris (2000) compared sex offenders who committed a new sex offense during parole supervision with sex offenders (matched to the first group on several known risk factors) not known to have committed a new offense. The recidivists were much more likely to have been prescribed an antiandrogen. Of course, it is likely that those men perceived to be higher risk were more likely to have been seen as candidates for the drugs. Nevertheless, mandating antiandrogen drugs during community supervision neither eliminated recidivism nor reduced it to low levels.

Behavioral and Cognitive–Behavioral Treatments

The third general approach to treating rapists and other sex offenders has been the use of behavioral and cognitive–behavioral techniques. Currently the most commonly used technique, originally developed for treating problem drinkers, is called *relapse prevention* (e.g., Marques, Day, Nelson, & West, 1994). Relapse prevention programs emphasize helping the offender to construct an offense cycle. The basic idea is to look at the chain of events that led to offending behavior in the past and to develop other thoughts and behaviors that can replace those that led to offending. Many treatment programs also contain behavioral techniques to normalize deviant sexual preferences. The particular methods used to alter sexual preferences vary, but most (e.g., covert sensitization, masturbatory reconditioning, operant conditioning) attempt to associate aversive events with arousal to deviant stimuli or fantasies.

Many treatment programs also include training in social competence. Some contain other components, including sex education (M. E. Rice, Quinsey, & Harris, 1991), anger management (Marshall & Barbaree, 1988), nonspecific counseling (Hanson, Steffy, & Gauthier, 1993), or family systems therapy (Borduin, Henggeler, Blaske, & Stein, 1990). Many also contain non-cognitive–behavioral elements such as insight-oriented psychotherapy (Davidson, 1984) or victim awareness and empathy (Marshall, Jones, Ward, Johnston, & Barbaree, 1991).

One Canadian prison-based cognitive–behavioral treatment program for sex offenders has been the subject of three evaluation studies. The studies provide a particularly revealing example of the methodological problems that characterize this field because although they used overlapping samples from the same population, they reported contradictory results about treatment effectiveness. Davidson (1984) compared the outcomes of 101 treated men with those of a matched control group of untreated men. The treated men had prior sex offenses on their criminal records and were treated in the Regional Treatment Centre (RTC) of the Kingston Penitentiary in Ontario, Canada, between 1974 and 1982 and released before August 1982. The comparison participants were drawn from men admitted to Ontario penitentiaries between 1966 and 1974 and released by 1977. The comparison sample was matched to the treated sample on age and sex of victim and whether the offender was an incest offender. This practice of choosing comparison participants from a different cohort has been common in treatment outcome studies for sex offenders. Groups were followed for criminal recidivism (using police records) for up to 5 years after release. There was no difference between groups in the likelihood of a new conviction for a sexual offense, although treated offenders were more likely to incur a new charge for a sexual offense and significantly less likely to be convicted of any new violent (including sexual) offense or any new offense.

In a second study, Quinsey, Khanna, and Malcolm (1998) studied the postrelease recidivism (average follow-up of 44 months) of 213 men who completed the treatment program at the same institution as the Davidson (1984) study. In addition, they studied 183 men who were assessed as not requiring treatment, 52 who refused to be assessed, 27 who were assessed but deemed to be unsuitable for treatment, and 9 who were considered to require treatment but who did not receive it for a variety of reasons. All participants were assessed or treated between 1976 and 1989 and released prior to 1992. Treated offenders were the most likely to be rearrested for sexual offenses (as in the Davidson study), and even after statistically controlling for several variables that predicted reoffending, the treatment program was associated with more sexual rearrests but not violent (including sexual) rearrests. Furthermore, therapists' ratings of progress and need for further treatment were unrelated to recidivism. The authors suggested that treatment might have increased sexual recidivism.

In contrast, the third study (Looman, Abracen, & Nicholaichuk, 2000) concluded that their investigation "clearly indicates that the RTC program was effective in terms of reducing the risk of future recidivism" (p. 288) and reported a significantly lower sexual recidivism rate (24% on the basis of national police records) among the treated offenders, compared with 52% for the untreated group. This study used matched offenders from a different cohort but drawn from a different region of the country. They were matched to treated participants on age at index offense, date of index offence, and number of past criminal convictions. The treated participants were a subset (42%) of the treated sample from the Quinsey, Khanna, et al. (1998) study that excluded men treated outside the residential program setting (13%), whose treatment format (group, individual, or outpatient) was unclear (17%), whose treatment occurred outside the period 1976 to 1989 (6%), who received treatment at another institution (4%), or who could not be matched (18%). The Looman et al. (2000) follow-up time was relatively long (nearly 10 years on average).

There are numerous other evaluations of behavioral and cognitive–behavioral treatments. However, like the studies reviewed in this section, all but two used designs that did not permit firm conclusions about treatment efficacy. Two random assignment studies of sex offenders deserve special mention. The first obtained very positive results for adolescent sex offenders using community-based multisystemic therapy (MST) compared with individual therapy (Borduin et al., 1990). The treatment was a problem-focused service aimed at family preservation by resolving school problems, social deficits, peer difficulties, and family contact. No treatment for deviant sexual preferences was provided. Treatment assignment was random, but no information was provided about treatment dropouts. Although the number of participants was small (eight in each group), officially recorded rearrest data for sexual and nonsexual offenses indicated a large positive effect of multisystemic therapy. This effect was related to an unusually high recidivism rate among the control participants. Borduin and his colleagues recently expanded the study samples to 24 in each group and extended the follow-up to 8 years (Borduin & Schaeffer, 2001) with similarly positive results regarding the effects of treatment (12% vs. 42% sexual recidivism for MST treatment vs. usual services). These are very encouraging results and suggest that multisystemic treatment is definitely worth studying further for adolescent offenders. On the other hand, the treatment components of multisystemic therapy would be difficult to use with the vast majority of rapists and other sex offenders who are neither in school nor living with their parents.

The other study was a very ambitious cognitive–behavioral program for incarcerated adult child molesters and rapists (Marques et al., 1994). The treatment combined relapse prevention training, relaxation training, social skills training, stress and anger management, counseling for substance abuse problems, behavioral treatment for deviant preferences, and aftercare. Random assignment to treatment was done from a larger pool of volunteers, and a second comparison group was formed by matching treatment refusers to treated participants. Offenders who dropped out of treatment were also recorded and followed. Attrition was high, and participants who failed to complete treatment after beginning were especially likely to have a subsequent sexual or violent arrest (Marques et al., 1994). When participants assigned to treatment were compared with the untreated volunteers, there were no significant positive effects of treatment.

It is unfortunate that no methodologically adequate study of adult sex offenders has obtained large or even moderate positive treatment effects. We believe, like earlier reviewers of sex offender treatment (Furby, Weinrott, & Blackshaw, 1989; Quinsey et al., 1993), that the effectiveness of adult sex offender treatment has yet to be demonstrated. Furthermore, findings showing that therapists' judgments about clinical progress are unrelated (or even positively related) to recidivism (Quinsey, Khanna, et al., 1998; Seto & Barbaree, 1999) raise more doubts about the value of current treatments.

Our views about the effectiveness of treatment are at odds with those of an influential recent meta-analysis of psychological treatment for sex offenders sponsored by the Association for the Treatment of Sexual Abusers (Hanson et al., 2002). That study reported that random assignment studies showed a zero effect, but "incidental assignment" indicated that treatment was associated with lower recidivism. Incidental assignment studies were those in which there was "no obvious reason to expect pre-treatment [treatment vs. comparison] group differences" (p. 172). In our view, however, inspection of the original studies reveals several obvious reasons. Most commonly, the treated group included those who completed treatment, whereas the comparison group was not offered treatment (e.g., Bakker, Hudson, Wales, & Riley, 1999; Looman et al., 2000; I. Martin, 1998; Nicholaichuk, Gordon, Gu, & Wong, 2000; Proctor, 1996); that is, the comparison group included an unknown number of men who would have refused or dropped out of treatment had it been offered. In addition, there were other obvious reasons to expect pretreatment group differences. These included a longer follow-up period for the comparison group (Procter, 1996), exclusion of offenders from the treatment but not the comparison group (Allam, 1998; Worling & Curwen, 2000), disproportionately high-risk offenders (i.e., exhibitionists) in the comparison group (Lindsay & Smith, 1998), disproportionately low-risk offenders (i.e., incestuous child molesters) in the treated group (R. J. McGrath, Hoke, & Vojtisek, 1998), or allowing comparison group offenders to choose relatively undemanding counseling instead of specialized sex offender treatment (Guarino-Ghezzi & Kimball, 1998; Marshall, Eccles, & Barbaree, 1991; R. J. McGrath et al., 1998).

R. K. Hanson et al. (2002) concluded "that the balance of available evidence suggests that current treatments reduce recidivism, but that firm conclusions await more and better research" (p. 186). We, on the other hand, conclude that the balance of available evidence suggests that current treatments *do not* reduce recidivism, but that firm conclusions await more and better research. Moreover, the research literature is of almost no help in giving clues as to what treatment might be effective with what kinds of sex offenders. The preferred or recommended treatment continues to change (e.g., Hall, Shondrick, & Hirschman, 1993a; Hollin & Howells, 1991; Marshall, 1993, 2001), but the changes are not based on an empirical foundation of demonstrably effective treatment. Without an empirically supported theory of why men commit sexual offenses, development of effective treatment programs is severely hampered.

CONCLUSION

Because evidence of treatment efficacy is so weak, careful risk appraisal must be a cornerstone of the management of sex offenders (Quinsey, Harris, et al., 1998). Because there is scant evidence that a high-risk rapist can be turned into a low-risk offender by participation in any current treatment, the best advice is to use treatments that (a) fit with what is known about rapists specifically and about offenders and sex offenders more generally, (b) have been shown to produce pre- and posttreatment changes in empirically relevant measures, (c) are acceptable to offenders and ethically supportable, (d) are carefully described so that program integrity can be evaluated, and (e) can be incorporated into ongoing supervision programs. Community supervision programs (and empirically based ways to deny access to the community) are especially important given the current lack of knowledge about effective treatments.

In the next chapter we make some suggestions about clinical treatment for rapists implied by our review of the individual differences associated with rape and by our hypotheses about the three pathways to the development and expression of antisociality and mating effort that we believe underlie most rapes in peacetime society. We conclude this chapter with a brief discussion of clinical assessment of rapists.

There are several somewhat independent goals of clinical assessment for rapists: appraising risk of recidivism, classifying rapists into subtypes, identifying criminogenic treatment targets, monitoring clinical progress, and assessing compliance with the conditions of supervision. The basis for most of these goals is the same—an accurate account of the rapist's life up to that point. Such a biography, called a *psychosocial history* in clinical and medical circles, needs to cover certain details to ascertain which path a rapist has followed. We have provided comprehensive instructions for compiling a psychosocial history elsewhere (Quinsey, Harris, et al., 1998). Briefly, a psychosocial history needs to list an offender's adult criminal history (what charges and convictions for which behaviors with which consequences), academic achievement (intellectual abilities, record of repeated grades, suspensions and expulsions, highest level achieved), vocational adjustment (employment record, levels achieved, frequency of job changes, whether fired and for what, financial problems), interpersonal functioning (number and quality of relationships, friends, preferred activities, substance abuse problems), and sexual history (age at puberty, age at first sexual intercourse, number of sexual partners, history of coercive sex). Significant biomedical data are also relevant (neurological difficulties, learning disabilities, other medical conditions including perinatal and obstetrical problems). Perhaps the most important category pertains to antisociality evident in the offender's childhood and family (frequency and severity of preschool aggression, antisocial and aggressive conduct in elementary and high school, criminal charges and convictions as a juvenile, conduct disorder diagnosis criteria, criminal conduct by parents, childhood abuse, childhood neglect or other extreme deprivation). Sufficient accurate information about the offender's life history would permit the scoring of the 20-item Psychopathy Checklist—Revised (PCL–R; Hare, 1991), the best available measure of the probability that an offender is a member of the psychopathy group.

Rapists with evidence of life-course-persistent antisociality but low or average scores on the PCL–R would be expected to exhibit neurodevelopmental difficulties; to come from socially disadvantaged backgrounds; and to show low levels of academic, vocational, and interpersonal skills. These characteristics would correspond to competitively disadvantaged rapists. Young rapists with concurrent nonsexual antisocial conduct but no evidence of early childhood aggression and antisociality can be thought of as adolescence-limited offenders or as displaying the young male syndrome. Further information would be required to determine that a rapist was a sexual sadist. Recognizing that sexual sadism could theoretically occur in any of these types, one can assume that the critical test concerns the degree to which the rapist has committed gratuitous violence and acts designed to humiliate others, especially victims of rape. As well, a clear preference for nonsexual violence and brutal rape stimuli in fantasy material and in phallometric assessment might suggest sexual sadism.

Assessing the risk of violent or sexual recidivism is based on the same accurate life history material as would be used for classification, except the clinician is not constrained by the use of informal guidelines as implied by the previous paragraph. That is, the empirically derived risk assessments available (like the VRAG and SORAG) are based entirely on biographical material. It is crucial, however, that this documentation of the offender's life history be biographical, not autobiographical. An offender might forget or minimize the most serious and important aspects of his past. Thus, as we have described in detail elsewhere (Quinsey, Harris, et al., 1998), for purposes of classification into subtype, assessment of risk, and identification of criminogenic needs, an offender's history must include data obtained from intimates, family members, schools, social service agencies, police, probation and parole officials, correctional facilities, and other institutions, as well as phallometric assessment.

In chapter 9, we review our proposed explanation for individual differences underlying rape, describe interventions we think are implied by the explanation, and suggest avenues for fruitful new research.

9

SYNTHESIS AND IMPLICATIONS
FOR TREATMENT

The field of sex offender research and clinical practice shows little *consilience*—a term used by E. O. Wilson (1998) to describe the linking of facts and theories across disciplines to form a "unity of knowledge." Many other fields in the social sciences experience lack of consilience, but this field has been particularly affected. The research reviewed in chapters 2 to 8 has been informed by mostly separate intellectual traditions, with little cross-fertilization. In this book we attempted to integrate findings and concepts from different fields to enrich an understanding of why some men rape and especially to uncover new ideas and hypotheses that could lead to novel and fruitful theoretical developments. It is clear that much remains to be learned, but we hope that this book provides useful starting points.

There are some facts about sexual coercion that must be accounted for by any theory of rape. First, rape is not a new phenomenon. It is likely that men have committed rape in most, if not all, societies at some time in their histories. Second, forced sex is not unique to the human species. Behaviors similar to rape have been observed in many species across the animal world and appear to form part of one of many conditional male reproductive strategies. Third, men who rape are generally antisocial. They often engage in other delinquent behaviors, show general antisocial tendencies, and rarely specialize in rape. Fourth, men who rape tend to engage in high mating effort, a precocious and short-term approach to heterosexual relationships with little emotional involvement; rapists are typically not deprived of mating opportunities. Fifth, a significant proportion of rapists show strong relative sexual arousal in the laboratory to sexually violent material involving an unwilling female victim. This pattern of arousal is rarely observed among other men, even among other delinquent or assaultive men; relative sexual arousal to rape is the only characteristic that reliably distinguishes rapists from other types of offenders, at least so far. Sixth, men who rape do not appear to have experienced gross neurological problems or any of the major psychopathologies. Finally, rape and other forms of sexual coercion differentially involve particular targets (young unmarried women) and are more likely in certain situations, such as when the costs are low (e.g., war or little likelihood of being reported), when the costs are discounted by hostile attributions or alcohol, or when coercion is supported by peers. These findings are generalizations based on group differences and variable correlations, and thus do not apply to all rapists or all cases of rape.

The studies we reviewed in chapter 4 strongly suggest that rape is part of a general antisocial, aggressive, and risk-tolerant lifestyle and that very few rapists specialize in rape. It is clear that to understand rape, one has to understand antisocial propensities more generally. The only reliably observed difference between rapists and other criminal offenders is sexual arousal to sexually violent material (rapists also appear to abuse alcohol more than other offenders, but this finding is based on a small number of studies using offender reports). What this unique pattern of sexual arousal represents is unclear but is likely to be important in understanding motivations underlying rape. We suggest that there are three general courses underlying the development and expression of antisocial tendencies, including the use of sexually coercive tactics. These three courses likely account for much of sexually coercive behavior.

The first and most common course involves the initiation and termination of antisocial activities during adolescence and early adulthood. Young men are particularly likely to engage in risky and often delinquent activities, likely as a result of increased competition for things that were statistically associated with reproductive success during human evolution. The acquisition of resources, status, and mateship brings desistence and a switch from high mating effort to high parenting effort (or at least a reduction in the ratio of mating to parenting effort). The characteristics of risk taking, mating effort, and willingness to engage in antisocial activities are all associated with the use of sexually coercive tactics among self-identified and adjudicated rapists. If this view is correct, rape, for these men, may be part of a conditional social strategy cued by increased competition during late adolescence and early adulthood.

The second course applies to a small group of men who have experienced neurodevelopmental and social adversity, putting them at a disadvantage in social competition. Antisocial tactics (e.g., fighting to achieve dominance) are used as alternatives to more prosocial tactics of competition (e.g., doing well in school). Aggressive and antisocial tendencies begin early and desistence is rare; high mating effort is rarely replaced by high parenting effort. Our review of psychopathology among rapists in chapter 6 suggests that this group accounts for a very small number of rapists, but research using more subtle neuropsychological measures has rarely been done. If this view is correct, rape for these men may be part of a conditional social strategy cued by low embodied capital.[1]

The third course involves a small group of men who begin their antisocial and aggressive lifestyle early and persist throughout their life span. These psychopathic men have not, as far as we can tell, experienced neurodevelopmental problems, and social adversity, based on the few studies available, does not appear to modulate their behavior. Psychopathy is characterized by high mating effort and extremely antisocial features. It is possible that psychopathy represents an alternative strategy of social defection that was reproductively viable in ancestral environments.

This three-pathway model of antisociality and rape leads in turn to certain expectations about the sexual interest of rapists. Traditionally, arousal to rape cues in phallometric assessment has been seen as a manifestation of sadistic, pathological sexual interests. There is, in fact, very little empirical evidence for this view. In chapter 5 we proposed that relative arousal to rape cues might be a manifestation of antisociality, which leads to the hypothesis that arousal to rape should be observed more among younger than older men in the general population. By the same account, arousal to rape should not show a decline with age among persistently antisocial individuals. Also, arousal to rape should be associated with measures of psychopathy and with measures of competitive disadvantage among nonpsychopathic offenders. Future studies on the phallometric assessment of rapists could distinguish between the three main groups of antisocial men to test those predictions.

This model proposes that nonspousal rape is part of one of three different social and reproductive strategies and thus suggests that rape had positive reproductive consequences during human evolution.[2] The issue is not whether rape was evolutionarily adaptive, but whether the decision rules underlying

---

[1]In addition to this facultative response to low embodied capital, it is possible that some sexual coercion is directly due to brain injury; damage to specific brain centers that normally modulate behavior causes uninhibited, impulsive conduct, including sexual aggression. In addition to traumatic injury, it is also possible that chronic exposure to alcohol, other intoxicants, and toxic agents could cause such brain damage. Although we suspect this is rare, there is little good neurological research on this topic. This hypothetical neurodevelopmental cause (an unspecified collection of causes, actually) does not imply the facultative adoption of a short-term life strategy, however.

[2]We also discussed the fact that some men engage in spousal rape as a response to cues of infidelity. Some data suggest that this is a tactic disproportionately used by generally antisocial men.

the use of aggressive tactics to obtain sex under certain conditions conferred reproductive advantages in the ancestral environment compared with other decision rules, such as those leading to always or never using coercive tactics. We saw in chapter 3 that there was much evidence that forced copulation had reproductive consequences in many species. The indirect evidence for humans is so far consistent with the notion that rape may have had positive reproductive consequences and thus may be part of one or more reproductive strategies among male humans. Rape victims tend to be of fertile age (see chap. 8),[3] many rapes involve penile–vaginal penetration (e.g., Grossin et al., 2003), rape victims often have semen in their genital tract (Evrard & Gold, 1979; Grossin et al., 2003; Groth & Burgess, 1977; Tintinalli & Hoelzer, 1985), and the pregnancy rate among rape victims is similar to the pregnancy rate for consensual sex and may even be higher (Gottschall & Gottshall, 2003; also reviewed in Heise, 1994; Koss, Woodruff, & Koss, 1991).[4] The pregnancy rate of rape victims can be viewed as especially high when one considers that women engage in fewer activities that present a risk for rape when ovulating (Bröder & Hohmann, 2003; Chavanne & Gallup, 1998). These findings do not prove that sexual coercion is part of male reproductive strategies, but they do suggest the possibility.

None of the findings reviewed in this book, in fact, demand that any male humans have a psyche specifically and uniquely adapted for coercive sex. All are compatible with the view that rape could be a by-product of men's strong motivation for having sex with reproductively competent partners (Palmer, 1991). As we noted earlier, Thornhill and Palmer (2000) listed psychological mechanisms that would constitute a rape-specific adaptation in men: mechanisms involved in evaluating potential victim vulnerability, motivating men to rape under specific conditions (e.g., lack of resources or access to female partners); differential evaluations of the sexual attractiveness of rape victims and consensual partners; differential sperm counts of ejaculates produced by interactions with rape victims and consensual partners in conditions of sperm competition; and differential arousal caused by depictions of rape and consensual copulations.

There is little evidence for or against the existence of any of these mechanisms except the last, and it is clear that nonrapists (most of whom have not been antisocial in any way) prefer depictions of consenting sex to those of rape. However, this same research reveals large individual differences among men in their relative sexual interest in rape. These differences could be explained by a facultative adaptation (e.g., in response to competitive disad-

[3]In a study of rape victims who were already pregnant at the time of the event, most were at the beginning of their pregnancies (Satin, Hemsell, Stone, Theriot, & Wendel, 1991).
[4]In a survey of 445 teenage mothers, 23% became pregnant by someone who had once sexually assaulted them (Gershenson et al., 1989). Holmes, Resnick, Kilpatrick, and Best (1996) estimated that there were about 32,000 rape-related pregnancies in the United States in the early 1990s.

vantage), some sort of pathology (e.g., a brain tumor or neurodevelopmental anomaly), or as a by-product of something else (such as antisociality).

As we have discussed in this volume, the evidence supports a link between rape and both mating effort and antisociality. Mating effort and antisociality are themselves closely linked. These characteristics may cause rape because they induce striving for sexual encounters and disregard for female preferences. However, these characteristics are not expected to lead to brutal sexual assaults and sexual murders. Rapists with strongly sadistic interests may have an exaggeration of what could be considered the male dominance component of courtship. The fraternal birth order effect observed among rapists and the relation of birth order to phallometrically measured arousal to violence suggests that this component is altered during early neurodevelopment.

Thus, the majority of rapists appear to be men engaging in high mating effort who disregard female interests because of a variety of personal characteristics, such as general antisociality, tendency to overestimate the interest of potential partners, misogynist attitudes, or particular circumstances such as opportunity mixed with alcohol. We regard most of the male variability in rape proclivity as resulting from nonpathological variation in mating effort and antisociality.

In contrast, we suspect that serial rapists are likely to be differentially sexually interested in coercive and sadistic activities and to be antisocial in orientation (if they were prosocial, they would seek consensual sadomasochistic relationships). Of course, it can be assumed that some highly antisocial men with sadistic or exaggeratedly dominant sexual interests are fortuitously apprehended following their first or second rape. Differences between these two groups of rapists are further obscured by cases in which antisocial men with normative sexual activity preferences physically injure their victims to subdue them, to intimidate them from reporting the crime, or to eliminate them as witnesses.

Returning to the issue of pathology, men who sexually prefer injuring their sexual partners would be considered to have a pathology in the sense of Wakefield's (1992, 1999) definition. It is likely that a sense of sexual agency, a striving for sexual relationships, and dominance-related behaviors facilitated male reproductive success in ancestral environments. These aspects of normal male sexual behavior, however, can be tuned too high, leading to pathological reproductive outcomes. An analogy can be drawn with another aspect of the male reproductive psychology, mate guarding. Mate guarding is likely the expression of a psychological adaptation that is designed to increase paternity certainty and of which sexual jealousy is the proximal motivator. For most men, this adaptation functions without serious consequences. However, in some men extreme jealousy can lead to the murder of their wives.

Obviously, much work remains to be done to understand how the major individual factors lead to rape. We have offered several possibilities in this book that we hope will stimulate research. We now turn to practical implications of the understanding detailed in this book for interventions. Because individual differences in male propensity to rape seem important, it makes sense to consider individual-based assessment and treatment approaches.

TREATMENT OF RAPISTS

If there is one thing that is clear from the previous chapter's summary of the empirical literature on the treatment of sex offenders, it is that there is no clarity about whether anyone has demonstrated a specific effect of treatment in lowering sexual offender recidivism. The situation is even worse with respect to rapists in particular. There is simply no convincing evidence that treatment has ever caused rapists to desist or even to reduce their offending behavior. It is fair to say that the available literature does not clearly identify treatments that seem promising for rapists. Of course, this paucity of evidence does not mean that one can be sure that existing treatments are worthless. There are two main possibilities: Treatment effects exist but simply have not yet been demonstrated, or no treatment effects exist. The obvious solution to the first possibility is to perform better outcome evaluation research. The obvious solution to the second is to develop effective treatments based, presumably, on a better understanding of the phenomenon of rape.

We have dealt at length with the first possibility elsewhere (Quinsey, Harris, Rice, & Lalumière, 1993; M. E. Rice & Harris, 2003), and we summarized our criteria for informative evaluation research in the previous chapter. What about the second possibility, that no treatment effects exist? In fact, the two possibilities blend somewhat. It is possible, for example, that treatment effects exist, but only for some subgroups of rapists, so that effects are almost impossible to detect when rapists (or, even worse, men who are both rapists and child molesters or exhibitionists) are treated as a homogeneous group. The following subsections briefly review our account of the various pathways to rape and suggest interventions implied by each. Along the way, we will also again make reference to the principles of effective service. That is, correctional treatment is most effective when the intensity of service varies with risk, when services target criminogenic needs (personal characteristics empirically related to rape, in this case), and when treatment is organized in a skills training, psychoeducational approach. What, then, are the interventions implied by the three pathway model of rape we hypothesize? We focus here on interventions for men who have already come to official attention (usually by being convicted of rape or sexual assault).

The Young Male Syndrome

In late adolescence and early adulthood, men are exposed to the most intense competition. At this age, young men are maximally attracted to risky activities and are most likely to engage in antisocial behavior and high mating effort. Rape is sometimes the result of this adolescence-limited antisociality. Indeed, adolescent rapists exhibit high rates of criminal conduct (Hagan & Gust-Brey, 1999; Seto & Lalumière, in press) even if most of this conduct appears not to involve sexual aggression. The rape behavior of adolescence-limited rapists is expected to be impulsive, instrumental, and exploitative.

For these men the risk of rape abates with age. Thus, the goal of intervention might best be seen as promoting earlier desistance—getting the client to abandon antisocial, high-mating-effort, young male tactics in favor of prosocial, high-parental-investment tactics characteristic of most older men. How might this be accomplished?

One of the best predictors of criminal conduct is the association with antisocial peers. Given that competition with peers is a driving force behind the young male syndrome, it makes sense that peer influences are especially important for rapists in the adolescence-limited category. Thus, interventions aimed at breaking up and promoting avoidance of antisocial peer groups are indicated (e.g., Borduin & Henggeler, 1990). Encouraging rapists to form all-male cohesive social groups with other young men high in mating effort and aggression (as might occur in unstructured therapeutic communities, correctional institutions, boot camps, some military organizations, some fraternities, and so on) could be expected to increase the risk of further rapes. As well, any peer group in which women are regarded as of low value or hostile to male interests could be expected to increase the likelihood that young male rapists will persist in rape. Vicarious involvement with peers, such as playing video games that involve rewards for aggression toward women, or exposure to peer models perpetrating sexual aggression against women in different media might also be expected to increase the likelihood of rape.

There has also been some evidence that breaking down antisocial values and beliefs that support and excuse law breaking can reduce criminal conduct in young offenders. This attitude change is achieved not by preaching and scolding, but rather by modeling of appropriate, prosocial attitudes by group leaders. Thus, it makes good sense to expose adolescence-limited rapists to slightly older men who exhibit competitive success and who adhere to investment in longer term tactics and espouse and enact the attitudes and values consistent with such tactics (e.g., ambition, conscientiousness, emotional stability, valuing of education and intellectual curiosity, desire for long-term monogamous relationships). In this regard, the multisystemic approach to treating young offenders has obvious application to helping adolescence-limited rapists to desist. Similarly, other psychoeducational approaches, especially if they are presented by prosocial adult male models, might be expected to have positive effects (O'Donahue, Yeater, & Fanetti, 2003). As we discuss next, however, such a therapeutic approach might not be expected to have much impact on the sexual aggression of other types of rapist.

Competitive Disadvantage

We hypothesize that another cause of rape is a facultative (or conditioned) antisocial response to low embodied capital. Thus, men who experience neurodevelopmental problems (perhaps evidenced by obstetrical complications, brain damage, learning disabilities, low IQ, or poor academic achievement) or experience poor social conditions (perhaps evidenced by abuse, lack of parental investment, criminal parents, or extreme neighborhood conditions) receive information early in life (unconsciously) that they will not easily acquire resources and mating success by conventional means. This information can act as a cue to such men to use shorter-term, more antisocial tactics throughout (a probably short) life. By this account, rape is a facultative consequence to the discovery (usually early in life) that one will otherwise experience competitive disadvantage.

The obvious intervention is to boost the offender's embodied capital to increase the likelihood of a facultative switch back to the preferred tactics associated with a long-term, prosocial lifestyle. Again, the obvious targets are the conventional routes to success—academic abilities, vocational skills, and interpersonal social skills. There is a long tradition of providing such training to offenders of all types, and it makes sense to try to improve the lot of rapists with low embodied capital. However, such advice cannot be given with absolute confidence. First, not all deficits can be directly remedied. The value of education and training are obvious, but no one knows how to remedy low intellectual ability directly. The cognitive deficits associated with many neurological deficits[5] can be ameliorated with careful training, even though the neurological damage itself might not be reparable. Social skills training can help improve interpersonal functioning, but it is probably impossible to alter the physical manifestations of many aspects of low embodied capital (e.g., high bilateral asymmetry, morphological anomalies, lesser attractiveness) that interfere with social success and especially mutually consenting heterosocial contact. The implications for prevention, in particular increasing prenatal and postnatal health as well as parental care and family stability, are more obvious.

---

[5]Although good neurological research on the question has not yet been done, we suggested earlier that neurological damage might cause rape in rare instances where regulatory brain mechanisms malfunction leading to uninhibited, aggressive, and even sexually aggressive behavior. In addition to the therapeutic ideas mentioned in this section, more straightforward behavioral treatments (e.g., Ducharme, 2000; Fluharty & Glassman, 2001) are probably indicated in such cases. We also recognize that sadism or sexual hyperdominance might be paraphilias that underlie some rape. As such, these conditions may represent the operation of more subtle neurodevelopmental perturbations for which other behavioral treatments, discussed later in this chapter, are also indicated.

Thus, it is to be expected that the efforts made need to be intensive and long term. In addition, the goal of treatment is to trigger a facultative switch in behaviors that presumably will occur only after the client "discovers" that the investments in training and education have actually resulted in improved social (including mating) success. Again, change can be expected to occur slowly. Of course, no one knows how much evidence is required to engage this hypothetical switch in life tactics, but if the original selection of tactics is associated with a critical period of development (developmentally fixed conditional strategy), it might be expected that much more effort would be required to achieve the switch in tactics later in life.

As a final caveat, this group of rapists does not exist in a vacuum. Such men may commit sexual aggression as a result of an implicit comparison between themselves and others. Thus, enhancing the embodied capital of one such rapist might get him to desist, but at the cost of reducing the relative competitive status of someone else, who might then have to switch to shorter term, antisocial tactics. Of course, this might not be very likely if the selection of tactics naturally occurs only at very young ages. And we certainly do not mean to argue against intervening with such rapists, but we recognize the possibility that treatment effects might be attenuated at the societal level by the zero-sum nature of competition. This said, a reduction in the total variance in embodied capital might reduce perceptions of competitive disadvantage.

Psychopathy

As we described in chapter 4, a small proportion of offenders (less, and perhaps much less, than 5% of the male population) are responsible for many serious violent crimes, including rape. The rapes committed by members of this group are the most predatory and most likely to involve strangers. There is little doubt that these rapists constitute the most dangerous men. Like the previous group, these are life-course-persistent offenders. Unlike the previous group, their behavior is probably not triggered by cues of low embodied capital. We proposed the hypothesis that psychopathy is an alternative and obligate strategy (in the language of chap. 3, a *morph*) characterized by aggression throughout the life span, dishonesty, extreme selfishness, high mating effort, callousness, and interpersonal exploitation. Such individuals form a qualitatively distinct group of offenders with much more violence in their histories and much greater risk of violent recidivism even than other violent offenders.

Research has shown that such individuals, although probably neurologically different from other offenders, exhibit no evidence of neurological lesions or defects. Our studies have shown that the medical histories, physical characteristics, reproductive success, and offense patterns of such individuals are all consistent with a reproductively viable life strategy. That is, though very different from other offenders, members of this group exhibit no biomedical evidence of pathology and appear to be operating as designed by natural selection.

The idea that this distinct group of offenders is qualitatively different helps explain the way they seem to respond to therapy. For this distinct class of offenders, intensive long-term psychotherapy (associated with marginal reductions in violence among other offenders) is associated with increased risk of violent recidivism compared with prison. Educational, vocational, and social skills training appear to increase their likelihood of committing subsequent crimes (Hare, Clark, Grann, & Thornton, 2000). Perceived progress in therapy has also been shown to be associated with increased risk of violent recidivism among psychopaths who are also sex offenders (Seto & Barbaree, 1999). So far, no one has been able to show any positive effects of treatment for psychopathic offenders, and most of the interventions implied for the previous two groups of rapists are contraindicated for these. The danger associated with providing inappropriate treatment for this group again points to the crucial importance of assessment.

What interventions are implied by our understanding of this group of rapists? We do not expect that such rapists can be induced to make a facultative switch to a longer-term, prosocial life strategy with currently available interventions. This does not mean, however, that the behavior of psychopaths is any less influenced by the social environment than that of other people. Thus, we expect that the well-understood principles of learning still apply. There is no reason to believe that such individuals are unaffected by reinforcement contingencies, for example, even if the relative potency of reinforcers might be different from that found among other people. This implies that tightly controlled contingency management coupled with careful measurement of behaviors makes sense both for institutional regimens and the community supervision of psychopathic rapists. The most obvious necessity is that behavioral measurement not rely on offender self-report. As well, such individuals are impulsive and relatively insensitive to punishment; community supervision cannot much rely on fear of aversive consequences. Long-term, intensive supervision may be required for this group of rapist. Because rapists of this type are so dangerous, we also regard long custodial sentences and preventative detention as appropriate if they can be arranged. Actuarial methods of risk assessment (discussed in chap. 8) can be useful in making the case that such incapacitation is warranted.

Are There Other Groups?

The three paths to sexual aggression covered by the previous sections subsume, in our view, the most important causes of rape in humans. However, there may be some other individual sources of rape. First, it is possible that some rapes are committed by men after adolescence who are not psychopaths and not competitively disadvantaged. Such men might engage in high mating effort and short-term mating tactics even though they have been generally successful in life's long-term endeavors. For example, there are media reports of very successful (and powerful) sports figures, businessmen, and politicians (even world leaders in these domains) who engage in remarkably high mating effort and some amount of sexual coercion. Such men do seem to be somewhat prone to risk taking and a casual approach to the truth, but they are not otherwise antisocial. It is unclear how much rape can be attributed to such men, who might be called the *competitively overadvantaged*. The most obvious intervention (in addition to other criminal justice sanctions) for such individuals is public exposure of their conduct and other consequences affecting their social status to lessen their competitive advantage and force a switch back to expected longer-term mating tactics.

As discussed earlier, some men rape their own wives. We expect that marital rape is commonly used by antisocial men (from either of the three paths) when they suspect or fear cuckholdry. However, it seems that some men who are not otherwise antisocial commit rape against their wives. Perhaps this is attributable to our more general observation, based on the historic and ethnographic record, that rape is relatively likely when the reproductive interests of women are devalued and when perceived costs are low. If so, we would expect that helping women expose such behavior, by providing assistance and resources to the victims of marital rape, and ensuring that the criminal justice system treats marital rape as a crime would deter nonantisocial marital rapists. That is, we expect that marital rape would be lessened by increasing the formal (criminal justice sanctions) and informal (condemnation and retaliation from victims' friends and relatives) costs and by increasing the societal value of women's reproductive interests. We do not necessarily expect much effect of such interventions on the sexual coercion engaged in by life-course-persistent antisocial men. Interventions to reduce or manage jealous responses might be beneficial for most spousal rapists.

Phallometric studies of rapists show that some might actually prefer (i.e., exhibit maximal erectile responses to) stimuli depicting rape, and some show large responses even to descriptions of nonsexual beatings of women. Furthermore, such responses are somewhat correlated with the amount of injury caused to rapists' victims in some studies. Of course, the possession of a sexual preference does not necessarily imply that it is acted upon. Thus, it seems clear that some amount of antisociality is necessary for rape and other sex crimes to occur, sexual preferences notwithstanding. Such sexual interests, at least among those apprehended for rape, qualify as criminogenic needs. Behavioral techniques to help such clients gain control of their sexual arousal make sense. We suggest that such techniques do not alter the preferences; rather, they permit conscious control of sexual arousal, which, one hopes, can be used to help manage ongoing risk. Although we would certainly want to see such an approach to treatment very carefully monitored and evaluated, we wonder whether a harm reduction approach to the treatment of nonantisocial rapists who exhibit such preferences might be successful. This approach would include giving rapists "permission" to fantasize about rape without feeling guilty but also reinforcing the distinction between fantasy and reality and emphasizing the negative consequences of acting on such fantasies. Obviously, such treatment is not expected to alter the risk of those rapists whose sexual coercion is an aspect of antisociality. We continue our discussion of subgroups of rapists in Exhibit 9.1.

ARE THERE TREATMENTS RECOMMENDED FOR ALL RAPISTS?

Discussion of behavioral therapies for deviant sexual interests to equip sex offenders with self-management skills leads to consideration of the most popular form of psychological treatment for sex offenders—relapse prevention. Relapse prevention has primarily been applied to sex offender treatment as a cognitive–behavioral means to organize therapy. In the case of rape, the goal of therapy is the teaching of self-management skills to help rapists interrupt the chain of events that lead to reoffending. Relapse prevention was first applied to addictions but seems to have application to other apparently compulsive behaviors because of the parallels of immediate gratification and delayed costs and negative emotional states as precursors of undesirable conduct (Marques & Nelson, 1992).

According to this approach, the goal of therapy is to identify the individual steps that lead to rape and to develop and practice skills to cope with individual risk factors that would otherwise lead to rape. Obvious possible individual risk factors include substance abuse, use of pornography, deviant sexual interests and fantasies, views of women only as sex objects, antagonistic attitudes toward women, boredom and dysphoria, prowling and cruising for sexual opportunities, and committing other criminal and sexual offenses (e.g., burglary, voyeurism). In general, behavioral and psychoeducational methods are used to teach coping skills with the idea that effective self-management is achieved to the extent that a sex offender intervenes early in his own "relapse chain." It seems to us that relapse prevention could be a useful way to organize interventions for some rapists, especially when the self-control skills are aimed at individual factors empirically related to rape *and* related in the individual case. This approach might have greatest application for low embodied capital rapists.

Discussion of sexual arousal patterns also leads to an obvious suggestion—why not castrate rapists? Is it not obvious that the great reduction in circulating testosterone would cause a parallel reduction in all sexual behavior, including sexual aggression, and even greatly reduce aggression in general? This treatment might not even need to be informed by the particular subtype of rapist at hand; perhaps castration could be expected to reduce aggression and sexual aggression regardless of the cause of rape. As discussed at length in chapter 8, there is some evidence from uncontrolled European studies that castration would greatly reduce sexual behavior and sexual aggression. And there is convincing evidence from research with nonhuman animals that sexual behavior is drastically reduced among castrati.

As discussed in detail, however, as a simple solution to rape castration has many drawbacks. It can be several years after surgery before sex drive is eliminated. Many courts would regard its imposition as cruel and unusual punishment, and it would be difficult to demonstrate in a legal forum even that volunteers for castration had not been coerced, at least implicitly. As well, synthetic testosterone is easily available on the illicit market, so that frequent testing would be required to ensure that the beneficial effects of castration were not subverted. As well, it can be assumed that the likelihood of such subversion would be greatest among the most dangerous rapists, psychopaths, who can be expected to be least amenable to all forms of supervision.

The legal and ethical difficulties associated with surgical castration might be lowered with so-called chemical castration, the use of drugs to block the action of androgens in the body. Estrogen and other chemicals have been tried. In general, it appears that such drugs do lower levels of circulating testosterone. Unfortunately, there is no empirical support for the idea that prescribing such drugs has lowered recidivism among rapists. As well, there is no reason to expect that such drugs can alter the direction of sexual interests. Adverse medical and psychological side effects mean that few sex offenders will take such drugs without some degree of coercion, and most men who take antiandrogen drugs will eventually have to stop because these side effects become serious health risks. Finally, the prescription of antiandrogens certainly does not abolish sex offending. In our view, antiandrogen drugs do not represent a long-term solution to the problem of rape. They might have some value as part of a short-term plan (perhaps during transition from institution to community, for example), but they have never received a scientifically useful test. We see value in performing such a test.

What about treatment for alcohol abuse? Research reviewed in chapters 6 and 7 showed that men who engage in sexual coercion often abuse alcohol. Alcohol intoxication for both the perpetrator and the victim (along with the expectations people have about alcohol use) appears to be a facilitating factor. It seems obvious that getting potential perpetrators and victims to drink less would reduce the amount of rape. As we discussed in those chapters, it is not necessarily clear that alcohol causes rape. The people who drink a lot are different in many ways from those who are abstemious, and one of those differences might be a common cause of rape and drinking. Most obvious, psychopaths are well known to abuse alcohol (and other drugs) at higher levels than other offenders. But it is only among other, nonpsychopathic offenders that history of alcohol abuse predicts violent

EXHIBIT 9.1
Subtypes of Rapists and Other Path Models

In this book we present three pathways to the development and expression of antisociality and rape and discuss other possible routes to rape. There have been other attempts to identify natural types of rapists relevant to the next generation of clinical assessment and treatment techniques. Knight and his colleagues have worked on developing and validating a typology that has received some empirical support (Knight, 1999; Knight & Prentky, 1987, 1990). The starting point was clinical observation (M. L. Cohen, Garofalo, Boucher, & Seghorn, 1971). Over the years, the typology has been revised on the basis of its fit with data gathered from rapists primarily at the Massachusetts Treatment Centre. The current version postulates eight types categorized according to four dichotomous variables. Two of these variables are postulated to be dimensional (social competence and "callousness–unemotionality") and the other two to represent truly dichotomous taxa (hypersexuality and impulsivity).

The first two types of rapists, *impulsive rapists* and *predatory rapists,* differ only in social competence and are called opportunistic rapists. For these offenders, rape is but one of many antisocial and predatory acts. Neither of the opportunistic types is hypersexual; they are not motivated by sexual fantasy and show lower phallometric rape indexes (Barbaree, Seto, Serin, Amos, & Preston, 1994; Preston, 1996). In addition, opportunists are said to often be narcissistic. The third type, *pervasively angry rapists,* are of all levels of social competence but are impulsive and not hypersexual. They are high on the dimension of callousness–unemotionality and are also high in expressive aggression and violence. They have relatively high scores on the PCL–R (S. L. Brown & Forth, 1997) and high levels of generalized anger. The fourth type is *sadistic rapists,* who are also of all levels of social competence but are impulsive and hypersexual as well as high on callousness and psychopathy (Barbaree et al., 1994). These offenders produce the highest phallometric rape indexes (Barbaree et al., 1994; Preston, 1996). The next two types (varying in social competence) are *vindictive* rapists, but they are not impulsive. For both, women are the exclusive focus of their anger. These offenders tend to inflict physical injury on their victims (Preston, 1996) and have relatively low PCL–R scores (Preston, 1996). The final two types (again varying in social competence) are non-sadistic sexual rapists postulated to be motivated and preoccupied by sexual fantasies. They are hypersexual but not impulsive or callous.

Much of the early research developing and refining the typology used exclusively archival information to gather data about each case. Later work incorporated data from the self-report Multidimensional Assessment of Sex and Aggression (MASA; Knight, Prentky, & Cerce, 1994), which was designed to assess domains identified in the typology. Initially it had questions about sex drive, fantasies, paraphilias, and pornography and was expanded to assess social competence, sadism, offense planning, anger, expressive aggression, and antisocial behavior. Knight (1999) related aspects of the typology to sex offender treatment targets. Types low in social competence are candidates for interpersonal skills training. Hypersexual types require techniques to manage deviant arousal. Sadistic, pervasively angry, and vindictive rapists are candidates for anger management. Impulsive types are candidates for therapy to reduce impulsivity. Finally, all but the opportunists are candidates for relapse prevention. There are no convincing data that any of these treatments are effective, but the key falsifiable prediction is that treatment will be effective only when delivered prescriptively according to type.

Recently, Knight and colleagues developed and tested a related three-path model of sexual aggression against women (Knight & Sims-Knight, in press-a; Knight & Sims-Knight, in 2003). History of physical or verbal abuse or both plays a central role. In the

continues

first path, abuse combines with callousness and unemotionality to lead to early anti-social behavior and aggression, which later escalate to various forms of trickery, deception, and aggression, including sexually coercive behavior against women. The sexually coercive behavior may be exacerbated by aggressive and sadistic fantasies. In the second path, abuse history leads directly to the development of callous–unemotional traits that, in turn, disinhibit sex drive and lead to hypersexuality. Sexual fantasies eventually include hostility culminating in sexual coercion. The third path leads from abuse to hypersexuality and the disinhibition of sexual drives and sexual fantasies. As in the second path, sexual fantasies eventually include aggression and sadism, culminating in rape.

Knight's types and paths relate somewhat to the hypotheses we presented in this book. There are obvious points of convergence, including the central roles of coercive sexual interests and the personality traits associated with psychopathy (e.g., callousness, narcissism). Also, it is quite possible that competitive disadvantage and low social competence are correlated. Similarly, we have provided some evidence that parental abuse and neglect are associated with psychopathy (Harris et al., 2001). We look forward to formal tests of our hypotheses in conjunction with postulates from other path and typological models (see also Malamuth & Heilmann, 1998).

---

recidivism; among psychopaths, alcohol abuse is not a risk factor for violence (M. E. Rice & Harris, 1995b). Thus, among psychopaths, reducing alcohol use would not be expected to reduce rape frequency. Indeed, a cold sober psychopathic rapist might be more dangerous than a drunken one. In addition, no treatment for alcohol abuse has been shown to reduce recidivism among any adult offenders, let alone rapists. Any form of insight-oriented, psychodynamic, emotionally evocative therapy (for any problem including alcohol abuse) would certainly be strongly contraindicated for psychopaths.

Among nonpsychopathic rapists (and among potential victims), it makes sense to test the hypothesis that alcohol abuse is a cause of rape by delivering interventions to reduce it. It is hard to imagine that reducing alcohol use among risk-taking adolescents, sexual sadists, and rapists of low embodied capital would be harmful. As with the provision of antiandrogen drugs, this hypothesis has not yet received a scientifically useful demonstration, however. We see real value in a scientifically sound evaluation of the effects of substance abuse therapy on the recidivism of rapists and the prevention of first rape.

Many of the ideas presented in this section are based on our account of rape as part of one of three main antisocial strategies adopted by different men. We recommend careful scientific examination of any innovation in the treatment of rapists or the more general prevention of rape. Theories, to the extent that they are empirically supported, should inform interventions, but interventions should be tested on their own merit. Ideally, interventions are designed in such a way as to provide a test of the theory upon which they are based.

FINAL WORD

As scientists we are committed to the view that progress in understanding and dealing with rape requires creativity, intellectual consilience, hypothesis testing, theory-driven interventions, rigorous evaluations of intervention programs that ideally further inform theory development, and modifications of one's views and theories and practices based on new empirical data. Much new research on topics relevant to rape will inform future developments, including the study of romantic relationships and conflicts, sexual preferences, antisocial behavior, ultimate (selective) causes of human violence, behavioral and adaptive flexibility, and so on. In this book we have attempted to integrate disparate literatures relevant to rape to provide a better understanding of why some men rape. The knowledgeable reader will notice that despite the fact that our reference list contains close to 1,000 entries, we have covered only a part of the relevant literatures. Nevertheless, we hope that the ideas presented in this book will stimulate future research and new theoretical developments. The general theory of rape and the best preventive and remediation interventions remain to be discovered, but the intellectual field is ripe for major improvements.

APPENDIX:
FORCED COPULATION

In this appendix we provide further examples of forced copulation in nonhuman species. Our purpose is not merely to impress readers with the sheer number of species in which forced copulation has been observed; these examples provide compelling illustrations of the conditions facilitating forced copulation, along with some interesting exceptions to the generalizations we offer in chapter 3.

INSECTS

In many insect species, males offer females a nuptial gift prior to or during mating. A nuptial gift consists of food and can take different forms: prey, glandular products, or even parts of the male's body. In sagebrush crickets (*Cyphoderris strepitans*), the nuptial gift is the male's hind wings, which females eat during copulation. They also consume the body fluid that flows from the injury. Not surprisingly, females prefer fully winged males. In the laboratory and in the wild, males with intact hind wings are more likely to mate, mate faster, and attain better transfer of the spermatophore (Eggert & Sakaluk, 1994; J. Johnson, Ivy, & Sakaluk, 1999; Sakaluk, Bangert, Eggert, Gack, & Swanson, 1995; Snedden, 1996).

Despite the permanent loss of his wings, a male has much to gain by exchanging them for copulation. Of course, he also has much to lose if he does not achieve sperm transfer. A female has much to gain by obtaining as much food as possible and much to lose if she receives the spermatophore without also getting the nourishment necessary for producing all of her eggs. This situation creates a conflict of interest between the sexes.

A male sagebrush cricket attracts females with sound. Once a female locates him, she mounts him and begins chewing on his wings. The male then uses a double pair of spines, called the *gin trap*, to secure the female. The gin trap prevents the female from leaving before the male completes sperm transfer. If the male's hind wings are already partially depleted, the female may not mount and might seek another male. Although sagebrush cricket females often choose the males with which they mate, they are often unable to terminate copulation once it has begun.

Sakaluk et al. (1995) studied the possibility that the gin trap might have evolved to allow males to better transfer sperm in the absence of full female cooperation. They systematically removed the males' hind wings, gin trap, or both. For males lacking wings, those with intact gin traps were much more likely to achieve sperm transfer than those lacking gin traps. No difference was found among males with intact hind wings. This suggests that the gin trap functions to force sperm transfer on uncooperative females. The researchers were able to discard such alternative functional hypotheses for the gin trap as aligning the genitalia.

Although forced copulation has not been reported in other cricket species, in some other cricket species males guard females after copulation to prevent mating with other males. The use of the gin trap in sagebrush crickets seems to be one of the many tactics male crickets use to circumvent female choice. Many other insect males have genital or other body parts to hold females during copulation. In the firefly *Pteroptyx valida*, the female inserts her terminalia into the male genital pocket and is then "gripped in the jaws of the male's copulatory gland" (Wing, Lloyd, & Hongtrakul, 1983, p. 87). The female's genital structure is even reinforced to accommodate the clamp. The exact role of the clamp in this and many other species of flying and nonflying insects is unclear but may include, as is the case with the sagebrush cricket, the control of females' mating behavior.

Tsubaki and Ono (1986) described the mating behavior of a miniature dragonfly, *Nannophya pygmaea*, commonly found in East Asia. Males fight over egg-laying territories and grab females as they fly by. Females do not choose males but choose territories for egg laying. When there are many males in an area, and when the best territories are already defended, some males adopt a "sneaky" tactic of waiting near a good territory and grabbing females before they encounter the resident male. Sneaky males are not always successful and are often attacked by the resident male. The authors surmised that the sneaky tactic might be at least as successful as the territory-holding tactic when territory availability is poor. Males may adopt both tactics during their lifetimes. Unfortunately, no information on female resistance was reported.

Males of the damselfly *Calopteryx haemorrhoidalis* are quite persistent and aggressive in mating. Cordero (1999) reported that over 50% of copulations were forced in one population of Italian damselfly. Females resisted mating by lowering their heads, opening their wings, and "impeding tandem formation" (p. 31). When a forceful attempt was successful, however, the female stopped struggling. Like many other species, males fight for territories, and females visit successful males who court them. When population density is high, males without territories disrupt courtship and mating. At a very high density, all males abandon territoriality and all attempt mating by force. Again, males adopt tactics (courtship and forced mating) depending on circumstances and guard females after all matings. This example clearly illustrates the conditionality of the use of forced copulation.

The Mediterranean fruit fly *Ceratitis capitata* mates on both leaves and fruit, but mating on fruit—where females deposit their eggs—seems to be forced on females (Prokopy & Hendrichs, 1979). When on leaves, males form small leks and attract females with a pheromone and the sound of their fanning wings. For up to 10 days after mating, females are not attracted to the male pheromone. Females typically fly toward males on leaves but avoid them on fruit. The authors noted that "sperm introduced during second matings of medfly females substantially, though not completely, displaces sperm from 1st matings" (p. 646).

The Coquillett fly (*Culicoides melleus*) reproduces quite soon after reaching adulthood, sometimes 6 minutes after emerging from the pupa. On the basis of extensive laboratory work, Linley and Adams (1972) observed that females show clear signs of mating cooperation when first approached by a male—she lowers her head and lifts her abdomen, which raises her genitalia. Mating takes about 10 seconds, and she remains immobile throughout. After separation a male may grab another female with his very efficient grasping apparatus and guard her until he is ready to transfer a new spermatophore (most males can produce and transfer at least three spermatophores). Although males seem willing to mate with as many females as possible, females resist mating with another male by running away, tipping down their posterior abdomen, or kicking the male with their hind legs. Females continue to resist even after males manage genital contact. These forced copulations usually last longer than other copulations due to female resistance. Not all attempts at forced copulation result in insemination. The Coquillett male "has few equals in his persistence in sexual endeavor, and will repeatedly attempt to copulate with an unreceptive female" (Linley & Adams, 1972, p. 110).

The male African ball-rolling scarab (*Kheper platynotus*) uses one of two mating tactics. The most successful involves pairing up with a female as she is engaged in rolling a ball (used for feeding the brood). Males fight for access to females, and the larger males usually win. Females involved in brood ball making seem to accept any male. The second and less successful tactic involves what Sato and Hiramatsu (1993) called *forced copulation*, in which a male approaches a female in the process of making a food ball (used by the female for food). The female tends "to break free from the male" (no other behavioral description is given) and often prevents copulation. Males engage in both tactics regardless of their size.[1] It appears that males generally seek receptive females but adopt coercive tactics when females are unreceptive.

Other insect examples include the brown planthopper (Oh, 1979), the fruit fly (Manning, 1967), and seed-eating bugs (Kelley McLain & Pratt, 1999).

BIRDS

There have been many studies of forced copulation in birds, and this appendix does not provide anywhere near an exhaustive review. Partial re-

---

[1]Paired-up males may provide assistance to females, but their pairing behavior seems to be all about mate guarding and paternity assurance (Sato & Imamori, 1987), because single females are just as reproductively successful as paired-up females.

views of this literature can be found in Gladstone (1979); Gowaty and Buschhaus (1998); McKinney (1985); McKinney, Cheng, and Bruggers (1984); and McKinney and Evarts (1997).

Snow geese (*Chen caerulescens*) have been well studied. They are communal breeders, assembling in large nesting groups. Males and females perform precopulatory displays and form pair bonds maintained through the breeding season. Long ago researchers noticed that there were many extra-pair copulations usually with little or no precopulatory display and much female resistance.

In an early study, Mineau and Cooke (1979) studied "rape attempts," which they defined as the absence of precopulatory display and two unpaired individuals. Female resistance or escape, though often observed, could not be used as an indicator of forced copulation, because females may not always struggle when protecting a nest. Over two breeding seasons, Mineau and Cooke observed 116 rape attempts. In contrast to pair-bonded copulations, which occured on the water, rape attempts occurred at the nest or elsewhere on the land. During these attempted rapes, treading—the trampling of the female's back to adjust position—occurred for a much longer time, suggesting that the females were not cooperating. In only nine cases, females raised their tails, accepting copulation. Offenders were usually neighbors taking advantage of females whose mates were absent, and offenders were almost always deterred by the mate's return. Removing pair-bonded males dramatically increased rape attempts. The researchers also observed multiple-male rapes and calculated that during one breeding season, "each female was victim of an attempted rape on average every 5 days" (p. 288).

Mineau and Cooke (1979) could not determine the number of forced copulation attempts that led to sperm transfer or the number of offspring that resulted. Using the same population over a longer period, Lank, Mineau, Rockwell, and Cooke (1989) did determine, using plumage color of parents and offspring, that at least 2.4% of offspring were the result of extra-pair copulations. P. O. Dunn, Afton, Gloutney, and Alisauskas (1999) went a step further using DNA fingerprinting. They observed 21 extra-pair copulation attempts in snow geese and 11 in Ross's geese (*Chen rossi*). Again, these extra-pair copulations differed from intra-pair copulations in that they occurred on land (often at the nest of the female) and during the egg-laying or early incubation period. Females appeared to resist and made loud vocalizations, and there were no precopulatory displays. Females stretched their necks to prevent males from grasping with their beaks and sometimes flew away (when not on the nest). Pair-bonded males always attacked offenders; all of the offenders were neighbors.

Half of extra-pair copulation attempts included genital contact, and DNA showed that 5% of offspring in snow geese and 2% in Ross's geese were the result of extra-pair copulations. These values might have been higher but for the fact that females were not always fertile, males forced copulation on their mates after extra-pair copulation, or sperm transfer was not efficient during forced copulation. P. O. Dunn et al. (1999) also observed that synchronicity of breeding seems to reduce extra-pair copulation attempts.

Mineau and Cooke (1979) discussed possible explanations for forced copulation in geese. Attacks on neighboring females might be the by-product of a high male sex drive combined with the fact that females are unreceptive during incubation. This idea, however, cannot explain why males almost always target females other than their own mates. Alternatively, forced copulation might be part of a male strategy of courting and bonding with a female before and during egg laying and then finding another partner. This strategy might be effective because goslings are precocious and require little paternal care. Because geese breed synchronously, males in search of new partners would find that most females are already mated and unwilling to copulate. It is also possible that females could benefit from extra-pair copulation through increased genetic diversity in their offspring, but this cannot explain why females resist. Forced copulation in geese, as in many bird species, seems an opportunistic tactic used by paired males to increase reproductive success.

Forced copulation has also been noted in the lesser black-backed gull (*Larus fuscus*; MacRoberts, 1973), the lesser black-headed gull (*L. ridibundus*; van Rhijn & Groothuis, 1985), the laughing gull (*L. atricilla*; Burger, 1976), the red-billed gull (*L. novaehollandiae scopulinus*; Mills, 1994), and the western gull (*L. occidentalis*; Pierotti, 1981). The general pattern in gulls involves an intruding male, who is often a paired neighbor, hovering over a nesting female and attempting copulation by descending on her, usually when the mate is absent. If the female is already incubating an egg, she remains on the nest and attempts to dislodge the attacker by pecking at his chest. Females successfully rebuff many attempts. Females are quite wary of males other than their own mate: "When approached by a strange male, the female behaviour is, if anything, the antithesis of that seen in normal premounting interactions" (MacRoberts, 1973, p. 72). Unpaired males do not attempt forced copulations, and among paired males, some engage in this behavior much more frequently than others (and some not at all). Pierotti suggested, in an evocative quote, that when ecological conditions are favorable, males can diminish their parental care and thus better "exploit the polygamy potential of their environment" (p. 547).

In many other bird species we see that paired males (rather than bachelors) engage in forced copulation and usually target fertile females. S. T. Emlen and Wrege (1986) studied white-fronted bee-eaters (*Merops bullockoides*) in Kenya. White-fronted bee-eaters are monogamous and colonial and live in extended family groups. They breed fairly synchronously (mostly over a 14-day period). Most nonbreeding individuals provide help at the nest. The female spends much time away from the nest until she is ready to copulate and lay eggs, after which she remains at the nest and is usually fed by her mate. When leaving the nest, either to feed or to dump eggs in other females' nests, the female calls her mate for escort. A female leaving the nest escorted by her mate is rarely subjected to harassment by other males. In contrast, a female leaving the nest alone "literally has to run the gauntlet of the assembled males" (p. 7) and is chased by them: "These chases sometimes end with the female being forced to the ground and mounted by numerous males" (p. 7).

Females defend themselves by pressing their cloaca to the ground and spreading their wings for balance, thereby usually avoiding sperm transfer. Males form a melee and leave sperm on each other and on the female. Not all lone females leaving the nest are equally likely to be harassed and attacked. Males tend to harass females during their most fertile period. Male harassers and attackers are not, as the authors originally expected, nonbreeders. They are the very males that are engaged in protection of their own egg-laying mates. Despite being involved in feeding and protecting their mates, these males find the time to engage in extra-pair forced copulations due to the close proximity of fertile females.

As we saw for ducks and geese, forced copulation can lead to reproduction. C. R. Brown (1978) observed "rape chases" by groups of purple martin males (*Progne subis*). Successful copulation was rarely observed, and paired males actively defended their mates. Morton (1987), in contrast, observed that as many as 30% of forced extra-pair copulations resulted in cloacal contact. Using DNA fingerprinting, Morton, Forman, and Braun (1990) found that male purple martins increased their number of fertilized eggs by as much as 80% through forced extra-pair copulations. In a subsequent study, Wagner, Schug, and Morton (1996) found much higher rates of extra-pair paternity in the clutches of young males (47%) than in the clutches of old males (8%). They suggested that although females resist extra-pair copulation attempts, they might selectively allow sperm transfer based on the characteristics of the aggressors (older and bigger) and of their own mates (younger and smaller). Given the male predilection for forced copulation, perhaps purple martin females get back some reproductive choice through selective resistance.

There are many other examples of female resistance to extra-pair copulation attempts. Björklund and Westman (1983) removed pied flycatcher males (*Ficedula hypoleuca*) for a brief period (45–120 minutes) 1 to 3 days before egg laying. Compared to a control condition, in which males were not removed, females that were left alone were visited by other males much more frequently, mostly by neighbors. Some males announced their presence by singing, whereas others silently approached the females by sneaking through the vegetation. A number of extra-pair copulations were observed, and the females resisted some of these attempts. Sneakers were more successful at achieving copulation than advertisers. Alatalo, Gottlander, and Lundberg (1987) noted that whereas female flycatchers may passively accept, solicit, or resist intra-pair copulation attempts, they never solicit extra-pair sex and are equally likely to passively accept or to resist extra-pair attempts. Both intra- and extra-pair copulations occur during the most fertile period. It is quite possible that males force some if not most extra-pair copulations.

The pied flycatcher and the related collared flycatcher (*Ficedula albicollis*) have a polyterritorial mating system in which some males defend and mate concurrently on two rather distant territories. Males mate polygynously but incur the risk of cuckoldry. Alatalo, Gustafsson, and Lundberg (1984) observed that offspring in both species resemble their mothers more than their fathers. They also resemble neighbor males more than outsiders. It is thus not surprising that about 24% of offspring are not the product of the resident male. Polyterritorial males arrive at the nesting territory earlier than monogamous males and produce more offspring, suggesting that they might be of higher phenotypic quality. Nonmating, nonterritorial males do not seem to solicit or attempt extra-pair copulations. Some mimic females in plumage colors, probably to avoid aggression from territorial males (Slagsvold & Sætre, 1991).

Fujioka and Yamagishi (1981) observed female resistance to extra-pair copulation attempts in the cattle egret (*Bubulcus ibis*). These birds nest synchronously in dense colonies. Neighboring males attempt copulations when females are left alone at the nest. Females may aggressively resist by attacking the males, emit cries to attract the mate (who invariably interferes and chases away the intruder), or passively accept the male. If the male manages to mount the female, she invariably moves her tail away to allow cloacal contact. Females never initiate copulation, and males target only fertile females.

The common murre or guillemot (*Uria aalga*) is a synchronously breeding colonial seabird with a fairly high frequency of extra-pair copulation. Birkhead, Johnson, and Nettleship (1985) categorized extra-pair copulation as forced when "the female attempted to avoid the male" and unforced when "the female apparently 'co-operated' with the male" (p. 609). Forced extra-pair copulations often involved more than one male. Paired males actively defended mates, and females actively resisted. Male absence from the nest almost always resulted in forced extra-pair copulation attempts. Because males tend to stay at the nest while females feed, the sex ratio of the colony increased over the breeding period and was positively related to the frequency of forced extra-pair copulations (the more males relative to females, the higher the frequency). Colony density was also positively related to the frequency of forced extra-pair copulations.

Although male murres suffer from lack of food when they remain at the breeding site, they seem to benefit by engaging in mate guarding and in forced extra-pair copulations with other females. As has been observed in other birds, Birkhead et al. (1985) found that the most successful mate guarders were also the most successful at forced copulation. The converse was observed in Hatchwell's (1988) study, but males who engaged in forced copulations were still more reproductively successful than those who did not.

The little blue heron *(Florida caerulea)* is another colonial nesting bird that engages in forced extra-pair copulation. Werschkul (1982; see also Meanly, 1955; Rodgers, 1980) observed 64 "extramarital copulations" over a period of 3 years. Males were already paired and almost always targeted fertile females from a nearby nest. Females attempted to escape and gave alarm calls. Most copulation attempts were averted, but when males achieved mounting, females stopped resisting, probably to save the eggs. All extra-pair copulations occurred in the absence of the paired male. No unpaired male attempted forced copulation. Some copulation attempts involved more than one male, and the mated male always successfully supplanted the intruders if he returned in time. The extra-pair copulations were approximately 33% shorter in duration than copulations among pairs. Some females were more often involved in these interactions than others.

The male little blue heron, like many so-called monogamous birds, has a strategy of first attracting a female to a nest and then protecting her from other males and predators while attempting to copulate with other females. Males are heavily involved in the rearing of the chicks, which might explain why extra-pair copulation attempts are not as common as in other species with less paternal involvement. Grey herons *(Ardea cinerea)* are very similar. Ramo (1993) observed 39 extra-pair copulation attempts, most of which "appeared to be forced, males seizing the head or neck vigorously, and sometimes removing feathers" (p. 117). Females never solicited extra-pair copulations. Both parties were already paired, and the female was fertile. Risk of forced copulation was directly related to female vulnerability (the length of time the mate was absent).

The female white ibis *(Eudocimus albus)* regularly engages in willing extra-pair copulations. Sometimes, however, a female resists extra-pair copulation by refusing to raise the tail and by lying flat on the ground, preventing cloacal contact. Males are about one-third larger than females. In a study of several white ibis groups, Frederick (1987a, 1987b; see also Kushland, 1973) observed that most extra-pair copulations occurred during the fertile period; one fifth involved male attacks before or during extra-pair copulations; intruders usually attempted to steal nesting material after the copulation; pair-bonded males disrupted the copulation and often chased away intruders; and males attempted extra-pair copulations at the end of their own mates' fertile period. Females who were attacked were less receptive to further copulatory attempts by the same males.

Again, the most successful males (in terms of extra-pair copulations) were also the least likely to be cuckolded. They had superior fighting abilities and were better foragers. Female protest was, however, unrelated to these male characteristics. Unpaired males, again, did not attempt copulations with females. Between-group analyses revealed that nest density, time spent at the nest, and the sex ratio were all negatively related to number of extra-pair copulations. The author speculated that female protest was due not to unwillingness to mate but rather to an effort to stimulate male competition.

Røskaft (1983) observed female resistance in about 75% of extra-pair copulation attempts by male rooks (*Corvus frugilegus*). Older males were more likely to attempt extra-pair copulations, and younger females were more likely to be the recipients (being often paired with younger males). Neighbors engaged in most extra-pair copulations, sometimes in groups and only when the mate was absent. These attempts occurred almost exclusively during the fertile period.

The hihi or stichbird (*Notiomystis cincta*) is a very unique bird. It is a New Zealand honeyeater that engages in a rare behavior among birds: face-to-face copulation. In fact, the wild hihi copulates in one of two ways: male on top, which involves the full cooperation of the female, and face-to-face, which is strongly resisted by females. Face-to-face copulation usually involves one or more males chasing a female, pinning her to the ground, spreading her wings, and making direct cloacal contact. Females resist by kicking and emitting distress calls. After forced copulation, both birds fly away separately without any of the usual postcopulatory display.

The hihi is unusual in other ways—males are 33% larger than females and have very large testes (4% of his body mass; this would be equivalent to an average human male having 6-lb testicles), both sexes have a protruding cloaca, and the mating system is sometimes polygynandrous[2] (Castro, Minot, Fordham, & Birkhead, 1996). In a study of seven pairs, males diminished their parental investment as a function of the frequency of forced extra-pair copulations involving their mates (Ewen & Armstrong, 2000). Many males are unpaired, and many of the unpaired males produce offspring (Ewen, Armstrong, & Lambert, 1999). Forced copulation seems to be the result of intense competition for females, little mate guarding, little male parental investment, and low breeding synchrony.

Other bird species in which forced copulation has been reported include the cape vulture, *Gyps coprotheres* (Robertson, 1986); the house sparrow, *Passer domesticus*, in which males with the largest badges—a signal of social dominance—are the most successful at forced extra-pair copulations (Møller, 1990); the Japanese quail, *Coturnix japonica* (in the laboratory; Adkins-Regan, 1995); the northern oriole, *Icterus galbula* (Edinger, 1988); the canvasback, *Aythya valisineria* (M. G. Anderson, 1985); the indigo bunting, *Passerina cyanea* (Westneat, 1987); the Laysian albatross, *Diomedea immutabilis* (H. I. Fisher, 1971); the red-wing blackbird, *Agelaius phoeniceus*, all involving paired males and all successfully rebuffed by females (E. M. Gray, 1996);

---

[2]Some males mate with multiple females, and some females mate with multiple males.

the anhinga, *Anhinga anhinga* (Burger, Miller, & Hajin, 1978); and the Canada goose, *Branta canadensis* (Whitford, 1993).[3]

FISH

Forced copulations and sneak fertilizations have been well studied in fish. One interesting aspect of these studies is that they have shown that males adopt different mating tactics, including forced and sneak fertilizations, depending on the features of the environment in which they grew up, the features of their current environment, their current physical condition, or a combination of these. These studies have led to some of the most productive conceptual advances in the animal literature with regard to the evolution and the development of individual differences in behavior and morphology within the sexes.

For many fish species of the family *Poeciliidae*—a family comprising guppies and many other popular aquarium fish—looks matter. Larger males establish and defend a territory, are usually brightly colored, court females, and are generally accepted by females. Smaller males have a subordinate status, do not have territories, are not colored, do not court females, and seem to be ignored or avoided by females. Males have an intromittent organ, called a *gonopodium*, and females are fertilized internally and give birth to live offspring. The gonopodium has hooks and grapples that to some extent probably prevent females from cutting the copulation short.

One well-studied species is the guppy (*Poecilia reticulata*). Male guppies either court females by curving and shaking their body or attempt gonopodial thrusting without courtship. The latter tactic has been described as forced copulation. Males use both tactics and vary their use as a function of female receptivity, which is about two days per month. Males often manage to inseminate females through forced copulation (Evans, Pilastro, & Ramnarine, 2003; Matthews & Magurran, 2000; Pilastro & Bisazza, 1999).

The use of different mating tactics in guppies depends on a complex interplay of many different factors. For instance, forced copulation is more often observed and courtship less often observed when females are unreceptive (Braun & Harper, 1993; Dill, Hedrick, & Fraser, 1999; Farr, 1980), when risk of predation to the male is high (Endler, 1987; Godin, 1995; Magurran & Seghers, 1990; Reynolds, Gross, & Coombs, 1993; Rodd & Sokolowski, 1995), and when males are raised in a mostly male environment (Evans &

---

[3]There are very few studies in which researchers looked for forced copulation in birds but did not observe it. Notable exceptions include Creelman and Storey (1991; Atlantic puffins, *Fratercula arctica*); Hunter and Jones (1999; various auklets, *Arthia pusilla*, *A. cristatella*, *A. pygmaea*, *Cyclorrhynchus psittacula*); S. M. Smith (1988; black-capped chickadee, *Parus atrcapillus*); and Venier, Dunn, Lifjeld, and Robertson (1993; tree swallows, *Tachycineta bicolor*). The absence of this important part of the literature is more likely due to a lack of interest in pursuing this research than to a lack of such species.

Magurran, 1999). Evans and Magurran found that male guppies reared in tanks with a male-biased sex ratio used courtship displays less often and single thrusting more often than males reared in a tank with an equal or female-biased sex ratio. Adult males subsequently placed in a tank with a balanced sex ratio did not modify their mating behavior. Thus, males' mating tactics appeared to be conditional but developmentally fixed with regard to this particular environmental cue.

In the gila topminnow (*Poediliopsis occidentalis*), small males dash toward females and attempt "sneak copulations" (Constantz, 1975). In contrast to dominant males, who have prolonged bouts of gonopodial thrusting, small sneaky males sometimes manage to achieve only a single thrust. Interestingly, small males have longer gonopodia than large males. Constantz noted that when dominant males are removed, small males quickly adopt a territorial role, change color, court females, and stop sneaking. In topminnows, then, sneak copulation is condition dependent (and developmentally flexible).

A similar state of affairs occurs in the sailfin molly (*Poecilia latipinna*). Large males have a long dorsal fin, and males with longer fins are more often involved in courtship. Smaller males attempt gonopodial thrusting without courtship. Farr, Travis, and Trexler (1986) studied different populations of sailfin mollies and found that the relative size of the fin (rather than the absolute size) is related to propensity for courtship versus gonopodial thrusting alone. In other words, the behavior of the male varies as a function of the size of its fin relative to that of other males.

In one mosquitofish species (*Gambusia affinis*), the social environment at the time of puberty determines size, and size at maturity determines the mating tactics used (courting vs. forced copulation). Large males are more successful when females are receptive, and small males are more successful at other times (Hughes, 1985). Thus, the mating tactics adopted by males are conditional and developmentally fixed, because large males tend to court even unreceptive females, and small males tend to attempt forced copulation even with receptive females.[4]

Sneak fertilization, or kleptogamy, has been frequently reported among egg laying fish. Sneak fertilization does not meet our definition of forced copulation, because little is known of the female response to sneaking attempts (and there is no copulation per se). Nevertheless, it is interesting to examine sneak fertilization in these species, because it reveals alternative mating tactics adopted by males who are ignored or even avoided by spawning females.

---

[4]In another mosquitofish (*Gambusia holbrooki*), in which females can be successfully inseminated at any time because they can store sperm, females rarely if ever cooperate with males' copulatory attempts—a case of resisted mating (Bisazza, Marconato, & Marin, 1989).

In the leaf fish (*Polycentrus schomburgkii*), for example, a small, subordinate male might sneak into a territory occupied by a spawning couple by pretending to be female—both morphologically and behaviorally—and fertilize some of the eggs (Barlow, 1967). The territorial male may thus end up tending some eggs that he did not fertilize. Males shift between the territorial and the sneaking tactic based on their dominance status. In the pupfish (*Cyprinodon sp.*), small nonterritorial males either court small females in undefended territories or sneak and release sperm into the territories of larger males (Kodric-Brown, 1977). Small males are too young to have achieved the size necessary to fight for territories. In the damselfish (*Stegastes nigricans*), the resident male accepts only one female at a time in his territory, probably to avoid sneak fertilization by female-looking males (Karino & Nakazono, 1993). Male damselfish can adopt both territorial and sneaking tactics within a single day, a nice example of a conditional and developmentally flexible strategy.

The phenomenon of some males looking like females once led to some confusion. Morris (1952) thought he had discovered homosexuality among male ten-spined sticklebacks (*Pygosteus pungitius L.*) unable to build a nest. These males take on the appearance of females, both in morphology and behavior, and convince nesting males to let them enter the nest. These males are of course not homosexuals but rather sneak fertilizers. Similar sneaky behavior has been observed in four-spined, *Apeltes quadracus* (Rowland, 1979), and three-spined sticklebacks, *Gasterosteus aculeatus*, as aptly described by van den Assem (1967):

> Sneaking starts suddenly. A male that has taken part in courtship competition, or has seen courtship behavior by another male in another territory may suddenly freeze; sometimes the change in behaviour is very dramatic. He then sinks to the bottom; no fins seems to be moved, only the dorsal spines are erected. In a very short time the male loses his bright nuptial colors . . . and adopts a cryptic pattern with dark bands across the back prevailing, much like the pattern of a female. . . . He may lie motionless for some time, then he starts sneaking very slowly—virtually millimetre by millimetre so that one hardly notices his moving forward at all—in the direction of a rival's nest, while the rival is courting the female at that time. . . . A sneaker will make a sudden dash for the rival's nest as the last part of his invasive action. (p. 101)

Sneaking behavior seems unrelated to rank or territory holding in three-spined sticklebacks. Stickleback sneaking seems highly situation dependent. A study using DNA fingerprinting of offspring from nests in a natural habitat found that a small proportion of the offspring were not produced by the nest owner (Rico, Kuhnlein, & Fitzgerald, 1992).

Salmonid males compete intensely for access to females. Males prefer large females because they produce more eggs, and females prefer males that are the same size or larger than they are. A large female paired with a smaller male may delay egg laying until a larger male comes along and chases away the small male. A large male paired with a large female, however, faces the cost of having to fight off many unpaired males. In brook trout *(Salvelinus fontinalis)*, small males manage to sneak in many spawnings involving large males. Genetic data shows that large males, however, fertilize most eggs (Blanchfield & Ridgway, 1999; Blanchfield, Ridgway, & Wilson, 2003).

The female sockeye salmon *(Oncorhynchus nerka)* selects and defends a spawning territory while males fight for dominance and the opportunity to spawn with her (A. J. Hanson & Smith, 1967). The dominant male mates with the female, but a subdominant male (called a *jack*), who is usually younger and smaller, will eject sperm "within a split second of the alpha male and always on the opposite, free, side of the spawning female" (Foote, Brown, & Wood, 1997, p. 1785). In a small study in a seminatural habitat, Foote et al. found that "jack males fertilized 42% of the eggs laid when they participated in a spawning involving a single large male" (p. 1790).

The male coho salmon *(Oncorhynchus kisutch)* also develops as a sneaking jack or a fighting large male depending on his size as a juvenile (Gross, 1991b). Small males mature faster than large males, thus gaining an advantage by being more likely to survive to sexual maturity but losing most battles for access to spawning females. Small males are able to fertilize eggs under certain conditions, such as when there are hiding structures near spawning grounds and when they are rare in the population. Gross (1985) reported that the two types have similar lifetime reproductive success. Similarly, the small sneaky male in Atlantic salmon *(Salmo salar)*, called *parr*, has been found to fertilize a sizeable proportion of eggs in the laboratory (Hutchings & Myers, 1988) and in seminatural habitats (Jordan & Youngson, 1992). Females defend their redd (nest) and reject small males. Although small male salmon appear to be at a competitive disadvantage in competition for females, their alternative mating behavior appears reproductively viable because large fighting males, although dominant if they live to breed, are more likely to die getting there.

There are many other observations of sneaking behavior in fish (e.g., Katano, 1992; Maekawa & Onozato, 1986), especially in wrasses, cichlids, and salmonids (reviewed in Taborsky, 1994).

In sum, forced copulation has been well documented in some species of viviparous fish, and sneak fertilization is common in oviparous species. Males adopt different mating tactics based on their conditions as juveniles, the features of their rearing environment, their current conditions, the features of their current environment, or a combination of these. Unfortunately, we know little of the female's response to sneak fertilization. In a study of longear sunfish, Keenleyside (1972) observed that females do not leave the nest when there is an intrusion. In Atlantic salmon, however, females are aggressive toward sneakers and appear to reject them. In most species, females prefer large and territorial males and ignore small and satellite males (Taborsky, 1994). We do not know whether the reproductive success of the female is negatively affected by fertilization by the nonpreferred, sneaker males.

MAMMALS

In laboratory studies, Nadler and Miller (1982) observed that male gorillas *(Gorilla gorilla beringei)* were quite aggressive in tests of mating. When females were near males and unable to leave, copulations took place frequently and outside the fertile period. In the wild, copulations occur for only a day or two during ovulation. Nadler and Miller suggested that male aggression stimulates females to present to the male and to accept copulation.

Nadler's (1989) later observation of mountain gorillas in the wild led him to modify this interpretation. In the wild, females will approach a silverback (dominant male) during ovulation, leading the male to invite copulation with chest beating and staring. The male then stands on his four limbs and the female gets even closer, sometimes backing up toward the male until the genitals touch. Copulation rarely takes place outside the fertile period. It seems that the unusual female proximity in cages during the laboratory tests stimulated an otherwise normal male response. When females can control proximity to the male in laboratory tests, copulatory frequency is closer to that observed in the wild.[5]

The mating behavior of chimpanzees *(Pan troglodytes)* has also been studied in the laboratory, with similar results. Nadler, Dahl, Collins, and Gould (1994) placed males and females together in cages every day over a period of a few weeks. In one situation females could determine whether they entered the male cage, and in another they were placed in the male cage with nowhere to go. Copulation was more frequent in the latter condition, especially when the male was dominant. The frequency of copulation when females had freedom was determined by the social compatibility of the two individuals. Genital swelling (indicating ovulation) was the main determinant of frequency of copulation in both conditions. These results suggest that female chimpanzees can be forced to copulate under some circumstances.

Nadler (1988) suggested that natural conditions prevent most male primates from engaging in forced copulation more often. The rarity of forced copulation in most primate species should not be taken to mean that mating is free of aggression. Smuts and Smuts (1993) argued that male aggression toward females outside of the mating context might serve to decrease female resistance to future male mating attempts or to maintain exclusive mating access. Support for this argument comes from the fact that male nonsexual aggression is more often directed at fertile, or soon to be fertile, females. In chimpanzees, a male may aggressively force a female into a consortship, which isolates her from the main group. Many conceptions result from consortships (Goodall, 1986).

---

[5]Female gorillas' protection from other males depends on the silverback protecting the group. When a silverback is supplanted, the new male typically kills the offspring, which brings the females into estrus and induces them to mate. Infanticide is another way males directly affect female reproduction.

REFERENCES

Abbey, A. L., McAuslan, P., & Ross, L. T. (1998). Sexual assault perpetration by college men: The role of alcohol, misperception of sexual intent, and sexual beliefs and experiences. *Journal of Social and Clinical Psychology, 17,* 167–195.

Abbey, A., McAuslan, P., Zawacki, T., Clinton, A. M., & Buck, P. O. (2001). Attitudinal, experiential, and situational predictors of sexual assault perpetration. *Journal of Interpersonal Violence, 16,* 784–807.

Abbey, A., Ross, L. T., McDuffie, D., & McAuslan, P. (1996). Alcohol, misperception, and sexual assault: How and why are they linked? In D. M. Buss & N. M. Malamuth (Eds.), *Sex, power, conflict: Evolutionary and feminist perspectives* (pp. 138–161). New York: Oxford University Press.

Abel, G. G., Barlow, D. H., Blanchard, E. B., & Guild, D. (1977). The components of rapists' sexual arousal. *Archives of General Psychiatry, 34,* 895–903.

Abel, G. G., Becker, J. V., Mittelman, M., Cunningham-Rathner, J., Rouleau, J. L., & Murphy, W. D. (1987). Self-reported sex crimes of nonincarcerated paraphiliacs. *Journal of Interpersonal Violence, 2,* 3–25.

Abel, G. G., Mittelman, M., Becker, J. V., Rathner, J., & Rouleau, J. L. (1988). Predicting child molesters' response to treatment. In R. Prentky & V. L. Quinsey (Eds.), *Human sexual aggression: Current perspectives* (pp. 223–243). New York: Annals of the New York Academy of Sciences.

Abler, T. S. (1992). Scalping, torture, cannibalism and rape: An ethnohistorical analysis of conflicting cultural values in war. *Anthropologica, 34,* 3–20.

Abracen, J., Looman, J., & Anderson, D. (2000). Alcohol and drug abuse in sexual and nonsexual violent offenders. *Sexual Abuse: A Journal of Research and Treatment, 12,* 263–274.

Adkins-Regan, E. (1995). Predictors of fertilization in the Japanese quail, *Coturnix japonica. Animal Behaviour, 50,* 1405–1415.

Afton, A. D. (1985). Forced copulation as a reproductive strategy of male lesser scaup: A field test of some predictions. *Behaviour, 92,* 146–167.

Agresti, A. (1996). *An introduction to categorical data analysis.* Toronto, Canada: Wiley.

Aigner, M., Eher, R., Fruehwald, S., Frottier, P., Guttierez-Lobos, K., & Dwyer, S. M. (2000). Brain abnormalities and violent behavior. *Journal of Psychology and Human Sexuality, 11,* 57–64.

Aizenman, M., & Kelley, G. (1988). The incidence of violence and acquaintance rape in dating relationships among college men and women. *Journal of College Student Development, 29,* 305–311.

Alatalo, R. V., Gottlander, K., & Lundberg, A. (1987). Extra-pair copulations and mate guarding in the polyterritorial pied flycatcher, *Ficedula hypoleuca. Behaviour, 101,* 139–155.

Alatalo, R. V., Gustafsson, L., & Lundberg, A. (1984). High frequency of cuckoldry in pied and collared flycatchers. *OIKOS, 42,* 41–47.

Alcorn, D. J., & Buelna, E. K. (1989). *The Hawaiian monk seal on Laysan Island, 1983* (Technical Memorandum NOAA-TM-NMFS-SWFC-124). Honolulu, HI: U.S. Department of Commerce.

Alexander, M., Gunn, J., Taylor, P. J., & Finch, J. (1993). Should a sexual offender be allowed castration? *British Medical Journal, 307,* 307–308.

Alison, L., Santtila, P., Sandnabba, N. K., & Nordling, N. (2001). Sadomasochistically oriented behavior: Diversity in practice and meaning. *Archives of Sexual Behavior, 30,* 1–12.

Allam, J. (1998). *Community-based treatment for sex offenders: An evaluation.* Birmingham, England: University of Birmingham.

Allen, M., D'Alessio, D., & Brezgel, K. (1995). A meta-analysis summarizing the effects of pornography: II. Aggression after exposure. *Human Communication Research, 22,* 258–283.

Allen, M., D'Alessio, D., & Emmers-Sommer, T. M. (2000). Reactions of criminal sexual offenders to pornography: A meta-analytic summary. In M. Roloff (Ed.), *Communication yearbook 22* (pp. 139–169). Thousand Oaks, CA: Sage.

Allen, G. R., & Simmons, L. W. (1996). Coercive mating, fluctuating asymmetry and male mating success in the dung fly *Sepsis cynipsea. Animal Behaviour, 52,* 737–741.

Allen, R. E. (1990). *Concise Oxford dictionary of current English* (8th ed.). Oxford, England: Clarendon Press.

Allnutt, S. H., Bradford, J. W., Greenberg, D. M., & Curry, S. (1996). Co-morbidity of alcoholism and the paraphilias. *Journal of Forensic Science, 41,* 234–239.

Alonzo, S. H., & Warner, R. R. (2000). Female choice, conflict between the sexes and the evolution of male alternative reproductive behaviours. *Evolutionary Ecology Research, 2,* 149–170.

Altemeyer, R. A. (1981). *Right-wing authoritarianism.* Winnipeg, Manitoba, Canada: University of Manitoba Press.

Altemeyer, R. A. (1988). *Enemies of freedom: Understanding right-wing authoritarianism.* San Francisco: Jossey-Bass.

Altemeyer, R. A. (1996). *The authoritarian specter.* Cambridge, MA: Harvard University Press.

American Psychiatric Association. (1994). *Diagnostic and statistical manual of mental disorders* (4th ed.). Washington, DC: Author.

Anderson, C. G., & Anderson, K. B. (1998). Temperature and aggression: Paradox, controversy, and a (fairly) clear picture. In R. G. Geen & E. Donnerstein (Eds.), *Human aggression: Theories, research and implications for social policy* (pp. 247–298). San Diego, CA: Academic Press.

Anderson, D. (2002). The utility of interpersonal circumplex theory in research and treatment of sexual offenders. *Forum on Corrections Research, 14,* 28–30.

Anderson, M. G. (1985). Variations on monogamy in canvasbacks (*Aythya valisineria*). *Ornithological Monographs, 37,* 57–67.

Andrews, D. A., & Bonta, J. (2003). *The psychology of criminal conduct* (3rd ed.). Cincinnati, OH: Anderson.

Andrews, D. A., Zinger, I., Hoge, R. D., Bonta, J., Gendreau, P., & Cullen, F. T. (1990). Does correctional treatment work? A clinically relevant and psychologically informed meta-analysis. *Criminology, 28,* 369–404.

Anglin, M. D. (1982). Alcohol and criminality. In M. Pattison & E. Kaufman (Eds.), *Encyclopedic handbook of alcoholism* (pp. 383–394). New York: Gardner Press.

Armentrout, J. A., & Hauer, A. L. (1978). MMPIs of rapists of adults, rapists of children, and non-rapist sex offenders. *Journal of Consulting Psychology, 34,* 330–332.

Arnqvist, G. (1988). Mate guarding and sperm displacement in the water strider *Gerris lateralis* Schumm (*Heteroptera: Gerridae*). *Freshwater Biology, 19,* 269–274.

Arnqvist, G. (1989a). Multiple mating in a water strider: Mutual benefits or intersexual conflict? *Animal Behaviour, 38,* 749–756.

Arnqvist, G. (1989b). Sexual selection in a water strider: The function, mechanism of selection and heritability of a male grasping apparatus. *OIKOS, 56,* 344–350.

Arnqvist, G. (1992a). Pre-copulatory fighting in a water strider: Inter-sexual conflict or mate assessment? *Animal Behaviour, 43,* 559–567.

Arnqvist, G. (1992b). Spatial variation in selective regimes: Sexual selection in the water strider, *Gerris odontogaster. Evolution, 46,* 914–929.

Arnqvist, G. (1997). The evolution of water strider mating systems: Causes and consequences of sexual conflicts. In J. C. Choe & B. J. Crespi (Eds.), *Mating systems in insects and arachnids* (pp. 146–163). Cambridge, England: Cambridge University Press.

Arnqvist, G., & Nilsson, T. (2000). The evolution of polyandry: Multiple mating and female fitness in insects. *Animal Behaviour, 60,* 145–164.

Arnqvist, G., & Rowe, L. (1995). Sexual conflict and arms race between the sexes: A morphological adaptation for control of mating in a female insect. *Proceedings of the Royal Society of London B, 261,* 123–127.

Arnqvist, G., & Rowe, L. (2002). Antagonistic coevolution between the sexes in a group of insects. *Nature, 415,* 787–789.

Arnqvist, G., Thornhill, R., & Rowe, L. (1997). Evolution of animal genitalia: Morphological correlates of fitness components in a water strider. *Journal of Evolutionary Biology, 10,* 613–640.

Arsenault, L., Tremblay, R. E., Boulerice, B., & Saucier, J.-F. (2002). Obstetrical complications and violent delinquency: Testing two developmental pathways. *Child Development, 73,* 496–508.

Austin, R. L., & Kim, Y. S. (2000). A cross-national examination of the relationship between gender equality and official rape rates. *International Journal of Offender Therapy & Comparative Criminology, 44,* 204–221.

Bagley, C., & Shewchuk-Dann, D. (1991, Fall). Characteristics of 60 children and adolescents who have a history of sexual assault against others: Evidence from a controlled study. *Journal of Child and Youth Care,* pp. 43–52.

Baier, J. L., Rosenzweig, M. G., & Whipple, E. G. (1991). Patterns of sexual behavior, coercion, and victimization of university students. *Journal of College Student Development, 32,* 310–322.

Bailey, R. O., Seymour, N. R., & Stewart, G. R. (1978). Rape behavior in blue-winged teal. *Auk, 95,* 188–190.

Bain, J., Langevin, R., Dickey, R., & Ben-Aron, M. (1987). Sex hormones in murderers and assaulters. *Behavioral Sciences and the Law, 5,* 95–101.

Bakker, L., Hudson, S., Wales, D., & Riley, D. (1999). *"And there was light": An evaluation of the Kia Marama Treatment Programme for New Zealand sex offenders against children.* Unpublished report. Kia Marama, New Zealand: Kia Marama Treatment Programme.

Balyk, E. D. (1997). Paraphilias as a subtype of obsessive–compulsive disorder: A hypothetical bio-social model. *Journal of Orthomolecular Medicine, 12,* 29–42.

Barash, D. P. (1977). Sociobiology of rape in mallards (*Ana platyrhynchos*): Responses of the mated male. *Science, 197,* 788–789.

Barbaree, H. E. (1990). Stimulus control of sexual arousal: Its role in sexual assault. In W. L. Marshall, D. R. Laws, & H. E. Barbaree (Eds.), *Handbook of sexual assault: Issues, theories, and treatment of the offender* (pp. 115–142). New York: Plenum Press.

Barbaree, H. E., Marshall, W. L., & Lanthier, R. D. (1979). Deviant sexual arousal in rapists. *Behavior Research and Therapy, 17,* 215–222.

Barbaree, H. E., Marshall, W. L., Yates, E., & Lightfoot, L. O. (1983). Alcohol intoxication and deviant sexual arousal in male social drinkers. *Behavior Research and Therapy, 21,* 365–373.

Barbaree, H. E., & Seto, M. C. (1998). *The ongoing follow-up of sex offenders treated at the Warkworth Sexual Behaviour Clinic.* Research report prepared for the Correctional Service of Canada, Ottawa, Ontario.

Barbaree, H. E., Seto, M. C., Langton, C. M., & Peacock, E. J. (2001). Evaluating the predictive accuracy of six risk instruments for adult sex offenders. *Criminal Justice and Behavior, 28,* 490–521.

Barbaree, H. E., Seto, M. C., Serin, R. C., Amos, N. L., & Preston, D. L. (1994). Comparisons between sexual and nonsexual rapist subtypes: Sexual arousal to rape, offense precursors, and offense characteristics. *Criminal Justice and Behavior, 21,* 95–114.

Barber, N. (2000). The sex ratio as a predictor of cross-national variation in violent crime. *Cross-Cultural Research, 34,* 264–282.

Bard, L. A., Carter, D. L., Cerce, D. D., Knight, R. A., Rosenberg, R., & Schneider, B. (1987). A descriptive study of rapists and child molesters: Developmental, clinical, and criminal characteristics. *Behavioral Sciences and the Law, 5,* 203–220.

Bardis, P. (1973). Violence: Theory and quantification. *Journal of Political and Military Sociology, 1,* 121–146.

Barlow, G. W. (1967). Social behavior of a South American leaf fish, *Polycentrus Schomburgkii,* with an account of recurring pseudofemale behavior. *American Midland Naturalist, 78,* 215–234.

Barnett, P. E. (1993). "And shortly for to seyn they were aton": Chaucer's deflection of rape in the Reeve's and Franklin's tales. *Women's Studies, 22,* 145–162.

Baron, L., Straus, M. A., & Jaffee, D. (1988). Legitimate violence, violent attitudes, and rape: A test of the cultural spillover theory. In R. A. Prentky & V. L. Quinsey (Eds.), *Human sexual aggression: Current perspectives* (pp. 79–110). New York: Annals of the New York Academy.

Barsetti, I., Earls, C. M., Lalumière, M. L., & Bélanger, N. (1998). The differentiation of intrafamilial and extrafamilial heterosexual child molesters. *Journal of Interpersonal Violence, 13,* 275–286.

Baumeister, R. F. (1988). Gender differences in masochistic scripts. *Journal of Sex Research, 25,* 478–499.

Baxter, D. J., Marshall, W. L., Barbaree, H. E., Davidson, P. R., & Malcolm, P. B. (1984). Deviant sexual behavior: Differentiating sex offenders by criminal and personal history, psychometric measures, and sexual response. *Criminal Justice and Behavior, 11,* 477–501.

Becker, J. V., Kaplan, M. S., Tenke, C. E., & Tartaglini, A. (1991). The incidence of depressive symptomatology in juvenile sex offenders with a history of abuse. *Child Abuse and Neglect, 15,* 531–536.

Beevor, A. (2002). *The fall of Berlin 1945.* New York: Viking

Bélanger, N., & Earls, C. M. (1996, May). Sex offender recidivism prediction. *Forum,* 22–24.

Belovsky, G. E., Slade, J. B., & Chase, J. M. (1996). Mating strategies based on foraging ability: An experiment with grasshoppers. *Behavioral Ecology, 7,* 438–444.

Bentler, P. M. (1968). Heterosexual behavior assessment—1: Males. *Behavior Research and Therapy, 6,* 217–230.

Bercovitch, F. B., Sladky, K. K., Roy, M. M., & Goy, R. W. (1987). Intersexual aggression and male sexual activity in captive rhesus macaques. *Aggressive Behavior, 13,* 347–358.

Bernat, J. A., Calhoun, K. S., & Adams, H. E. (1999). Sexually aggressive and nonaggressive men: Sexual arousal and judgments in response to acquaintance rape and consensual analogues. *Journal of Abnormal Psychology, 108,* 662–673.

Berryman-Fink, C., & Riley, K. V. (1997). The effect of sex and feminist orientation on perceptions in sexually harassing communication. *Women's Studies in Communication, 20,* 25–44.

Betzig, L. (1992). Roman polygyny. *Ethology and Sociobiology, 13,* 309–349.

Bingham, C. R., & Crockett, L. J. (1996). Longitudinal adjustment patterns of boys and girls experiencing early, middle, and late sexual intercourse. *Developmental Psychology, 32,* 647–658.

Bingman, V. P. (1980). Novel rape avoidance in the mallards. *Wilson Bulletin, 92,* 409.

Birkhead, T. R. (2000). *Promiscuity: A natural history of sperm competition*. Cambridge, MA: Harvard University Press.

Birkhead, T. R., Clarkson, K., & Zann, R. (1988). Extra-pair courtship, copulation and mate guarding in wild zebra finches *Taeniopygia guttata*. *Animal Behaviour, 36,* 1853–1855.

Birkhead, T. R., & Fletcher, F. (1995). Male phenotype and ejaculate quality in the zebra finch *Taeniopygia guttata*. *Proceedings of the Royal Society of London B, 262,* 329–334.

Birkhead, T. R., Hunter, F. M., & Pellatt, J. E. (1989). Sperm competition in the zebra finch, *Taeniopygia guttata*. *Animal Behaviour, 38,* 935–950.

Birkhead, T. R., Johnson, S. D., & Nettleship, D. N. (1985). Extra-pair matings and mate guarding in the common murre *Uria aalge*. *Animal Behaviour, 33,* 608–619.

Bisazza, A., Marconato, A., & Marin, G. (1989). Male mate preferences in the mosquitofish *Gambusia holbrooki*. *Ethology, 83,* 335–343.

Bjöklund, M., & Westman, B. (1983). Extra-pair copulations in the pied flycatcher (*Ficedula hypoleuca*). *Behavioral Ecology and Sociobiology, 13,* 271–275.

Blader, J. C., & Marshall, W. L. (1989). Is assessment of sexual arousal in rapists worthwhile? A critique of current methods and the development of a response compatibility approach. *Clinical Psychology Review, 9,* 569–587.

Blanchard, R. (2001). Fraternal birth order and the maternal immune hypothesis of male homosexuality. *Hormones & Behavior, 40,* 105–114.

Blanchard, R., Barbaree, H. E., Bogaert, A. F., Dickey, R., Klassen, P., Kuban, M. E., & Zucker, K. J. (2000). Fraternal birth order and sexual orientation in pedophiles. *Archives of Sexual Behavior, 29,* 463–478.

Blanchard, R., & Klassen, P. (1997). H-Y antigen and homosexuality in men. *Journal of Theoretical Biology, 185,* 373–378.

Blanchfield, P. J., & Ridgway, M. S. (1999). The cost of peripheral males in a brook trout mating system. *Animal Behaviour, 57,* 537–544.

Blanchfield, P. J., Ridgway, M. S., & Wilson, C. C. (2003). Breeding success of male brook trout (*Salvelinus fontinalis*) in the wild. *Molecular Ecology, 12,* 2417–2428.

Blonigen, D. M., Carlson, S. R., Krueger, R. F., & Patrick, C. J. (2003). A twin study of self-reported psychopathic personality traits. *Personality and Individual Differences, 35,* 179–197.

Blumstein, A., & Wallman, J. (2000). *The crime drop in America*. New York: Cambridge University Press.

Bock, J. (2002). Evolutionary demography and intrahousehold time allocation: School attendance and child labor among the Okavango Delta peoples of Botswana. *American Journal of Human Biology, 14,* 206–221.

Bogaert, A. F., Bezeau, S., Kuban, M., & Blanchard, R. (1997). Pedophilia, sexual orientation, and birth order. *Journal of Abnormal Psychology, 106,* 331–335.

Bonta, J., Law, M., & Hanson, K. (1998). The prediction of criminal and violent recidivism among mentally disordered offenders: A meta-analysis. *Psychological Bulletin, 123,* 123–142.

Book, A. S., Starzyk, K. B., & Quinsey, V. L. (2001). The relationship between testosterone and aggression: A meta-analysis. *Aggression and Violent Behavior, 6,* 579–599.

Borduin, C. M., & Henggeler, S. W. (1990). A multisystemic approach to the treatment of serious delinquent behavior. In R. J. McMahon & R. D. Peters (Eds), *Behavior disorders of adolescence: Research, intervention, and policy in clinical and school settings* (pp. 63–80). New York: Plenum Press.

Borduin, C. M., Henggeler, S. W., Blaske, D. M., & Stein, R. J. (1990). Multisystemic treatment of adolescent sexual offenders. *International Journal of Offender Therapy and Comparative Criminology, 34,* 105–113.

Borduin, C. M., & Schaeffer, C. M. (2001). Multisystemic treatment of juvenile sex offenders: A progress report. *Journal of Psychology and Human Sexuality, 13,* 25–42.

Borgia, G. (1995). Why do bowerbirds build bowers? *American Scientist, 83,* 542–547.

Bossema, I., & Roemers, E. (1985). Mating strategy, including mate choice, in mallards. *Ardea, 73,* 147–157.

Boswell, A. A., & Spade, J. Z. (1996). Fraternities and collegiate rape culture: Why are some fraternities more dangerous places for women? *Gender and Society, 10,* 133–147.

Boudreaux, E., Kilpatrick, D. G., Resnick, H. S., Best, C. L., & Saunders, B. E. (1998). Criminal victimization, posttraumatic stress disorder and comorbid psychopathology among a community sample of women. *Journal of Traumatic Stress, 11,* 665–678.

Bownes, I. T., O'Gorman, E. C., & Sayers, A. (1991). Rape—A comparison of stranger and acquaintance assaults. *Medical Science and Law, 2,* 102–109.

Bradford, J. M. W. (1999). The paraphilias, obsessive compulsive spectrum disorder and the treatment of sexually deviant behaviour. *Psychiatric Quarterly, 70,* 209–219.

Bradford, J. M. W. (2001). The neurobiology, neuropharmacology, and pharmacological treatment of the paraphilias and compulsive sexual behaviour. *Canadian Journal of Psychiatry, 46,* 26–34.

Bradford, J. M. W., & McLean, D. (1984). Sexual offenders, violence and testosterone: A clinical study. *Canadian Journal of Psychiatry, 29,* 335–343.

Braukmann, C. J., & Morris, E. K. (1987). Behavioral approaches to crime and delinquency. In E. K. Morris & C. J. Braukmann (Eds.), *Behavioral approaches to crime and delinquency: A handbook of application, research, and concepts* (pp. 326). New York: Plenum Press.

Braun, K., & Harper, R. G. (1993). Effects of predator size and female receptivity in courtship behavior of captive-bred male guppies. *Transactions of the Illinois State Academy of Science, 86,* 127–132.

Brecklin, L. R., & Ullman, S. E. (2001). The role of offender alcohol use in rape attacks: An analysis of national crime victimization survey data. *Journal of Interpersonal Violence, 16,* 3–21.

Bremer, J. (1959). *Asexualization: A follow-up study of 244 cases.* New York: Macmillan.

Brennan, P. A., Hall, J., Bor, W., Najman, J. M., & Williams, G. (2003). Integrating biological and social processes in relation to early-onset persistent aggression in boys and girls. *Developmental Psychology, 39,* 309–323.

Brewer, G. L. (1997). Displays and breeding behaviour of the chiloe widgeon *Anas sibilatrix. Wildfowl, 47,* 97–127.

Briskie, J. V. (1998). Avian genitalia. *Auk, 115,* 826–828.

Briskie, J. V., & Montgomerie, R. (1997). Sexual selection and the intromittent organ of birds. *Journal of Avian Biology, 28,* 73–86.

Britt, C. L. (1996). The measurement of specialization and escalation in the criminal career: An alternative modeling strategy. *Journal of Quantitative Criminology, 12,* 193–222.

Bröder, A., & Hohmann, N. (2003). Variation in risk taking behavior over the menstrual cycle: An improved replication. *Evolution and Human Behavior, 24,* 391–398.

Broude, G. J., & Greene, S. J. (1976). Cross-cultural codes on twenty sexual attitudes and practices. *Ethnology, 15,* 419–429.

Brower, K. J. (1993). Anabolic steroids. *Psychiatric Clinics of North America, 16,* 97–103.

Brown, C. K. (1996). Episodic patterns and the perpetrator: The structure and meaning of Chaucer's *Wife of Bath's Tale. The Chaucer Review, 31,* 18–35.

Brown, C. R. (1978). Sexual chase in purple martins. *Auk, 95,* 588–590.

Brown, P. (1986). Simbu aggression and the drive to win. *Anthropological Quarterly, 59,* 165–170.

Brown, S. L., & Forth, A. E. (1997). Psychopathy and sexual assault: Static risk factors, emotional precursors, and rapist subtypes. *Journal of Consulting and Clinical Psychology, 65,* 848–857.

Brown, W. D., Crespi, B. J., & Choe, J. C. (1997). Sexual conflict and the evolution of mating systems. In J. C. Choe & B. J. Crespi (Eds.), *Mating systems in insects and arachnids* (pp. 352–377). Cambridge, England: Cambridge University Press.

Browne, A., & Finkelhor, D. (1986). Impact of child sexual abuse: A review of the research. *Psychological Bulletin, 99,* 66–77.

Brownmiller, S. (1975). *Against our will: Men, women and rape.* New York: Simon & Schuster.

Burch, R. L., & Gallup, G. G. (2000). Perceptions of paternal resemblance predict family violence. *Evolution and Human Behavior, 21,* 429–435.

Burger, J. (1976). Daily and seasonal activity patterns in breeding laughing gulls. *Auk, 93,* 308–323.

Burger, J., Miller, L. M., & Hajin, D. C. (1978). Behavior and sex roles of nesting anhingas at San Blas, Mexico. *Wilson Bulletin, 90,* 359–375.

Burgess, A. W., Hazelwood, R. R., Roukas, F. E., Hartman, C. R., & Burgess, A. G. (1987, January). *Serial rapists and their victims: Reenactment and repetition.* Paper presented at the New York Academy of Sciences Conference on Human Sexual Aggression: Current Perspectives, New York.

Burley, N. T., Enstrom, D. A., & Chitwood, L. (1994). Extra-pair relations in zebra finches: Differential male success results from female tactics. *Animal Behaviour, 48,* 1031–1041.

Burley, N. T., Parker, P. G., & Lundy, K. (1996). Sexual selection and extrapair fertilization in a socially monogamous passerine, the zebra finch (*Taeniopygia guttata*). *Behavioral Ecology, 7,* 218–226.

Burns, J. T., Cheng, K. M., & McKinney, F. (1980). Forced copulation in captive mallards: I. Fertilization of eggs. *Auk, 97,* 875–879.

Burt, M. R. (1980). Cultural myths and supports for rape. *Journal of Personality and Social Psychology, 38,* 217–230.

Bushman, B. J., & Cooper, H. M. (1990). Effects of alcohol on human aggression: An integrative research review. *Psychological Bulletin, 107,* 341–354.

Buss, A. H., & Perry, M. (1992). The aggression questionnaire. *Journal of Personality and Social Psychology, 63,* 452–459.

Buss, D. E. (1998). Women at the borders: Rape and nationalism in international law. *Feminist Legal Studies, 6,* 171–203.

Buss, D. M. (1999). *Evolutionary psychology: The new science of the mind.* Toronto, Ontario, Canada: Allyn & Bacon.

Buss, D. M., & Malamuth, N. M. (1996). *Sex, power, conflict: Evolutionary and feminist perspectives.* New York: Oxford University Press.

Buss, D. M., & Schmitt, D. P. (1993). Sexual strategies theory: An evolutionary perspective on human mating. *Psychological Review, 100,* 204–232.

Byers, E., & Lewis, K. (1988). Dating couples' disagreements over the desired level of sexual intimacy. *Journal of Sex Research, 24,* 15–29.

Byers, E. S., & Eno, R. J. (1991). Predicting men's sexual coercion and aggression from attitudes, dating history, and sexual response. *Journal of Psychology & Human Sexuality, 4,* 55–70.

Byers, J. A., Moodie, J. D., & Hall, N. (1994). Pronghorn females choose vigorous mates. *Animal Behaviour, 47,* 33–43.

Calhoun, K. S., Bernat, J. A., Clum, G. A., & Frame, C. L. (1997). Sexual coercion and attraction to sexual aggression in a community sample of young men. *Journal of Interpersonal Violence, 12,* 392–406.

Campagna, C., Le Boeuf, B. J., & Cappozzo, H. L. (1988). Group raids: A mating strategy of male Southern sea lions. *Behaviour, 105,* 224–249.

Campbell, A. (1995). A few good men: Evolutionary psychology and female adolescent aggression. *Ethology and Sociobiology, 16,* 99–123.

Canterbury, R. J., Grossman, S. J., & Lloyd, J. (1993). Drinking behaviors and drinking incidents of date rape among high school graduates entering college. *College Student Journal, 27,* 75–84.

Capp, B. (1999). The double standard revisited: Plebeian women and male sexual reputation in early modern England. *Past and Present, 162,* 70–100.

Carey, G., & Goldman, D. (1997). The genetics of antisocial behavior. In D. M. Stoff, J. Breiling, & J. D. Maser (Eds.), *Handbook of antisocial behavior* (pp. 243–254). New York: Wiley.

Carstairs, G. M. (1964). Cultural differences in sexual deviation. In I. Rosen (Ed.), *The pathology and treatment of sexual deviation: A methodological approach* (pp. 419–449). London: Oxford University Press.

Carter, J. M. (1982). Rape and medieval English society: The evidence of Yorkshire, Wiltshire and London, 1218–76. *Comitatus, 8,* 33–63.

Caspi, A., Moffitt, T. E., Entner Wright, B. R., & Silva, P. A. (1998). Early failure in the labor market: Childhood and adolescent predictors of unemployment in the transition to adulthood. *American Sociological Review, 63,* 424–451.

Castro, I., Minot, E. O., Fordham, R. A., & Birkhead, T. R. (1996). Polygynandry, face-to-face copulation and sperm competition in the Hihi *Notiomystic cincta* (Aves: Meliphagidae). *IBIS, 138,* 765–771.

Centerwall, B. S. (1992). Television and violence. *Journal of the American Medical Association, 267,* 3059–3063.

Chagnon, N. A. (1977). *Yanomamo: The fierce people.* Toronto, Canada: Holt, Rinehart & Winston.

Chambless, D. L., & Hollon, S. D. (1998). Defining empirically supported therapies. *Journal of Consulting and Clinical Psychology, 66,* 7–18.

Chang, I. (1998). *The rape of Nanking: The forgotten holocaust of World War II.* New York: Basic Books.

Chantry, K., & Craig, R. J. (1994). Psychological screening of sexually violent offenders with the MCMI. *Journal of Clinical Psychology, 50,* 430–435.

Chaplin, T. C., Rice, M. E., & Harris, G. T. (1995). Salient victim suffering and the sexual responses of child molesters. *Journal of Consulting and Clinical Psychology, 163,* 249–255.

Chappell, D. (1976). Cross-cultural research on forcible rape. *International Journal of Criminology and Penology, 4,* 295–304.

Chavanne, T. J., & Gallup, G. G. (1998). Variation in risk taking behavior among female college students as a function of the menstrual cycle. *Evolution and Human Behavior, 19,* 27–32.

Check, J. V. P., Malamuth, N. M., Elias, B., & Barton, S. (1985). On hostile ground. *Psychology Today, 19,* 56–61.

Cheng, K. M., Burns, J. T., & McKinney, F. (1982). Forced copulation in captive mallards *(Anas platyrhynchos)*: II. Temporal factors. *Animal Behaviour, 30,* 695–699.

Cheng, K. M., Burns, J. T., & McKinney, F. (1983). Forced copulation in captive mallards: III. Sperm competition. *Auk, 100,* 302–310.

Christiansen, K., & Knussmann, R. (1987). Androgen levels and components of aggressive behavior in men. *Hormones and Behavior, 21,* 170–180.

Christopher, F. S., Owens, L. A., & Stecker, H. L. (1993). Exploring the dark side of courtship: A test of a model of male premarital sexual aggressiveness. *Journal of Marriage and the Family, 55,* 469–479.

Cluss, P. A., Broughton, J., Frank, E., Stewart, B. D., & West, D. (1983). The rape victim: Psychological correlates of participation in the legal process. *Criminal Justice and Behavior, 10*, 342–357.

Clutton-Brock, T. H., & Vincent, A. C. J. (1991). Sexual selection and the potential reproductive rate of males and females. *Nature, 351*, 58–60.

Cohen, J. (1992). A power primer. *Psychological Bulletin, 112*, 155–159.

Cohen, M. L., Garofalo, R. F., Boucher, R., & Seghorn, T. (1971). The psychology of rapists. *Seminars in Psychiatry, 3*, 307–327.

Coid, J. (1993). Current concepts and classifications of psychopathic disorder. In P. Tyrer & G. Stein (Eds.), *Personality disorder reviewed* (pp. 113–164). London: Gaskell.

Coleman, M. (1985). Shame: A powerful underlying factor in violence and war. *Journal of Psychoanalytic Anthropology, 8*, 67–79.

Combs-Lane, A., & Smith, D. W. (2002). Risk of sexual victimization in college women: The role of behavioral intentions and risk-taking behaviors. *Journal of Interpersonal Violence, 17*, 165–183.

Conley, C. (1986). Rape and justice in Victorian England. *Victorian Studies, 29*, 519–536.

Connor, R. C., Heithaus, M. R., & Barre, L. M. (2001). Complex social structure, alliance stability and mating access in a bottlenose dolphin "super-alliance." *Proceedings of the Royal Society of London B, 268*, 263–267.

Connor, R. C., Richards, A. F., Smolker, R. A., & Mann, J. (1996). Patterns of female attractiveness in Indian Ocean bottlenose dolphins. *Behaviour, 133*, 37–69.

Connor, R. C., Smolker, R. A., & Richards, A. F. (1992). Two levels of alliance formation among male bottlenose dolphins (*Tursiops sp.*). *Proceedings of the National Academy of Sciences USA, 89*, 987–990.

Constantz, G. D. (1975). Behavioral ecology of mating in the male Gila topminnow, *Poeciliopsis occidentalis* (Cyprinodontiforms: Poecillidae). *Ecology, 56*, 966–973.

Cook, S. E., Vernon, J. G., Bateson, M., & Guildford, T. (1994). Mate choice in the polymorphic African swallowtail butterfly, *Papilio dardanus*: Male-like females may avoid sexual harassment. *Animal Behaviour, 47*, 389–397.

Cooper, A. J. (1987). Sadistic homosexual pedophilia treatment with cyproterone acetate. *Canadian Journal of Psychiatry, 32*, 738–740.

Copenhaver, S., & Grauerholz, E. (1991). Sexual victimization among sorority women: Exploring the link between sexual violence and institutional practices. *Sex Roles, 24*, 31–41.

Cordero, A. (1992). Density-dependent mating success and colour polymorphism in females of the damselfly *Ischnura graellsii* (Odonata: Coenagrionidae). *Journal of Animal Ecology, 61*, 769–780.

Cordero, A. (1999). Forced copulations and female contact guarding at a high male density in a Calopterygid damselfly. *Journal of Insect Behavior, 12*, 27–37.

Côté, K., Earls, C. M., & Lalumière, M. L. (2002). Birth order, birth interval, and deviant sexual preferences among sex offenders. *Sexual Abuse: A Journal of Research and Treatment, 14,* 67–81.

Court, J. H. (1976). Pornography and sex-crimes: A re-evaluation in the light of recent trends around the world. *International Journal of Criminology and Penology, 5,* 129–157.

Cox, C. R., & Le Boeuf, B. J. (1977). Female incitation of male competition: A mechanism in sexual selection. *American Naturalist, 111,* 317–335.

Craig Shea, M. E. (1993). The effects of selective evaluation on the perception of female cues in sexually coercive and noncoercive males. *Archives of Sexual Behavior, 22,* 415–433.

Crawford, C., & Galdikas, B. M. F. (1986). Rape in non-human animals: An evolutionary perspective. *Canadian Psychology, 27,* 215–230.

Crawford, D. A. (1979, December). *Applications of penile response monitoring to the assessment of sexual offenders.* Paper presented at the 12th Cropwood Round-Table Conference, Sex Offenders in the Criminal Justice System, Cambridge, England.

Creelman, E., & Storey, A. E. (1991). Sex differences in reproductive behavior of Atlantic puffins. *Condor, 93,* 390–398.

Cronin, E. W., & Sherman, P. W. (1976). A resource-based mating system: The orange-rumped honeyguide. In D. A. Lancaster & J. R. Johnson (Eds.), *The living bird* (pp. 5–32). Ithaca, NY: Laboratory of Ornithology, Cornell University.

Crowe, L. C., & George, W. H. (1989). Alcohol and human sexuality: Review and integration. *Psychological Bulletin, 105,* 374–386.

Dabbs, J. M., & Dabbs, M. G. (2000). *Heroes, rogues, and lovers: Testosterone and behavior.* New York: McGraw-Hill.

Daly, M., & Wilson, M. (1983). *Sex, evolution, and behavior* (2nd ed.). Belmont, CA: Wadsworth.

Daly, M., & Wilson, M. (1988). *Homicide.* New York: Aldine de Gruyter.

Daly, M., & Wilson, M. I. (1999). Human evolutionary psychology and animal behaviour. *Animal Behaviour, 57,* 509–519.

Daly, M., & Wilson, M. I. (2001). Risk-taking, intrasexual competition, and homicide. *Nebraska Symposium on Motivation, 47,* 1–36.

Daly, M., Wilson, M., & Vasdev, S. (2001). Income inequality and homicide rates in Canada and the United States. *Canadian Journal of Criminology, 43,* 219–236.

Davidson, P. R. (1984). *Behavioral treatment for incarcerated sex offenders: Post-release outcome.* Paper presented at the Conference on the Assessment and Treatment of the Sex Offender, Kingston, Ontario, Canada.

Davis, E. S. (2002a). Female choice and the benefits of mate guarding by male mallards. *Animal Behaviour, 64,* 619–628.

Davis, E. S. (2002b). Male reproductive tactics in the mallard, *Anas platyrhynchos:* Social and hormonal mechanisms. *Behavioral Ecology and Sociobiology, 52,* 224–231.

Davis, W. A., Jr. (1997). The rape of Tess: Hardy, English law, and the case for sexual assault. *Nineteenth/Century Literature, 52,* 221–231.

Day, R., & Wong, S. (1996). Anomalous perceptual asymmetries for negative emotional stimuli in the psychopath. *Journal of Abnormal Psychology, 105,* 648–652.

Dean, K. E., & Malamuth, N. M. (1997). Characteristics of men who aggress sexually and men who imagine aggressing: Risk and moderating variables. *Journal of Personality and Social Psychology, 72,* 449–455.

DeBloois, N. (1997). Rape, marriage, or death? Gender perspectives in the Homeric Hymn to Demeter. *Philological Quarterly, 76,* 245–262.

DeMaris, A. (1997). Elevated sexual activity in violent marriages: Hypersexuality or sexual extortion? *Journal of Sex Research, 34,* 361–373.

Dempster, R. J., Hart, S. D., & Boer, D. P. (2001). *Prediction of sexually violent recidivism: A comparison of risk assessment instruments.* Manuscript in preparation.

Diamond, M., & Uchiyama, A. (1999). Pornography, rape, and sex crimes in Japan. *International Journal of Law and Psychiatry, 22,* 1–22.

Dill, L. M., Hedrick, A. V., & Fraser, A. (1999). Male mating strategies under predation risk: Do females call the shots? *Behavioral Ecology, 10,* 452–461.

Dixson, A. F. (1998). *Primate sexuality: Comparative studies of the prosimians, monkeys, apes, and human beings.* Oxford, England: Oxford University Press.

Dominey, W. J. (1980). Female mimicry in male bluegill sunfish—A genetic polymorphism? *Nature, 284,* 546–548.

Dominey, W. J. (1984). Alternative mating tactics and evolutionary stable strategies. *American Zoologist, 24,* 385–396.

Donohue J. J., III, & Levitt, S. D. (2001). The impact of legalized abortion on crime. *Quarterly Journal of Economics, 116,* 379–420.

Donovan, J. E., Jessor, R., & Costa, F. M. (1988). Syndrome of problem behavior in adolescence: A replication. *Journal of Consulting and Clinical Psychology, 56,* 762–765.

Dubinsky, K. (1993). *Improper advances: Rape and heterosexual conflict in Ontario, 1880–1929.* Chicago: University of Chicago Press.

Ducharme, J. M. (2000). Treatment of maladaptive behavior in acquired brain injury: Remedial approaches in postacute settings. *Clinical Psychology Review, 20,* 405–426.

Dunn, C. W. (1952). *A Chaucer reader.* New York: Harcourt, Brace.

Dunn, P. O., Afton, A. D., Gloutney, M. L., & Alisauskas, R. T. (1999). Forced copulation results in few extra-pair fertilizations in Ross's lesser snow geese. *Animal Behaviour, 57,* 1071–1081.

Earls, C. M., & Proulx, J. (1986). The differentiation of francophone rapists and non-rapists using penile circumferential measures. *Criminal Justice and Behavior, 13,* 419–429.

Earls, C. M., Quinsey, V. L., & Castonguay, L. G. (1987). A comparison of three methods of scoring penile circumference changes. *Archives of Sexual Behavior, 16,* 493–500.

East, P. L., & Jacobson, L. J. (2001). The younger siblings of teenage mothers: A follow-up of their pregnancy risk. *Developmental Psychology, 37*, 254–264.

Eastman, N. (1993). Surgical castration for sex offenders. *British Medical Journal, 307*, 141.

Eberhard, W. G. (2002). The function of female resistance behavior: Intromission by male coercion vs. female cooperation in sepsid flies (Diptera: Sepsidae). *International Journal of Tropical Biology and Conservation, 50*, 485–505.

Edinger, B. B. (1988). Extra-pair courtship and copulation attempts in northern orioles. *Condor, 90*, 546–554.

Eggert, A.-K., & Sakaluk, S. K. (1994). Sexual cannibalism and its relation to male mating success in sagebrush crickets, *Cyphoderris strepitans* (Haglidae: Orthoptera). *Animal Behaviour, 47*, 1171–1177.

Elliott, D. S. (1994). Serious violent offenders: Onset, developmental course, and termination—The American Society of Criminology 1993 Presidential Address. *Criminology, 32*, 1–21.

Elliott, D. S., Huizinga, D., & Morse, B. (1987). Self-reported analysis of violent offending: A descriptive analysis of juvenile violent offenders and their offending careers. *Journal of Interpersonal Violence, 1*, 472–513.

Ellis, L. (1987). Relationships of criminality and psychopathy with eight other apparent behavioral manifestations of sub-optimal arousal. *Personality and Individual Differences, 8*, 905–925.

Ellis, L., & Blanchard, R. (2001). Birth order, sibling sex ration, and maternal miscarriages in homosexual and heterosexual men and women. *Personality and Individual Differences, 30*, 543–552.

Ellis, L., & Coontz, P. D. (1990). Androgens, brain functioning, and criminality: The neurohormonal foundations of antisociality. In L. Ellis & H. Hoffman (Eds.), *Crime in biological social and moral contexts* (pp. 162–193). New York: Praeger.

Ellis, L., & Walsh, A. (2000). *Criminology: A global perspective.* Toronto, Ontario, Canada: Allyn and Bacon.

Emlen, D. J. (1994). Environmental control of horn length dimorphism in the beetle *Onthophagus acuminatus* (Coleoptera: Scarabaeidae). *Proceedings of the Royal Society of London B, 256*, 131–136.

Emlen, S. T., & Wrege, P. H. (1986). Forced copulation and intra-specific parasitism: Two costs of social living in the white-fronted bee-eater. *Ethology, 71*, 2–29.

Emm, D., & McKenry, P. C. (1988). Coping with victimization: The impact of rape on female survivors, male significant others, and parents. *Contemporary Family Therapy: An International Journal, 10*, 272–279.

Emory, L. E., Cole, C. M., & Myer, W. J. (1992). The Texas experience with depo provera: 1980–1990. *Journal of the Offender Rehabilitation, 18*, 125–139.

Endler, J. A. (1987). Predation, light intensity and courtship behaviour in *Poecilia reticulata* (Pisces: Poeciliidae). *Animal Behaviour, 35*, 1376–1385.

Epp, M. (1997). The memory of violence: Soviet and East European Mennonite refugees and rape in the Second World War. *Journal of Women's History, 9*, 58–87.

Erickson, C. J., & Zenone, P. G. (1976). Courtship differences in male ring doves: Avoidance of cuckoldry? *Science, 192,* 1353–1354.

Estep, D. Q., & Bruce, K. E. M. (1981). The concept of rape in non-humans: A critique. *Animal Behaviour, 29,* 1272–1273.

Evans, J. P., & Magurran, A. E. (1999). Male mating behaviour and sperm production characteristics under varying sperm competition risk in guppies. *Animal Behaviour, 58,* 1001–1006.

Evans, J. P., Pilastro, A., & Ramnarine, I. W. (2003). Sperm transfer through forced matings and its evolutionary implications in natural guppies *(Poecilia reticulata)* populations. *Biological Journal of the Linnean Society, 78,* 605–612.

Evarts, S., & Williams, C. J. (1987). Multiple paternity in a wild population of mallards. *Auk, 104,* 597–602.

Evrard, J. R., & Gold, E. M. (1979). Epidemiology and management of sexual assault victims. *Obstetrics and Gynecology, 53,* 381–387.

Ewen, J. C., & Armstrong, D. P. (2000). Male provisioning is negatively correlated with attempted extrapair copulation frequency in the stitchbird (or hihi). *Animal Behaviour, 60,* 429–433.

Ewen, J. C., Armstrong, D. P., & Lambert, D. M. (1999). Floater males gain reproductive success through extrapair fertilizations in the stitchbird. *Animal Behaviour, 58,* 321–328.

Fagan, J., & Wexler, S. (1988). Explanations of sexual assault among violent delinquents. *Journal of Adolescent Research, 3,* 363–385.

Fagot, B. I., Pears, K. C., Capaldi, D. M., Crosby, L., & Leve, C. S. (1998). Becoming an adolescent father: Precursors and parenting. *Developmental Psychology, 34,* 1209–1219.

Fairbairn, D. L. (1993). Costs of loading associated with mate-carrying in the waterstrider, *Aquarius remigis. Behavioral Ecology, 4,* 224–231.

Farr, J. A. (1980). The effects of sexual experience and female receptivity on courtship-rape decisions in male guppies, *Poecilia reticulata* (Pisces: Poeciliidae). *Animal Behaviour, 28,* 1195–1201.

Farr, J. A., Travis, J., & Trexler, J. C. (1986). Behavioural allometry and interdemic variation in sexual behaviour of the sailfin molly, *Poecilia latipinna* (Pisces: Poeciliidae). *Animal Behaviour, 34,* 497–509.

Fedora, O., Reddon, J. R., Morrison, J. W., Fedora, S. K., Pascoe, H., & Yeudall, L. T. (1992). Sadism and other paraphilias in normal controls and aggressive and nonaggressive sex offenders. *Archives of Sexual Behavior, 21,* 1–15.

Feild, H. S. (1978). Attitudes toward rape: A comparative analysis of police, rapists, crisis counselors, and citizens. *Journal of Personality and Social Psychology, 36,* 156–179.

Felson, R. B., & Hayne, D. L. (2002). Pubertal development, social factors, and delinquency among adolescent boys. *Criminology, 40,* 967–988.

Felson, R. B., & Krohn, M. (1990). Motives for rape. *Journal of Research in Crime and Delinquency, 27,* 222–242.

Fiebert, M. S., & Tucci, L. M. (1998). Sexual coercion: men victimized by women. *Journal of Men's Studies, 6,* 127–133.

Figueredo, A. J., Sales, B. D., Russell, K. P., Becker, J. V., & Kaplan, M. (2000). A Brunswikian evolutionary–developmental theory of adolescent sex offending. *Behavioral Sciences and the Law, 18,* 2–3.

Finkelhor, D. (1986). Abusers: Special topics. In D. Finkelhor (Ed.), *A sourcebook on child sexual abuse* (pp. 119–142). Newbury Park, CA: Sage.

Finkelhor, D., & Jones, L. M. (2004, January). Explanations for the decline in child sexual abuse cases. *Juvenile Justice Bulletin,* pp. 1–12.

Firestone, P., Bradford, J. M., Greenberg, D. M., & Serran, G. A. (2000). The relationship of deviant sexual arousal and psychopathy in incest offenders, extrafamilial child molesters, and rapists. *Journal of the American Academy of Psychiatry and the Law, 28,* 303–308.

Fisher, B. S., Cullen, F. T., & Turner, M. G. (2000). *The sexual victimization of college women* (Publication No. NCJ 182369). Washington, DC: U.S. Department of Justice.

Fisher, H. I. (1971). The laysian albatross: Its incubating, hatching, and associated behaviors. In O. S. Pettingill Jr. & D. A. Lancaster (Eds.), *The living bird* (pp. 19–78). Ithaca, NY: Laboratory of Ornithology, Cornell University.

Fisher, W., & Grenier, G. (1994). Violent pornography, antiwoman thoughts, and antiwoman acts: In search of reliable effects. *Journal of Sex Research, 31,* 23–38.

Flick, S. N. (1988). Managing attrition in clinical research. *Clinical Psychology Review, 8,* 499–515.

Fluharty, G., & Glassman, N. (2001). Use of antecedent control to improve the outcome of rehabilitation for a client with frontal lobe injury and intolerance for auditory and tactile stimuli. *Brain Injury, 15,* 995–1002.

Foerster, K., Delhey, K., Johnsen, A., Lifjeld, J. T., & Kempenaers, B. (2003). Females increase offspring heterozygosity and fitness through extra-pair matings. *Nature, 425,* 714–717.

Foote, C. J., Brown, G. S., & Wood, C. C. (1997). Spawning success of males using alternative mating tactics in sockeye salmon, *Oncorhynchus nerka. Canadian Journal of Fisheries and Aquatic Sciences, 54,* 1785–1795.

Fox, E. A. (2002). Female tactics to reduce sexual harassment in the Sumantran orangutan (*Pongo pygmaeus abelii*). *Behavioral Ecology and Sociobiology, 52,* 93–101.

Frank, E., & Anderson, B. P. (1987). Psychiatric disorders in rape victims: Past history and current symptomatology. *Comprehensive Psychiatry, 28,* 77–82.

Frederick, P. C. (1987a). Extrapair copulations in the mating system of white ibis (*Eudocimus albus*). *Behaviour, 100,* 170–201.

Frederick, P. C. (1987b). Responses of male white ibises to their mate's extra-pair copulations. *Behavioral Ecology and Sociobiology, 21,* 223–228.

French, D. C., & Dishion, T. J. (2003). Predictors of early initiation of sexual intercourse among high-risk adolescents. *Journal of Early Adolescence, 23,* 295–315.

Freund, K. (1980). Therapeutic sex drive reduction. *Acta Psychiatrica Scandinavica, 62*, 5–38.

Freund, K. (1988). Courtship disorder: Is this hypothesis valid? In R. A. Prentky & V. L. Quinsey (Eds.), *Human sexual aggression: Current perspectives* (pp. 172–182). New York: New York Academy of Sciences.

Freund, K. (1990). Courtship disorder. In W. L. Marshall, D. R. Laws, & H. E. Barbaree (Eds.), *Handbook of sexual assault: Issues, theories, and treatment of the offender* (pp. 195–207). New York: Plenum Press.

Freund, K., & Kuban, M. (1993). Toward a testable developmental model of pedophilia: The development of erotic age preference. *Child Abuse and Neglect, 17*, 315–324.

Freund, K., Scher, H., & Hucker, S. (1983). The courtship disorders. *Archives of Sexual Behavior, 12*, 369–379.

Freund, K., Scher, H., Racansky, I. G., Campbell, K., & Heasman, G. (1986). Males disposed to commit rape. *Archives of Sexual Behavior, 15*, 23–35.

Freund, K., & Seto, M. C. (1998). Preferential rape in the theory of courtship disorder. *Archives of Sexual Behavior, 27*, 433–443.

Freund, K., Seto, M. C., & Kuban, M. (1997). Frotteurism and the theory of courtship disorder. In D. R. Laws, & W. T. O'Donohue (Eds.), *Sexual deviance: Theory, assessment and treatment* (pp. 111–130). New York: Guilford Press.

Freund, K., & Watson, R. J. (1993). Gender identity disorder and courtship disorder. *Archives of Sexual Behavior, 22*, 13–21.

Frick, P. J., O'Brien, B. S., Wootton, J. M., & McBurnett, K. (1994). Psychopathy and conduct problems in children. *Journal of Abnormal Psychology, 103*, 700–707.

Friedrich, W. N., Gerber, P. N., Koplin, B., Davis, M., Giese, J., Mykelbust, C., et al. (2001). Multimodal assessment of dissociation in adolescents: Inpatients and juvenile sex offenders. *Sexual Abuse: A Journal of Research and Treatment, 13*, 167–177.

Frisbie, L. V. (1969). *Another look at sex offenders in California* (Research Monograph No. 12). California Department of Mental Hygiene.

Frisbie, L. V., & Dondis, E. H. (1965). *Recidivism among treated sex offenders* (Research Monograph No. 5). California Department of Mental Hygiene.

Fu, P., Neff, B. D., & Gross, M. R. (2001). Tactic-specific success in sperm competition. *Proceedings of the Royal Society of London B, 268*, 1105–1112.

Fujioka, M., & Yamagishi, S. (1981). Extramarital and pair copulations in the cattle egret. *Auk, 98*, 134–144.

Furby, L., Weinrott, M. R., & Blackshaw, L. (1989). Sex offender recidivism: A review. *Psychological Bulletin, 105*, 3–30.

Gacono, C. (2000). *The clinical and forensic assessment of psychopathy: A practitioner's guide*. Mahwah, NJ: Erlbaum.

Gade, K. E. (1986). Homosexuality and rape of males in Old Norse law and literature. *Scandinavian Studies, 58*, 124–141.

Gadpaille, W. J. (1980). Cross species and cross-cultural contributions to understanding homosexual activity. *Archives of General Psychiatry, 37,* 349–356.

Galdikas, B. M. F. (1979). Orangutan adaptation at Tanjung Puting Reserve: Mating and ecology. In D. A. Hamburg & E. R. McCown (Eds.), *The great apes* (pp. 195–233). Menlo Park, CA: Benjamin Cummings.

Galdikas, B. M. F. (1981). Orangutan reproduction in the wild. In C. E. Graham (Ed.), *The reproductive biology of the great apes: Comparative and biomedical perspective* (pp. 281–300). New York: Academic Press.

Galdikas, B. M. F. (1985a). Adult male sociality and reproductive tactics among orangutans at Tanjung Puting. *Folia Primatology, 45,* 9–24.

Galdikas, B. M. F. (1985b). Orangutan sociality at Tanjung Puting. *American Journal of Primatology, 9,* 101–119.

Galdikas, B. M. F. (1985c). Subadult male orangutan sociality and reproductive behavior at Tanjung Puting. *American Journal of Primatology, 8,* 87–99.

Galdikas, B. M. F. (1995). *Reflections of Eden: My years with the orangutans of Borneo.* New York: Little Brown.

Gangestad, S. W., & Simpson, J. A. (2000). The evolution of human mating: Trade-offs and strategic pluralism. *Behavioral and Brain Sciences, 23,* 573–644.

Gauthier, G. (1988). Territorial behaviour, forced copulation and mixed reproductive strategy in ducks. *Wildfowl, 39,* 102–114.

Gebhard, P. H., Gagnon, J. H., Pomeroy, W. B., & Christenson, C. V. (1965). *Sex offenders: An analysis of types.* New York: Harper Row.

Gelles, R. J. (1982). Child abuse and family violence: Implications for medical professionals. In E. H. Newberger (Ed.), *Child abuse* (pp. 25–41). Boston: Little Brown.

Gendreau, P., & Ross, R. (1979). Effective correctional treatment: Bibliotherapy for cynics. *Crime and Delinquency, 25,* 463–489.

George, W. H., & Marlatt, G. A. (1986). The effects of alcohol and anger on interest in violence, erotica, and deviance. *Journal of Abnormal Psychology, 95,* 150–158.

Gershenson, H. P., Musick, J., Ruch-Ross, H., Magee, V., Kamiya Rubino, K., & Rosenberg, D. (1989). The prevalence of coercive sexual experience among teenage mothers. *Journal of Interpersonal Violence, 4,* 204–219.

Ghiglieri, M. P. (1999). *The dark side of man.* Reading, MA: Perseus Books.

Gibbens, T. C. N., Soothill, K. L., & Way, C. K. (1981). Sex offences against young girls: A long-term record study. *Psychological Medicine, 11,* 351–357.

Gidycz, C. A., Nelson Coble, C., Latham, L., & Layman, M. J. (1993). Sexual assault experience in adulthood and prior victimization experiences. *Psychology of Women Quarterly, 17,* 151–168.

Ginn, S. R., Walker, K., Poulson, R. L., Singletary, S. K., Cyrus, V. K., & Picarelli, J. A. (1998). Coercive sexual behavior and the influence of alcohol consumption and religiosity among college students in the Bible Belt. *Journal of Social Behavior and Personality, 13,* 151–165.

Giotakos, O., Markianos, M., Vaidakis, N., & Christodoulou, G. N. (2003). Aggression, impulsivity, plasma sex hormones, and biogenic turnover in forensic population of rapists. *Journal of Sex and Marital Therapy, 29*, 215–225.

Gladstone, D. E. (1979). Promiscuity in monogamous colonial birds. *American Naturalist, 114*, 545–557.

Godin, J.-G. J. (1995). Predation risk and alternative mating tactics in male Trinidadian guppies *(Poecilia reticulata)*. *Oecologia, 103*, 224–229.

Gold, S. R., & Clegg, C. L. (1990). Sexual fantasies of college students with coercive experiences and coercive attitudes. *Journal of Interpersonal Violence, 5*, 464–473.

Golden, C. J. (1979). *The Luria-Nebraska Neuropsychological Battery: A manual for clinical and experimental uses.* Lincoln, NE: University of Nebraska Press.

Goodall, J. (1986). *The chimpanzees of Gombe: Patterns of behavior.* Cambridge, MA: Harvard University Press.

Goodburn, S. F. (1984). Mate guarding in the mallard Anas plathyrhyncos. *Ornis Scandinavica, 15*, 261–265.

Goodman, L. A., Koss, M. P., & Russo, N. F. (1993). Violence against women: Physical and mental health effects: Part I. Research findings. *Applied & Preventive Psychology, 2*, 79–89.

Gottfredson, M. R., & Hirschi, T. (1990). *A general theory of crime.* Stanford, CA: Stanford University Press.

Gottschall, J. A., & Gottschall, T. A. (2003). Are per-incident rape-pregnancy rates higher than per-incident consensual pregnancy rates? *Human Nature, 14*, 1–20.

Gottschall, T. (2003, June). *Income inequality and rape: An economic analysis.* Poster presented at the 15th annual meeting of the Human Behavior and Evolution Society, Lincoln, Nebraska.

Gowaty, P. A., & Buschhaus, N. (1998). Ultimate causation or aggressive and forced copulation in birds: Female resistance, the CODE hypothesis, and social monogamy. *American Zoologist, 38*, 207–225.

Graber, B., Hartmann, K., Coffman, J. A., Huey, C. J., & Golden, C. J. (1982). Brain damage among mentally disordered sex offenders. *Journal of Forensic Sciences, 27*, 125–134.

Gravdal, K. (1991). Law and literature in the French Middle Ages: Rape law on trial in Le Roman de Renart. *Romanic Review, 82*, 1–24.

Gray, E. M. (1996). Female control of offspring paternity in a western population of red-winged blackbirds *(Agelaius phoeniceus)*. *Behavioral Ecology and Sociobiology, 38*, 267–278.

Gray, P. B., Kahlenberg, S. M., Barrett, E. S., Lipson, S. F., & Ellison, P. T. (2002). Marriage and fatherhood are associated with lower testosterone in males. *Evolution and Human Behavior, 23*, 193–201.

Greendlinger, V., & Byrne, D. (1987). Coercive sexual fantasies of college men as predictors of self-reported likelihood to rape and overt sexual aggression. *Journal of Sex Research, 23*, 1–11.

Greenfeld, L. A. (1997). *Sex offenses and offenders: An analysis of data on rape and sexual assault* (Publication No. NCJ-163392). Washington, DC: U.S. Department of Justice.

Gross, M. R. (1985). Disruptive selection for alternative life histories in salmon. *Nature, 313*, 47–48.

Gross, M. R. (1991a). Evolution of alternative reproductive strategies: Frequency-dependent sexual selection in male bluegill sunfish. *Philosophical Transactions of the Royal Society of London B, 332*, 59–66.

Gross, M. R. (1991b). Salmon breeding behavior and life history evolution in changing environments. *Ecology, 72*, 1179–1186.

Gross, M. R. (1996). Alternative reproductive strategies and tactics: Diversity within sexes. *Trends in Ecology and Evolution, 11*, 92–98.

Gross, M. R., & Charnov, E. L. (1980). Alternative life histories in bluegill sunfish. *Proceedings of the National Academy of Sciences USA, 77*, 6937–6940.

Grossin, C., Sibille, I., Lorin de la Grandmaison, G., Banasr, A., Brion, F., & Durigon, M. (2003). Analysis of 418 cases of sexual assault. *Forensic Science International, 131*, 125–130.

Groth, A. N. (1979). Psychodynamics of rape. In A. N. Groth (Ed.), *Men who rape: The psychology of the offender* (pp. 12–83). New York: Plenum Press.

Groth, A. N., & Burgess, A. W. (1977). Sexual dysfunction during rape. *New England Journal of Medicine, 297*, 764–766.

Grove, W. M., & Meehl, P. E. (1996). Comparative efficiency of informal (subjective, impressionistic) and formal (mechanical, algorithmic) prediction procedures: The clinical-statistical controversy. *Psychology, Public Policy, and Law, 2*, 293–323.

Gualtieri, T., & Hicks, R. E. (1985). An immunoreactive theory of selective male affliction. *Behavioral and Brain Sciences, 8*, 427–441.

Guarino-Ghezzi, S., & Kimball, L. M. (1998). Juvenile sex offenders in treatment. *Corrections Management Quarterly, 2*, 45–54.

Gullace, N. F. (1997). Sexual violence and family honor: British propaganda and international law during the First World War. *American Historical Review, 102*, 714–747.

Gwynne, D. T. (1991). Sexual competition among females: What causes courtship-role reversal? *Trends in Ecology and Evolution, 6*, 118–121.

Hagan, M. P., & Gust-Brey, K. L. (1999). A ten-year longitudinal study of adolescent rapists upon return to the community. *International Journal of Offender Therapy & Comparative Criminology, 43*, 448–458.

Hall, G. C. N., Shondrick, D. D., & Hirschman, R. (1993a). Conceptually derived treatments for sexual aggressors. *Professional Psychology: Research and Practice, 24*, 62–69.

Hall, G. C. N., Shondrick, D. D., & Hirschman, R. (1993b). The role of sexual arousal in sexually aggressive behavior: A meta-analysis. *Journal of Consulting and Clinical Psychology, 61*, 1091–1095.

Hanawalt, B. A. (1987). Review of rape in medieval England: An historical and sociological study. *Journal of Interdisciplinary History, 17,* 656–657.

Hanson, A. J., & Smith, H. D. (1967). Mate selection in a population of sockeye salmon *(Oncorhynchus nerka)* of mixed age-groups. *Journal of Fishery Research Board of Canada, 24,* 1955–1977.

Hanson, K. (1997). *The development of a brief actuarial risk scale for sexual offense recidivism.* Ottawa, Ontario, Canada: Department of the Solicitor General.

Hanson, R. K., & Bussière, M. T. (1998). Predicting relapse: A meta-analysis of sexual offender recidivism studies. *Journal of Consulting and Clinical Psychology, 66,* 348–362.

Hanson, R. K., Gordon, A., Harris, A. J. R., Marques, J. K., Murphy, W., Quinsey, V. L., et al. (2002). First report of the Collaborative Outcome Data Project on the effectiveness of psychological treatment for sex offenders. *Sexual Abuse: A Journal of Research and Treatment, 14,* 169–194.

Hanson, R. K., & Harris, A. J. (2000). Where should we intervene? Dynamic predictors of sexual offense recidivism. *Criminal Justice and Behavior, 27,* 6–35.

Hanson, R. K., Morton, K. E., & Harris, A. J. R. (2003). Sexual offender recidivism risk. In R. A. Prentky, E. Janus, & M. C. Seto (Eds.), *Sexually coercive behavior: Understanding and management* (pp. 154–166). New York: Annals of the New York Academy of Sciences.

Hanson, R. K., & Slater, S. (1988). Sexual victimization in the history of child sexual abusers: A review. *Annals of Sex Research, 1,* 485–499.

Hanson, R. K., Steffy, R. A., & Gauthier, R. (1993). Long-term recidivism of child molesters. *Journal of Consulting and Clinical Psychology, 61,* 656–652.

Hanson, R. K., & Thornton, D. (2000). Improving risk assessments for sex offenders: A comparison of three actuarial scales. *Law and Human Behavior, 24,* 119–136.

Hare, R. D. (1978). Psychopathy and electrodermal responses to nonsignal stimulation. *Biological Psychology, 6,* 237–246.

Hare, R. D. (1984). Performance of psychopaths on cognitive tasks related to frontal lobe function. *Journal of Abnormal Psychology, 93,* 133–140.

Hare, R. D. (1991). *The Hare Psychopathy Checklist—Revised.* Toronto, Ontario, Canada: Multi-Health Systems.

Hare, R. D., Clark, D., Grann, M., & Thornton, D. (2000). Psychopathy and the predictive validity of the PCL–R: An international perspective. *Behavioral Sciences and the Law, 18,* 623–645.

Hare, R. D., & McPherson, L. M. (1984). Psychopathy and perceptual asymmetry during verbal dichotic listening. *Journal of Abnormal Psychology, 93,* 141–149.

Harned, M. S. (2002). A multivariate analysis of risk markers for dating violence victimization. *Journal of Interpersonal Violence, 17,* 1179–1197.

Harpending, H. C., & Sobus, J. (1987). Sociopathy as an adaptation. *Ethology and Sociobiology, 8,* 63S–72S.

Harris, G. T. (1998, October). *Psychopathy and sexual deviance.* Paper presented at the 17th Annual Research and Treatment Conference of the Association for the Treatment of Sexual Abusers, Vancouver, British Columbia, Canada.

Harris, G. T., & Rice, M. E. (1996). The science in phallometric testing of male sexual interest. *Current Directions in Psychological Science, 5,* 156–160.

Harris, G. T., Rice, M. E., Chaplin, T. C., & Quinsey, V. L. (1999). Dissimulation in phallometric testing of rapists' sexual preferences. *Archives of Sexual Behavior, 28,* 223–232.

Harris, G. T., Rice, M. E., & Cormier, C. A. (1994). Psychopaths: Is a therapeutic community therapeutic? *Therapeutic Communities, 15,* 283–300.

Harris, G. T., Rice, M. E., & Cormier, C. A. (2002). Prospective validation of the Violence Risk Appraisal Guide in predicting violent recidivism among forensic patients. *Law and Human Behavior, 26,* 377–394.

Harris, G. T., Rice, M. E., & Lalumière, M. L. (2001). Criminal violence: The roles of neurodevelopmental insults, psychopathy, and antisocial parenting. *Criminal Justice and Behavior, 28,* 402–426.

Harris, G. T., Rice, M. E., & Quinsey, V. L. (1993). Violent recidivism of mentally disordered offenders: The development of a statistical prediction instrument. *Criminal Justice and Behavior, 20,* 315–335.

Harris, G. T., Rice, M. E., & Quinsey, V. L. (1994). Psychopathy as a taxon: Evidence that psychopaths are a discrete class. *Journal of Consulting and Clinical Psychology, 62,* 387–397.

Harris, G. T., Rice, M. E., & Quinsey, V. L. (1998). Appraisal and management of risk in sexual aggressors: Implications for criminal justice policy. *Psychology, Public Policy, and Law, 4,* 73–115.

Harris, G. T., Rice, M. E., Quinsey, V. L., & Chaplin, T. C. (1996). Viewing time as a measure of sexual interest among child molesters and normal heterosexual men. *Behavioural Research and Therapy, 34,* 389–394.

Harris, G. T., Rice, M. E., Quinsey, V. L., Chaplin, T. C., & Earls, C. M. (1992). Maximizing the discriminant validity of phallometric assessment. *Psychological Assessment, 4,* 502–511.

Harris, G. T., Rice, M. E., Quinsey, V. L., Lalumière, M. L., Boer, D., & Lang, C. (2003). A multi-site comparison of actuarial risk instruments for sex offenders. *Psychological Assessment, 15,* 413–425.

Harris, G. T., Skilling, T. A., & Rice, M. E. (2001). The construct of psychopathy. *Crime and Justice: A Review of Research, 28,* 197–264.

Harris, J. A. (1999). Review and methodological considerations in research on testosterone and aggression. *Aggression and Violent Behavior, 4,* 273–291.

Harris, R. (1993). The "child of the barbarian:" Rape, race and nationalism in France during the First World War. *Past and Present, 141,* 170–206.

Hart, S. D., Forth, A. E., & Hare, R. D. (1990). Performance of criminal psychopaths on selected neuropsychological tests. *Journal of Abnormal Psychology, 99,* 374–379.

Haselton, M. G., & Buss, D. M. (2000). Error management theory: A new perspective on biases in cross-sex mind reading. *Journal of Personality and Social Psychology, 78,* 81–91.

Haselton, M. G., & Buss, D. M. (2001). The affective shift hypothesis: The functions of emotional changes following sexual intercourse. *Personal Relationships, 8,* 357–369.

Hatchwell, B. J. (1988). Intraspecific variation in extra-pair copulation and mate defense in common guillemots *Uria aalge. Behaviour, 107,* 157–185.

Hathaway, S. R., & McKinley, J. C. (1967). *Manual for the Minnesota Multiphasic Personality Inventory.* New York: Psychological Corporation.

Hatziolos, M. E., & Caldwell, R. L. (1983). Role reversal in courtship in the stomatopod *Pseudosquilla ciliata* (Crustacea). *Animal Behaviour, 31,* 1077–1087.

Heim, N. (1981). Sexual behavior of castrated sex offenders. *Archives of Sexual Behavior, 10,* 11–19.

Heim, N., & Hursch, C. J. (1979). Castration of sex offenders: Treatment or punishment? A review and critique of recent European literature. *Archives of Sexual Behavior, 8,* 281–304.

Heise, L. L. (1994). Gender-based violence and women's reproductive health. *International Journal of Gynecology & Obstetrics, 46,* 221–229.

Henmi, Y., Koga, T., & Murai, M. (1993). Mating behavior of the sand bubbler crab *Scopimera globosa. Journal of Crustacean Biology, 13,* 736–744.

Henn, F. A., Herjanic, M., & Vanderpearl, R. H. (1976). Forensic psychiatry: Profiles of two types of sex offenders. *American Journal of Psychiatry, 133,* 694–696.

Herdt, G., & McClintock, M. (2000). The magical age of 10. *Archives of Sexual Behavior, 29,* 587–606.

Hiebert, R. J. V. (1994). Deuteronomy 22:28–29 and its premishnaic interpretations. *Catholic Biblical Quarterly, 56,* 203–220.

Hilton, D. F. J. (1982). Is it rape or forced copulation? *Bioscience, 32,* 641.

Hilton, N. Z., Harris, G. T., & Rice, M. E. (1998). On the validity of self-reported rates of interpersonal violence. *Journal of Interpersonal Violence, 13,* 58–72.

Hilton, N. Z., Harris, G. T., & Rice, M. E. (2000). The functions of aggression by male teenagers. *Journal of Personality and Social Psychology, 79,* 988–994.

Hilton, N. Z., Harris, G. T., & Rice, M. E. (2003). Adolescents' perceptions of the seriousness of sexual aggression: Influence of gender, traditional attitudes, and self-reported experience. *Sexual Abuse: A Journal of Research and Treatment, 15,* 201–214.

Himelein, M. J. (1995). Risk factors for sexual victimization in dating: A longitudinal study of college women. *Psychology of Women Quarterly, 19,* 31–48.

Hogg, J. T. (1984). Mating in bighorn sheep: Multiple creative male strategies. *Science, 225,* 526–529.

Hogg, J. T. (1987). Intrasexual competition and mate choice in Rocky Mountain bighorn sheep. *Ethology, 75,* 119–144.

Hogg, J. T. (1988). Copulatory tactics in relation to sperm competition in Rocky Mountain bighorn sheep. *Behavioral Ecology and Sociobiology, 22,* 49–59.

Hogg, J. T., & Forbes, S. H. (1997). Mating in bighorn sheep: Frequent male reproduction via a high-risk "unconventional" tactic. *Behavioral Ecology and Sociobiology, 41*, 33–48.

Hollin, C. R., & Howells, K. (Eds.). (1991). *Clinical approaches to sex offenders and their victims.* Chichester, England: Wiley.

Holmes, M. M., Resnick, H. S., Kilpatrick, D. G., & Best, C. L. (1996). Rape-related pregnancy: Estimates and descriptive characteristics from a national sample of women. *American Journal of Obstetrics and Gynecology, 175*, 320–324.

Home Office. (1979). *Committee on obscenity and film censorship.* London: Her Majesty's Stationery Office.

Hough, C. (1997). Alfred's domboc and the language of rape: A reconsideration of Alfred Ch. 11. *Medium Ævum, 66*, 1–27.

Howard, R., Payamal, L. T., & Neo, L. H. (1997). Response modulation deficits in psychopaths: A failure to confirm and a reconsideration of the Patterson–Newman model. *Personality and Individual Differences, 22*, 707–717.

Howland, E. W., Kosson, D. S., Patterson, D. S., & Newman, J. P. (1993). Altering a dominant response: Performance of psychopaths and low-socialization college students on a cued reaction time task. *Journal of Abnormal Psychology, 102*, 379–387.

Hucker, S., Langevin, R., & Bain, J. (1988). A double blind trial of sex drive reducing medication in pedophiles. *Annals of Sex Research, 1*, 227–342.

Hucker, S. J., Langevin, R., & Handy, L. C. (1988). Cerebral damage and dysfunction in sexually aggressive men. *Annals of Sex Research, 1*, 33–47.

Hucker, S. J., Langevin, R., Wortzman, G., Dickey, R., Bain, J., Handy, L., et al. (1988). Cerebral damage and dysfunction in sexually aggressive men. *Annals of Sex Research, 1*, 33–47.

Hudson, S. M., & Ward, T. (1997). Intimacy, loneliness, and attachment style in sexual offenders. *Journal of Interpersonal Violence, 12*, 323–339.

Hughes, A. L. (1985). Male size, mating success, and mating strategy in the mosquitofish *Gambusia affinis* (Poeciliidae). *Behavioral Ecology and Sociobiology, 17*, 271–278.

Humphrey, S. E., & Kahn, A. S. (2000). Fraternities, athletic teams, and rape: Importance of identification with a risky group. *Journal of Interpersonal Violence, 15*, 1313–1322.

Hunter, F. M., & Jones, I. L. (1999). The frequency and function of aquatic courtship and copulation in least, crested, whiskered, and parakeet auklets. *The Condor, 101*, 518–528.

Hutchings, J. A., & Myers, R. A. (1988). Mating success of alternative maturation phenotypes in male Atlantic salmon, *Salmo salar. Oecologia, 75*, 169–174.

Intrator, J., Hare, R. D., Stritzke, P., Brichtswein, K., Dorfman, D., Harpur, T., et al. (1997). A brain imaging (single photon emission computerized tomography) study of semantic and affective processing in psychopaths. *Biological Psychiatry, 42*, 96–103.

Ives, E. W. (1978). 'Agaynst taking awaye of Women': The inception and operation of the Abduction Act of 1487. In E. W. Ives, R. J. Knecht, & J. J. Scansbrick (Eds.), *Wealth and power in Tudor England: Essays presented to S. T. Bindoff* (pp. 21–44). London: Knecht & Scansbrick .

Jackson, J. E. (1992). Meaning and message of symbolic sexual violence in Tukanoan ritual. *Anthropological Quarterly, 65,* 1–18.

Jackson, T. L. (1996). *Acquaintance rape: Assessment, treatment, and prevention.* Sarasota, FL: Professional Resource Press.

Jaffee, D., & Straus, M. (1987). Sexual climate and reported rape: A state-level analysis. *Archives of Sexual Behavior, 16,* 107–123.

Janzen, D. H. (1977). A note on optimal male selection by plants. *American Naturalist, 111,* 365–371.

Jensen, A. R. (1998). *The g factor: The science of mental ability.* London: Praeger.

Jessor, R., Costa, F., Jessor, L., & Donovan, J. E. (1983). Time of first intercourse: A prospective study. *Journal of Personality and Social Psychology, 44,* 618–626.

Johnson, J. C., Ivy, T. M., & Sakaluk, S. K. (1999). Female remating propensity contingent on sexual cannibalism in sagebrush crickets, *Cyphoderris strepitans:* A mechanism of cryptic female choice. *Behavioral Ecology, 10,* 227–233.

Johnson, S. D., Gibson, L., & Linden, R. (1978). Alcohol and rape in Winnipeg 1966–1975. *Journal of Studies on Alcohol, 39,* 1887–1894.

Johnson, W. R. (1996). The rapes of Callisto. *Classical Journal, 92,* 9–24.

Johnston, T. D., & Edwards, L. (2002). Genes, interactions, and the development of behavior. *Psychological Review, 109,* 26–34.

Jones, C., & Aronson, E. (1973). Attribution of fault to a rape victim as a function of respectability of the victim. *Journal of Personality and Social Psychology, 26,* 415–419.

Jones, C. B. (1985). Reproductive patterns in mantled howler monkeys: Estrus, mate choice and copulation. *Primates, 26,* 130–142.

Jones, L. M., & Finkelhor, D. (2001, January). The decline in child sexual abuse cases. *Juvenile Justice Bulletin,* pp. 1–12.

Jones, O. D. (1999). Sex, abuse, and the biology of rape: Toward explanation and prevention. *California Law Review, 87,* 827–942.

Jordan, W. C., & Youngson, A. F. (1992). The use of genetic marking to assess the reproductive success of mature male Atlantic salmon parr (*Salmo salar,* L.) under natural spawning conditions. *Journal of Fish Biology, 41,* 613–618.

Kalin, R., & Tilby, P. J. (1978). Development and validation of a sex-role ideology scale. *Psychological Reports, 42,* 731–738.

Kanin, E. J. (1957). Male aggression in dating-courtship relations. *American Journal of Sociology, 63,* 197–204.

Kanin, E. J. (1983). Rape as a function of relative sexual frustration. *Psychological Reports, 51,* 133–134.

Kanin, E. J. (1984). Date rape: Unofficial criminals and victims. *Victimology, 9,* 95–108.

Kanin, E. J. (1985). Date rapists: Differential sexual socialization and relative deprivation. *Archives of Sexual Behavior, 14*, 219–231.

Karino, K., & Nakazono, A. (1993). Reproductive behavior of the territorial herbivore *Stegastes nigricans* (Pisces: Pomacentridae) in relation to colony formation. *Journal of Ethology, 11*, 99–110.

Katano, O. (1992). Spawning tactics of paired males of the dark chub, *Zacco temmincki*, reflects potential fitness costs of satellites. *Environmental Biology of Fishes, 35*, 343–350.

Kaufman, J., & Zigler, E. (1987). Do abused children become abusive parents? *American Journal of Orthopsychiatry, 57*, 186–192.

Keenleyside, M. H. A. (1972). Intraspecific intrusions into nests of spawning longear sunfish (Pisces: Centrarchidae). *Copeia*, 272–278.

Kelley McLain, D., & Pratt, A. E. (1999). The cost of sexual coercion and heterospecific sexual harassment on the fecundity of a host-specific, seed-eating insect (*Neacoryphus bicrucis*). *Behavioral Ecology and Sociobiology, 46*, 164–170.

Kelly, A. (1950). *Eleanor of Aquitaine and the four kings*. Cambridge, MA: Harvard University Press.

Kiehl, K. A., Hare, R. D., Liddle, P. F., & McDonald, J. J. (1999). Reduced P300 responses in criminal psychopaths during a visual oddball task. *Biological Psychiatry, 45*, 1498–1507.

Kilpatrick, D. G., Best, C. L., Saunders, B. E., & Veronen, L. J. (1988). Rape in marriage and in dating relationships: How bad is it for mental health? In R. A. Prentky & V. L. Quinsey (Eds.), *Human sexual aggression: Current perspectives* (pp. 335–358). New York: Annals of the New York Academy of Sciences.

Kilpatrick, D. G., Saunders, B. E., Amick-McMullan, A., Best, C. L., Vernonen, L. J., & Resnick, H. S. (1989). Victim and crime factors associated with the development of crime-related post-traumatic stress disorder. *Behavior Therapy, 20*, 199–214.

Kimmel, M. S., & Linders, A. (1996). Does censorship make a difference? An aggregate empirical analysis of pornography and rape. *Journal of Psychology and Human Sexuality, 8*, 1–20.

King, K. C. (1987). *Achilles: Paradigms of the war hero from Homer to the Middle Ages*. Berkeley: University of California Press.

Knight, R. A. (1999). Validation of a typology for rapists. *Journal of Interpersonal Violence, 14*, 297–323.

Knight, R. A. (in press). Typologies/profiles of rapists. In J. R. Conte (Ed.), *Encyclopedia of trauma and abuse*. New York: Sage.

Knight, R. A., & Prentky, R. A. (1987). The developmental antecedents and adult adaptations of rapist subtypes. *Criminal Justice and Behavior, 14*, 403–426.

Knight, R. A., & Prentky, R. A. (1990). Classifying sexual offenders: The development and corroboration of taxonomic models. In W. L. Marshall, D. R. Laws, &

H. E. Barbaree (Eds.), *Handbook of sexual assault: Issues, theories and treatment of the offender* (pp. 23–52). New York: Plenum Press.

Knight, R. A., Prentky, R. A., & Cerce, D. (1994). The development, reliability, and validity of an inventory for the multidimensional assessment of sex and aggression. *Criminal Justice and Behavior, 21,* 72–94.

Knight, R. A., & Sims-Knight, J. E. (in press). The developmental antecedents of sexual coercion against women in adolescents. In R. Geffner & K. Franey (Eds.), *Sex offenders: Assessment and treatment.* New York: Haworth Press.

Knight, R. A., & Sims-Knight, J. E. (2003). The developmental antecedents of sexual coercion against women: Testing alternative hypotheses with structural equation modeling. In R. A. Prentky, E. Janus, & M. Seto (Eds.), *Sexually coercive behavior: Understanding and management* (pp. 72–85). New York: Academy of Sciences.

Kodric-Brown, A. (1977). Reproductive success and the evolution of breeding territories in pupfish (*Cyprinondon*). *Evolution, 31,* 750–766.

Koss, M. P. (1988). Hidden rape: Sexual aggression and victimization in a national sample of students in higher education. In A. W. Burgess (Ed.), *Rape and sexual assault II* (pp. 3–25). New York: Garland Press.

Koss, M. P., & Dinero, T. E. (1988). Predictors of sexual aggression among a national sample of male college students. In R. A. Prentky & V. L. Quinsey (Eds.), *Human sexual aggression: Current perspectives* (pp. 133–147). New York: Annals of the New York Academy of Sciences.

Koss, M. P., & Gaines, J. A. (1993). The prediction of sexual aggression by alcohol use, athletic participation, and fraternity affiliation. *Journal of Interpersonal Violence, 8,* 94–108.

Koss, M. P., Gidycz, C. A., & Wisniewski, N. (1987). The scope of rape: Incidence and prevalence of sexual aggression and victimization in a national sample of higher education students. *Journal of Consulting and Clinical Psychology, 55,* 162–170.

Koss, M. P., & Leonard, K. E. (1984). Sexually aggressive men: Empirical findings and theoretical implications. In N. Malamuth & E. Donnerstein (Eds.), *Pornography and sexual aggression* (pp. 213–232). New York: Academic Press.

Koss, M. P., Leonard, K. E., Beezley, D. A., & Oros, C. J. (1985). Nonstranger sexual aggression: A discriminant analysis of the psychological characteristics of undetected offenders. *Sex Roles, 12,* 981–992.

Koss, M. P., & Oros, C. (1982). Sexual experiences survey: A research instrument investigating sexual aggression and victimization. *Journal of Consulting and Clinical Psychology, 50,* 455–457.

Koss, M. P., Woodruff, W. J., & Koss, P. G. (1991). Criminal victimization among primary care medical patients: Prevalence, incidence, and physician usage. *Behavioral Sciences and the Law, 9,* 85–96.

Kosson, D. S., Kelly, J. C., & White, J. W. (1997). Psychopathy-related traits predict self-reported sexual aggression among college men. *Journal of Interpersonal Violence, 12,* 241–254.

Krahé, B., Scheinberger-Olwig, R., & Bieneck, S. (2003). Men's report of nonconsensual sexual interactions with women: Prevalence and impact. *Archives of Sexual Behavior, 32*, 165–175.

Krahé, B., Waizenhöfer, E., & Möller, I. (2003). Women's sexual aggression against men: Prevalence and predictors. *Sex Roles, 49*, 219–232.

Kramer, H., & Sprenger, J. (1948). *The Malleus Maleficarum* (M. Summers, Trans.). London: Dover. (Original work published 1486)

Kroner, D. G., & Mills, J. F. (2001). The accuracy of five risk appraisal instruments in predicting institutional misconduct and new convictions. *Criminal Justice and Behavior, 28*, 471–489.

Kushland, J. A. (1973). Promiscuous mating behavior in the white ibis. *Wilson Bulletin, 85*, 331–332.

Kutchinsky, B. (1991). Pornography and rape: Theory and practice? *International Journal of Law and Psychiatry, 14*, 47–64.

Laakso, M. P., Vaurio, O., Koivisto, E., Savolainen, L., Eronen, M., Aronen, M. J., et al. (2001). Psychopathy and the posterior hippocampus. *Behavioural Brain Research, 118*, 187–193.

Lalumière, M. L., Chalmers, L., Quinsey, V. L., & Seto, M. C. (1996). A test of the mate deprivation hypothesis of sexual coercion. *Ethology and Sociobiology, 17*, 299–318.

Lalumière, M. L., & Earls, C. M. (1992). Voluntary control of penile responses as a function of stimulus duration and instructions. *Behavioral Assessment, 14*, 121–132.

Lalumière, M. L., & Harris, G. T. (1998). Common questions about phallometric assessment. *Sexual Abuse: A Journal of Research and Treatment, 10*, 227–237.

Lalumière, M. L., Harris, G. T., Quinsey, V. L., & Rice, M. E. (1998). Sexual deviance and number of older brothers among sexual offenders. *Sexual Abuse: A Journal of Research and Treatment, 10*, 5–15.

Lalumière, M. L., Harris, G. T., & Rice, M. E. (2001). Psychopathy and developmental instability. *Evolution and Human Behavior, 22*, 75–92.

Lalumière, M. L., & Quinsey, V. L. (1993). The sensitivity of phallometric measures with rapists. *Annals of Sex Research, 6*, 123–138.

Lalumière, M. L., & Quinsey, V. L. (1994). The discriminability of rapists from nonsex offenders using phallometric measures: A meta-analysis. *Criminal Justice and Behavior, 21*, 150–175.

Lalumière, M. L., & Quinsey, V. L. (1996). Sexual deviance, antisociality, mating effort, and the use of sexually coercive behaviors. *Personality and Individual Differences, 21*, 33–48.

Lalumière, M. L., & Quinsey, V. L. (1998a, October). *Mating effort and sexually coercive behavior*. Paper presented at the 17th Annual Research and Treatment Conference of the Association for the Treatment of Sexual Abusers, Vancouver, British Columbia, Canada.

Lalumière, M. L., & Quinsey, V. L. (1998b). Pavlovian conditioning of sexual interests in human males. *Archives of Sexual Behavior, 27*, 241–252.

Lalumière, M. L., & Quinsey, V. L. (1999). A Darwinian interpretation of individual differences in male propensity for sexual aggression. *Jurimetric, 39*, 201–216.

Lalumière, M. L., & Quinsey, V. L. (2000). Good genes, mating effort, and delinquency. *Behavioral and Brain Sciences, 23*, 608–609.

Lalumière, M. L., Quinsey, V. L., & Craig, W. M. (1996). Why children from the same family are so different from one another: A Darwinian note. *Human Nature, 7*, 281–290.

Lalumière, M. L., Quinsey, V., Harris, G., Rice, M., Coleman, G., & Côté, K. (2000). *Birth order and rape.* Paper presented at the Annual Forensic Day of the University of Toronto, Penetanguishene, Ontario, Canada.

Lalumière, M. L., Quinsey, V. L., Harris, G. T., Rice, M. E., & Trautrimas, C. (2003). Are rapists differentially aroused by coercive sex in phallometric assessments? In R. Prentky, E. Janus, & M. C. Seto (Eds.), *Sexually coercive behavior: Understanding and management* (pp. 211–224). New York: Annals of the New York Academy of Sciences.

Landolt, M. A., Lalumière, M. L., & Quinsey, V. L. (1995). Sex differences and intra-sex variations in human mating tactics: An evolutionary approach. *Ethology and Sociobiology, 16*, 3–23.

Langan, P. A., Schmitt, E. L., & Durose, M. R. (2003). *Recidivism of sex offenders released from prison in 1994* (Publication No. NCJ 198281). Washington, DC: Bureau of Justice Statistics.

Langevin, R. (1983). *Sexual strands: Understanding and treating sexual anomalies in men.* Hillsdale, NJ: Erlbaum.

Langevin, R., Ben-Aron, M. H., Coulthard, R., Heasman, G., Purins, J. E., Handy, L., et al. (1985). Sexual aggression: Constructing a predictive equation: A controlled pilot study. In R. Langevin (Ed.), *Erotic preference, gender identity, and aggression in men: New research studies* (pp. 39–76). Hillsdale, NJ: Erlbaum.

Langevin, R., & Lang, R. A. (1990). Substance abuse among sex offenders. *Annals of Sex Research, 3*, 397–424.

Langevin, R., Paitich, D., & Russon, A. E. (1985). Are rapists sexually anomalous, aggressive, or both? In R. Langevin (Ed.), *Erotic preference, gender identity, and aggression in men: New research studies* (pp. 13–38). Hillsdale, NJ: Erlbaum.

Langevin, R., Wright, P., & Handy, I. (1988). What treatment do sex offenders want? *Annals of Sex Research, 1*, 353–385.

Langevin, R., Wright, P., & Handy, I. (1989). Characteristics of sex offenders who were sexually victimized as children. *Annals of Sex Research, 2*, 227–253.

Lank, D. B., Mineau, P., Rockwell, R. F., & Cooke, F. (1989). Intraspecific nest parasitism and extra-pair copulation in lesser snow geese. *Animal Behaviour, 37*, 74–89.

Lansky, D., & Wilson, G. T. (1981). Alcohol, expectations, and sexual arousal in males: An information processing analysis. *Journal of Abnormal Psychology, 90*, 35–45.

Laub, J. H., Nagin, D. S., & Sampson, R. J. (1998). Trajectories of change in criminal offending: Good marriages and the desistance process. *American Sociological Review, 63*, 225–238.

Lawson, J. E. (1989). "She's a pretty woman . . . for a gook": The misogyny of the Vietnam War. *Journal of American Culture, 12*, 55–65.

Le Boeuf, B. J., & Mesnick, S. (1990). Sexual behavior of male Northern elephant seals: I. Lethal injuries to adult females. *Behaviour, 116*, 143–162.

Lee, B. S. (1995). Exploitation and excommunication in The wife of Bath's tale. *Philological Quarterly, 74*, 17–35.

Lefkowitz, M. R., & Fant, M. B. (1992). *Women's life in Greece and Rome: A sourcebook in translation* (2nd ed.). Baltimore: Johns Hopkins University Press.

Leitenberg, H., & Henning, K. (1995). Sexual fantasy. *Psychological Bulletin, 117*, 469–496.

Levenson, M. R., Kiehl, K. A., & Fitzpatrick, C. M. (1995). Assessing psychopathic attributes in a noninstitutionalized population. *Journal of Personality and Social Psychology, 68*, 151–158.

LeVine, R. A. (1959). Gusii sex offenders: A study in social control. *American Anthropologist, 61*, 965–990.

Lightfoot, L. O., & Barbaree, H. E. (1993). The relationship between substance use and abuse and sexual offending in adolescents. In H. E. Barbaree, W. L. William, & S. M. Hudson (Eds.), *The juvenile sex offender* (pp. 203–224). New York: Guilford Press.

Lilienfeld, S. O., & Marino, L. (1999). Essentialism revisited: Evolutionary theory and the concept of mental disorder. *Journal of Abnormal Psychology, 108*, 400–411.

Lim, I. E. C., Gwee, K. P., Woo, M., & Parker, G. (2001). Men who commit rape in Singapore. *Annals Academy of Medicine Singapore, 30*, 620–624.

Lindsay, W. R., & Smith, A. H. (1998). Responses to treatment for sex offenders with intellectual disability: A comparison of men with 1- and 2-year probation sentences. *Journal of Intellectual Disability Research, 42*, 346–353.

Linley, J. R., & Adams, G. M. (1972). A study of mating behaviour of *Culicoides melleus* (Coquillett) (Diptera: Ceratopogonidae). *Transactions of the Royal Entomological Society of London, 124*, 81–121.

Linton, D. K., & Wiener, N. I. (2002). Personality and potential conceptions: Mating success in a modern Western male sample. *Personality and Individual Differences, 31*, 675–688.

Lipsey, M. W. (1992). Juvenile delinquency treatment: A meta-analytic inquiry into the variability of effects. In T. D. Cook (Ed.), *Meta-analysis for explanation: A casebook* (pp. 83–126). New York: Russell Sage.

Lipton, D. N., McDonel, E. C., & McFall, R. M. (1987). Heterosocial perception in rapists. *Journal of Consulting and Clinical Psychology, 55*, 17–21.

Lisak, D., & Ivan, C. (1995). Deficits in intimacy and empathy in sexually aggressive men. *Journal of Interpersonal Violence, 10*, 296–308.

Lisak, D., & Miller, P. M. (2002). Repeat rape and multiple offending among undetected rapists. *Violence and Victims, 17*, 73–84.

Lohr, B. A., Adams, H. E., & Davis, J. M. (1997). Sexual arousal to erotic and aggressive stimuli in sexually coercive and noncoercive men. *Journal of Abnormal Psychology, 106,* 230–242.

Looman, J., Abracen, J., & Nicholaichuk, T. P. (2000). Recidivism among treated sexual offenders and matched controls. *Journal of Interpersonal Violence, 15,* 279–290.

Low, B. S. (2000). *Why sex matters: A Darwinian look at human behavior.* New Haven, CT: Princeton University Press.

Lykken, D. T. (1957). A study of anxiety in the sociopathic personality. *Journal of Abnormal and Social Psychology, 55,* 6–10.

Lykken, D. T. (2001). Parental licensure. *American Psychologist, 56,* 885–894.

MacKinnon, J. (1979). Reproductive behavior in wild orangutan populations. In D. A. Hamburg & E. R. McCown (Eds.), *The great apes* (pp. 257–273). Menlo Park, CA: Benjamin Cummings.

MacRoberts, M. H. (1973). Extramarital courting in lesser black-backed and herring gulls. *Z. Tierpsychology, 32,* 62–74.

Maekawa, K., & Onozato, H. (1986). Reproductive tactics and fertilization success of mature male Miyabe charr, *Salvelinus malma miyabei. Environmental Biology of Fishes, 15,* 119–129.

Maggioncalda, A. N., & Sapolsky, R. M. (2002). Disturbing behaviors of the orangutan. *Scientific American,* 60–65.

Magrath, M. J. L., & Komdeur, J. (2003). Is male care compromised by additional mating opportunity? *Trends in Ecology and Evolution, 18,* 424–430.

Magurran, A. E., & Seghers, B. H. (1990). Risk sensitive courtship in the guppy (*Poecilia reticulata*). *Behaviour, 112,* 194–201.

Mahoney, E. R., Shively, M. D., & Traw, M. (1986). Sexual coercion and assault: Male socialization and female risk. *Sexual Coercion & Assault, 1,* 2–8.

Mahoney, P., & Williams, L. M. (1998). Sexual assault in marriage: Prevalence, consequences, and treatment of wife rape. In J. L. Jasinski & L. M. Williams (Eds.), *Partner violence: A comprehensive review of 20 years of research* (pp. 113–158). Thousand Oaks, CA: Sage.

Malamuth, N. M. (1986). Predictors of naturalistic sexual aggression. *Journal of Personality and Social Psychology, 50,* 953–962.

Malamuth, N. M. (1988a). A multidimensional approach to sexual aggression: Combining measures of past behavior with present likelihood. In R. A. Prentky & V. L. Quinsey (Eds.), *Human sexual aggression: Current perspectives* (pp. 123–132). New York: Annals of the New York Academy of Sciences.

Malamuth, N. M. (1988b). Predicting laboratory aggression against female and male targets: Implications for sexual aggression. *Journal of Research in Personality, 22,* 474–495.

Malamuth, N. M. (2003). Criminal and noncriminal sexual aggressors : Integrating psychopathy in a hierarchical-mediational confluence model. In R. Prentky, E.

Janus, & M. C. Seto (Eds.), *Sexual coercive behavior: Understanding and management* (pp. 33–58). New York: Annals of the New York Academy of Sciences.

Malamuth, N. M., Addison, T., & Koss, M. (2000). Pornography and sexual aggression: Are there reliable effects and can we understand them? *Annual Review of Sex Research, 11,* 26–91.

Malamuth, N. M., & Brown, L. M. (1994). Sexually aggressive men's perceptions of women's communications: Testing three explanations. *Journal of Personality and Social Psychology, 67,* 699–712.

Malamuth, N. M., & Ceniti, J. (1986). Repeated exposure to violent and nonviolent pornography: Likelihood of raping ratings and laboratory aggression against women. *Aggressive Behavior, 12,* 129–137.

Malamuth, N. M., & Check, J. V. (1983). Sexual arousal to rape depictions: Individual differences. *Journal of Abnormal Psychology, 92,* 55–67.

Malamuth, N. M., Heavey, C. L., & Linz, D. (1993). Predicting men's antisocial behavior against women: The interaction model of sexual aggression. In G. C. Nagayama Hall & R. Hirschman (Eds.), *Sexual aggression: Issues in etiology, assessment, and treatment* (pp. 63–97). Philadelphia: Taylor & Francis.

Malamuth, N. M., & Heilmann, M. F. (1998). Evolutionary psychology and sexual aggression. In C. Crawford & D. L. Krebs (Eds.), *Handbook of evolutionary psychology: Ideas, issues, and applications* (pp. 515–542). Mahwah, NJ: Erlbaum.

Malamuth, N. M., Linz, D., Heavey, C. L., Barnes, G., & Acker, M. (1995). Using the confluence model of sexual aggression to predict men's conflicts with women: A 10-year follow-up study. *Journal of Personality and Social Psychology, 69,* 353–369.

Malamuth, N. M., Sockloskie, R. J., Koss, M. P., & Tanaka, J. S. (1991). Characteristics of aggressors against women: Testing a model using a national sample of college students. *Journal of Consulting and Clinical Psychology, 59,* 670–681.

Malamuth, N. M., & Thornhill, N. W. (1994). Hostile masculinity, sexual aggression, and gender-biased domineeringness in conversations. *Aggressive Behavior, 20,* 185–193.

Maletzky, B. M. (1991). The use of medroxyprogesterone acetate to assist in the treatment of sexual offenders. *Annals of Sex Research, 4,* 117–129.

Malinowski, B. (1929). *The sexual life of savages in North-Western Melanesia.* New York: Eugenics Publishing Co.

Manning, A. (1967). The control of sexual receptivity in female *Drosophila. Animal Behaviour, 15,* 239–250.

Mark, V. H., & Ervin, F. R. (1970). *Violence and the brain.* New York: Harper & Row.

Marlow, B. J. (1975). The comparative behaviour of the Australian sea lions *Neophoca cinerea* and *Phocarctos hookeri* (Pinnipedia: Otariidae). *Mammalia, 39,* 159–230.

Marques, J. K., Day, D. M., Nelson, C., & West, M. (1994). Effects of cognitive–behavioral treatment on sex offender recidivism. *Criminal Justice and Behavior, 21,* 28–54.

Marques, J. K., & Nelson, C. (1992). The relapse prevention model: Can it work with sex offenders? In R. D. Peters, R. J. McMahon, & V. L. Quinsey (Eds.), *Aggression and violence throughout the life span* (pp. 222–243). Thousand Oaks, CA: Sage Publications.

Marshall, J. M. (1985). *Rape in medieval England: An historical and sociological study.* Lanham, MD: University Press of America.

Marshall, W. L. (1993). A revised approach to the treatment of men who sexually assault adult females. In G. C. Nagayama Hall, R. Hirschman, J. R. Graham, & M. S. Zaragoza (Eds.), *Sexual aggression: Issues in etiology, assessment, and treatment* (pp. 143–166). Washington, DC: Taylor & Francis.

Marshall, W. L. (2001). Adult sexual offenders against women. In C. R. Hollin (Ed.), *Handbook of offender assessment and treatment* (pp. 333–348). New York: Wiley.

Marshall, W. L., & Barbaree, H. E. (1988). The long-term evaluation of a behavioral treatment program for child molesters. *Behaviour Research and Therapy, 26*, 499–511.

Marshall, W. L., Eccles, A., & Barbaree, H. E. (1991). The treatment of exhibitionists: A focus on sexual deviance versus cognitive and relationship features. *Behavior Research and Therapy, 29*, 129–135.

Marshall, W. L., & Fernandez, Y. M. (2000). Phallometric testing with sexual offenders: Limits to its value. *Clinical Psychology Review, 20*, 807–822.

Marshall, W. L., & Hall, G. C. (1995). The value of the MMPI in deciding forensic issues in accused sexual offenders. *Sexual Abuse: A Journal of Research and Treatment, 7*, 205–219.

Marshall, W. L., Jones, R., Ward, T., Johnston, P., & Barbaree, H. E. (1991). Treatment outcome with sex offenders. *Clinical Psychology Review, 11*, 465–485.

Marshall, W. L., Kennedy, P., & Yates, P. (2002). Issues concerning the reliability and validity of the diagnosis of sexual sadism applied in prison settings. *Sexual Abuse: A Journal of Research and Treatment, 14*, 301–311.

Marshall, W. L., Kennedy, P., Yates, P., & Serran, G. (2002). Diagnosing sexual sadism in sexual offenders: Reliability across diagnosticians. *International Journal of Offender Therapy and Comparative Criminology, 46*, 668–677.

Martin, I. (1998). *Efficacité d'un programme cognitif–behavioural institutionnel pour délinquents sexuels.* Unpublished doctoral dissertation, Department of Psychology, University of Montreal, Quebec, Canada.

Martin, P. Y., & Hummer, R. A. (1998). Fraternities and rape on campus. In M. E. Odem & J. Clay-Warner (Eds.), *Confronting rape and sexual assault* (pp. 165–180). Wilmington, DE: Scholarly Resources.

Marx, B. P., Gross, A. M., & Adams, H. E. (1999). The effect of alcohol on the responses of sexually coercive and noncoercive men to an experimental rape analogue. *Sexual Abuse: A Journal of Research and Treatment, 11*, 131–145.

Marx, B. P., Van Wie, V., & Gross, A. M. (1996). Date rape risk factors: A review and methodological critique of the literature. *Aggression and Violent Behavior, 1*, 27–45.

Matthews, I. M., & Magurran, A. E. (2000). Evidence for sperm transfer during sneaky mating in wild Trinidadian guppies. *Journal of Fish Biology, 56,* 1381–1386.

Mazur, A., & Booth, A. (1998). Testosterone and dominance in men. *Behavioral and Brain Sciences, 21,* 353–397.

Mazur, A., Halpern, C., & Udry, J. R. (1994). Dominant looking males teenagers copulate earlier. *Ethology and Sociobiology, 15,* 87–94.

McCauley, D. E. (1981). Application of the Kence–Bryant model of mating behavior to a natural population of soldier beetles. *American Naturalist, 117,* 400–402.

McCauley, D. E., & Wade, M. J. (1978). Female choice and the mating structure of a natural population of the soldier beetle, *Chauliognathus pennsylvanicus. Evolution, 32,* 771–775.

McConaghy, N. (1999). Methodological issues concerning evaluation of treatment for sexual offenders: Randomization, treatment, dropouts, untreated controls, and within-treatment studies. *Sexual Abuse: A Journal of Research and Treatment, 11,* 183–193.

McConaghy, N., Blaszczynski, A., & Kidson, W. (1988). Treatment of sex offenders with imaginal desensitization and/or medroxyprogesterone. *Acta Psychiatrica Scandinavica, 77,* 199–206.

McCord, J. (1978). A thirty-year follow-up of treatment effects. *American Psychologist, 33,* 284–289.

McCormack, A., Rokous, F. E., Hazelwood, R. R., & Burgess, A. W. (1992). An exploration of incest in the childhood development of serial rapists. *Journal of Family Violence, 7,* 219–228.

McCrae, R. R., Costa, P. T., Jr., Ostendorf, F., Angleitner, A., Hřebíčková, M., Avia, M. D., et al. (2000). Nature over nurture: Temperament, personality and lifespan development. *Journal of Personality and Social Psychology, 78,* 173–186.

McDonald, A., & Paitich, D. (1983). Psychological profile of the rapists. *American Journal of Forensic Psychiatry, 111,* 159–172.

McDonel, E. C., & McFall, R. M. (1991). Construct validity of two heterosocial perception skill measures for assessing rape proclivity. *Violence and Victims, 6,* 17–30.

McGrath, R. J., Hoke, S. E., & Vojtisek, J. E. (1998). Cognitive–behavioral treatment of sex offenders. *Criminal Justice and Behavior, 25,* 203–225.

McKinney, F. (1985). Primary and secondary male reproductive strategies of dabbling ducks. *Ornithological Monographs, 37,* 68–82.

McKinney, F., Cheng, K. M., & Bruggers, D. J. (1984). Sperm competition in apparently monogamous birds. In R. L. Smith (Ed.), *Sperm competition and the evolution of animal mating systems* (pp. 523–545). New York: Academic Press.

McKinney, F., & Evarts, S. (1997). Sexual coercion in waterfowl and other birds. In P. G. Parker & N. T. Burley (Eds.), *Avian reproductive tactics: Female and male perspectives* (pp. 163–195). Lawrence, KS: Allen Press.

McKinney, F., & Stolen, P. (1982). Extra-pair-bond courtship and forced copulation among captive green-winged teal *(Anas crecca carolinensis)*. *Animal Behaviour, 30*, 461–474.

McLain, D. K. (1982). Density dependent sexual selection and positive phenotypic assortative mating in natural populations of the soldier beetle, *Chauliognathus pennsylvanicus. Evolution, 36*, 1227–1235.

Mealey, L. (1995). The sociobiology of psychopathy: An integrated evolutionary model. *Behavioral and Brain Sciences, 18*, 523–599.

Mealey, L. (2000). *Sex difference: Developmental and evolutionary strategies.* New York: Academic Press.

Mealey, L. (2003). Combating rape: Views from an evolutionary psychologist. In R. W. Bloom & N. Dess (Eds.), *Evolutionary psychology and violence: A primer for policymakers and public policy advocates.* Oxford, England: Praeger.

Meanly, B. (1955). A nesting study of the little blue heron in Eastern Arkansas. *Wilson Bulletin, 67*, 84–99.

Meehl, P. E., & Golden, R. R. (1982). Taxometric methods. In P. C. Kendall & J. N. Butcher (Eds.), *Handbook of research methods in clinical psychology* (pp. 127–181). New York: Wiley.

Meese, A. G. E. (1986). *Attorney general (Edwin Meese) commission report.* Washington, DC: U.S. Government Printing Office.

Mesnick, S. L. (1997). Sexual alliances: Evidence and evolutionary implications. In P. Gowaty (Ed.), *Feminism and evolutionary biology* (pp. 207–260). New York: Chapman Hall.

Mesnick, S. L., & Le Boeuf, B. J. (1991). Sexual behavior of male northern elephant seals: II. Female response to potentially injurious encounters. *Behaviour, 117*, 262–280.

Mezey, G. (1994). Rape in war. *Journal of Forensic Psychiatry, 5*, 583–596.

Michael, R. P., & Zumpe, D. (1983). Sexual violence in the United States and the role of season. *American Journal of Psychiatry, 7*, 883–886.

Millon, T. (1977). *Millon Clinical Multiaxial Inventory: Manual.* Minneapolis, MN: NCS Interpretive Scoring Systems.

Mills, J. A. (1994). Extra-pair copulations in the red-billed gull: Females with high-quality, attentive males resist. *Behaviour, 128*, 41–64.

Milton, K. (1985). Mating patters of woolly spider monkeys, *Brachyteles arachnoides:* Implications for female choice. *Behavioral Ecology and Sociobiology, 17*, 53–59.

Mineau, P., & Cooke, F. (1979). Rape in the lesser snow goose. *Behaviour, 70*, 280–291.

Miner, M. H., West, M. A., & Day, D. M. (1995). Sexual preference for child and aggressive stimuli: Comparison of rapists and child molesters using auditory and visual stimuli. *Behavior Research and Therapy, 33*, 545–551.

Mitani, J. C. (1985). Mating behaviour of male orangutans in the Kutai Game Reserve, Indonesia. *Animal Behaviour, 33*, 392–402.

Mitchell, F. J. (1973). Studies on the ecology of the agamid lizard *Amphibolurus maculosus* (Mitchell). *Transactions of the Royal Society of South Australia, 97*, 47–76.

Moffitt, T. E. (1993). Adolescence-limited and life-course-persistent antisocial behavior: A developmental taxonomy. *Psychological Bulletin, 100*, 674–701.

Moffitt, T. E., & Caspi, A. (2001). Childhood predictors differentiate life-course persistent and adolescence-limited antisocial pathways among males and females. *Developmental and Psychopathology, 13*, 84–100.

Moffitt, T. E., Caspi, A., Harrington, H., & Milne, B. J. (2002). Males on the life-course-persistent and adolescence-limited antisocial pathways: Follow-up at age 26 years. *Development and Psychopathology, 14*, 179–207.

Møller, A. P. (1990). Sexual behavior is related to badge size in the house sparrow *Passer domesticus. Behavioral Ecology and Sociobiology, 27*, 23–29.

Money, J. (1995). Forensic sexology: Paraphilic serial rape (biastophilia) and lust murder (erotophonophilia). *Acta Sexologica, 1*, 47–62.

Monson, C. M., & Langhinrichsen-Rohling, J. (1998). Sexual and nonsexual marital aggression: Legal considerations, epidemiology, and an integrated typology of perpetrators. *Aggression and Violent Behavior, 3*, 369–389.

Morris, D. (1952). Homosexuality in the ten-spined stickleback *(Pygosteus pungitius L.). Behaviour, 4*, 233–261.

Morton, E. S. (1987). Variation in mate guarding intensity by male purple martins. *Behaviour, 101*, 211–224.

Morton, E. S., Forman, L., & Braun, M. (1990). Extrapair fertilizations and the evolution of colonial breeding in purple martins. *Auk, 107*, 275–283.

Mossman, D. (1994). Assessing predictions of violence: Being accurate about accuracy. *Journal of Consulting and Clinical Psychology, 61*, 293–323.

Muehlenhard, C. L., & Linton, M. A. (1987). Date rape and sexual aggression in dating situations: Incidence and risk factors. *Journal of Counseling Psychology, 34*, 186–196.

Muir, G., & MacLeod, M. D. (2003). The demographic and spatial patterns of recorded rape in a large UK metropolitan area. *Psychology, Crime, & Law, 9*, 345–355.

Murdock, G. P., & White, D. R. (1969). Standard cross-cultural sample. *Ethnology, 13*, 329–369.

Murnen, S. K., Wright, C., & Kaluzny, G. (2002). If "boys will be boys," then girls will be victims? A meta-analytic review of the research that relates masculine ideology to sexual aggression. *Sex Roles, 46*, 359–375.

Murphy, W. D., Krisak, J., Stalgaitis, S., & Anderson, K. (1984). The use of penile tumescence measures with incarcerated rapists: Further validity issues. *Archives of Sexual Behavior, 13*, 545–554.

Nacci, P. L., & Kane, R. R. (1984). Inmate sexual aggression: Some evolving propositions, empirical findings, and mitigating counter-forces. *Journal of Offender Counseling, Services & Rehabilitation, 9*, 1–20.

Nadler, R. D. (1977). Sexual behavior of captive orangutans. *Archives of Sexual Behavior, 6,* 457–475.

Nadler, R. D. (1988). Sexual aggression in the great apes. *Annals of the New York Academy of Sciences USA, 528,* 154–162.

Nadler, R. D. (1989). Sexual initiation in wild mountain gorillas. *International Journal of Primatology, 10,* 81–92.

Nadler, R. D., & Collins, D. C. (1991). Copulatory frequency, urinary pregnanediol, and fertility in great apes. *American Journal of Primatology, 24,* 167–179.

Nadler, R. D., Dahl, J. F., Collins, D. C., & Gould, K. G. (1994). Sexual behavior of chimpanzees *(Pan troglodytes):* Male versus female regulation. *Journal of Comparative Psychology, 108,* 58–67.

Nadler, R. D., & Miller, L. C. (1982). Influence of male aggression on mating of gorillas in the laboratory. *Folia Primatologica, 38,* 233–239.

Neff, B. D. (2001). Genetic paternity analysis and breeding success in bluegill sunfish *(Lepomis macrochirus). Journal of Heredity, 92,* 111–119.

Nelson, P. A. (1979). *Personality, sexual functions, and sexual behavior: An experiment in methodology.* Unpublished doctoral dissertation, University of Florida, Gainesville.

Newman, J. P., & Kosson, D. S. (1986). Passive avoidance learning in psychopathic and nonpsychopathic offenders. *Journal of Abnormal Psychology, 95,* 252–256.

Newman, J. P., Kosson, D. S., & Patterson, C. M. (1992). Delay of gratification in psychopathic and nonpsychopathic offenders. *Journal of Abnormal Psychology, 101,* 630–636.

Newman, J. P., Patterson, C. M., & Kosson, D. S. (1987). Response perseveration in psychopaths. *Journal of Abnormal Psychology, 96,* 145–148.

Ng, V. W. (1987). Ideology and sexuality: Rape laws in Qing China. *Journal of Asian Studies, 46,* 57–70.

Niarchos, C. N. (1995). Women, war, and rape: Challenges facing the International Tribunal for the former Yugoslavia. *Human Rights Quarterly, 17,* 649–690.

Nicholaichuk, T., Gordon, A., Gu, D., & Wong, S. (2000). Outcome of an institutional sexual offender treatment program: A comparison between treated and matched untreated offenders. *Sexual Abuse: A Journal of Research and Treatment, 12,* 139–153.

Noffsinger, S. G., & Resnick, P. J. (2000). Sexual predator laws and offenders with addictions. *Psychiatric Annals, 30,* 602–608.

Nunes, K. L., Firestone, P., Bradford, J. M., Greenberg, D. M., & Broom, I. (2002). A comparison of modified versions of the Static-99 and Sex Offender Risk Appraisal Guide. *Sexual Abuse: A Journal of Research and Treatment, 14,* 253–269.

O'Brien, R. M. (2003). UCR violent crime rates, 1958–2000: Recorded and offender-generated trends. *Social Science Research, 32,* 499–518.

O'Donohue, W., Yeater, E. A., & Fanetti, M. (2003). Rape prevention with college males: The roles of rape myth acceptance, victim empathy, and outcome expectancies. *Journal of Interpersonal Violence, 18,* 513–531.

Ogloff, J. R. P., & Wong, S. (1990). Electrodermal and cardiovascular evidence of coping response in psychopaths. *Criminal Justice and Behavior, 17*, 231–245.

Oh, R. J. (1979). Repeated copulation in the brown planthopper, *Nilaparvata lugens* Stål (Homoptera; Delphacidae). *Ecological Entomology, 4*, 345–353.

Olsson, M. (1995). Forced copulation and costly female resistance behavior in the Lake Eyre dragon, *Ctenophorus maculosus. Herpetologica, 51*, 19–24.

Olweus, D., Mattsson, A., Schalling, D., & Löw, H. (1988). Circulating testosterone levels and aggression in adolescent males: A causal analysis. *Psychosomatic Medicine, 50*, 261–272.

Orlando, J. A., & Koss, M. P. (1983). The effects of sexual victimization on sexual satisfaction: A study of the negative-association hypothesis. *Journal of Abnormal Psychology, 92*, 104–106.

Otterbein, K. F. (1979). A cross-cultural study of rape. *Aggressive Behavior, 5*, 425–435.

Ouimet, M. (2002). Explaining the American and Canadian crime "drop" in the 1990s. *Canadian Journal of Criminology*, 33–50.

Ouimette, P. C. (1997). Psychopathology and sexual aggression in nonincarcerated men. *Violence and Victims, 12*, 389–395.

Packer, C., & Pusey, A. E. (1983a). Adaptations of female lions to infanticide by incoming males. *American Naturalist, 121*, 716–728.

Packer, C., & Pusey, A. E. (1983b). Male takeovers and female reproductive parameters: A simulation of oestrous synchrony in lions *(Panthera leo). Animal Behaviour, 31*, 334–340.

Palmer, C. T. (1989a). Is rape a cultural universal? A re-examination of the ethnographic evidence. *Ethnology, 28*, 1–16.

Palmer, C. T. (1989b). Rape in nonhuman animal species: Definitions, evidence, and implications. *Journal of Sex Research, 26*, 355–374.

Palmer, C. T. (1991). Human rape: Adaptation or by-product? *Journal of Sex Research, 28*, 365–386.

Palmer, C. T., & Tilley, C. F. (1995). Sexual access to females as a motivation for joining gangs: An evolutionary approach. *Journal of Sex Research, 32*, 213–217.

Patrick, C. J. (1994). Emotion and psychopathy: Startling new insights. *Psychophysiology, 31*, 319–330.

Patton, W., & Mannison, M. (1995a). Sexual coercion in dating situations among university students: Preliminary Australian data. *Australian Journal of Psychology, 47*, 66–72.

Patton, W., & Mannison, M. (1995b). Sexual coercion in high school dating. *Sex Roles, 33*, 447–457.

Petty, G. M., & Dawson, B. (1989). Sexual aggression in normal men: Incidence, beliefs, and personality characteristics. *Personality and Individual Differences, 10*, 355–362.

Pezza Leith, K., & Baumeister, R. F. (1996). Why do bad moods increase self-defeating behavior? Emotion, risk taking, and self-regulation. *Journal of Personality and Social Psychology, 71*, 1250–1267.

Pierotti, R. (1981). Male and female parental roles in the western gull under different environmental conditions. *Auk, 98,* 532–549.

Pilastro, A., & Bisazza, A. (1999). Insemination efficiency of two alternative male mating tactics in the guppy (*Poecilia reticulata*). *Proceedings of the Royal Society of London B, 266,* 1887–1891.

Pistono, S. P. (1988). Susan Brownmiller and the history of rape. *Women's Studies, 14,* 265–276.

Plaud, J. J., & Bigwood, S. J. (1997). The relationship of male self-report of rape supportive attitudes, sexual fantasies, social desirability and physiological arousal to sexual coercive stimuli. *Journal of Clinical Psychology, 53,* 935–942.

Plomin, R. (1989). Environment and genes. *American Psychologist, 44,* 105–111.

Plomin, R., & Daniels, D. (1987). Why are children in the same family so different from one another? *Behavioral and Brain Sciences, 10,* 1–60.

Pokorny, A. D., Miller, B. A., & Kaplan, H. B. (1972). The brief MAST: A shortened version of the Michigan Alcoholism Screening Test. *American Journal of Psychiatry, 129,* 342–345.

Pollock, N. L., & Hashmall, J. M. (1991). The excuses of child molesters. *Behavioral Sciences and the Law, 9,* 53–59.

Pope, H. G., Kouri, E. M., & Hudson, J. I. (2000). Effects of supraphysiologic doses of testosterone on mood and aggression in normal men: A randomized controlled trial. *Archives of General Psychiatry, 57,* 133–140.

Porter, J. F., & Critelli, J. W., & Tang, C. S. K. (1992). Sexual and aggressive motives in sexually aggressive college males. *Archives of Sexual Behavior, 21,* 457–468.

Post, J. B. (1980). Sir Thomas West and the Statute of Rapes, 1382. *Bulletin of the Institute of Historical Research, 53,* 24–30.

Prebble, J. (1967). *Culloden.* Markham, Ontario, Canada: Penguin.

Prentky, R. A., & Knight, R. A. (2000, November). *Psychopathy baserates among subtypes of sex offenders.* Paper presented at the 19th Annual Meeting of the Association for the Treatment of Sexual Abusers, San Diego, CA.

Prentky, R. A., Knight, R. A., & Lee, A. F. S. (1997). Risk factors associated with recidivism among extrafamilial child molesters. *Journal of Consulting and Clinical Psychology, 65,* 141–149.

Preston, D. L. (1996). Patterns of sexual arousal among rapist subtypes. *Dissertation Abstracts International: Section B: The Sciences and Engineering, 56*(11-B), 6445.

Preziosi, R. F., & Fairbairn, D. J. (1996). Sexual size dimorphism and selection in the wild in the waterstrider *Aquarius remigis*: Body size, components of body size and male mating success. *Journal of Evolutionary Biology, 9,* 317–336.

Price, J. A., & Price, J. H. (1983). Alcohol and sexual functioning: A review. *Advances in Alcohol and Substance Abuse, 2,* 43–56.

Price, S. G. (1999). Social reconciliation theory—Developing a new foundation for community-based responses to sex offenders. In B. K. Schwartz (Ed.), *The sex offender: Theoretical advances, treating special populations and legal developments* (Vol. 3, pp. 1.1–1.16). Kingston, NJ: Civic Research Institute.

Proctor, E. (1996). A five year outcome evaluation of a community-based treatment programme for convicted sexual offenders run by the probation service. *Journal of Sexual Aggression, 2,* 3–16.

Proeve, M., & Howells, K. (2002). Shame and guilt in child sexual offenders. *International Journal of Offender Therapy and Comparative Criminology, 46,* 657–667.

Prokopy, R. J., & Hendrichs, J. (1979). Mating behavior of Ceratitis capitata on a field-caged host tree. *Entomological Society of America, 72,* 642–648.

Propp, W. H. (1993). Kinship in 2 Samuel 13. *Catholic Biblical Quarterly, 55,* 39–53.

Proulx, J., Aubut, J., McKibben, A., & Côté, M. (1994). Penile responses of rapists and nonrapists to rape stimuli involving physical violence or humiliation. *Archives of Sexual Behavior, 23,* 295–310.

Purcell, D. W., Blanchard, R., & Zucker, K. J. (2000). Birth order in a contemporary sample of gay men. *Archives of Sexual Behavior, 29,* 349–356.

Quinsey, V. L. (1977). The assessment and treatment of child molesters: A review. *Canadian Psychological Review, 18,* 204–220.

Quinsey, V. L. (1984). Sexual aggression: Studies of offenders against women. In D. Weisstub (Ed.), *Law and mental health: International perspectives* (pp. 84–121). New York: Pergamon.

Quinsey, V. L. (2003). The etiology of anomalous sexual preferences in men. In R. A. Prentky, M. C. Seto, & A. Burgess (Eds.), *Understanding and managing sexually coercive behavior* (pp. 105–117). New York: Annals of the New York Academy of Sciences.

Quinsey, V. L., & Ambtman, R. (1979). Variables affecting psychiatrists' and teachers' assessments of the dangerousness of mentally ill offenders. *Journal of Consulting and Clinical Psychology, 47,* 353–362.

Quinsey, V. L., Arnold, L. S., & Pruesse, M. G. (1980). MMPI profiles of men referred for a pretrial psychiatric assessment as a function of offense type. *Journal of Clinical Psychology, 36,* 410–417.

Quinsey, V. L., Book, A., & Lalumière, M. L. (2001). A factor analysis of traits related to individual differences in antisocial behavior. *Criminal Justice and Behavior, 28,* 522–536.

Quinsey, V. L., Book, A., & Skilling, T. A. (in press). A follow-up deinstitutionalized developmentally handicapped men with histories of antisocial behavior. *Journal of Developmental Disabilities.*

Quinsey, V. L., & Chaplin, T. C. (1982). Penile responses to nonsexual violence among rapists. *Criminal Justice and Behavior, 9,* 312–324.

Quinsey, V. L., & Chaplin, T. C. (1984). Stimulus control of rapists' and non-sex offenders' sexual arousal. *Behavioral Assessment, 6,* 169–176.

Quinsey, V. L., & Chaplin, T. C. (1988a). Penile responses of child molesters and normals to descriptions of encounters with children involving sex and violence. *Journal of Interpersonal Violence, 3,* 259–274.

Quinsey, V. L., & Chaplin, T. C. (1988b). Preventing faking in phallometric assessments of sexual preference. In R. A. Prentky & V. L. Quinsey (Eds.), *Human sexual aggression: Current perspectives* (pp. 49–58). New York: Annals of New York Academy of Sciences.

Quinsey, V. L., Chaplin, T. C., & Upfold, D. (1984). Sexual arousal to nonsexual violence and sadomasochistic themes among rapists and non-sex offenders. *Journal of Consulting and Clinical Psychology, 52*, 651–657.

Quinsey, V. L., Chaplin, T. C., & Varney, G. (1981). A comparison of rapists' and non-sex offenders' sexual preferences for mutually consenting sex, rape, and physical abuse of women. *Behavioral Assessment, 3*, 12.

Quinsey, V. L., Harris, G. T., Rice, M. E., & Cormier, C. A. (1998). *Violent offenders: Appraising and managing risk*. Washington, DC: American Psychological Association.

Quinsey, V. L., Harris, G. T., Rice, M. E., & Lalumière, M. L. (1993). Assessing treatment efficacy in outcome studies of sex offenders. *Journal of Interpersonal Violence, 8*, 512–523.

Quinsey, V. L., Khanna, A., & Malcolm, P. B. (1998). A retrospective evaluation of the Regional Treatment Centre Sex Offender Treatment Program. *Journal of Interpersonal Violence, 13*, 621–644.

Quinsey, V. L., & Lalumière, M. L. (1995). Evolutionary perspectives on sexual offending. *Sexual Abuse: A Journal of Research and Treatment, 7*, 301–315.

Quinsey, V. L., & Lalumière, M. L. (2001). *Assessment of sexual offenders against children* (2nd ed.). Thousand Oaks, CA: Sage.

Quinsey, V. L., Lalumière, M. L., Rice, M. E., & Harris, G. T. (1995). Predicting sexual offenses. In J. C. Campbell (Ed.), *Assessing dangerousness: Violence by sexual offenders, batterers, and child abusers* (pp. 114–137). Thousand Oaks, CA: Sage.

Quinsey, V. L., Rice, M. E., & Harris, G. T. (1995). Actuarial prediction of sexual recidivism. *Journal of Interpersonal Violence, 10*, 85–105.

Quinsey, V. L., Skilling, T. A., Lalumière, M. L., & Craig, W. (2004). *Juvenile delinquency: Understanding individual differences*. Washington, DC: American Psychological Association.

Quinsey, V. L., & Upfold, D. (1985). Rape completion and victim injury as a function of female resistance strategy. *Canadian Journal of Behavioural Science, 17*, 40–50.

Rabinowitz Greenberg, S. R., Firestone, P., Bradford, J. M., & Greenberg, D. M. (2002). Prediction of recidivism in exhibitionists: Psychological, phallometric, and offense factors. *Sexual Abuse: A Journal of Research and Treatment, 14*, 329–348.

Raboch, J., Cerna, H., & Zemek, P. (1987). Sexual aggressivity and androgens. *British Journal of Psychiatry, 151*, 398–400.

Rada, R. T. (1975). Alcoholism and forcible rape. *American Journal of Psychiatry, 132*, 444–446.

Rada, R. T., Laws, D. R., & Kellner, R. (1976). Plasma testosterone levels in the rapist. *Psychosomatic Medicine, 38,* 257–268.

Rada, R. T., Laws, D. R., Kellner, R., Stivastava, L., & Peake, G. (1983). Plasma androgens in violent and nonviolent sex offenders. *American Academy of Psychiatry and the Law, 11,* 149–158.

Radzinowicz, L. (1957). *Sexual offences: A report of the Cambridge department of criminal science.* Toronto, Ontario, Canada: MacMillan.

Raider, C. M. (1977). MMPI profile types of exposers, rapists, and assaulters in a court services population. *Journal of Consulting and Clinical Psychology, 45,* 61–69.

Raine, A., Lencz, T., Bihrle, S., LaCasse, L., & Colletti, P. (2000). Reduced prefrontal gray matter volume and reduced autonomic activity in antisocial personality disorder. *Archives of General Psychiatry, 57,* 119–127.

Raine, A., O'Brien, M., Smiley, N., Scerbo, A., & Chan, C. (1990). Reduced lateralization in verbal dichotic listening in adolescent psychopaths. *Journal of Abnormal Psychology, 99,* 272–277.

Ramo, C. (1993). Extra-pair copulations of grey herons nesting as high density. *Ardea, 81,* 115–120.

Rapaport, K. (1984). *Sexually aggressive males: Characterological features and sexual responsiveness to rape depictions.* Unpublished doctoral dissertation, Auburn University, Alabama.

Rapaport, K., & Burkhart, B. (1984). Personality and attitudinal characteristics of sexually coercive college males. *Journal of Abnormal Psychology, 93,* 216–221.

Resnick, H. S., Kilpatrick, D. G., Walsh, C., & Veronen, L. J. (1991). *Marital rape.* New York: Plenum Press.

Ressler, R. K., Burgess, A. W., & Douglas, J. E. (1988). *Sexual homicide: Patterns and motives.* Toronto, Ontario, Canada: Lexington.

Reynolds, J. D., Gross, M. R., & Coombs, M. J. (1993). Environmental conditions and male morphology determine alternative mating behaviour in Trinidadian guppies. *Animal Behaviour, 45,* 145–152.

Rhodes, J. E., Ebert, L., & Meyers, A. B. (1993). Sexual victimization in young, pregnant and parenting African-American women: Psychological and social outcomes. *Violence and Victims, 8,* 153–163.

Rice, M. E., Chaplin, T. C., Harris, G. T., & Coutts, J. (1994). Empathy for the victim and sexual arousal among rapists and nonrapists. *Journal of Interpersonal Violence, 9,* 435–449.

Rice, M. E., & Harris, G. T. (1995a). Violent recidivism: Assessing predictive validity. *Journal of Consulting and Clinical Psychology, 63,* 737–748.

Rice, M. E., & Harris, G. T. (1995b). Psychopathy, schizophrenia, alcohol abuse, and violent recidivism. *International Journal of Law and Psychiatry, 18,* 333–342.

Rice, M. E., & Harris, G. T. (1997). Cross-validation and extension of the Violence Risk Appraisal Guide for child molesters and rapists. *Law and Human Behavior, 21,* 231–241.

Rice, M. E., & Harris, G. T. (1999). Sexual aggressors. In D. L. Faigman, D. H. Kaye, M. J. Saks, & J. Sanders (Eds.), *Modern scientific evidence: The law and science of expert testimony* (Vol. 3, pp. 89–121). St. Paul, MN: West.

Rice, M. E., & Harris, G. T. (2002). Men who molest their sexually immature daughters: Is a special explanation required? *Journal of Abnormal Psychology, 111*, 329–339.

Rice, M. E., & Harris, G. T. (2003a). What we know and don't know about treating sex offenders. In B. J. Winick & J. Q. LaFond (Eds.), *Protecting society from sexually dangerous offenders: Law, justice, and therapy* (pp. 101–117). Washington, DC: American Psychological Association.

Rice, M. E. & Harris, G. T. (2003b). The size and sign of treatment effects in therapy for sex offenders. In R. Prentky, E. Janus, & M. C. Seto (Eds.), *Sexually coercive behavior: Understanding and management* (pp. 428–440). New York: Annals of the New York Academy of Sciences.

Rice, M. E., & Harris, G. T. (2004). *Comparing effect sizes in follow-up studies: ROC area, Cohen's d and r.* Manuscript submitted for publication.

Rice, M. E., Harris, G. T., & Cormier, C. A. (1992). Evaluation of a maximum security therapeutic community for psychopaths and other mentally disordered offenders. *Law and Human Behavior, 16*, 399–412.

Rice, M. E., Harris, G. T., & Quinsey, V. L. (1990). A followup of rapists assessed in a maximum security psychiatric facility. *Journal of Interpersonal Violence, 5*, 435–448.

Rice, M. E., Harris, G. T., & Quinsey, V. L. (2001). Treating the adult sex offender. In J. B. Ashford, B. D. Sales, & W. Reid (Eds.), *Treating offenders with special needs* (pp. 291–312). Washington, DC: American Psychological Association.

Rice, M. E., Quinsey, V. L., & Harris, G. T. (1991). Sexual recidivism among child molesters released from a maximum security psychiatric institution. *Journal of Consulting and Clinical Psychology, 59*, 381–386.

Rice, W. R. (1996). Sexually antagonistic male adaptation triggered by experimental arrest of female evolution. *Nature, 381*, 232–234.

Rice, W. R. (1998). Male fitness increases when females are eliminated from gene pool: Implications for the Y chromosome. *Proceedings of the National Academy of Sciences USA, 95*, 6217–6221.

Rico, C., Kuhnlein, U., & Fitzgerald, G. J. (1992). Male reproductive tactics in the threespine stickleback—An evaluation by DNA fingerprinting. *Molecular Ecology, 1*, 79–87.

Ridley, M. (1994). *The red queen: Sex and the evolution of human nature.* New York: Macmillan.

Rind, B., Tromovitch, P., & Bauserman, R. (1998). A meta-analytic examination of assumed properties of child sexual abuse using college samples. *Psychological Bulletin, 124*, 22–53.

Robertson, A. (1986). Copulations throughout breeding in a colonial accipitrid vulture. *Condor, 88*, 535–539.

Rodd, F. H., & Sokolowski, M. B. (1995). Complex origins of variation in the sexual behaviour of male Trinidadian guppies, *Poecilia reticulata:* Interactions between social environment, heredity, body size and age. *Animal Behaviour, 49,* 1139–1159.

Rodgers, J. A. (1980). Little blue heron breeding behavior. *Auk, 97,* 371–384.

Rodman, P. S. (1979). Individual activity patterns and the solitary nature of orangutans. In D. A. Hamburg & E. R. McCown (Eds.), *The great apes* (pp. 235–255). Menlo Park, CA: Benjamin Cummings.

Rodman, P. S., & Mitani, J. C. (1987). Orangutans: Sexual dimorphism in a solitary species. In B. B. Smuts, D. L. Cheney, R. M. Seyfarth, R. W. Wrangham, & T. T. Struthsaker (Eds.), *Primate societies* (pp. 146–154). Chicago: University of Chicago Press.

Roland, C. G. (1997). Massacre and rape in Hong Kong: Two case studies involving medical personnel and patients. *Journal of Contemporary History, 32,* 43–61.

Romero, J. J., & Williams, L. M. (1983). Group psychotherapy and intensive probation supervision with sex offenders. *Federal Probation, 47,* 36–42.

Rosenberg, M. (1979). *Conceiving the self.* New York: Basic Books.

Rosenman, S. (2000). The spawning grounds of the Japanese rapists of Nanking. *Journal of Psychohistory, 28,* 2–23.

Røskaft, E. (1983). Male promiscuity and female adultery by the rook *Corvus frugilegus. Ornis Scandinavica, 14,* 175–179.

Ross, L., & Nisbett, R. E. (1991). *The person and the situation.* New York: McGraw-Hill.

Rotton, J., & Cohn, E. G. (2003). Global warming and U.S. crime rates: An application of routine activity theory. *Environment and Behavior, 35,* 802–825.

Rowe, D. C. (2002). *Biology and crime.* Los Angeles: Roxbury.

Rowe, D. C., & Rodgers, J. L. (1989). Behavioral genetics, adolescent deviance, and "d": Contributions and issues. In G. R. Adams, R. Montemayor, & T. P. Gullotta (Eds.), *Biology of adolescent behavior and development* (pp. 38–67). Newbury Park, CA: Sage.

Rowe, D. C., Rodgers, J. L., Meseck-Bushey, S., & St. John, C. (1989). Sexual behavior and nonsexual deviance: A sibling study of their relationship. *Developmental Psychology, 25,* 61–69.

Rowland, W. J. (1979). Stealing fertilization in the fourspine stickleback, *Apeltes quadracus. American Naturalist,* 602–604.

Rozée, P. D. (1993). Forbidden or forgiven? Rape in cross-cultural perspective. *Psychology of Women Quarterly, 17,* 499–514.

Rubenstein, D. I. (1984). Resource acquisition and alternative mating strategies in water striders. *American Zoologist, 24,* 345–353.

Rubenstein, M., Yeager, C. A., Goodstein, C., & Lewis, D. O. (1993). Sexually assaultive male juveniles: A follow-up. *American Journal of Psychiatry, 150,* 262–265.

Ruggiero, G. (1980). *Violence in early renaissance Venice.* Piscataway, NJ: Rutgers University Press.

Russell, B. L., & Oswald, D. L. (2002). Sexual coercion and victimization of college men: The role of love styles. *Journal of Interpersonal Violence, 17,* 273–285.

Rutter, M., Giller, H., & Hagell, A. (1997). *Antisocial behavior by young people.* New York: Cambridge University Press.

Ryan, M. J., & Causey, B. A. (1989). "Alternative" mating behavior in the swordtails *Xiphophorus nigrensis* and *Xiphophorus pygmaeus* (Pisces: Poeciliidae). *Behavioral Ecology and Sociobiology, 24,* 341–348.

Ryan, M. J., Pease, C. M., & Morris, M. R. (1992). A genetic polymorphism in the swordtail *Xiphophorus nigrensis:* Testing the prediction of equal fitness. *American Naturalist, 139,* 21–31.

Sadler, A. G., Booth, B. M., Cook, B. L., & Doebbeling, B. N. (2003). Factors associated with women's risk of rape in the military environment. *American Journal of Industrial Medicine, 43,* 262–273.

Sakaluk, S. K., Bangert, P. J., Eggert, A.-K., Gack, C., & Swanson, L. V. (1995). The gin trap as a device facilitating coercive mating in sagebrush crickets. *Proceedings of the Royal Society of London B, 261,* 65–71.

Sampson, R. J., & Laub, J. H. (1993). *Crime in the making: Pathways and turning points through life.* Cambridge, MA: Harvard University Press.

Sanday, P. (1981). The sociocultural context of rape: A cross-cultural study. *Journal of Social Issues, 37,* 5–27.

Sanday, P. R. (1990). *Fraternity gang rape: Sex, brotherhood, and privilege on campus.* New York: York University Press.

Sarwer, D. B., Kalichman, S. C., Johnson, J. R., Early, J., & Ali, S. A. (1993). Sexual aggression and love styles: An exploratory study. *Archives of Sexual Behavior, 22,* 265–276.

Satin, A. J., Hemsell, D. L., Stone, I. C., Theriot, S., & Wendel, G. D. (1991). Sexual assault in pregnancy. *Obstetrics and Gynecology, 77,* 710–714.

Sato, H., & Hiramatsu, K. (1993). Mating behavior and sexual selection in the African ball-rolling scarab *Kheper platynotus* (Bates) (Coleoptera: Scarabaeidae). *Journal of Natural History, 27,* 657–668.

Sato, H., & Imamori, M. (1987). Nesting behavior of a subsocial African ball-roller *Kheper platynotus* (Coleoptera, Scarabaeidae). *Ecological Entomology, 12,* 415–425.

Scaramella, L. V., Conger, R. D., Simons, R. L., & Whitbeck, L. B. (1998). Predicting risk for pregnancy by late adolescence: A social contextual perspective. *Developmental Psychology, 34,* 1233–1245.

Scaramella, T. J., & Brown, W. A. (1978). Serum testosterone and aggressiveness in hockey players. *Psychomatic Medicine, 40,* 262–265.

Schlegel, A., & Barry, H. (1986). The cultural consequences of female contributions to subsistence. *American Anthropologist, 88,* 142–150.

Schmauk, F. J. (1970). Punishment, arousal, and avoidance learning in sociopaths. *Journal of Abnormal Psychology, 76,* 325–335.

Schmitt, D. P. (2003, July). *Sociosexuality across 48 nations: A cross-cultural study of sex, gender equity, and the reproductive ecology of human mating strategies.* Paper presented at the 29th Annual Meeting of the International Academy of Sex Research, Bloomington, IN.

Schroeder, J. A. (1997). The rape of Dinah: Luther's interpretation of a biblical narrative. *Sixteenth Century Journal, 28,* 775–791.

Schulsinger, F. (1972). Psychopathy: Heredity and environment. *International Journal of Mental Health, 1,* 190–206.

Schürmann, C. L., & van Hooff, J. A. R. A. M. (1986). Reproductive strategies of the orangutan: New data and a reconsideration of existing sociosexual models. *International Journal of Primatology, 7,* 265–287.

Schwartz, M. D., DeKeseredy, W. S., Tait, D., & Alvi, S. (2001). Male peer support and a feminist routine activity theory: Understanding sexual assault on the college campus. *Justice Quaterly, 18,* 623–649.

Scott, M. L., Cole, J. K., McKay, S. E., Golden, C. J., & Liggett, K. R. (1984). Neuropsychological performance of sexual assaulters and pedophiles. *Journal of Forensic Sciences, 29,* 1114–1118.

Scott, R. L., & Tetreault, L. A. (1987). Attitudes of rapists and other violent offenders toward women. *Journal of Social Psychology, 127,* 375–380.

Seghorn, T. K., Prentky, R. A., & Boucher, R. J. (1987). Childhood sexual abuse in the lives of sexually aggressive offenders. *Journal of the American Academy of Child Adolescent Psychiatry, 26,* 262–267.

Seifert, R. (1996). The second front: The logic of sexual violence in wars. *Women's Studies International Forum, 19,* 35–43.

Senn, C. Y., Desmarais, S., Verberg, N., & Wood, E. (2000). Predicting coercive sexual behavior across the lifespan in a random sample of Canadian men. *Journal of Social and Personality Relationships, 17,* 95–113.

Serbin, L. A., Cooperman, J. M., Peters, P. L., Lehoux, P. M., Stack, D. M., & Schwartzman, A. E. (1998). Intergenerational transfer of psychosocial risk in women with childhood histories of aggression, withdrawal, or aggression and withdrawal. *Developmental Psychology, 34,* 1246–1262.

Serin, R. C., Mailloux, D. L., & Malcolm, P. B. (2001). Psychopathy, deviant sexual arousal, and recidivism among sexual offenders. *Journal of Interpersonal Violence, 16,* 234–246.

Serin, R. C., Malcolm, P. B., Khanna, A., & Barbaree, H. E. (1994). Psychopathy and deviant sexual arousal in incarcerated sexual offenders. *Journal of Interpersonal Violence, 9,* 3–11.

Seto, M. C. (2001). The value of phallometry in the assessment of male sex offenders. *Journal of Forensic Psychology Practice, 1,* 65–75.

Seto, M. C., & Barbaree, H. E. (1993). Victim blame and sexual arousal to rape cues in rapists and nonoffenders. *Annals of Sex Research, 6,* 167–183.

Seto, M. C., & Barbaree, H. E. (1995). The role of alcohol in sexual aggression. *Clinical Psychology Review, 15,* 545–566.

Seto, M. C., & Barbaree, H. E. (1999). Psychopathy, treatment behavior, and sex offender recidivism. *Journal of Interpersonal Violence, 14,* 1235–1248.

Seto, M. C., Khattar, N. A., Lalumière, M. L., & Quinsey, V. L. (1997). Deception and sexual strategy in psychopathy. *Personality and Individual Differences, 22,* 301–307.

Seto, M. C., & Kuban, M. (1996). Criterion-related validity of a phallometric test for paraphilic rape and sadism. *Behaviour Research and Therapy, 34,* 175–183.

Seto, M. C., & Lalumière, M. L. (in press). Conduct problems and juvenile sexual offending. In H. E. Barbaree & W. L. Marshall (Eds.), *The juvenile sex offender* (2nd ed.). New York: Guilford Press.

Seto, M. C., Lalumière, M. L., & Quinsey, V. L. (1995). Sensation seeking and males' sexual strategy. *Personality and Individual Differences, 19,* 669–676.

Seto, M. C., Maric, A., & Barbaree, H. E. (2001). The role of pornography in the etiology of sexual aggression. *Aggression and Violent Behavior, 6,* 35–53.

Seymour, N. R., & Titman, R. D. (1979). Behaviour of unpaired male black ducks (*Anas rupribes*) during the breeding season in a Nova Scotia tidal marsh. *Canadian Journal of Zoology, 57,* 2421–2428.

Shackelford, T. K. (2002a). Are young women the special targets of rape-murder? *Aggressive Behavior, 28,* 224–232.

Shackelford, T. K. (2002b). Risk of multiple-offender rape–murder varies with female age. *Journal of Criminal Justice, 30,* 135–141.

Sheldon, B. C. (1994). Sperm competition in the chaffinch: The role of the female. *Animal Behaviour, 47,* 163–173.

Shields, N. M., & Hanneke, C. R. (1983). Battered wives' reactions to marital rape. In D. A. Finkelhor, R. J. Gelles, G. Hotaling, & J. S. Strauss (Eds.), *The dark side of families* (pp. 131–148). Beverly Hills, CA: Sage.

Shields, W. M., & Shields, L. M. (1983). Forcible rape: An evolutionary perspective. *Ethology and Sociobiology, 4,* 115–136.

Shine, R., Langkilde, T., & Mason, R. T. (2003). Cryptic forcible insemination: Male snakes exploit female physiology, anatomy, and behavior to obtain coercive matings. *American Naturalist, 162,* 653–667.

Simpson, G., Tate, R., Ferry, K., Hodgkinson, A., & Blaszczynski, A. (2001). Social, neuroradiologic, medical and neuropsychologic correlates of sexually aberrant behavior after traumatic brain injury: A controlled study. *Journal of Head Trauma Rehabilitation, 16,* 556–572.

Simpson, J. A., & Gangestad, S. W. (1991). Individual differences in sociosexuality: Evidence for convergent and discriminant validity. *Journal of Personality and Social Psychology, 60,* 870–883.

Siniff, D. B., Stirling, I., Bengston, J. L., & Reichle, R. A. (1979). Social and reproductive behavior of crabeater seal (*Lobodon carcinophagus*) during the austral spring. *Canadian Journal of Zoology, 57,* 2243–2255.

Sjöstedt, G., & Långström, N. (2002). Assessment of risk for criminal recidivism among rapists: A comparison of four different measures. *Psychology, Crime & Law, 8,* 25–40.

Skilling, T. A., Harris, G. T., Rice, M. E., & Quinsey, V. L. (2002). Identifying persistently antisocial offenders using the Hare Psychopathy Checklist and *DSM* Antisocial Personality Disorder criteria. *Psychological Assessment, 14,* 27–38.

Skilling, T. A., Quinsey, V. L., & Craig, W. (2001). Evidence of a taxon underlying serious antisocial behavior in boys. *Criminal Justice and Behavior, 28,* 450–470.

Skinner, H. A. (1982). The Drug Abuse Screening Test (DAST–20). *The Addictive Behaviors, 7,* 363–371.

Slagsvold, T., & Sætre, G.-P. (1991). Evolution of plumage color in male pied fly-catchers *(Ficedula hypoleuca)*: Evidence for female mimicry. *Evolution, 45,* 910–917.

Smith, D. C., & Prokopy, R. J. (1980). Mating behavior of *Rhagoletis pomonella (Diptera: Tephritidae)*: VI. Site of early-season encounters. *Canadian Entomologist, 112,* 585–590.

Smith, S. M. (1988). Extra-pair copulations in black-capped chickadees: The role of the female. *Behaviour, 107,* 15–23.

Smuts, B. (1995). The evolutionary origins of patriarchy. *Human Nature, 6,* 1–32.

Smuts, B. (1996). Male aggression against women: An evolutionary perspective. In D. M. Buss & N. M. Malamuth (Eds.), *Sex, power, conflict: Evolutionary and feminist perspectives* (pp. 231–268). New York: Oxford University Press.

Smuts, B. B., Cheney, D. L., Seyfarth, R. M., Wrangham, R. W., & Struhsaker, T. T. (1987). *Primate societies.* Chicago: University of Chicago Press.

Smuts, B. B., & Smuts, R. W. (1993). Male aggression and sexual coercion of females in nonhuman primates and other mammals: Evidence and theoretical implications. *Advances in the Study of Behavior, 22,* 1–63.

Snedden, W. A. (1996). Lifetime mating success in male sagebrush crickets: Sexual selection constrained by a virgin male mating advantage. *Animal Behaviour, 51,* 1119–1125.

Soltis, J., Mitsunaga, F., Shimizu, K., Yanagihara, Y., & Nozaki, M. (1997). Sexual selection in Japanese macaques: I. Female mate choice or male sexual coercion? *Animal Behaviour, 54,* 725–736.

Soothill, K., Francis, B., Sanderson, B., & Ackerley, E. (2000). Sex offenders: Specialists, generalists—Or both? *British Journal of Criminology, 40,* 56–67.

Soothill, K. L., Jack, A., & Gibbens, T. C. N. (1976). Rape: A 22-year cohort study. *Medicine, Science, and the Law, 16,* 62–68.

Sorenson, L. G. (1994a). Forced extra-pair copulation and mate guarding in the white-cheeked pintail: Timing and trade-offs in an asynchronously breeding duck. *Animal Behaviour, 48,* 519–533.

Sorenson, L. G. (1994b). Forced extra-pair copulation in the white-cheeked pintail: Male tactics and female responses. *Condor, 96,* 400–410.

Spence, J. T., Losoff, M., & Robbins, A. S. (1991). Sexually aggressive tactics in dating relationships: Personality and attitudinal correlates. *Journal of Social and Clinical Psychology, 10*, 289–304.

Spitzberg, B. H., & Rhea, J. (1999). Obsessive relational intrusion and sexual coercion victimization. *Journal of Interpersonal Violence, 14*, 3–20.

Starks, P. T., & Blackie, C. A. (2000). The relationship between serial monogamy and rape in the United States (1960–1995). *Proceedings of the Royal Society of London B, 267*, 1259–1263.

Stermac, L. E., DuMont, J. A., & Kalemba, V. (1995). Comparison of sexual assaults by strangers and known assailants in an urban population of women. *Canadian Medical Association Journal, 153*, 1089–1094.

Sternberg, R. J., & Grigorenko, E. L. (1997). *Intelligence, heredity, and environment.* New York: Cambridge University Press.

Stewart, G. R., & Titman, R. D. (1980). Territorial behaviour by prairie pothole blue-winged teal. *Canadian Journal of Zoology, 58*, 639–649.

Stone, M. H., & Thompson, E. H. (2001). Executive function impairment in sexual offenders. *Journal of Individual Psychology, 57*, 51–59.

Storey, A. E., Walsh, C. J., Quinton, R. L., & Wynne-Edwards, K. E. (2000). Hormonal correlates of paternal responsiveness in new and expectant fathers. *Evolution and Human Behavior, 21*, 79–85.

Stouthamer-Loeber, M., & Wei, E. H. (1998). The precursors of young fatherhood and its effect on delinquency of teenage males. *Journal of Adolescent Health, 22*, 56–65.

Streiner, D. L. (2002). The 2 "Es" of research: Efficacy and effectiveness trials. *Canadian Journal of Psychiatry, 47*, 552–556.

Sturgeon, H. V., & Taylor, J. (1980). Report of a five-year follow-up study of mentally disordered sex offenders released from Atascadero State hospital. *Criminal Justice Journal, 4*, 31–61.

Stürup, G. K. (1968). Treatment of sexual offenders in Herstedvester Denmark. *Acta Psychiatrica Scandinavica, 44*, 5–63.

Sulloway, F. J. (1996). *Born to rebel: Birth order, family dynamics, and creative lives.* New York: Pantheon Books.

Swets, J. A., Dawes, R. M., & Monahan, J. (2000). Better decisions through science. *Scientific American*, 70–76.

Swiss, S., & Giller, J. E. (1993). Rape as a crime of war—A medical perspective. *Journal of the American Medical Association, 270*, 612–615.

Symons, D. (1979). *The evolution of human sexuality.* New York: Oxford.

Taborsky, M. (1994). Sneakers, satellites, and helpers: Parasitic and cooperative behavior in fish reproduction. *Advances in the Study of Behavior, 23*, 1–100.

Tays, T. M., Earle, R. H., Wells, K., Murray, M., & Garret, B. (1999). Treating sex offenders using the sex addiction model. *Sexual Addiction and Compulsivity, 6*, 281–288.

Testa, M. (2002). The impact of men's alcohol consumption on perpetration of sexual aggression. *Clinical Psychology Review, 22*, 1239–1263.

Testa, M., & Dermen, K. H. (1999). The differential correlates of sexual coercion and rape. *Journal of Interpersonal Violence, 14*, 548–561.

Testa, M., & Parks, K. A. (1996). The role of women's alcohol consumption in sexual victimization. *Aggression and Violent Behavior, 1*, 217–234.

Thiessen, D. (1990). Hormonal correlates of sexual aggression. In L. Ellis & H. Hoffman (Eds.), *Crime in biological, social and moral contexts* (pp. 153–161). New York: Praeger.

Thornhill, R. (1980). Rape in *Panorpa* scorpionflies and a general rape hypothesis. *Animal Behaviour, 28*, 52–59.

Thornhill, R. (1981). *Panorpa* (Mecoptera: Panorpidae) scorpionflies: Systems for understanding resource-defense polygyny and alternative male reproductive efforts. *Annual Review of Ecology and Systematics, 12*, 355–386.

Thornhill, R. (1983). Cryptic female choice and its implications in the scorpionfly *Harpobittacus nigriceps*. *American Naturalist, 122*, 765–788.

Thornhill, R. (1987). The relative importance of intra- and interspecific competition in scorpionfly mating systems. *American Naturalist, 130*, 711–729.

Thornhill, R. (1992). Fluctuating asymmetry and the mating system of the Japanese scorpionfly, *Panorpa japonica*. *Animal Behaviour, 44*, 867–879.

Thornhill, R., & Palmer, C. T. (2000). *A natural history of rape: Biological bases of sexual coercion*. Cambridge, MA: MIT Press.

Thornhill, R., & Sauer, K. P. (1991). The notal organ of the scorpionfly (*Panorpa vulgaris*): An adaptation to coerce mating duration. *Behavioral Ecology, 2*, 156–164.

Thornhill, R., & Thornhill, N. W. (1983). Human rape: An evolutionary analysis. *Ethology and Sociobiology, 4*, 137–173.

Tigges, W. (1992). 'Lat the womman telle hire tale': A reading of The Wife of Bath's Tale. *English Studies, 73*, 97–103.

Tintinalli, J. E., & Hoelzer, M. (1985). Clinical findings and legal resolution in sexual assault. *Annals of Emergency Medicine, 14*, 113–119.

Titman, R. D. (1983). Spacing and three-bird flights of mallards breeding in pothole habitat. *Canadian Journal of Zoology, 61*, 839–847.

Titman, R. D., & Lowther, J. K. (1975). The breeding behavior of a crowded population of mallards. *Canadian Journal of Zoology, 53*, 1270–1283.

Trivers, R. L. (1972). Parental investment and sexual selection. In B. Campbell (Ed.), *Sexual selection and the descent of man* (pp. 136–179). Chicago: Aldine.

Tsubaki, V., & Ono, T. (1986). Competition for territorial sites and alternative mating tactics in the dragonfly Nsnnophya-pygmaea odonata libellulideae. *Behaviour, 97*, 234–252.

Turnbull, C. M. (1961). *The forest people: A study of the pygmies of the Congo*. New York: Simon and Schuster.

Turnbull, C. M. (1972). *The mountain people.* New York: Simon and Schuster.

Ullman, S. E., Karabatsos, G., & Koss, M. P. (1999). Alcohol and sexual assault in a national sample of college women. *Journal of Interpersonal Violence, 14,* 603–625.

Utami, S. S., Goossens, B., Bruford, M. W., de Ruiter, J. R., & van Hooff, J. A. R. A. M. (2002). Male bimaturism and reproductive success in Sumantran orang-utans. *Behavioral Ecology, 13,* 643–652.

Valera, F., Hoi, H., & Kristin, A. (2003). Male shrikes punish unfaithful females. *Behavioral Ecology, 14,* 403–408.

van den Assem, J. (1967). *Territory in the three-spined stickleback* Gasterosteus aculeatus l.: *An experimental study in intra-specific competition.* Leiden, the Netherlands: E. J. Brill.

van der Heijden, M. (2000). Women as victims of sexual and domestic violence in seventeenth-century Holland: Criminal cases of rape, incest, and maltreatment in Rotterdam and Delft. *Journal of Social History, 33,* 623–644.

van Goozen, S. H. M., Cohen-Kettenis, P. T., Matthys, W., & van Engeland, H. (2002). Preference for aggressive and sexual stimuli in children with disruptive behavior disorder and normal controls. *Archives of Sexual Behavior, 31,* 247–253.

van Rhijn, J., & Groothuis, T. (1985). Biparental care and the basis for alternative bond-types among gulls, with special reference to black-headed gulls. *Ardea, 73,* 159–174.

Venier, L. A., Dunn, P. O., Lifjeld, J. T., & Robertson, R. J. (1993). Behavioral patterns of extra-pair copulation in tree swallows. *Animal Behaviour, 45,* 412–415.

Vieraitis, L. M., & Williams, M. R. (2002). Assessing the impact of gender inequality on female homicide victimization across U.S. cities: A racially disaggregated analysis. *Violence Against Women, 8,* 35–63.

Vitz, E. B. (1997). Rereading rape in medieval literature: Literary, historical, and theoretical reflections. *Romanic Review, 88,* 1–26.

Wagner, R. H. (1991). The use of extrapair copulations for mate appraisal by razorbills, *Alca torda. Behavioral Ecology, 2,* 198–203.

Wagner, R. H., Schug, M. D., & Morton, E. S. (1996). Condition-dependent control of paternity by female purple martins: Implications for coloniality. *Behavioral Ecology and Sociobiology, 38,* 379–389.

Wakefield, J. C. (1992). Disorder as harmful dysfunction: A conceptual critique of *DSM-III-R's* definition of mental disorder. *Psychological Review, 99,* 232–247.

Wakefield, J. C. (1993). Limits of operationalization: A critique of Spitzer and Endicott's (1978) proposed operational criteria for mental disorder. *Journal of Abnormal Psychology, 102,* 160–172.

Wakefield, J. D. (1999). Evolutionary versus prototype analyses of the concept of disorder. *Journal of Abnormal Psychology, 108,* 374–399.

Walker, E. A., Katon, W. J., Roy-Byrne, P. P., Jemelka, R. P., & Russo, J. (1993). Histories of sexual victimization in patients with irritable bowel syndrome or inflammatory bowel disease. *American Journal of Psychiatry, 150,* 1502–1506.

Walker, E. A., Katon, W. J., Hansom, J., Harrop-Griffiths, J., Holm, L., Jones, M. L., et al. (1995). Psychiatric diagnoses and sexual victimization in women with chronic pelvic pain. *Psychosomatics, 36,* 531–540.

Walker, W. D. (1997). *Patterns in sexual offending.* Unpublished doctoral dissertation, Queen's University, Kingston.

Walker, W. D., & Quinsey, V. L. (1998). *Escalation in sexual offending.* Poster presented at the Annual Meeting of the Association for the Treatment of Sexual Abusers Annual Meeting, Vancouver, British Columbia, Canada.

Walker, W. D., Rowe, R. C., & Quinsey, V. L. (1993). Authoritarianism and sexual aggression. *Journal of Personality and Social Psychology, 65,* 1036–1045.

Warr, M. (1998). Life-course transitions and desistance from crime. *Criminology, 36,* 183–216.

Warren, J. I., & Hazelwood, R. R. (2002). Relational patterns associated with sexual sadism: A study of 20 wives and girlfriends. *Journal of Family Violence, 17,* 75–89.

Watson, P. J., Arnqvist, G., & Stallmann, R. R. (1998). Sexual conflict and the energetic costs mating and mate choice in water striders. *American Naturalist, 151,* 46–58.

Weigensberg, I., & Fairbairn, D. J. (1996). The sexual arms race and phenotypic correlates of mating success in the waterstrider, *Aquarius remigis* (Hemiptera: Gerridae). *Journal of Insect Behavior, 9,* 307–319.

Weinrott, M. R., & Saylor, M. (1991). Self-report of crimes committed by sex offenders. *Journal of Interpersonal Violence, 6,* 286–300.

Werner, D. I. (1978). On the biology of *Tropidurus delanonis,* Baur (Iguanidae). *Z. Tierpsychoogy, 47,* 337–395.

Werner, E. E. (1989). High-risk children in young adulthood: A longitudinal study from birth to 32 years. *American Journal of Orthopsychiatry, 59,* 72–81.

Werschkul, D. F. (1982). Nesting ecology of the little blue heron: Promiscuous behavior. *Condor, 84,* 381–384.

Westneat, D. F. (1987). Extra-pair copulation in a predominantly monogamous bird: Observations of behavior. *Animal Behaviour, 35,* 865–876.

Westneat, D. F., Sherman, P. W., & Morton, M. L. (1990). The ecology and evolution of extra-pair copulations in birds. *Current Ornithology, 7,* 331–369.

Wheeler, J. G., George, W. H., & Dahl, B. J. (2002). Sexually aggressive college males: Empathy as a moderator in the "confluence model" of sexual aggression. *Personality and Individual Differences, 33,* 759–775.

White, H. R. (1997). Alcohol, illicit drugs and violence. In D. M. Stoff, J. Breiling, & J. D. Maser (Eds.), *Handbook of antisocial behavior* (pp. 511–523). New York: Wiley.

Whitford, P. C. (1993). Observations of attempted rape (forced copulation) in Canada geese. *Passenger Pigeon, 55*, 359–361.

Widom, C. S. (1999). Childhood victimization and the development of personality disorders. *Archives of General Psychiatry, 56*, 607.

Widom, C. S., & Ames, M. A. (1994). Criminal consequences of childhood sexual victimization. *Child Abuse and Neglect, 18*, 303–318.

Widom, C. S., & Morris, S. (1997). Accuracy of adult recollections of childhood victimization: Part 2. Childhood sexual abuse. *Psychological Assessment, 9*, 34–46.

Wille, R., & Beier, K. M. (1989). Castration in Germany. *Annals of Sex Research, 2*, 103–133.

Williamson, S., Harpur, T. J., & Hare, R. D. (1991). Abnormal processing of affective words by psychopaths. *Journal of Psychophysiological Research, 28*, 260–273.

Wilson, A. E., Calhoun, K. S., & McNair, L. D. (2002). Alcohol consumption and expectancies among sexually coercive college men. *Journal of Interpersonal Violence, 17*, 1145–1159.

Wilson, E. O. (1998). *Consilience: The unity of knowledge.* Boston: Little Brown.

Wilson, G. T., Lawson, D. M., & Abrams, D. B. (1978). Effects of alcohol on sexual arousal in male alcoholics. *Journal of Abnormal Psychology, 87*, 609–616.

Wilson, G. T., & Niaura, R. (1984). Alcohol and the disinhibition of sexual responsiveness. *Journal of Studies on Alcohol, 45*, 219–224.

Wilson, M., & Daly, M. (1985). Competitiveness, risk-taking, and violence: The young male syndrome. *Ethology and Sociobiology, 6*, 59–73.

Wilson, M., & Daly, M. (1997). Life expectancy, economic inequality, homicide, and reproductive timing in Chicago neighborhoods. *British Medical Journal, 314*, 1271–1274.

Wilson, M., Daly, M., & Scheib, J. E. (1997). Femicide: An evolutionary psychological perspective. In P. Gowaty (Ed.), *Feminism and evolutionary biology* (pp. 431–465). New York: Chapman Hall.

Wilson, M., & Mesnick, S. L. (1997). An empirical test of the body guard hypothesis. In P. Gowaty (Ed.), *Feminism and evolutionary biology* (pp. 505–511). New York: Chapman Hall.

Wing, S., Lloyd, J. E., & Hongtrakul, T. (1983). Male competition in *Pteroptyx* fireflies: Wing-cover clamps, female anatomy, and mating plugs. *Florida Entomologist, 66*, 86–91.

Wolfgang, M. E., Figlio, R. M., Tracy, P. E., & Singer, S. I. (1985). *The National Survey of Crime Severity.* Washington, DC: U.S. Department of Justice Statistics.

Wootton, J. M., Frick, P. J., Shelton, K. K., & Silverthorn, P. (1997). Ineffective parenting and childhood conduct problems: The moderating role of callous-unemotional traits. *Journal of Consulting and Clinical Psychology, 65*, 301–308.

Worling, J. R. (1995). Sexual abuse histories of adolescent male sex offenders: Differences on the basis of the age and gender of their victims. *Journal of Abnormal Psychology, 104*, 610–613.

Worling, J. R., & Curwen, T. (2000). Adolescent sexual offender recidivism: Success of specialized treatment and implications for risk prediction. *Child Abuse and Neglect, 24,* 965–982.

Wright, P., Nobrega, J., Langevin, R., & Wortzman, G. (1990). Brain density and symmetry in pedophilic and sexually aggressive offenders. *Annals of Sex Research, 3,* 319–328.

Wydra, A., Marshall, W. L., Earls, C. M., & Barbaree, H. E. (1983). Identification of cues and control of sexual arousal by rapists. *Behavior Research and Therapy, 21,* 469–476.

Yang, D. (1999). Convergence or divergence? Recent historical writings on the Rape of Nanjing. *American Historical Review, 104,* 842–865.

Yarvis, R. M. (1995). Diagnostic patterns among three violent offender types. *Bulletin of the American Academy of Psychiatry and the Law, 23,* 411–419.

Zahavi, A., & Zahavi, A. (1997). *The handicap principle: A missing piece of Darwin's puzzle.* New York: Oxford University Press.

Zajonc, R. B. (2001). The family dynamics of intellectual development. *American Psychologist, 56,* 490–496.

Zamble, E., & Quinsey, V. L. (1997). *The criminal recidivism process.* Cambridge, England: Cambridge University Press.

Zenone, P. G., Sims, M. E., & Erickson, C. J. (1979). Male ring dove behavior and the defense of genetic paternity. *The American Naturalist, 114,* 615–626.

Zgourides, G., Monto, M., & Harris, R. (1997). Correlates of adolescent male sexual offense: Prior adult sexual contact, sexual attitudes, and use of sexually explicit materials. *International Journal of Offender Therapy and Comparative Criminology, 41,* 272–283.

Zimmerer, E. J., & Kallman, K. D. (1989). Genetic basis for alternative reproductive tactics in the pygmy swordtail, *Xiphophorus nigrensis. Evolution, 43,* 1298–1307.

Zuckerman, M. (1979). *Beyond the optimal level of arousal.* Mahwah, NJ: Erlbaum.

Zuk, M., & Simmons, L. W. (1997). Reproductive strategies of the crickets (Orthoptera: Gryllidae). In J. C. Choe & B. J. Crespi (Eds.), *Mating systems in insects and arachnids* (pp. 89–109). Cambridge, England: Cambridge University Press.

Zweig, J. M., Sayer, A., Crockett, L. J., & Vicary, J. R. (2002). Adolescent risk factors for sexual victimization: A longitudinal analysis of rural women. *Journal of Adolescent Research, 17,* 586–603.

AUTHOR INDEX

Abbey, A. L., 151
Abel, G. G., 113, 115
Abler, T. S., 10, 26
Abracen, J., *127*, 139, 178
Abrams, D. B., 152
Acker, M., 77, 78
Ackerly, E., 81
Adams, G. M., *201*
Adams, H. E., 116, 121, 122, 151
Addison, T., 146, 148
Adkins-Regan, E., 49, 207
Afton, A. D., *47*, 202, 203
Agresti, A., 82
Aigner, M., 131
Aizenman, M., 150
Alatalo, R. V., 204, 205
Alcorn, D. J., 38n
Alexander, M., 174
Ali, S. A., 73, 75
Alisauskas, R. T., 202, 203
Alison, L., 128
Allam, J., 179
Allen, G. R., 37
Allen, M., 147, 148
Allnutt, S. H., 138
Alonzo, S. H., 45
Altemeyer, R. A., 76
Alvi, S., 139, 150, 153
Ambtman, R., 167
American Psychiatric Association, 100, *106*, 119
Ames, M. A., 138
Amick-McMullan, A., 154, 155
Amos, N. L., 120, 196
Anderson, B. P., 3
Anderson, C. G., 145
Anderson, D., 80, 139
Anderson, K., 116
Anderson, K. B., 145
Anderson, M. G., 208
Andrews, D. A., 162, 169, 173
Angleitner, A., 87
Anglin, M. D., 138
Armentrout, J. A., 79
Armstrong, D. P., 207
Arnold, L. S., 79

Arnqvist, G., 36, *39*, 42
Aronson, E., 3
Arsenault, L., 93
Aubut, J., 119
Austin, R. L., 146

Bagley, C., 135
Baier, J. L., 150
Bailey, R. O., 47
Bain, J., 131, 133, 175
Bakker, L., 178
Balyk, E. D., 130
Bangert, P. J., 199
Barash, D. P., 46, 50
Barbaree, H. E., 68, 79, 113, 116, 116n, 120, 121, 122, 125, 126, 139, 146, 152, 168, 176, 178, 179, 182, 196
Barber, N., 62
Bard, L. A., 79, 80
Bardis, P., 74
Barlow, D. H., 113, 115
Barlow, G. W., 209
Barnes, C. L., 77, 78
Barnett, P. E., 16
Baron, L., 145
Barrett, E. S., 86
Barry, H., 12
Barsetti, I., 113
Barton, S., 74
Bateson, M., 43
Baumeister, R. F., 128
Bauserman, R., 135, 138
Baxter, D. J., 116, 116n
Becker, J. V., 135, 140, 155, 171
Beevor, A., 27
Beezley, D. A., 73, 75
Beier, K. M., 174
Bélanger, N., 113, 168
Belovsky, G. E., *52*
Ben-Aron, M. H., 120, 133
Bengston, J. L., 38
Bentler, P. M., 74
Bercovitch, F. B., 54n
Bernat, J. A., 74, 116, 121, 122
Berryman-Fink, C., 22
Best, C. L., 3, 154, 155, 186n

SUBJECT INDEX

Lloyd, J. E., *200*
Looman, J., *127*
Ludus, antisociality and high mating effort, 75

MacKinnon, J., *40*
MacRoberts, M. H., *203*
Male fraternities, sexual coercion and, 153
Mallards
    forced copulation in, 46–47
    mating resistance in, 49n
Mammals, forced copulation in, 212
Marques, J. K., *179*
Mate guarding, 185
Maternal immune response, and neurodevelopment of rapists, 127
Mating effort
    acquaintance rape as aspect of, 151
    and antisociality, 72–81
    characteristics associated with, 88
    of competitively disadvantaged males, 96–97
    parental investment *versus*, 63, 65
    rape and, 80, 88, 184
    risk taking and antisociality in
        in older men, 89
    in young men, 88–90
Mating resistance
    of bighorn mountain ewes, 55–56
    of coquillett fly, 201
    of orangutans, 40
    as tool of selection, 89
Maturity gap, in adolescence-limited delinquency, 87n
McKinney, F., *46, 47*
Mediterranean fruit fly, forced copulation in, 200
Medroxyprogesterone acetate
    controlled outcome evaluations of, 174–175
    recidivism with, 175
Meese, A. G. E., *146*
Mineau, P., *202*
Modern Europe double standard in, 1500–1800, 20–21
Monkeys, forced copulation and, 55n–56n
Morphs, forced copulation and genetic differences in, 56–57
Mosquito fish, sneak fertilization in, 209
Mothers, adolescent, 70–71
Murder and assault, rape and, 62
Murphy, W., *179*

Murre
    extra-pair copulation in, 205
    forced copulation in, 205

Nicholaichuk, T., *127*
North America
    double standard in, 19th and early 20th centuries, 22
    sexual assault in, 22–23, 24
Nuptial gifts, of scorpion fly, 53

Obstetrical complications, neurodevelopmental problems and, 99–100
Onozato, H., *211*
Opportunistic spouse
    definition of, 46
    in extra-pair copulation, 46
Orangutans
    consortships of, 40, 41
    forced copulation and female resistance in, 40
    forced copulation by competitively disadvantaged male, 55–56
    large *vs.* small males, 40–41
    male and female mating preferences of, 40–41
    sexual behavior of captive pairs, 41
Ovid, Jupiter's rape of Callisto, 15

Paitch, D., *118*
Palmer, C. T., *34n*
Paraphilias
    as compulsions *versus* addictions, 140
    obsessive-compulsive disorder and, 130
    in rapist, 121
    as a sexual disorder, 106–108
    versus sexual dysfunctions, 106
Parental investment, mating effort *versus*, 63, 65
Parenting, abusive, effects of, 135–138
Patrick, C. J., *99*
Pedophiles
    brain deficits in, 131
    comparison with normal heterosexual men, 110–111
Pedophilia
    and birth order of brothers, 126, 127
    in disruption of sexual development, 112
    as paraphilic sexual disorder, 107, 111–112

association with mating effot and antisociality, 187

in biblical sources, 13–15

by competitively overadvantaged men, 192–193

contextual and situational factors in alcohol use, 151–153

membership in male organizations, 153

misperception of sexual cues, 150–151

pornography, 146–149

cross-cultural data on, 10–11

cross-gender antagonism and

status of women and, 12, 13

definitions of, 10, *29, 34n,* 105n

in biblical accounts, 14–15

Elizabeth I, England, 20

Kent County court, 19th century, *21*

ethnographic record of preliterate societies and, 10–13

fraternal interest groups and, 11

frequency of

factors in, 10

interpersonal violence correlation with, 11–12

historical and ethnographic literature on aspects of, 5, 9–30

in historical record, 13–20

male dominance ideology and, 12

marital, 197

in Medieval Europe

England, 16–18

Germany and France, 19–20

Italy, 18–19

of men, 28–30

by heterosexual men, 156

in modern era, 20–23

Asia, 21–22

Europe, 20–21

in North America

recent trends in, 22–23, 24

19th and early 20th centuries, 22

physical and emotional consequences of, 3

in preliterate societies, 10–13

social class and, 29

specialization and escalation of, 81–84

three pathway model of

antisociality in adolescence and early adulthood, 184

life-course-persistent delinquency, 185

neurodevelopmental and social adversity and competitive disadvantage, 185

in wartime, 23–28, 29

Rape of men

female sexual coercion and, 28

by men, 28, 154

Rape proneness, in pedophilia, 118–119

Rapid Risk Assessment for Sex Offender Recidivism (RRASOR)

for prediction of sex offense recidivism, 168–169

Rapists

alcoholism in, 139

antisociality of, 78–80

and birth order of brothers, 126–127

characteristics of, 183–184

childhood sexual abuse and, 137

versus child molesters, 79–80

clinical assessment of, 161

adolescence-limited offenders and, 180

antisociality evaluation in, 180

biomedical data in, 180

goals of, 180

life-course-persistent antisociality in, 180

psychosocial history in, 180

sexual sadism in, 180

comparison of sadistic and nonsadistic, 119–120

on brain imaging, 131

on neuropsychiatric test battery, 131

comparison with nonrapists

for sexual arousal patterns, 115–116

criminal history of, 79

definition of, 113

effectiveness of

as generalists, 81

mating effort of, 80

phallometric assessment of, 112–117

psychopathology of, 129–130

recidivism of, 80

rates for, 162, 163

similarity to other violent offenders, 5

subtypes of, 196

treatments for, 196

treatment of

castration, 194–195

goal of, 194

pharmacological, 174–177

in Homer's Iliad, 24–25
by Japanese, 26–27
in modern times, 25–28
Old Testament accounts, 23–24
by Russians in Germany, 27
by soldiers of occupation, 25–26
Water striders
evolutionary arms race in, 39, 43
female anatomy of, 39
male anatomy of, 36, 39
resisted mating in, 34, 36, 39
White-cheeked pintail duck, forced copulation in, 31–32
White-fronted bee-eaters, extra-pair copulation in, 203–204
Wing, S., *200*
Women and rape
complicity in, 14–15

responsibility for, 15, 16
Wood, C. C., *211*

Young adulthood, switch from mating effort to parenting effort in, 86–87
Young male syndrome
determinants of risk acceptance in, 87–88
rape in, 85–86
risk-taking for status, resources, mates in, 85–86
treatment of
multisystemic approach to, 189
psychoeducational approaches to, 189–190
substitution of antisocial peer groups with prosocial adult male models, 189, 190

ABOUT THE AUTHORS

Martin L. Lalumière, PhD, was a research psychologist at the Centre for Addiction and Mental Health and associate professor of psychiatry and criminology at the University of Toronto during the preparation of this book. He is now associate professor in the department of psychology and neuroscience at the University of Lethbridge. His research interests include the etiology of sexual aggression, the development of sexual preferences, the physiological assessment of sexual arousal, the nature of psychopathy, and the link between early neurodevelopmental perturbations and men's propensity for violence. He received the Governor General's Academic Gold Medal for his graduate work at Queen's University. He is on the editorial board of the journals *Archives of Sexual Behavior* and *Sexual Abuse*. Some of his recent work was published in *Evolution and Human Behavior, Journal of Abnormal Psychology, Proceedings of the Royal Society of London: Biological Sciences*, and *Psychological Bulletin*.

Grant T. Harris, PhD, is the director of research at the Mental Health Centre, Ontario, Canada. He is also an associate professor of psychology at Queen's University in Kingston, and associate professor of psychiatry at the University of Toronto. He is a fellow of the Canadian Psychological Association and was awarded the Amethyst Award for Outstanding Achievement by an Ontario Public Servant. He has been awarded several research grants on the topics of actuarial violence risk assessment, sexual aggression, the nature of psychopathy, and the assessment and treatment of violent offenders. This research has resulted in more than 100 publications on forensic topics.

Vernon L. Quinsey, PhD, is professor of psychology, biology, and psychiatry at Queen's University in Kingston. He is a fellow of the Canadian Psychological Association and has served on the editorial boards of a variety of journals. He has chaired research review panels of the American National Institute of Mental Health and the Ontario Mental Health Foundation. He was awarded the Significant Achievement Award of the Association for the Treatment of Sexual Abusers in 1994 and was the recipient of a Senior Research Fellowship from the Ontario Mental Health Foundation. He has authored or coauthored more than 100 publications on forensic topics, including eight books.

Marnie E. Rice, PhD, is the scientific director of the Centre for the Study of Aggression and Mental Disorder and is the former director of the Research Department of the Mental Health Centre, Penetanguishene, Ontario, Canada, where she continues her research parttime. She is also part-time professor of psychiatry and behavioral neurosciences at McMaster University, adjunct professor of psychiatry at the University of Toronto, and adjunct associate professor of psychology at Queen's University. She was the 1995 recipient of the American Psychological Association's award for Distinguished Contribution to Research in Public Policy, was the 1997 recipient of a government of Ontario Amethyst Award for outstanding contribution by an Ontario public servant, and was recently elected Fellow of the Royal Society of Canada in recognition of her scholarly contributions.